ESTATE PLANNING FORMS

L. Rush Hunt

GP | Solo
ABA General Practice, Solo & Small Firm Division

ABA
**Defending Liberty
Pursuing Justice**

Cover design by ABA Publishing.

The materials contained herein represent the opinions and views of the authors and/or the editors, and should not be construed to be the views or opinions of the law firms or companies with whom such persons are in partnership with, associated with, or employed by, nor of the American Bar Association or the General Practice, Solo and Small Firm Division, unless adopted pursuant to the bylaws of the Association.

Nothing contained in this book is to be considered as the rendering of legal advice, either generally or in connection with any specific issue or case; nor do these materials purport to explain or interpret any specific bond or policy, or any provisions thereof, issued by any particular franchise company, or to render franchise or other professional advice. Readers are responsible for obtaining advice from their own lawyers or other professionals. This book and any forms and agreements herein are intended for educational and informational purposes only.

Printed in the United States of America

15 14 14   5 4 3 2

Cataloging-in-Publication Data is on file with the Library of Congress.

Estate Planning Forms Book
L. Rush Hunt
ISBN 978-1-60442-384-6

Discounts are available for books ordered in bulk. Special consideration is given to state bars, CLE programs, and other bar-related organizations. Inquire at Book Publishing, ABA Publishing, American Bar Association, 321 North Clark Street, Chicago, Illinois 60654-7598.

www.ShopABA.org

Dedication

I dedicate this book to my two favorite lawyers, Lara Hunt, my daughter, and Lee Hunt, my son.

Table of Contents

Acknowledgments

I appreciate the confidence of the American Bar Association in publishing this book. The encouragement and guidance of ABA Publishing, the professionalism and friendliness of their staff makes it a real joy to work with them. In particular I especially want to thank Rick Paszkiet for his encouragement and patience.

I also appreciate very much the diligent effort of Rebecca Warren who doggedly worked on the preparation of this manuscript. Rebecca and I have worked on this manuscript with her as near as my front office and as far away as India and Egypt as she took her laptop with her wherever she went and continued her faithful typing and editing of the manuscript.

About the Author

L. Rush Hunt is currently engaged in the private practice of law in Madisonville, Kentucky, where he devotes much of his time to areas of estate and trust law. Mr. Hunt brings more than thirty years of experience in estate planning and related areas of the law to the writing of this text, including not only his legal experience but also his experience as a certified financial planner and his previous employment as a vice-president of trust services for Citizens Bank of Kentucky, where he supervised trust administration and investments.

Mr. Hunt earned his B.S. in accounting from Murray State University, his J.D. from the University of Louisville School of Law, and his Ph.D. in public law at Southern Illinois University. A frequent lecturer at continuing legal education seminars for both lawyers and accountants, Mr. Hunt is a member of the General Practice, Solo and Small Firm Section of the American Bar Association; the Kentucky Bar Association; and the Christian Legal Society.

Introduction

This book is intended to be a user friendly will and trust manual. I have sought to make the book user friendly by having numerous comments throughout the various provisions of each of the documents. Just consider these comments my conversation with you as you use the forms. Also, I have made references to a number of excellent ABA publications that can assist the reader with some of the more intricate substantive issues of the law concerning wills and trusts. These are excellent publications and will make an important addition to your library.

The book is divided into five basic parts. Part one provides samples of various documents that can be used in client interviews and samples of engagement letters. The assumption is that the reader already uses forms for these purposes, but it is my hope that by providing you with these documents, you will be able to modify your existing forms. While many lawyers do not use engagement letters for will and trust work, it is suggested that you consider an engagement letter for this area of practice. As litigation in the estate and trust area is increasing, it is a wise practice for the lawyer to use an engagement letter to better define the limits of representation and as an aid to your liability protection. The forms provided are based upon an hourly rate being charged. Simple modifications can be made if the fee agreement is a flat fee.

Part two provides a number of basic documents that the lawyer can use for most estate plans. These forms include a master will, a pour over will, a master inter vivos trust for a single grantor and a master inter vivos trust for multiple grantors. These forms have more options than will be needed in most estate plans. You must review these documents in detail in order to be familiar with the various provisions. Then you can delete those provisions not needed when drafting for a given client's estate plan. Also, you will find basic forms for a power of attorney, an advanced health care directive and several marital agreements.

While part two provides general forms for estate planning, the other three sections deal with specific drafting situations. For example, part three provides multiple options that the lawyer may wish to use for clients who have young children. These include forms specifically designed for families with young children, including both a testamentary and an inter vivos trust. The other two options are ones that are sometimes used by clients when establishing a trust fund for a child's education. While these forms are not inclusive of all options, they do provide two options that are frequently used.

Part four provides several different options when drafting for a client who has a child with special needs. Both a testamentary trust and an inter vivos trust are provided as sample documents. Both documents include supplemental care trust provisions that will keep the trust beneficiary from losing SSI or Medicaid benefits. The qualifying income trust, or Miller trust, is of limited applicability, but is used in those situations in which the client could qualify for Medicaid to pay nursing home expenses but has income in excess of the state's income cap, thus prohibiting the person from receiving Medicaid benefits. The sample trust will allow the person to qualify for Medicaid benefits. The final form in this section is a spendthrift trust. The form is the basic type of trust used for trust beneficiaries who should not receive an inheritance outright due to any number of reasons such as, health, marital, financial, or addiction problems.

Part five provides an irrevocable life insurance trust and a marital-credit shelter trust. These trusts are used when there are federal estate tax considerations that require special drafting. These are basic forms to get the lawyer started. There are a number of variations of each of these trusts. The ones provided are intended to provide one set of options. If the lawyer is going to become deeply involved in estate tax planning, then these forms are a good starting point. But the lawyer is cautioned that there is much more to learn when tax planning is involved. The reader will find the cited ABA resources to be most helpful.

As with all form books, the reader is cautioned to not use them blindly. They are intended to be an aid to you as you customize an estate plan to meet your client's own particular needs. These forms should be a helpful supplement to those forms you currently use, or for the less experienced lawyer these forms should be a springboard to establishing your own forms.

PART I—INTAKE FORMS

Family Questionnaire

Asset Questionnaire

Engagement Letter for Individual

Engagement Letter for Couple

Additional Terms and Conditions of Client Employment

Privacy Notice

FAMILY QUESTIONNAIRE

1. Client Facts	
a. Full Name	
b. Name Commonly Used	
c. Social Security No.	
d. Home Address	
e. Primary Telephone	
f. Secondary(Cell)Telephone	
g. E-mail Address	
h. Occupation	
i. Work address	
j. Birthdate	
k. Birthplace	
l. Period of residence [state]	

Additional Information (Client)

a. Do you have any physical or mental health conditions? Yes / No

    If yes, please explain:_____

    _____

    _____

b. In what state do you vote, have your driver's license, car registered, own real estate, and file state income taxes? _____

c. Have you ever lived in a community property state (AZ, CA, ID, LA, NV, NM, TX, WA, WI)? Yes / No _____If yes, please list: _____

d. Do you have a pre-nuptial or post-nuptial agreement? Yes / No

    If so, please provide a copy of that agreement with this questionnaire.

e. Do you have a divorce decree affecting any of your property rights or imposing a current legal obligation to support a former spouse or child? Yes / No

If so, please provide a copy of that divorce decree, property settlement agreement and any related court documents.

f. Are you a U.S. citizen? Yes / No

If not, in what country are you a citizen? _____

2. Spouse/Partner Facts	
a. Full Name	
b. Name Commonly Used	
c. Social Security No.	
d. Home Address	
e. Primary Telephone	
f. Secondary (Cell) Telephone	
g. E-mail Address	
h. Occupation	
i. Work address	
j. Birthdate	
k. Birthplace	
l. Period of residence [state]	

2. **Additional Information (Spouse)**

a. Do you have any physical or mental health conditions? Yes / No

    If yes, please explain:_____

    _____

    _____

b. In what state do you vote, have your driver's license, car registered, own real estate, and file state income taxes? _____

c. Have you ever lived in a community property state (AZ, CA, ID, LA, NV, NM, TX, WA, WI)? Yes / No

    If yes, please list: _____

d. Do you have a pre-nuptial or post-nuptial agreement? Yes / No

    If so, please provide a copy of that agreement with this questionnaire.

e. Do you have a divorce decree affecting any of your property rights or imposing a current legal obligation to support a former spouse or child? Yes / No

    If so, please provide a copy of that divorce decree, property settlement agreement and any related court documents.

f. Are you a U.S. citizen? Yes / No

    If not, in what country are you a citizen? _____

    _____

3. **Children and Grandchildren**

    Is there a physical possibility of your having more children? Yes / No

    Please list all children, noting any who are illegitimate or non-U.S. citizens.

    If a child is not of your present marriage, please note the name of the other parent (your prior spouse/partner).

Child #1 Facts	Deceased? Yes / No Adopted? Yes / No Handicapped /Poor Health? Yes / No	
Full Name		
Date of Birth		
Address		
Spouse's Name		
Child's Children	Name:	Date of Birth:
	Name:	Date of Birth:
	Name:	Date of Birth:
	Physical possibility of further children? Yes / No	

Child #2 Facts	Deceased? Yes / No Adopted? Yes / No Handicapped /Poor Health? Yes / No	
Full Name		
Date of Birth		
Address		
Spouse's Name		
Child's Children	Name:	Date of Birth:
	Name:	Date of Birth:
	Name:	Date of Birth:
	Physical possibility of further children? Yes / No	

Child #3 Facts	Deceased? Yes / No Adopted? Yes / No Handicapped /Poor Health? Yes / No	
Full Name		
Date of Birth		
Address		
Spouse's Name		
Child's Children	Name:	Date of Birth:
	Name:	Date of Birth:
	Name:	Date of Birth:
	Physical possibility of further children? Yes / No	

Child #4 Facts	Deceased? Yes / No Adopted? Yes / No Handicapped /Poor Health? Yes / No	
Full Name		
Date of Birth		
Address		
Spouse's Name		
Child's Children	Name:	Date of Birth:
	Name:	Date of Birth:
	Name:	Date of Birth:
	Physical possibility of further children? Yes / No	

4. Parents	Father	Mother
Client's Parents Name		
Address		
Age		
State of Health		
Financially Dependent?		
Expected Inheritance from Parent?		
Spouse's/Partner's Parents Name		
Address		
Age		
State of Health		
Financially Dependent?		
Expected Inheritance from Parent?		

5. Advisors	
a. Accountant	
b. Stockbroker	
c. Financial Advisor	
d. Insurance Underwriter	
e. Banker	
f. Other	
g. Other	

6. **Additional Information**

    a. Did you bring your existing estate planning documents? If not, please provide copies or originals for my review.

    b. Have you or your spouse/partner made any gifts to any other person that require the filing of a federal gift tax return? If so, please provide a copy of all gift tax returns.

    c. Are you or your spouse/partner beneficiaries under any trust agreements? If so, please provide a copy of those documents.

    d. Are you or your spouse/partner the holders of a power of appointment under any legal document? If so, please provide a copy of that document.

e. Do you or your spouse/partner anticipate receiving an inheritance or a large gift in the future? If so, in what amount, and please explain the details. _____

_____

_____

f. Do you or your spouse/partner own any property in a foreign country? If so, please give full details. _____

_____

_____

g. Are you or your spouse/partner subject to any existing or anticipated litigation; or are you in any business arrangements or occupations in which such liabilities are a possibility? If so, please explain. _____

_____

_____

h. Do you or your spouse/partner have any relatives who are dependent on your for support? If so, please explain. _____

_____

_____

i. Are you going to be disinheriting any family members? If so, please explain who and the reason for the disinheritance. _____

_____

_____

j. Do any of your children or grandchildren, or other family members who are inheriting from you, have special needs either due to being of young age, mental or physical health problems, substance abuse, marital problems, or other factors that should be taken into account in determining how such person should inherit? If so, please explain. _____

_____

_____

_____

_____

_____

ASSET QUESTIONNAIRE

(If more space is needed for any section, continue at number 12 below.)

1. **Cash Equivalents**
   Do you have any checking accounts and/or any other bank accounts or certificates of deposit?

	Name of Institution, Address, Account Number	Title in whose name	Approx. Balance
Checking Accounts	1.		
	2.		
	3.		
	4.		
Certificates of Deposit, Savings Accounts	1.		
	2.		
	3.		
	4.		
		TOTAL:	$

Safe deposit box no.	
Location	

2. **Stocks**
   Do you own any stocks?

Number of Shares	Company	Title in whose name	Current Market Value
		TOTAL:	$

3. **Bonds**
   Do you own any bonds?

Maturity Value	Description	Title in whose name	Current Market Value
		TOTAL:	$

4.   Mutual Funds

Do you own any mutual funds?

Number of Units	Company	Title in whose name	Current Market Value
		TOTAL:	$

5.   Real Estate (please bring deeds)

Do you own a home or any other real estate? Indicate which is your residence.

Description and location	Title in whose name	Current Market Value	Mortgage Amount
	TOTAL:	$	$

6.   Business

Do you own an interest in any business?

Description of Business	Percentage of Ownership	Name of Co-owners	Market Value
		TOTAL:	$

Is there an existing buy-sell agreement? If so, please provide a copy of that agreement.

7.   Retirement Benefits

Do you have any IRAs, 401Ks, or other retirement benefits?

Description	Beneficiary	Approximate Value
	TOTAL:	$

8.   Life Insurance
Do you have any life insurance policies and/or annuities?

Insurance Company	Policy Owner	Insured	First Beneficiary	Second Beneficiary	Death Benefit

9.   Other - Trusts, Anticipated Inheritance, Etc.

_____

_____

_____

10.   Personal Property
Do you own any other titled property such as a car, boat, etc?

Description	Title in whose name	Approximate Value	Amount of Lien
TOTAL:		$	$

Do you own any other personal property that is not titled?

Description	Title in whose name	Approximate Value
Home Furnishings		
Jewelry		
Collections		
Other		
Other		
	TOTAL:	$

11. Liabilities

Description	Lender/Debtor	Approximate Value
Home mortgage		
Other mortgages		
Other debts		

12. Continuation of Assets

Type of Asset	Description of Asset	Title in whose name	Current Market Value

ENGAGEMENT LETTER FOR INDIVIDUAL

Dear_____:

I am pleased that you have asked me and [name of firm] to assist you in developing your estate plan. This letter confirms my discussion with you regarding your employment of our firm and describes the basis upon which we will provide legal services to you. Accordingly, I submit for your approval the following provisions governing our employment. If you are in agreement, please sign a copy of this letter in the space provided below.

Scope of Representation. You have asked me to represent you with regard to the planning, preparation, and implementation of appropriate estate planning documents (such as wills, health care power of attorney, durable power of attorney and revocable trust agreements). You may limit or expand the scope of my representation from time to time, provided that any substantial expansion must be agreed to by me. While our firm would be interested in assisting you in other matters, unless our firm is specifically engaged for some other future matter this letter shall confirm that our representation of you is limited to the foregoing matters and shall end when they are concluded.

Fees. Our fees are based primarily upon the time expended by our attorneys and paralegals on the engagement. Attorneys and paralegals have been assigned hourly rates based upon their experience and level of expertise. The present rates of those attorneys and paralegals likely to work on these matters range from $_____ in the case of the paralegal who will work on this matter, $_____ in the case of the associate who will work on this matter, and $_____ in my case. Our hourly rates are reviewed periodically and may be increased from time to time, but will remain at these rates during this representation. We do not consider any billing for our services final until you are satisfied as to both the quality of our services and the amount charged. If you have any questions about a billing, please contact me directly.

Potential Conflicts. Our firm represents other businesses and individuals. This can create situations where work for one client on a matter may preclude us from assisting other clients on unrelated matters. It is at least possible that during the time that we are representing you some of our present or future clients may have disputes or transactions with you. In order to avoid the potential problems that this kind of restriction could have for our practice, we ask you to agree that we may continue to represent (or may undertake in the future to represent) existing or new clients in any matter that is not substantially related to matters in which we have represented you, even if the interests of such clients in those other matters might be adverse to yours. We do not intend, however, for you to waive your right to have our firm maintain confidences or secrets that you transmit to our firm, and we agree not to disclose them to any third party without your consent. We will, of course, take appropriate steps to insure that such information is kept confidential.

Additional Standard Terms. Our engagement is subject to the policies included in the enclosed memorandum.

Privacy Policy. Enclosed is a copy of the Firm's privacy policy. Please let us know if you have any questions about it.

If these terms of our engagement are acceptable to you, please sign a copy of this letter for my records. You may keep the original letter for your records.

Sincerely,

[name of firm]

_____

[name of attorney]

The foregoing is understood and accepted:

_____

Date: _____

ENGAGEMENT LETTER FOR COUPLE

Dear_____,

I am pleased that you have asked me and [name of firm], to assist you in developing your estate plan. This letter confirms my discussion with you regarding your employment of our firm and describes the basis upon which we will provide legal services to you. Accordingly, I submit for your approval the following provisions governing our employment. If you are in agreement, please sign a copy of this letter in the space provided below.

Scope of Representation. You have asked me to represent you with regard to the planning, preparation, execution and implementation of appropriate estate planning documents (such as wills, health care power of attorney, power of attorney and revocable trust agreements) for each of you concerning the management of your assets during your joint lives and the life of the survivor and the disposition of those assets to beneficiaries in connection with various contractual rights, such as life insurance policies and retirement plan accounts. You may limit or expand the scope of my representation from time to time, provided that any substantial expansion must be agreed to by me. While our firm would be interested in assisting you in other matters, unless we are specifically engaged for some other future matter this letter will confirm that our representation of you is limited to the foregoing matters and will end when they are concluded.

Joint Representation. Under the ethical rules that govern attorneys, I may represent both of you jointly so long as you are in agreement about your estate plan. It is normally quite beneficial for one attorney to represent both a husband and wife in the estate planning process, and my goal in doing so will be to help you implement a mutually agreeable plan for both the present and future. However, in the course of the estate planning process a husband and wife sometimes develop differences in their choices of beneficiaries, appointments of trustees, executors and representatives and in their overall interests and desires. Occasionally, couples initially agree on a plan and then later change their minds and go in different directions. Consequently, please understand that if I undertake to represent both of you jointly, I cannot take sides or favor one of you over the other, either now or in the future.

During the planning process, I will obtain confidential information from each of you, whether in conference with both of you together or with one of you alone. If I undertake to represent you jointly, please understand that I cannot withhold any such information from either of you even if one of you asks me to do so. The alternative is for me to represent only one of you separately without open sharing of information. The other one of you would then have to either engage separate counsel or choose not to be represented at all. Such separate representation is usually not practical and having one party unrepresented is usually not desirable. If during the course of my joint representation of you a conflict should develop that in my opinion would keep me from adequately representing both of you or if either of you asks me to take sides against the other, I will have no choice but to withdraw from further joint representation of the two of you and advise each of you to obtain separate counsel. By your signing this letter you are assuring me that you are comfortable with my representing both of you jointly.

Fees. Our fees are based primarily upon the time expended by our attorneys and paralegals on the engagement. Attorneys and paralegals have been assigned hourly rates based upon their experience and level of expertise. The present rates of those attorneys and paralegals likely to work on these matters range from $_____ in the case of the paralegal who will work on this matter, $_____ in the case of the associate who will work on this matter, and $_____ in my case. Our hourly rates are reviewed periodically and may be increased from time to time, but will remain at these rates during this representation. We do not consider any billing for our services final until you are satisfied as to both the quality of our services and the amount charged. If you have any questions about a billing, please contact me directly.

Potential Conflicts. Our firm represents other businesses and individuals. This can create situations where work for one client on a matter may preclude us from assisting other clients on unrelated matters. It is at least possible that during the time that we are representing you some of our present or future clients may have disputes or transactions with you. In order to avoid the potential problems that this kind of restriction could have for our practice, we ask you to agree that we may continue to represent (or may undertake in the future to represent) existing or new clients in any matter that is not substantially related to matters in which we have represented you, even if the interests of such clients in those other matters might be adverse to yours. We do not intend, however, for you to waive your right to have our firm maintain confidences or secrets that you transmit to our firm, and we agree not to disclose them to any third party without your consent. We will, of course, take appropriate steps to insure that such information is kept confidential.

Additional Standard Terms. Our engagement is also subject to the policies included in the enclosed memorandum.

Privacy Policy. Enclosed is a copy of the Firm's privacy policy. Please let us know if you have any questions about it.

If these terms of our engagement are acceptable to you, please sign a copy of this letter for my records. You may keep the original letter for your records.

If you have any questions regarding any of the matters discussed in this letter, please feel free to give me a call.

Sincerely,

[name of firm]

_____

[name of attorney]

The foregoing is understood and accepted:

_____

Date:_____

_____

Date:_____

ADDITIONAL TERMS AND CONDITIONS OF CLIENT EMPLOYMENT

1. <u>Expenses.</u> Expenses we incur on the engagement are charged to the Client's account. Expenses include such items as court costs, charges for computerized research services and the use of our facsimile and photocopying machines, long distance telephone calls, travel expenses, messenger service charges, overnight mail or delivery charges, extraordinary administrative support, filing fees, fees of court reporters and charges for depositions, fees for expert witnesses and other expenses we incur on your behalf. Our charges for these services reflect our actual out-of-pocket costs based on usage, and in some areas may also include our related administrative expenses.

2. <u>Monthly Statements.</u> Unless a different billing period is agreed upon with the Client, the firm will render monthly statements indicating the current status of the account as to both fees and expenses. In some situations we will need to bill at the conclusion of the legal work. The statements are payable upon receipt.

3. <u>Termination.</u> The Client has the right to terminate our representation at any time by notifying us of the Client's intention to do so. We will have the same right, subject to an obligation to give the client reasonable notice to arrange alternative representation. If either party should elect to terminate our relationship, our fees and expenses incurred up to that point still will be due to us. Upon payment to us of any balance due for fees and expenses, we will return to the Client, or to whomever the Client directs, any property or papers of the Client in our possession. We will retain our files pertaining to any matters on which we have been engaged to represent the Client.

4. <u>Withdrawal.</u> Under the rules of professional conduct by which we are governed, we may withdraw from our representation of the Client in the event of (for example): nonpayment of our fees and expenses; misrepresentation or failure to disclose material facts concerning the engagement; action taken by the Client contrary to our advice; and in situations involving a conflict of interest with another client. If such a situation occurs, which we do not anticipate, we will promptly give the Client written notice of our intention to withdraw.

5. <u>Post-Engagement Services.</u> The Client is engaging our Firm to provide legal services in connection with a specific matter or matters. After completion of that matter or matters, changes may occur in the applicable laws or regulations that could have an impact on the Client's future rights and liabilities. Unless the Client engages us after completion of a matter to provide additional advice on issues arising from the matter, the Firm has no continuing obligation to advise the Client with respect to future legal developments.

6. <u>Authorization.</u> By the Client's agreement to these terms of our representation, the Client authorizes us to take all action we deem advisable on the Client's behalf on this matter. Whenever possible, we will discuss with the Client in advance any significant actions we intent to take.

PRIVACY NOTICE

[Name of Firm] understands your privacy is important. We are sure that you are aware that your personal information will always be held in the strictest confidence within [Name of Firm]. You are receiving this notice in accordance with applicable federal law because you receive income, estate and gift tax advice, planning, or preparation services, from [Name of Firm]. This privacy notice outlines what information we collect and how we use it. In serving you we are committed to maintaining your privacy.

We collect "nonpublic personal information" about you from multiple sources including:

- Information we receive from you on questionnaires, forms or other documents supplied by you to us;

- Information about your transactions with us or with others;

- Information we receive from others involved in your financial or tax planning activity, such as your accountant, banker, or stockbroker.

The rules governing lawyers' professional conduct prohibit a lawyer from disclosing information obtained in connection with representing a client, except in limited circumstances. These rules are very stringent. The lawyers and staff at [Name of Firm] take great care to adhere to these rules, and have always protected your right to privacy. We do not disclose any nonpublic personal information about you or about former clients, except as agreed by you or as required by law or by the applicable rules governing lawyers' conduct.

We restrict access to nonpublic personal information about you to lawyers and employees at [Name of Firm]. Physical, electronic and procedural safeguards that comply with rules governing lawyers' professional conduct are maintained to guard your nonpublic personal information.

PART II–DRAFTING BASIC DOCUMENTS

Master Will

Pour Over Will

Single Person Inter Vivos Trust

Joint Trust

General Durable Power of Attorney

Health Care Power of Attorney

Pre-Marital Agreement

Post-Marital Agreement

Memorandum of Agreement

MASTER WILL WORKSHEET

1. Testator's and Family Information

1.1 Testator's Name _____

1.2 Testator's City and State_____

1.3 Name of Spouse _____

1.4 Names of Children _____

_____

_____

1.5 Are any of the above-named children step-children? <u>Yes / No</u>

(See Paragraph 1, Option 2)

1.6 Are provisions needed for after-born children? <u>Yes / No</u>

(See Paragraph 1, Option 3)

1.7 Are provisions needed for adopted and/or illegitimately born children? <u>Yes / No</u>

(See Paragraph 1, Option 4)

1.8 Are any children to be disinherited? <u>Yes / No</u>

(See Paragraph 1, Option 5)

Name of disinherited child: _____ _____

1.9 Are any loans or gifts/advancements to be considered for any child? <u>Yes / No</u>

Name of Child: _____

Is loan or gift/advancement to be considered in making distribution? <u>Yes / No</u>

_____

(See Paragraphs 4 and 5, Options 1 and 2)

2.   Payment of Death Taxes

2.1 Are taxes on probate and nonprobate assets, including apportionment property, to be paid from the residue? (Option 1) Yes / No

2.2 Are death taxes to be paid by beneficiary and taxes collected on apportionment property? (Option 2) Yes / No

2.3 Are death taxes to be paid from the residue, but taxes on apportionment property to be collected? (Option 3) Yes / No

2.4 Other tax provisions _____

_____

3.   Specific Bequests and Legacies

3.1 Specific Gifts (See Paragraph 3)

a. Description _____

b. Primary Beneficiary _____

c. Contingent Beneficiary _____

d. Survivorship Period _____

3.2 Tangible Personal Property (spouse, and if not surviving, to children)

a. Description _____

b. Primary Beneficiary _____

c. Contingent Beneficiary _____

d. Survivorship Period _____

3.3 Gift of land provision needed? Yes / No

3.4 Gift of residence provision needed? Yes / No

3.5 Gift of life estate in residence provision needed? Yes / No

3.6 If no agreement among children as to division of personal property:

(See Paragraph 6)

Personal Representative Decides? (Option 1) Yes / No

or Sell and Distribute Proceeds to Residue? (Option 2) Yes / No

3.7 Residuary estate:

Outright to spouse if surviving, then outright to children? (Option 1) Yes / No

To spouse if surviving, if not then to inter vivos trust? (Option 2) Yes / No

To inter vivos trust directly? (Option 3) Yes / No

To spouse if surviving, if not then to separate testamentary trusts? (Option 4) Yes / No

Ages of child for mandatory distributions: _____

Deceased child's share distributed to such child's estate? Yes / No

or Deceased child's share per stirpes to lineal descendants? Yes / No

To spouse if surviving, if not then to single testamentary trust? (Option 5) <u>Yes / No</u>

Age of youngest child for termination of trust: _____

Additional comments: _____

_____

3.8 Contingent trust if child deceased? <u>Yes / No</u>

Age for termination _____ years

If remote descendants are deceased:

Distributed to person's estate? (Option 1) <u>Yes / No</u>

Allocated per stirpes to lineal descendants? (Option 2) <u>Yes / No</u>

4.   Default Provisions, if all named beneficiaries are deceased: _____

_____

_____

_____

5.   Special Provisions

Residential Real Estate? <u>Yes / No</u>

Rule against Perpetuities? <u>Yes / No</u>

Subchapter S Stock? <u>Yes / No</u>

Reliance on Will? <u>Yes / No</u>

Method of Payment? <u>Yes / No</u>

Accrued Income and Termination:

Distributed to such interested person's estate? (Option 1) <u>Yes / No</u>

Remain an asset of the trust (not distributed)? (Option 2) <u>Yes / No</u>

Life Insurance Policies? <u>Yes / No</u>

6.   Powers

Environmental Powers? <u>Yes / No</u> (See Paragraph 15)

Farm Powers? <u>Yes / No</u> (See Paragraph 16)

Limitation on Trustee Powers? <u>Yes / No</u>

7.   Trustees

Name of initial trustee: _____

Name of successor trustee: _____

Corporate trustee compensation? <u>Yes / No</u>

Individual reimbursed for expenses but no compensation? <u>Yes / No</u>

Individual receives compensation? <u>Yes / No</u>

Amount of compensation: $_____

8.   **Personal Representative**

8.1 Spouse named initial personal representative? <u>Yes / No</u>

8.2 If spouse not initial personal representative:

Name_____ Address _____

8.3 Successor Personal Representative:

Name _____

Relationship _____

Address _____

8.4 Surety Bond Waived? <u>Yes / No</u>

8.5 Special Provisions needed to operate business? <u>Yes / No</u>

9.   **Incompetency**

One physician decides? (Option 1) <u>Yes / No</u>

Two physicians decide and one board certified? (Option 2) <u>Yes / No</u>

10.   **Miscellaneous**

Is no contest provision needed? <u>Yes / No</u> (See Paragraph 26)

Is employment of law firm needed? <u>Yes / No</u> (See Paragraph 27)

11.   **Guardian, if spouse not surviving**:

Name _____

Relationship _____

Address _____

Successor _____

Relationship _____

Address _____

Surety Bond Waived? <u>Yes / No</u>

Special provisions or bequests for guardian?_____

_____

12.   **Survivorship** (See Paragraph 29)

1. Simultaneous Death <u>Yes / No</u>

If yes, which spouse is presumed to die first? _____

2. General Survivorship _____ days

Does this apply to spouse? <u>Yes / No</u>

MASTER WILL

The master will is intended to provide numerous provisions that will from time to time be needed when preparing a will. The form includes typical provisions needed in a will and also includes testamentary trust provisions for the testator's children or other beneficiaries. This is not intended as a simple "boilerplate" will, but rather a master document that will have multiple provisions which should be considered and edited to fit the client's needs.

OF

[FULL NAME OF CLIENT]

I, [Full Name of Client], currently of [Client's City], [Client's State], make this my last will and testament, hereby revoking all wills and codicils previously made by me.

1. <u>Family Information.</u> My [husband or wife]'s name is [husband or wife's name], and all references in this will to "my [husband or wife]" are only to [him or her].

OPTION 1: Naming of all children My [child is or children are], [names of children], and all references in this will to "my [child is or children are]" only to [him her or them].

OPTION 2: Inclusion of step-children Even though some of these children are step-children it is my intent that each of the above-named children be treated for purposes of inheriting under this will as if they and their lineal descendants are my natural born children and descendants.

OPTION 3: After-born children If subsequent to the execution of this will there shall be an additional child or children born to me, then such child or children shall share in the benefits of my estate to the same extent as my above named children and their descendants; and the provisions of this will shall be deemed modified to the extent necessary to carry out this intent.

COMMENT: The full name of the other spouse and children should be inserted. If step-children are involved, Option 2 should be considered. Also, Option 3 may be appropriate if there is the possibility of additional children. The lawyer's state law should provide for this contingency, but it still may be appropriate to add this provision to the will.

OPTION 4: Adopted and illegitimately born children The words "child," "children," "descendant" or "descendants" shall exclude adopted persons unless they are adopted prior to [insert age] years; and shall include only persons legitimately born unless a decree of adoption terminates the parental rights of the natural mother during her lifetime, or the natural father signs a written notarized instrument during his lifetime in which he irrevocably states that the child is to be considered legitimately born for purposes of inheriting under this will.

COMMENT: Some clients will want to restrict distribution for an adopted child to preclude a child adopted as an adult. Thus, many will use the age 18 or perhaps a slightly older age such as 20 or 21. Other clients may wish to restrict the age to a younger adopted child, such as under the age of 10. The issue of illegitimate children should also be addressed. In many situations, a child or more remote descendant should be treated the same as any other child, in which case the portion of this paragraph that deals with illegitimate children can be deleted. In other situations there may be a limited or no relationship with the child, in which event no distribution should be made to that child. This form gives the father the right to allow the child to inherit by the father signing a written document allowing inheritance.

OPTION 5: Disinheritance I have made no provisions for the benefit of my <relationship>, <name>, for reasons that need not be expressed.

If a child is to be disinherited, then it is wise practice to mention the child's name to clarify the child is not to receive a share so that no claim can be made that the client intended for the child to inherit, but the lawyer drafting the document failed to name the child.

---

2. <u>Payment of Debts, Death Taxes and Funeral Expenses.</u> **OPTION 1: Death taxes paid from residue** I direct that all of my just debts, my funeral expenses, costs of estate administration, and death taxes, if any, be paid from the residue of my estate as soon as possible after my death. I further direct that any real property that is subject to a mortgage or lien shall pass under my will subject to such mortgage or lien, rather than such indebtedness being paid from my estate. Death taxes means any estate or inheritance taxes, but not generation-skipping transfer taxes, imposed under the laws of any jurisdiction due to my death on any property passing by reason of my death whether or not such property passes under this will. Any generation-skipping transfer taxes resulting from a transfer occurring under my will shall be paid from the property that incurred such tax and shall not be paid from my other estate assets.

COMMENT: This paragraph first provides for the payment of all debts and final expenses, then imposes any death taxes on the residue to the estate. Any mortgage indebtedness is not to be paid from the residue but is to pass to the beneficiary who is the recipient of that property subject to the debt. If the debt is to be paid, then this second sentence should be deleted.

OPTION 2: Death taxes paid by beneficiary and collecting taxes on apportionment property I direct that all of my just debts, my funeral expenses and costs of estate administration be paid from the residue of my estate as soon as possible after my death; provided, however, I direct that if any death taxes are owed by my estate that such taxes be charged against the share passing to the person whose share generated such tax. I further direct that any real property that is subject to a mortgage or lien shall pass under my will subject to such mortgage or lien, rather than such indebtedness being paid from my estate. Death taxes means any estate or inheritance taxes, but not generation-skipping transfer taxes, imposed under the laws of any jurisdiction due to my death on any property passing by reason of my death whether or not such property passes under this will. With regard to apportionment property, my personal representative shall take such actions as are necessary to obtain reimbursement with respect to apportionment property, including withholding distribution. Apportionment property means (a) any property with respect to which my personal representative may be entitled to recover federal estate tax under Internal Revenue Code Section 2207, 2207A, or 2207B and (b) any policies of insurance, or the proceeds of policies of insurance, on my life which are not owned by me at my death. Any generation-skipping transfer taxes resulting from a transfer occurring under my will shall be paid from the property that incurred such tax and shall not be paid from my other estate assets.

COMMENT: This paragraph first provides for the payment of all debts and final expenses, however in Option 2, state and federal death taxes are charged to each beneficiary based upon the amount received by such beneficiary. Thus the tax burden is shared among the estate beneficiaries based on the amount of their inheritance. This becomes important when there are beneficiaries receiving gifts who do not share in the residuary estate. To assess their taxes to the residue results in a reduction in the amount of the residue received by the residuary beneficiaries. Sometimes this is the result the client wants, but other times, they prefer for each beneficiary to pay their own tax burden. The issue of who pays should be addressed in determining the correct tax payment clause. Apportionment property refers to property that is subject to estate tax due to the decedent having a power of appointment over property, assets that are taxable in the decedent's estate due to having qualified for the marital deduction in the estate of the decedent's spouse, or property in which the decedent had a retained interest, or certain life insurance. Normally, reimbursement for estate taxes owed by the decedent's estate should be sought from the holders of such property. As in Option 1, any mortgage indebtedness is not to be paid from the residue but is to pass to the beneficiary who is the recipient of that property subject to the debt. If the debt should be paid, then this second sentence should be deleted.

OPTION 3: Death taxes paid from residue but collecting tax on apportionment property I direct that all of my just debts, my funeral expenses and costs of estate administration be paid from the residue of my estate as soon as possible after my death. I also direct that any real property that is subject to a mortgage or lien shall pass under my will subject to such mortgage or lien, rather than such indebtedness being paid from my estate.

I further direct that my death taxes, if any, be paid out of my residuary estate, other than apportionment property, without proration and my personal representative shall not seek contribution toward or recovery of any such payments. Death taxes means any estate or inheritance taxes, but not generation-skipping transfer taxes, imposed under the laws of any jurisdiction due to my death on any property passing by reason of my death whether or not such property passes under this will. With regard to apportionment property, my personal representative shall take such actions as are necessary to obtain reimbursement with respect to apportionment property, including withholding distribution. Apportionment property means (a) any property with respect to which my personal representative may be entitled to recover federal estate tax under Internal Revenue Code Section 2207, 2207A, or 2207B and (b) any policies of insurance, or the proceeds of policies of insurance, on my life which are not owned by me at my death. Any generation-skipping transfer taxes resulting from a transfer occurring under my will shall be paid from the property that incurred such tax and shall not be paid from my other estate assets.

COMMENT: Option 3 provides for the payment of all debts, final expenses, and death taxes being paid from the residue of the estate. Thus, any specific gifts other than gifts of the residue are received free of any state or federal death taxes. The only exception is apportionment property which is to pay its share of the estate taxes. Apportionment property refers to property that is subject to estate tax due to the decedent having a power of appointment over property, assets that are taxable in the decedent's estate due to having qualified for the marital deduction in the estate of the decedent's spouse, property in which the decedent had a retained interest, or certain life insurance. Normally, reimbursement for estate taxes owed by the decedent's estate should be sought from the holders of such property. As in the prior two options, any mortgage indebtedness is not to be paid from the residue but is to pass to the beneficiary who is the recipient of that property subject to the debt. If the debt should be paid, then this second sentence should be deleted.

---

3. <u>Specific Gift.</u> **OPTION 1: Single gift** I give to my [relationship],[name], if [he or she] survives me, [gift], if owned by me at my death.

OPTION 2: Multiple gifts To the individuals listed below, I give the following:

   a. To my [relationship],[name], if [he or she] survives me, [gift], if owned by me at my death.

b. To my [relationship], [name], if [he or she] survives me, [gift], if owned by me at my death.

OPTION 3: Gift of land I give to my [relationship], [name], if [he or she] survives me, a tract of land containing approximately [number of acres] acres situated in [name of county] County, [state], said tract having been conveyed to me on [date of deed] and is of record in the office of the [name of the recorder's office] in Deed Book [number], page [number], if owned by me at my death.

OPTION 4: Gift of residence I give to [relationship], [name], if [he or she] survives me, my personal residence, including all furniture, furnishings and appliances, located at [street address], [city], [state], such residence having been conveyed to me on [date of deed] and is of record in the office of the [name of the recorder's office] in Deed Book [number], page [number], if owned by me at my death.

OPTION 5: Gift of life estate in residence I give to [relationship], [name], if [he or she] survives me, a life estate in my personal residence located at [street address], [city], [state], such residence having been conveyed to me on [date of deed] and is of record in the office of the [name of the recorder's office] in Deed Book [number], page [number], if owned by me at my death. My [relationship], [name] shall be responsible for maintaining this property and shall pay all reasonable repair and maintenance expenses for this property; and in addition shall pay all property and casualty insurance premiums and property taxes assessed on this property.

COMMENT: Full names and a complete description of the specific gift should be inserted in the appropriate form used. The form as drafted includes the phrase "if [he or she] survives me" in order to ensure a lapse of the gift should the named person be deceased at the death of the testator. Also, the phrase "if owned by me at my death" is inserted to ensure a lapse of the gift if the asset is no longer owned. This provision avoids the application of the rule of ademption.

---

4. <u>Advancements.</u> I have made gifts to various of my children and may make additional gifts in the future, all of which I have made record of in my personal papers.

OPTION 1: Gifts not considered None of these gifts shall be considered an advancement and thus these gifts shall not be taken into account in determining the distribution of my estate.

OPTION 2: Gifts considered These gifts shall be considered an advancement without interest to the recipient and shall be taken into account in determining the distribution of my estate.

COMMENT: Oftentimes, the testator has made gifts to a child or other beneficiary prior to death. If that is the case, a decision needs to be made whether those gifts are to be considered a gift or an advancement against the inheritance.

---

5. <u>Loans.</u> I have made loans to various of my children and may make additional loans in the future, all of which I have made record of in my personal papers.

OPTION 1: Loans forgiven I forgive these loans, thus these loans shall not be taken into account in determining the distribution of my estate.

OPTION 2: Loans collected These loans shall be considered an advancement without interest to the recipient and shall be taken into account in determining the distribution of my estate.

COMMENT: If the client has made loans to the children or other estate beneficiaries, then a clear statement in the will as to whether that loan is forgiven or is to be collected will avoid administrative problems for the personal representative and will ensure that the testator has given proper consideration to the effect of gifts.

6. <u>Disposition of Tangible Personal Property.</u> I give to my [husband or wife], all of my personal and household effects, including but not limited to furniture, furnishings, appliances, clothing, jewelry, automobiles and any other similar tangible personal property. If my [husband or wife] does not survive me, I give all such tangible personal property to my [child or children], in as nearly equal shares as is possible.

OPTION 1: If no agreement personal representative decides If my children cannot agree upon this division within ninety (90) days after the appointment of my personal representative, then the division made by my personal representative shall be final and binding upon my children and shall not be subject to question by anyone or in any court.

OPTION 2: If no agreement sell and pass to residue If my children cannot agree upon this division within ninety (90) days after the appointment of my personal representative, then my personal representative shall sell all property with respect to which my children have not reached an agreement and the net sales proceeds shall be distributed as part of the residue of my estate.

COMMENT: Gifts of personal property can be the source of family disagreements and even litigation. While the initial gift of such property to the surviving spouse is not a problem, the problem arises when the personal property passes to the children. Options 1 and 2 provide two different approaches for handling distribution in the event of a disagreement. The lawyer may choose either of those options, write his/her own method of resolving the conflict or leave out these options and let the probate court deal with the problem. This writer has found that going to court over grandmother's clock is not something most clients want their children to do. Thus, Option 1, Option 2 or some variation may be helpful.

I may leave with my will or among my papers a handwritten letter or handwritten memorandum concerning the distribution of certain items of my tangible personal property. If so, I direct my personal representative to distribute those items of my tangible personal property as I have provided in that letter or memorandum.

COMMENT: Some clients have numerous items of personal property that they want to give to family and friends. Rather than having a lengthy will naming these items, some lawyers prefer the use of a handwritten letter that is dated and signed at the bottom of the page by the testator. This approach allows the ease of changing the document over the years. It has the disadvantage of possibly not being an enforceable document depending upon state law. If the document qualifies under state law as a holographic codicil, or due to enactment of Section 2-513 of the Uniform Probate Code, then it is enforceable and the personal representative is required to account for those items named in the letter and to ensure their distribution to the correct beneficiary. A problem with the handwritten letter is that it is unlikely that it will be written in a way to address the lapse of a gift if a beneficiary predeceases the testator and the applicability of the rule of ademption in the event the gift is no longer in existence at the testator's death.

7. <u>Residuary Estate.</u> **OPTION 1: Residue outright** I give the residue of my estate to my [husband or wife], if [he or she] survives me. If my [husband or wife] does not survive me, I give the residue of my estate in equal shares to my children. If a child should die before me, I give the share of my deceased child to such child's surviving lineal descendants, per stirpes. If a deceased child has no living lineal descendants, the share of my deceased child shall be given to my other descendants, per stirpes.

COMMENT: This is a basic provision that provides for the residue passing to the surviving spouse if living, and if not, then to the children or more remote living descendants if children are deceased. Care must be taken to be certain that the outright distribution to the non-spouse beneficiaries is properly defined.

OPTION 2: Residue to spouse or inter vivos trust I give the residue of my estate to my [husband or wife] if [he or she] survives me, and if not, I give the residue of my estate to the trustee of the [trust name] Trust, which I entered into on [month] [day], [year of trust], prior to the execution of this will, to be held, administered and distributed according to the terms of that trust agreement.

COMMENT: This option provides for an outright distribution to the surviving spouse, if living, and if not then to an inter vivos trust. Obviously, this option contemplates the use of one of the inter vivos trust documents in this book.

OPTION 3: Residue to inter vivos trust I give the residue of my estate to the trustee of the [trust name] Trust, which I entered into on [month] [day], [year of trust], prior to the execution of this will, to be held, administered and distributed according to the terms of that trust agreement.

COMMENT: This option provides for the entire estate to pass into an inter vivos trust, whether or not there is a surviving spouse. This option is much the same as the pour over will provided in this book.

OPTION 4: Residue to spouse or to separate testamentary trusts (Option 1 below) I give the residue of my estate to my [husband or wife], if [he or she] survives me, and if not, I give the residue of my estate to my lineal descendants per stirpes subject to the trust in paragraph [insert number] below in the case of my [child or children] and subject to the contingent trust in paragraph [insert number] below in the case of my more remote lineal descendants.

COMMENT: This option provides for the estate to be distributed to the surviving spouse, if living, and if there is no surviving spouse then the estate is distributed on a per stirpes basis with the children receiving separate shares subject to the trust provisions in paragraph 8 Option 1 below; and the more remote lineal descendants (such as grandchildren) receiving their separate shares due to their parent's death subject to the trust provisions in paragraph 9 below.

OPTION 5: Residue to spouse or single testamentary trust (Option 2 below) I give the residue of my estate to my [husband or wife], if [he or she] survives me, and if not, I give the residue of my estate to the trust in paragraph [insert number] below.

COMMENT: This option provides for the estate to pass outright to the surviving spouse, if living, but if not to a single trust for all of the testator's children as provided in paragraph 8 Option 2 below.

8. **OPTION 1: Separate trusts for children** <u>Child's Trust.</u> If a child entitled to a share under this will is below the age of [final age to inherit] years that child's share shall be retained in trust as a separate trust which shall be named for that child. If a child is already [final age to inherit] years old, then such child shall receive his or her share outright.

COMMENT: Option 1 creates separate trusts for each child. Paragraph 8.b provides for a distribution of principal one-half at each of two ages. If that method is followed, then the final age to inherit is inserted into the two places above.

a. The trustee may pay to or use all, part or none, of the income and principal of a child's trust as the trustee believes appropriate for the reasonable maintenance, support, health, and education (including college or graduate, professional or vocational school education) of such child, considering such child's income or assets and all other circumstances and factors the trustee believes pertinent. It is my desire that distributions of income and principal not impair my child's motivation to be productive and self-supporting, thus my trustee shall not make distributions of income and principal from a child's trust if my child is not productive, mature, and responsible. If any net income remains undistributed at the end of each calendar year (excluding income distributed during the sixty-five (65) day period under Internal Revenue Code Section 663), the trustee shall add it to the principal of my child's trust.

COMMENT: The first sentence provides broad discretion to the trustee in making distributions for the child. The second sentence is not essential, but is provided to illustrate a possible restriction that the testator may desire. The third sentence can be eliminated, but is provided for situations in which income is not distributed before year end; and to set the time at which accumulated income is added to trust principal.

b. When a child for whom a trust held under this paragraph is named reaches the age of [initial age to inherit] years, the trustee shall distribute to such child one-half (1/2) of the then principal of that child's trust; and when such child reaches the age of [final age to inherit] years, the child's trust shall terminate and the balance of such child's trust shall be distributed outright to such child.

COMMENT: The trust can terminate and be distributed outright at one age, or in any number of other increments. This instrument provides for distribution at two ages with one-half at an age such as 25 and the remaining one-half at a later age such as 30. Clients differ as to the proper ages.

c. **OPTION 1: Default to child's estate** If a child for whom a trust held under this paragraph is named dies prior to termination of such child's trust, then such child's trust shall terminate and shall be distributed to such child's own estate.

c. **OPTION 2: Default to descendants** On the death of a child for whom a trust held under this paragraph is named, any principal and undistributed income of such child's trust shall be divided and allocated per stirpes among the then living lineal descendants of such child, if any, otherwise such child's trust shall be divided and allocated per stirpes among the then living lineal descendants of the nearest lineal ancestor of such child who also was a descendant of mine and of whom one or more descendants then are living, or, if none, such child's trust shall be divided and allocated per stirpes among my then living lineal descendants.

COMMENT: A decision must be made as to the distribution of the trust should the child die before termination of the trust. Option 1 is the simplest, as it permits the trust assets to be distributed to that child's own estate for distribution pursuant to the child's will if the child is old enough to have written a will, or pursuant to intestate laws. That result may be appropriate or it could be a disaster. The lawyer must determine if Option 1 is appropriate. Option 2 is designed to maintain a per stirpes distribution. Care must be taken to be certain that the per stirpes distribution provided in this form is adequate. This provision should not be used routinely without an analysis of its effect under the facts of the particular estate plan, especially the phrase that refers to "lineal descendants of the nearest lineal ancestor of a child who was also a descendant of mine."

---

d. Notwithstanding paragraphs 8.a and 8.b, following high school graduation, if a child for whom a trust is held hereunder fails to pursue post-secondary education leading to a bachelor's degree from an accredited college or university, all trust distributions, except for health care needs, shall cease until such child reaches the age of twenty-three (23) years. A child pursuing post-secondary education must annually maintain a 2.50 GPA based on a 4.0 grading scale in order to receive trust distributions, except for health care needs, prior to the age of twenty-three (23) years. If a child for whom a trust is named earns a bachelor's degree from an accredited college or university before such child reaches the age of twenty-three (23) years, the trustee shall within ninety (90) days of my child's graduation distribute [enter number] percent ([enter number]%) of the trust assets to my child free of trust.

COMMENT: This provision is intended to provide a model for the lawyer to consider in addressing an incentive for a child to pursue post-secondary education and to maintain an adequate grade point average. This paragraph may need to be moved to become part of paragraph a or as a separate paragraph. In this form, the decision was made to place it in this location as it and the following paragraph are both offered as supplemental provisions that some clients will want and others will not. Be certain to modify the reference in the first sentence to the correct paragraph numbers.

---

e. In addition to the restrictions provided above in paragraphs 8.a through 8.d and as a condition precedent to distributions under those paragraphs, my trustee shall withhold or postpone any or all distributions of income or principal from a child's trust if my trustee believes a distribution to such child could result in the loss of some part or all of the distribution due to any possible civil or criminal legal action involving my child or my child's spouse, or due to my child or my child's spouse being addicted to alcohol or any legal or illegal controlled substance. The decision of my trustee shall be final and binding and shall not be subject to question by any person or in any court.

COMMENT: If the client is faced with a child who has substance abuse or other serious problems making distributions from the trust unwise, or if the client is concerned about such possibility, then paragraph e or a variation of it may be helpful. It is designed to give the trustee full authority to withhold all distributions of income and principal when a child is facing substance abuse or other significant personal problems.

OPTION 2: Single trust for children Children's Trust. If my youngest child is below the age of [final age to inherit] years my entire residuary estate shall be retained in trust for all of my aforenamed children.

COMMENT: This trust provides one single trust for all of the testator's children. Therefore, trust distributions can be made among all children and the trust does not terminate until the youngest child reaches a particular age. That age will be inserted at the appropriate place above.

a. Until my youngest child becomes [final age to inherit] years old, my trustee shall pay to or use all, part or none of the income and principal of the trust, without regard to quality of distribution, to or for the benefit of my children as the trustee believes appropriate for the reasonable maintenance, support, health, and education (including college or graduate, professional or vocational school education) of my children, considering each child's income or assets and all other circumstances and factors the trustee believes pertinent. If any net income remains undistributed at the end of each calendar year (excluding income distributed during the sixty-five (65) day period under Internal Revenue Code Section 663), the trustee shall add it to the principal of the trust. Disbursements of income and principal shall not be taken into account when my trustee makes final distribution of the trust property upon termination of the trust.

COMMENT: This trust allows the trustee to make distributions among all the testator's children without regard to equality of distribution. This gives the trustee broad discretion to make distributions among the children based upon their then current needs. Because of the broadness of the discretion granted to the trustee, paragraph d from Option 1 has not been included but can be modified and added if the lawyer so desires. The second sentence can be eliminated, but is provided for situations in which income is not distributed before year end; and to set the time at which accumulated income is added to trust principal. A decision must be made as to the use of the third sentence.

b. Upon my youngest child reaching [final age to inherit] years of age, the trust shall terminate and my trustee shall distribute the trust property to my children in equal shares. If a child is deceased my deceased child's share shall be distributed to that child's then living lineal descendants per stirpes, if any, otherwise such child's share shall be distributed to my then living lineal descendants, per stirpes.

COMMENT: The trust terminates upon the youngest child reaching a particular age, at which time the trust terminates and each child receives an equal share. If a child is deceased, that child's share is distributed equally to his or her descendants. Care must be taken to be certain that the per stirpes distribution provided in this form is adequate. This provision should not be used routinely without an analysis of its effect under the facts of the particular estate plan.

9. Contingent Trust. My personal representative shall retain any property otherwise distributable pursuant to this will to any of my descendants, other than my [child or children] who

[children is or are] provided for above, who have not reached the age of [age for remote descendants] years as a separate trust named for such person to be distributed to such person when he or she reaches the age of [age for remote descendants] years. If such person is already [age for remote descendants] years of age, then such person shall receive his or her share outright. Until such person reaches [age for remote descendants] years of age, the trustee may pay to or use all, part or none, of the income and principal of such person's trust as the trustee believes appropriate for the reasonable maintenance, support, health and education (including college or graduate, professional or vocational school education) of the person for whom the trust is named, considering such person's income or assets and all other circumstances and factors the trustee believes pertinent. It is my desire that distributions of income and principal not impair such person's motivation to be productive and self-supporting, thus my trustee shall not make distributions of income and principal from a person's trust if such person is not productive, mature, and responsible. If any net income remains undistributed at the end of each calendar year (excluding income distributed during the sixty-five (65) day period under Internal Revenue Code Section 663), the trustee shall add it to the principal of such person's trust.

OPTION 1: Default to person's estate If the person for whom a trust held under this paragraph is named dies prior to the termination of such person's trust, then such person's trust shall terminate and be distributed to such person's own estate.

OPTION 2: Default to descendants On the death of a person for whom a trust held under this paragraph is named such person's trust shall be divided and allocated per stirpes among the then living lineal descendants of such person, if any, otherwise such person's trust shall be divided and allocated per stirpes among the then living lineal descendants of the nearest lineal ancestor of such person who also was a descendant of mine and of whom one or more descendants then are living, or, if none, such person's trust shall be divided and allocated per stirpes among my then living lineal descendants.

COMMENT: Paragraph 9 is used with paragraph 8 option 4 or 5 and permits a distribution to more remote descendants who are under a specified minimum age to be held in trust until that person reaches the minimum age with the trust property to be used for that person until termination of the trust. If this option is used, then Option 1 or 2 above should be selected to determine to whom the trust property is distributed should that remote descendant die before termination of the trust. Care must be taken to be certain that the per stirpes distribution provided in this form is adequate. This provision should not be used routinely without an analysis of its effect under the facts of the particular estate plan.

---

10. <u>Protection from Creditors.</u> No trust beneficiary shall have the right to sell, transfer, assign, alienate, pledge, or in any way encumber trust assets, including income and principal, nor shall trust assets be subject to execution, levy, sale, garnishment, attachment, bankruptcy, or other legal proceedings. Any such actions by a trust beneficiary or a third party seeking to enforce a claim against the trust assets shall not be recognized under any circumstances by the trustee. These provisions do not prevent the trustee from making distributions for the benefit of a trust beneficiary in such amounts and at such times as the trustee determines necessary for the trust beneficiary's maintenance, support, health and education.

COMMENT: This is a standard paragraph that precludes the trust assets from being attached by claims of creditors. The lawyer should check state law before advising a client of the effect of this provision.

---

11. <u>Default Provisions.</u> If all beneficiaries under this instrument are deceased, my estate or trust assets shall be distributed to [default provisions].

COMMENT: If there are a limited number of beneficiaries, then it may be wise to insert a default provision providing for the ultimate recipient should all the beneficiaries in paragraphs 8 and 9 and their descendants be deceased. If this is too remote of a possibility, some clients may direct that this paragraph be deleted.

---

12. <u>Definition of Per Stirpes.</u> Whenever assets are to be divided and allocated per stirpes, the assets to be divided or allocated shall be divided into as many equal shares as are necessary to divide or allocate one share to each then living child of such person and to provide one share collectively for the then living descendants of each child of such person who then is deceased leaving one or more descendants then living. Any collective share shall be divided and allocated per stirpes among the descendants of such deceased person in accordance with the preceding sentence.

COMMENT: Since the term per stirpes is used often in this document, a definition is provided of that term. The lawyer should modify this definition to conform with his or her own state law should it differ from this definition. Of course, a definition is not essential, since the term will be defined under state law. But since it is a term that clients are not familiar with, it is often helpful to define it for them in the document. An excellent ABA resource that explains the term per stirpes and its variations is Jeffrey N. Penell and Alan Newman, *Estate and Trust Planning*, American Bar Association (Chicago, 2005) pp. 19–26.

---

13. <u>Special Provisions.</u> In addition to the other provisions of this trust agreement:

COMMENT: The following are various provisions that may be needed in a given situation, but rarely will all of these paragraphs be needed.

---

a. <u>Residential Real Estate.</u> In the event any residential real estate is included among the trust assets and my [husband or wife] is then living, [he or she] may occupy such residence rent-free during [his or her] lifetime. My [husband or wife] shall pay all property taxes, insurance premiums, and the expenses of ordinary maintenance and repair. Further, my [husband or wife] may purchase any such residential real estate at its then appraised value as determined by a professional real estate appraiser.

COMMENT: In the event the testator desires for his or her personal residence to be available for a trust beneficiary, then this paragraph, or a modification of it, may be appropriate.

---

b. <u>Rule Against Perpetuities.</u> If not sooner terminated, twenty-one years after the death of the last to die of my [husband or wife], myself, and my descendants who are living at the time of the death of the first to die of my [husband or wife] or me, my trustee shall distribute the trust property to each person for whom a trust is held under this trust agreement.

COMMENT: The lawyer will need to determine if there is any concern over the rule against perpetuities, and if so, the above provision, or a modification of it, will be necessary. In most drafting situations, there will not be the possibility of violating this rule, thus the lawyer may want to omit this paragraph.

c. <u>Subchapter S Stock.</u> In the event a trust under this agreement holds Subchapter S stock, then the terms of this trust are hereby modified so that this trust qualifies as a Qualified Subchapter S Trust ("QSST") under section 1361(d) of the Internal Revenue Code. Therefore, any trust that has more than one permissible beneficiary shall be divided on a prorata basis into separate trusts for those beneficiaries, resulting in each trust having only one beneficiary who shall be the only recipient of trust income and principal until the earlier of the beneficiary's death or the termination of the trust. This provision shall not preclude the limitations on distributions of income and principal as required in paragraphs 8 and 9.

COMMENT: One of the general tax law requirements for a corporation being taxed as a Subchapter S corporation, which allows the corporate income to flow to the owners and be taxed to them rather than facing the possible double-taxation of the traditional corporate tax law, is that a trust cannot be an owner. Of course, with the tax law there are always exceptions. There are several situations in which a trust can be a stockholder of a Subchapter S corporation. This paragraph is intended to ensure that the corporation will maintain its status as a Subchapter S corporation, even though some of its stock is held in trust. This is a technical and somewhat tricky tax trap. An excellent ABA resource addressing this issue is Thomas M. Featherston, Jr. et al., *Drafting for Tax and Administrative Issues*, American Bar Association (Chicago: 2000). Be sure to change the numbers in the last sentence if any paragraphs prior to paragraph 8 are deleted.

d. <u>Reliance on Will.</u> The trustee may rely on a will admitted to probate in any jurisdiction as the last will and testament of such person, or may assume (absent actual knowledge to the contrary) the person had no will if a will has not been admitted to probate within three months after such person's death.

COMMENT: This is a "boilerplate" provision that is helpful, but this provision must be reviewed to be certain that it is needed, and to make any modifications that are required.

e. <u>Method of Payment.</u> If a person entitled to receive income or principal distributions is unable to manage his or her financial affairs due to any type of mental or physical incapacity, then distributions may be made to or for such person's benefit, including making distributions to such person's guardian, conservator, committee, or a custodian under a Uniform Gift or Transfer to Minors Act.

COMMENT: This is a "boilerplate" provision that is usually inserted in a trust instrument.

f. <u>Accrued Income and Termination.</u> Income accrued and undistributed at the termination of a person's interest in trust property **OPTION 1** shall be distributed to such person's estate. **OPTION 2** shall remain an asset of the trust and shall not be distributed to such person's estate.

COMMENT: This is a helpful provision for administrative reasons to clarify for the trustee whether accumulated but undistributed income should remain in the trust after the beneficiary's death or if it should be distributed to that beneficiary's estate. One of the two options should be selected.

g. <u>Rights and Duties Relating to Life Insurance Policies.</u> After my death when life insurance policies become payable to the trust, my trustee shall promptly furnish proof of loss to the life insurance companies, and shall collect and receive the proceeds of the policies. My trustee shall have power to execute and deliver receipts and other instruments and to take such action as is appropriate for this collection. If my trustee deems it necessary to institute legal action for the collection of any policies, [he, she or it] shall be indemnified for all costs, including attorney's fees.

My trustee, in [his, her or its] sole discretion, may accept any of the optional modes of payment provided in any of such policies where such modes of payment are permitted to the trustee by the life insurance company. No life insurance company under any policy of insurance deposited with my trustee shall be responsible for the application or disposition of the proceeds of such policy by my trustee. Payment to my trustee of such life insurance proceeds shall be a full discharge of the liability of the life insurance company under such policy.

COMMENT: This paragraph is needed only if life insurance is made payable to the trust. The provisions are customary and are intended to avoid liability for the life insurance company and the trustee over receipt of life insurance death proceeds and the selection of the mode of payment. While these are routine provisions, the lawyer should review them to be certain that they are appropriate.

14. <u>Trustee Powers.</u> In the administration of the trusts, the trustee shall have the following powers and rights and all others granted by law:

a. To sell publicly or privately any trust property, for cash or on time, without an order of court and upon such terms and conditions as my trustee deems proper; and no person dealing with my trustee shall have any obligation to look to the application of the purchase money.

b. To invest and reinvest all or any part of the principal of the trust in any stocks, bonds, mortgages, shares or interests in common trust funds, mutual funds, or other securities or property, real, personal, or mixed, and of any kind or nature whatsoever, as the trustee deems proper, and without diversification if the trustee deems it advisable, irrespective of whether or not such securities or property are eligible for trust investment under state or any other law, and may change any investment received or made by the trustee, and may hold cash if the trustee deems it advisable.

c. To exercise broad discretion as to diversification of trust property, and shall not be required to reduce any concentrated holdings merely because of such concentration, and shall have full discretion as to the percentage to be invested in fixed income securities, and is specifically relieved from any requirements, legal or otherwise, as to the percentage of the trust assets to be invested in fixed income securities, and may invest or retain invested any trust estates wholly in common stocks.

d. To sell, convey, lease or mortgage, repair and improve, and take any and all other steps with regard to any real estate that may at any time be a part of the principal of the trust; and any lease of such real property or contract with regard thereto made by the trustee shall be binding for the full period of the lease or contract, even though the period shall extend beyond the termination of the trust.

e. To vote shares of stock held in the trust at stockholders' meetings in person or by special, limited, or general proxy, with or without power of substitution, as seems best to the trustee.

f. To participate in the liquidation, reorganization, consolidation, incorporation and reincorporation, or any other financial readjustment of any corporation, limited liability company or business in which the trust is, or shall be financially interested.

g. To borrow money from any source for any purpose connected with the protection, preservation, improvement or development of the trust hereunder, whenever in the trustee's judgment the trustee deems it advisable, and as security to mortgage or pledge any real estate or personal property forming a part of the trust upon such terms and conditions as the trustee may deem advisable.

h. To hold any and all securities in bearer form, in the trustee's own name, or the name of some other person, partnership, or corporation, or in the name of a duly appointed nominee, with or without disclosing the fiduciary ownership.

i. To divide the principal of the trust property into parts or shares and to distribute or allot same, and to make such division in cash or in kind or both. For the purpose of such division or allotment, the judgment of the trustee concerning the propriety thereof and relative value of property so distributed or allotted shall be binding and conclusive with respect to all interested persons.

j. To merge and consolidate the trust property of any separate trust held hereunder with other trusts and then to administer such trust property as a single trust provided the separate trust is for the benefit of the same persons with substantially the same terms, conditions and federal tax consequences.

k. To pay such income and principal during the minority or incapacity of any beneficiary for whose benefit income and principal may be expended, in any one or more of the following ways: (1) directly to the beneficiary; (2) to the legal guardian or committee of the beneficiary; (3) to a relative of the beneficiary to be expended by the relative for the maintenance, health, and education of the beneficiary; or (4) by expending the same directly for the maintenance, health, and education of the beneficiary. The trustee shall not be obliged to see to the application of the funds so expended, but the receipt of such person shall be full acquittance to the trustee.

l. To continue and operate any business owned by me at my death and to do any and all things deemed appropriate by the trustee, including the power to form a limited liability company or incorporate the business and to put additional capital into the business, for such time as the trustee deems advisable, without liability for loss resulting from the continuance or operation of the business except for the trustee's own negligence; and to close out, liquidate, or sell the business at such time and upon such terms as the trustee deems proper, and in this connection a sale may be made (pursuant to an agreement entered into by me during my lifetime, or otherwise) to a partner, officer, member, employee or beneficiary under this trust. I am aware of the fact that certain risks are inherent in the operation of any business and, therefore, my trustee shall not be liable for any loss resulting from the retention and operation of any business unless such loss results directly from my trustee's gross negligence or willful misconduct.

m. To have the same powers, authorities, and discretions in the management of the trust as I would have in the management and control of my own personal assets. The trustee may continue to exercise any powers and discretions granted in this instrument for a reasonable period after the termination of any trust under this instrument.

COMMENT: The above powers are a set of standard powers that appear throughout this book. The powers should be reviewed to be certain that you the lawyer understand each power, the client is in agreement with each of the powers granted and that the powers granted are needed. Because this is a generic and broad statement of powers, some of these powers may not be necessary. For example, powers to sell or lease real estate are not needed if the testator knows the trust will consist only of cash and other intangible investments.

---

15. <u>Environmental Interests.</u> In the administration of this trust, my trustee shall have the power and authority to inspect, assess and evaluate any assets held in this trust, or proposed to be added

to this trust, to determine if any environmental concerns exist with such asset or assets, and if so, my trustee may take any remedial action my trustee believes necessary to prevent, abate or remedy any environmental concerns whether or not my trustee is required to do so by any governmental agency. Further, my trustee may refuse to accept or may disclaim any asset or assets proposed to be added to the trust if my trustee believes there are possible environmental concerns that could result in liability to the trust or the trustee. Also, my trustee may settle or compromise any claims or lawsuits alleging environmental concerns which have been asserted by a private party or governmental agency. The decisions of my trustee regarding environmental concerns shall be final and binding on all parties and shall not be subject to question by anyone or in any court.

COMMENT: In many situations, it will be appropriate to address concerns of the trustee if the trust holds, or is expected to receive by will or other transfer, an asset that may have environmental concerns. This paragraph, or a variation of it, is helpful to the trustee in addressing this oftentimes difficult fiduciary problem. If there is any possibility the trust may hold assets that have environmental concerns, then the lawyer should address those issues fully with the client and with the trustee, including successor trustees, to avoid the situation in which a named trustee refuses to serve due to concerns over personal liability of the fiduciary for environmental cleanup costs.

16. <u>Trustee Powers as to Farms and Farm Real Estate.</u> In the administration of any farms and farmland held in this trust, the trustee shall have the following powers and rights:

a. To formulate and carry out a general farm plan of operation.

b. To make leases and enter into contracts with tenants, either on shares or for stated compensation, or to employ and pay such labor as might be employed.

c. To buy, breed, raise, and sell all kinds of livestock, either on shares with a tenant or solely on behalf of the trust estate.

d. To plant, cultivate, fertilize, produce, and market all crops raised on the farm, and to collect, receive and receipt for all shares, rent, and other income from the farm.

e. To ditch and drain so much of the land as might be considered desirable, and to make such repairs and improvements to building, land, and other items of property as may be consistent with good farm management.

f. To enter into contracts with the United States Department of Agriculture, or other Federal or State governmental agencies, for crop reductions or soil conservation practices.

g. To pay all taxes and assessments against the farm property and insure the improvements against loss by fire, windstorm, and other casualties.

h. To credit receipts and charge expenditures to and against the income account or the principal account as may be appropriate under applicable rules of trust accounting. In this regard, it is especially provided that any capital improvements made by the trustee in the exercise of prudent trust management shall be allocated between the income account and the principal account on the basis of the ratio of the life expectancy of the income beneficiary at that time to the normally expected useful life of the capital improvement.

i. To employ farm management services to the extent that this may be considered desirable for the proper formulation of farming plans and the active management of farm properties under the supervision and responsibility of the trustee.

j. To borrow monies which may be required from time to time to finance the farm operations, and to encumber trust assets to secure such loans.

k. To do any and all other things consistent with the provisions of this trust to facilitate an orderly distribution of our assets calculated to accomplish the purposes herein set out in an economically feasible manner.

COMMENT: In the event the trust will include a farm that will continue to be owned in trust, then these additional trust provisions should be considered. The general trustee powers should be sufficient, but when drafting for a farming client these more specific trustee powers are usually helpful.

---

17. <u>Limitation on Powers of Individual Trustee.</u> Notwithstanding any other powers granted to my trustee in this instrument, an individual trustee (a) shall have no power to make payments or distributions that would discharge the trustee's legal obligation to support the trust beneficiary, (b) shall not exercise any power or discretion in any manner that would be deemed to be a general power of appointment under Internal Revenue Code Section 2041, (c) shall be limited by the ascertainable standard of "maintenance, support, health and education" when making payments or distributions to the trustee personally or to anyone for whom the trustee has a beneficial interest, and (d) shall possess no incidence of ownership or powers with respect to life insurance in which the trustee is the insured and has fiduciary power over such life insurance.

COMMENT: There are some situations in which an individual trustee may have adverse estate or income tax consequences when given broad powers as trustee. If a corporate trustee is used, then this paragraph is not needed. But an individual trustee must be certain that acting as trustee does not result in any adverse estate or income tax consequences. This paragraph is intended to ensure that adverse tax consequences are avoided if overly broad powers are granted in the trust instrument. The lawyer is urged to exercise caution when using individual trustees coupled with broad discretionary powers of income and principal distribution to a trust beneficiary because of possible adverse tax consequences. An ABA resource to acquaint oneself with these issues is L. Rush Hunt and Lara Rae Hunt, *A Lawyer's Guide to Estate Planning*, American Bar Association (Chicago: 2004) §14.4.

---

18. <u>Trustee Resignation.</u> My trustee may resign at any time by giving written notice to my successor trustee named below, if any, and if none, then written notice shall be given to each current adult income beneficiary who is then living.

COMMENT: If a trustee resigns, there must be some method of notice and appointment of a successor trustee. This paragraph provides a method of notification. It is not an essential trust provision, but is a helpful one.

---

19. <u>Trustee Appointment and Succession.</u> The initial trustee shall be [trustee name]. If my initial trustee ceases to act as trustee due to death, incompetency, resignation or any other reason, then [successor trustee] shall be successor trustee. My successor trustee may name [his or her] own successor trustee by a written instrument delivered to the successor trustee, or by will. The successor trustee shall be an individual or a financial institution possessing trust powers under state or federal law. Any further vacancy in the office of trustee shall be filled by decision of the probate court where I resided at the time of my death. No trustee or successor trustee shall be required to post a surety bond for serving as trustee or successor trustee.

COMMENT: A decision must be made as to the succession of trustees and the method of appointing a successor trustee if all of those named successor trustees are unable to serve. It is also essential to clarify whether successor trustees must only be financial institutions or if individuals may also be considered. Once a decision is made as to the succession of trustees, then the last three sentences should be reviewed to be certain to what extent each of those are needed.

20. <u>Powers of Successor Trustee.</u> Each successor trustee shall have the same rights, titles, powers, duties, discretions, and immunities and otherwise be in the same position as if originally named trustee. No successor trustee shall be personally liable for any act or failure to act of a predecessor trustee. Further, a successor trustee may accept the account furnished and the property delivered by or for a predecessor trustee without liability for so doing, and such acceptance shall be a full and complete discharge to the predecessor trustee.

COMMENT: This paragraph clarifies that a successor trustee has the same powers as the initial trustee. Further, the paragraph relieves the successor trustee from liability for the prior acts of the resigning trustee and waives any requirements of audit or inquiry into the activities of the prior trustee. This is essential for any successor trustee.

21. <u>Compensation of Trustee.</u> **OPTION 1: Corporate trustee compensation** A corporate trustee shall receive compensation in accordance with its regular schedule of fees in effect at the time such services are rendered.

OPTION 2: Individual does not receive compensation An individual trustee shall not be paid any compensation, but shall be reimbursed for out-of-pocket expenses.

OPTION 3: Individual does receive compensation An individual trustee shall be paid [insert amount of compensation] as compensation for such services and shall be reimbursed for out-of-pocket expenses.

COMMENT: Three options are provided, but the actual drafting of this paragraph may be different than each of these options. If the only trustee to be used is a corporate trustee, then Option 1 is a standard trust provision. If there is a possibility of individual trustees, then care should be given to the method for setting this fee. If no fee is to be paid because the trustee is a close family member, then it is suggested that Option 2 be used. If the testator expects a fee to be charged, then Option 3 sets the fee at an amount or a percentage of income or principal. It is unwise to simply provide for compensation to be a reasonable fee, as that leaves an individual trustee with great uncertainty as to the fee to be charged. Without the testator clarifying compensation, the trustee could find him or herself in litigation with the beneficiary.

22. <u>Appointment of Personal Representative.</u> My [husband or wife], shall be the personal representative of my estate. If my [husband or wife] fails to qualify as personal representative, or having qualified, dies, becomes incompetent, resigns, or declines to continue to serve, then my [relationship of successor PR] [name of successor PR] shall serve as my successor personal representative. Neither my [husband or wife] nor my successor personal representative shall be required to furnish any surety bond for serving as my personal representative.

COMMENT: The full names of the personal representative and successor personal representative are required as is a decision concerning the waiver of a surety bond. The form, as drafted, assumes the intent to waive such bond.

23. <u>Powers of Personal Representative.</u> I hereby grant to my personal representative (including my successor personal representative) the absolute power to deal with any property, real or personal, held in my estate, as freely as I might in the handling of my own affairs. This power may be exercised independently and without the approval of any court, and no person dealing with my personal representative shall be required to inquire into the propriety of the actions of my personal representative. Without in any way limiting the generality of the foregoing provisions, I grant to my personal representative in addition to those powers specified under state law the following powers:

a. To sell, exchange, assign, transfer and convey any security or property, real or personal, held in my estate at public or private sale, at such time and at such reasonable price and upon such reasonable terms and conditions (including credit) as my personal representative may determine; and without regard to whether or not such sale is necessary in order to settle my estate.

b. To lease any real estate for such term, or terms, and upon such reasonable conditions and rentals and in such manner as my personal representative deems proper, and any lease so made shall be valid and binding for its full term even though such lease term extends beyond the duration of the administration of my estate; to make repairs, replacements and improvements, structural or otherwise, to any such real estate; to subdivide real estate, dedicate real estate to public use and grant easements as my personal representative deems proper.

c. To employ accountants, attorneys and such other agents as my personal representative deems necessary; to pay reasonable compensation for such services and to charge same to (or apportion same between) income and principal as my personal representative deems proper.

d. To make such elections under the tax laws applicable to my estate as my personal representative determines should be made; to elect to treat any fraction or all of any trust I have created as qualified terminable interest property for federal estate tax purposes to the extent my personal representative deems proper; and to make allocations of any available generation-skipping tax exemption as my personal representative deems proper. No adjustment shall be made between principal and income or in the relative interests of the beneficiaries to compensate for any such election or allocation made by my personal representative.

e. To join with my [husband or wife] on my behalf in filing income tax returns, or to consent for gift tax purposes to having gifts made by either of us during my life considered as made one-half by each of us, and any resulting tax liability shall be paid by my estate, except such portion as my personal representative and my [husband or wife] agree should be paid by my [husband or wife].

COMMENT: A statement of the powers of the personal representative is not essential, as those powers are specified by state law; however, those state laws may not be sufficiently broad. Often state laws do not include power to real estate. Paragraph 23.c may not be essential, but this writer prefers to clarify that the personal representative may hire at the expense of the estate professionals to assist in estate settlement. Paragraph 23.d deals with the signing of tax returns and, while not essential, still is appropriate in most situations.

---

24. <u>Power to Operate Business.</u> I grant to my personal representative the power to retain and continue to operate any limited liability company, corporation, or other business entity I own an interest in at my death, for such period of time as my personal representative determines and my personal representative shall be the sole decision maker as to the manner and extent of my personal representative's active participation in the operation of such business. I further grant to my personal representative the power to sell or liquidate all or part of my business at such time and price and upon such terms and conditions as my personal representative deems advisable

and in this connection a sale may be made (pursuant to an agreement entered into by me during my lifetime, or otherwise) to a partner, officer, member, employee or beneficiary under this will. I am aware of the fact that certain risks are inherent in the operation of any business and, therefore, my personal representative shall not be liable for any loss resulting from the retention and operation of any business unless such loss results directly from my personal representative's gross negligence or willful misconduct.

COMMENT: This provision is only needed if the testator owns a business that will continue to be operated for some period of time by the personal representative.

---

25. Certification of Incompetency. **OPTION 1: Decided by treating physician** Any person acting or named to act in a fiduciary capacity in this will is considered to be unable to serve or to continue serving when a physician whom such person has consulted within the prior three years has certified as to such consultation and the certification states that the person is incapable of managing the affairs of my estate or any trust I have established, regardless of cause and regardless of whether there is an adjudication of incompetency. No person is liable to anyone for actions taken in reliance on the physician's certification or for dealing with a personal representative or trustee other than the one removed for incompetency based on these certifications.

OPTION 2: Decided by two physicians Any person acting or named to act in a fiduciary capacity in this will is considered to be unable to serve or to continue serving when a written certification is received from two (2) physicians, both of whom have personally examined the person and at least one (1) of whom is board-certified in the specialty most closely associated with the health condition alleged to cause such incompetency. The certification must state that the person is incapable of managing his or her own finances, regardless of cause and regardless of whether there is an adjudication of incompetence, or need for a conservator, guardian, or other personal representative. No person is liable to anyone for actions taken in reliance on these certifications, or for dealing with a personal representative or trustee other than the one removed for incompetency based on these certifications.

COMMENT: This provision relates back to paragraph 19, 22 and 28 concerning the succession of trustees, personal representatives and guardians. It defines incompetency, which is one of those events requiring a successor trustee, personal representative or guardian. The first option involves consultation with the fiduciary's personal physician, whereas Option 2 involves a panel of two physicians, one of whom is board certified in the speciality most closely associated with the health condition of the fiduciary. Absent a strong preference by the testator, Option 1 is the provision most frequently used.

---

26. No-Contest Provision. If any beneficiary contests the probate or validity of my will or any of its provisions, including the provisions of any testamentary trust, or if any beneficiary joins in any such action, then all provisions in this instrument for the benefit of such beneficiary are revoked and his or her share shall be distributed as if such beneficiary predeceased me dying without any lineal descendants.

COMMENT: This provision or some variation of it should be considered if there is any concern that a beneficiary or heir-at-law may challenge the will or testamentary trust. The lawyer may need to modify this provision to meet any requirements of state law.

---

27. <u>Employment of Attorney.</u> I request but do not require that my personal representative employ the law firm of [insert name of law firm], [city], [state] to be my estate's attorney as the attorneys in that law firm are the most familiar with my intentions expressed in this will.

COMMENT: This paragraph may be appropriate when the client is expecting the lawyer who drafted the will to be available to settle the estate. Often the children do not know the parent's preference for a lawyer, thus the provision is inserted. The employment of the testator's lawyer is made permissive to avoid any appearance of self-dealing by the lawyer preparing the will. There will be situations in which the client insists the wording be made mandatory. If so, the lawyer may wish to document this fact by memo to the file, signed by the client.

---

28. <u>Appointment of Guardian.</u> If my [husband or wife] does not survive me, my [relationship], [Name of Guardian], shall be guardian of each child for whom it is necessary to appoint a guardian. If [Name of Guardian] does not act as guardian, or having qualified dies, becomes incompetent, resigns, or declines to continue to serve, then my [relationship], [Alternate guardian] shall be guardian of each child for whom it is necessary to appoint a guardian. No surety shall be required of my guardians.

COMMENT: This is a standard paragraph naming a guardian for any children for whom a guardian is necessary. If there is only one possible guardian and no alternate guardian, then the second sentence can be omitted. This paragraph omits the requirement of a surety bond.

---

29. **OPTION 1: Client dies first** <u>Simultaneous Death.</u> In the event that my [husband or wife] and I shall die simultaneously or under such circumstances as to render it impossible or difficult to determine which of us survived the other, I direct that it shall be deemed that I predeceased my [husband or wife], and this will and all of its provisions shall be construed on that assumption and basis.

OPTION 2: Other spouse dies first <u>Simultaneous Death.</u> In the event that my [husband or wife] and I shall die simultaneously or under such circumstances as to render it impossible or difficult to determine which of us survived the other, I direct that it shall be deemed that I survived my [husband or wife], and this will and any and all of its provisions shall be construed on that assumption and basis.

OPTION 3: <u>Survivorship</u> In the event my [husband or wife] does not survive me by [number of days] days this will shall be read and construed as though my [husband or wife] predeceased me.

COMMENT: In some situations, a survivorship clause may be desired. Three options have been provided. The lawyer will need to either select one of these, make a modification to them to fit the particular circumstances, or in some situations may feel there to be no need for such a clause.

IN TESTIMONY WHEREOF, I, [Name of Client], sign my name to this instrument this _____ day of _____, [current year], and being first duly sworn, do hereby declare to the undersigned authority that I sign and execute this instrument as my last will and that I sign it willingly, that I execute it as my free and voluntary act for the purposes therein expressed, and that I am 18 years of age or older, of sound mind, and under no constraint or undue influence.

_____
[Name of Client]

We _____ and _____, the witnesses, sign our names to this instrument, being first duly sworn, and do hereby declare to the undersigned authority that [Name of Client] signs and executes this instrument as [his or her] Last Will and Testament dated _____, [current year], and that [he or she] signs it willingly and that each of us, in the presence and hearing of [Name of Client] and in the presence of the other subscribing witness, hereby signs this Last Will and Testament as witness to [Name of Client]'s signing, and that to the best of their knowledge, [Name of Client] is eighteen (18) years of age or older, of sound mind and under no constraint or undue influence, all on this _____ day of _____, [current year].

_____   _____
Witness   Address

_____   _____
Witness   Address

STATE OF [State of Notary]   )
)SCT.
COUNTY OF [County of Notary])

Subscribed, sworn to, and acknowledged before me by [Name of Client], and subscribed and sworn to before me by _____ and _____, witnesses, this the _____ day of _____, [current year].

                                   _____
                                   Notary Public, State at Large

                                   My Commission Expires:_____

COMMENT: The above provisions are in compliance with the writer's own state law to avoid the necessity of locating witnesses to the will at a later date. This provision should be modified to meet the requirement of the lawyer's own state law.

PREPARED BY:

_____
[Name of Attorney]
[Name of Law Firm]
Attorneys at Law
[Street Address]
[City], [State] [Zip Code]
[Telephone Number]

POUR OVER WILL WORKSHEET

1. **Testator and Family Information**

   1.1 Name of Testator _____

   1.2 Testator City and State _____

   1.3 Name of Spouse _____

   1.4 Names of Children _____

   _____

   _____

   _____

   1.5 Are any of the above-named children step-children? <u>Yes / No</u>

   (Paragraph 1, Option 2)

   1.6 Are provisions needed for after-born children? <u>Yes / No</u>

   (Paragraph 1, Option 3)

   1.7 Are provisions needed for adopted and/or illegitimately born children? <u>Yes / No</u>

   (Paragraph 1, Option 4)

   1.8 Are any children to be disinherited? <u>Yes / No</u>

   (Paragraph 1, Option 5)

   Name of disinherited child: _____

   1.9 Are any loans or advancements to be considered for any child? <u>Yes / No</u>

   Name of Child: _____

   Is loan or gift/advancement to be considered in making distribution? <u>Yes / No</u>

   _____

   (See Master Will Paragraphs 4 and 5, Options 1 and 2, beginning at page 28)

2. **Specific Bequests and Legacies**

   2.1 Specific Gifts (See Master Will Paragraph 3, beginning at page 27)

   a. Description _____

   b. Primary Beneficiary _____

   c. Contingent Beneficiary _____

   d. Survivorship Period _____

   2.2 Tangible Personal Property (spouse, and if not surviving, to children)

   a. Description _____

   b. Primary Beneficiary _____

   c. Contingent Beneficiary _____

   d. Survivorship Period _____

2.3 Tangible Personal Property (spouse not surviving)

    If no agreement among children as to division:

        Personal Representative Decides? (Option 1) <u>Yes / No</u>

        Sell and Distribute Proceeds to Residue? (Option 2) <u>Yes / No</u>

3.   Payment of Death Taxes

3.1 Are taxes on probate and nonprobate assets, including apportionment property, to be paid from the residue? (Option 1)

3.2 Are death taxes to be paid by beneficiary and taxes collected on apportionment property? (Option 2)

3.3 Are death taxes to be paid from the residue but taxes collected on apportionment property? (Option 3)

Yes / No
Yes / No
Yes / No

3.4 Other tax provisions _____

_____

4.   Residue to Trust

Name and date of trust: _____

5.   Personal Representative

5.1 Spouse named initial personal representative? <u>Yes / No</u>

5.2 If spouse not initial personal representative:

    Name_____ Address _____

5.3 Successor Personal Representative:

    Name _____

    Relationship _____

    Address_____

5.4 Surety Bond Waived? <u>Yes / No</u>

5.5 Special Provisions needed to operate business? <u>Yes / No</u>

6.   Guardian, if spouse not surviving

6.1 Name _____ Address _____

6.2 Alternate _____ Address _____

6.3 Surety Bond Waived? <u>Yes / No</u>

6.4 Special provisions or bequests for guardian?_____

_____

7.   Survivorship

7.1 Simultaneous Death <u>Yes / No</u>

    If yes, which spouse is presumed to die first? _____

7.2 General Survivorship _____ days

    Does this apply to spouse? <u>Yes / No</u>
    (See Master Will Paragraph 29 at page 44)

POUR OVER WILL

This will is termed a pour over will. It is used whenever a trust receives all, or a majority of the testamentary distributions. In this pour over will, the entire estate other than tangible personal property is distributed to a separate inter vivos trust. This form can be used with the addition from the Master Will beginning at page 25 of wording for specific bequests provided in paragraph 3, paragraph 4 in the case of an advancement or paragraph 6 in the case of loans. Other than these minor provisions, the entire estate will pass into the inter vivos trust.

OF

[FULL NAME OF CLIENT]

I, [Full Name of Client], currently of [Client's City], [Client's State], make this my last will and testament, hereby revoking all wills and codicils previously made by me.

1. Family Information. My [husband or wife]'s name is [husband or wife's name], and all references in this will to "my [husband or wife]" are only to [him or her].

OPTION 1: Naming of all children My [child is or children are], [names of children], and all references in this will to "my [child is or children are]" only to [him her or them].

OPTION 2: Inclusion of step-children Even though some of these children are step-children it is my intent that each of the above-named children be treated for purposes of inheriting under this will as if they and their lineal descendants are my natural born children and descendants.

OPTION 3: After-born children If subsequent to the execution of this will there shall be an additional child or children born to me, then such child or children shall share in the benefits of my estate to the same extent as my above named children and their descendants; and the provisions of this will shall be deemed modified to the extent necessary to carry out this intent.

COMMENT: The full name of the other spouse and children should be inserted. If step-children are involved, Option 2 should be considered. Also, Option 3 may be appropriate if there is the possibility of additional children. The lawyer's state law should provide for this contingency, but it may still be appropriate to add this provision to the will.

OPTION 4: Adopted and illegitimately born children The words "child," "children," "descendant" or "descendants" shall exclude adopted persons unless they are adopted prior to [insert age] years; and shall include only persons legitimately born unless a decree of adoption terminates the parental rights of the natural mother during her lifetime, or the natural father signs a written notarized instrument during his lifetime in which he irrevocably states that the child is to be considered legitimately born for purposes of inheriting under this will.

COMMENT: Some clients will want to restrict distribution for an adopted descendant to preclude a child adopted as an adult. Thus, many clients will use the age 18 or perhaps a slightly older age such as 20 or 21. Other clients may wish to restrict the age to a younger adopted child, such as one under the age of 10. The issue of illegitimate descendants should also be considered. In many situations, a child or more remote descendant should be treated the same as any other child, in which case the portion of this paragraph that deals with illegitimate children should be deleted. In other situations there may be a limited or no relationship with the child, in which event no distribution should be made to that child. This form gives the father of the child the right to allow the child to inherit if the father signs a written document allowing the inheritance.

OPTION 5: Disinheritance I have made no provisions for the benefit of my [relationship], [name], for reasons that need not be expressed.

If a child is to be disinherited, then it is wise practice to mention the child's name to clarify the child is not to receive a share so that no claim can be made that the client intended for the child to inherit, but the lawyer drafting the document failed to name the child.

---

2. <u>Payment of Debts, Death Taxes and Funeral Expenses.</u> **OPTION 1: Death taxes paid from residue** I direct that all of my just debts, my funeral expenses, costs of estate administration, and death taxes, if any, be paid from the residue of my estate as soon as possible after my death. I further direct that any real property that is subject to a mortgage or lien shall pass under my will subject to such mortgage or lien, rather than such indebtedness being paid from my estate. Death taxes means any estate or inheritance taxes, but not generation-skipping transfer taxes, imposed under the laws of any jurisdiction due to my death on any property passing by reason of my death whether or not such property passes under this will. Any generation-skipping transfer taxes resulting from a transfer occurring under my will shall be paid from the property that incurred such tax and shall not be paid from my other estate assets.

COMMENT: This paragraph first provides for the payment of all debts and final expenses, then imposes any death taxes on the residue to the estate. Any mortgage indebtedness is not to be paid from the residue but is to pass to the beneficiary who is the recipient of that property subject to the debt. If the debt is to be paid, then this second sentence should be deleted. If wording concerning the generation-skipping tax is not needed, the final sentence can be omitted and the phrase in the third sentence that refers to the generation-skipping tax can be deleted.

OPTION 2: Death taxes paid by beneficiary and collecting taxes on apportionment property I direct that all of my just debts, my funeral expenses and costs of estate administration be paid from the residue of my estate as soon as possible after my death; provided, however, I direct that if any death taxes are owed by my estate that such taxes be charged against the share passing to the person whose share generated such tax. I further direct that any real property that is subject to a mortgage or lien shall pass under my will subject to such mortgage or lien, rather than such indebtedness being paid from my estate. Death taxes means any estate or inheritance taxes, but not generation-skipping transfer taxes, imposed under the laws of any jurisdiction due to my death on any property passing by reason of my death whether or not such property passes under this will. With regard to apportionment property, my personal representative shall take such actions as are necessary to obtain reimbursement with respect to apportionment property, including withholding distribution. Apportionment property means (a) any property with respect to which my personal representative may be entitled to recover federal estate tax under Internal Revenue Code Section 2207, 2207A, or 2207B and (b) any policies of insurance, or the proceeds of policies of insurance, on my life which are not owned by me at my death. Any generation-skipping transfer taxes resulting from a transfer occurring under my will shall be paid from the property that incurred such tax and shall not be paid from my other estate assets.

COMMENT: Option 2 first provides for the payment of all debts and final expenses from the residue, but state and federal death taxes are charged to each beneficiary based upon the amount received by such beneficiary. Thus the tax burden is shared among the estate beneficiaries based on the amount of their inheritance. This becomes important when there are beneficiaries receiving gifts who do not share in the residuary estate. To assess their taxes to the residue results in a reduction in the amount of the residue received by the residuary beneficiaries. Sometimes this is the result the client wants, but other times, they prefer for each beneficiary to pay their own tax burden. The issue of who pays the tax should be addressed in determining the correct tax payment clause. Apportionment property refers to property that is subject to estate tax due to the decedent having a power of appointment over property, assets that are taxable in the decedent's estate due to having qualified for the marital deduction in the estate of the decedent's spouse, property in which the decedent had a retained interest, or some life insurance proceeds. Normally, reimbursement for estate taxes owed by the decedent's estate should be sought from the holders of such property. As in Option 1, any mortgage indebtedness is not to be paid from the residue but is to pass to the beneficiary who is the recipient of that property subject to the debt. If the mortgage debt should be paid, then this second sentence should be deleted.

OPTION 3: Death taxes paid from residue but collecting taxes on apportionment property I direct that all of my just debts, my funeral expenses and costs of estate administration be paid from the residue of my estate as soon as possible after my death. I also direct that any real property that is subject to a mortgage or lien shall pass under my will subject to such mortgage or lien, rather than such indebtedness being paid from my estate.

I further direct that my death taxes, if any, be paid out of my residuary estate, other than apportionment property, without proration and my personal representative shall not seek contribution toward or recovery of any such payments. Death taxes means any estate or inheritance taxes, but not generation-skipping transfer taxes, imposed under the laws of any jurisdiction due to my death on any property passing by reason of my death whether or not such property passes under this will. With regard to apportionment property, my personal representative shall take such actions as are necessary to obtain reimbursement with respect to apportionment property, including withholding distribution. Apportionment property means (a) any property with respect to which my personal representative may be entitled to recover federal estate tax under Internal Revenue Code Section 2207, 2207A, or 2207B and (b) any policies of insurance, or the proceeds of policies of insurance, on my life which are not owned by me at my death. Any generation-skipping transfer taxes resulting from a transfer occurring under my will shall be paid from the property that incurred such tax and shall not be paid from my other estate assets.

COMMENT: Option 3 provides for the payment of all debts, final expenses, and death taxes from the residue of the estate, thus any specific gifts other than gifts of the residue are received free of any state or federal death taxes. The only exception is apportionment property which is to pay its share of the estate taxes. Apportionment property refers to property that is subject to estate tax due to the decedent having a power of appointment over property, assets that are taxable in the decedent's estate due to having qualified for the marital deduction in the estate of the decedent's spouse, property in which the decedent had a retained interest, or some life insurance proceeds. Normally, reimbursement for estate taxes owed by the decedent's estate should be sought from the holders of such property. As in the prior two options, any mortgage indebtedness is not to be paid from the residue but is to pass to the beneficiary who is the recipient of that property subject to the debt. If the mortgage debt should be paid, then this second sentence should be deleted.

3. <u>Disposition of Tangible Personal Property.</u> I give to my [husband or wife], all of my personal and household effects, including but not limited to furniture, furnishings, appliances, clothing,

jewelry, automobiles and any other similar tangible personal property. If my [husband or wife] does not survive me, I give all such tangible personal property to my [child or children], in as nearly equal shares as is possible.

OPTION 1: If no agreement personal representative makes decision If my children cannot agree upon this division within ninety (90) days after the appointment of my personal representative, then the division made by my personal representative shall be final and binding upon my children and shall not be subject to question by anyone or in any court.

OPTION 2: **If no agreement sell and proceeds to residue** If my children cannot agree upon this division within ninety (90) days after the appointment of my personal representative, then my personal representative shall sell all property with respect to which my children have not reached an agreement and the net sales proceeds shall be distributed as part of the residue of my estate.

COMMENT: Gifts of personal property can be the source of family disagreements and even litigation. While the initial gift of such property to the surviving spouse is not a problem, the problem arises when the surviving spouse dies and the personal property passes to the children. Options 1 and 2 provide two different approaches for handling distribution in the event of a disagreement. The lawyer may choose either of those options, write his/her own method of resolving the conflict or leave out these options and let the probate court deal with the problem. This writer has found that going to court over grandmother's clock is not something most clients want their children to do. Thus, Option 1, Option 2 or some variation may be helpful.

I may leave with my will or among my papers a handwritten letter or handwritten memorandum concerning the distribution of certain items of my tangible personal property. If so, I direct my personal representative to distribute those items of my tangible personal property as I have provided in that letter or memorandum.

COMMENT: Some clients have numerous items of personal property that they want to give to family and friends. Rather than having a lengthy will naming these items, some lawyers prefer the use of a handwritten letter that is dated and signed at the bottom of the page by the testator. This approach allows the ease of changing the document over the years. It has the disadvantage of possibly not being an enforceable document depending upon state law. If the document qualifies under state law as a holographic codicil, or due to enactment of Section 2-513 of the Uniform Probate Code, then it is enforceable and the personal representative is required to account for those items named in the letter and to ensure their distribution to the correct beneficiary. A problem with the handwritten letter is that it is unlikely that it will be written in a way to address the lapse of a gift if a beneficiary predeceases the testator and the applicability of the rule of ademption in the event the gift is no longer in existence at the testator's death.

---

4. <u>Residuary Estate.</u> I give the residue of my estate to the trustee of the [trust name] Trust, which I entered into on [month] [day], [year of trust], prior to the execution of this will, to be held, administered and distributed according to the terms of that trust agreement.

COMMENT: Since the entire estate passes to the inter vivos trust, all that is necessary is to name the trust and provide the date the trust was executed. If a spouse or other beneficiary is to receive the estate outright and the residue passing to a trust is an alternate disposition, then a minor change in wording is needed to make the outright bequest and then to use the above wording following the outright bequests if the named beneficiary is deceased. The trust must be executed prior to the signing of the will to avoid the illogical results of a will passing property to a trust that has yet to come into existence. Since the documents are often signed the same day, as a matter of office practice, the trust should be signed first followed by the will being signed.

---

5. <u>Appointment of Personal Representative.</u> My [husband or wife], shall be the personal representative of my estate. If my [husband or wife] fails to qualify as personal representative, or having qualified, dies, becomes incompetent, resigns, or declines to continue to serve, then my [relationship of successor PR] [name of successor PR] shall serve as my successor personal representative. Neither my [husband or wife] nor my successor personal representative shall be required to furnish any surety bond for serving as my personal representative.

COMMENT: The full names of the personal representative and successor personal representative are required as is a decision concerning the waiver of a surety bond. The form, as drafted, assumes the intent to waive such bond.

---

6. <u>Powers of Personal Representative.</u> I hereby grant to my personal representative (including my successor personal representative) the absolute power to deal with any property, real or personal, held in my estate, as freely as I might in the handling of my own affairs. This power may be exercised independently and without the approval of any court, and no person dealing with my personal representative shall be required to inquire into the propriety of the actions of my personal representative. Without in any way limiting the generality of the foregoing provisions, I grant to my personal representative in addition to those powers specified under state law the following powers:

a. To sell, exchange, assign, transfer and convey any security or property, real or personal, held in my estate at public or private sale, at such time and at such reasonable price and upon such reasonable terms and conditions (including credit) as my personal representative may determine; and without regard to whether or not such sale is necessary in order to settle my estate.

b. To lease any real estate for such term, or terms, and upon such reasonable conditions and rentals and in such manner as my personal representative deems proper, and any lease so made shall be valid and binding for its full term even though such lease term extends beyond the duration of the administration of my estate; to make repairs, replacements and improvements, structural or otherwise, to any such real estate; to subdivide real estate, dedicate real estate to public use and grant easements as my personal representative deems proper.

c. To employ accountants, attorneys and such other agents as my personal representative deems necessary; to pay reasonable compensation for such services and to charge same to (or apportion same between) income and principal as my personal representative deems proper.

d. To make such elections under the tax laws applicable to my estate as my personal representative determines should be made; to elect to treat any fraction or all of any trust I have created as qualified terminable interest property for federal estate tax purposes to the extent my personal representative deems proper; and to make allocations of any available generation-skipping tax exemption as my personal representative deems proper. No adjustment shall be made between principal and income or in the relative interests of the beneficiaries to compensate for any such election or allocation made by my personal representative.

e. To join with my [husband or wife] on my behalf in filing income tax returns, or to consent for gift tax purposes to having gifts made by either of us during my life considered as made one-half by each of us, and any resulting tax liability shall be paid by my estate, except such portion as my personal representative and my [husband or wife] agree should be paid by my [husband or wife].

COMMENT: A statement of the powers of the personal representative is not essential, as those powers are specified by state law; however, state laws may not be sufficiently broad. Often state laws do not include power over real estate. Paragraph 6.c may not be essential, but this writer prefers to clarify that the personal representative may hire at the expense of the estate professionals to assist in estate settlement. Paragraph 6.d deals with tax electives and especially the QTIP election. If the estate is not large enough to involve estate tax issues, this paragraph can be deleted. Paragraph 6.e deals with the signing of tax returns and, while not essential, still is appropriate in most situations.

---

7. <u>Appointment of Guardian.</u> If my [husband or wife] does not survive me, my [relationship], [Name of Guardian], shall be guardian of each child for whom it is necessary to appoint a guardian. If [Name of Guardian] does not act as guardian, or having qualified dies, becomes incompetent, resigns, or declines to continue to serve, then my [relationship], [Alternate guardian] shall be guardian of each child for whom it is necessary to appoint a guardian. No surety bond shall be required of my guardians.

COMMENT: This is a standard paragraph naming a guardian for any children for whom a guardian is necessary. If there is only one possible guardian and no alternate guardian, then the second sentence can be omitted. This paragraph omits the requirement of a surety bond.

---

8. <u>Employment of Attorney.</u> I request but do not require that my personal representative employ the law firm of [insert name of law firm], [city], [state] to be my estate's attorney as the attorneys in that law firm are the most familiar with my intentions expressed in this will.

COMMENT: This paragraph may be appropriate when the client is expecting the lawyer who drafted the will to be available to settle the estate. Often the children do not know the parent's preference for a lawyer, thus the provision is inserted. The employment of the testator's lawyer is made permissive to avoid any appearance of self-dealing by the lawyer preparing the will. There will be situations in which the client insists the wording be made mandatory. If so, the lawyer may wish to document this fact by memo to the file, signed by the client.

IN TESTIMONY WHEREOF, I, [Name of Client], sign my name to this instrument this _____ day of _____, [current year], and being first duly sworn, do hereby declare to the undersigned authority that I sign and execute this instrument as my last will and that I sign it willingly, that I execute it as my free and voluntary act for the purposes therein expressed, and that I am 18 years of age or older, of sound mind, and under no constraint or undue influence.

_____
[Name of Client]

We _____ and _____, the witnesses, sign our names to this instrument, being first duly sworn, and do hereby declare to the undersigned authority that [Name of Client] signs and executes this instrument as [his or her] Last Will and Testament dated _____, [current year], and that [he or she] signs it willingly and that each of us, in the presence and hearing of [Name of Client] and in the presence of the other subscribing witness, hereby signs this Last Will and Testament as witness to [Name of Client]'s signing, and that to the best of their knowledge, [Name of Client] is eighteen (18) years of age or older, of sound mind and under no constraint or undue influence, all on this _____ day of _____, [current year].

_____

Witness

_____

Witness

_____

Address

_____

Address

STATE OF [State of Notary]   )

)SCT.

COUNTY OF [County of Notary])

Subscribed, sworn to, and acknowledged before me by [Name of Client], and subscribed and sworn to before me by _____ and _____, witnesses, this the _____ day of _____, [current year].

_____

Notary Public, State at Large

My Commission Expires:_____

COMMENT: The above provisions are in compliance with the writer's own state law to avoid the necessity of locating witnesses to the will at a later date. This provision should be modified to meet the requirement of the lawyer's own state law.

PREPARED BY:

_____

[Name of Attorney]
[Name of Law Firm]
Attorneys at Law
[Street Address]
[City], [State] [Zip Code]
[Telephone Number]

SINGLE PERSON INTER VIVOS TRUST WORKSHEET

1.   Grantor and Trustee Information

Name _____

City and State _____

2.   Name of Trust

"_____ Trust"

3.   Children

3.1 Names of Children _____

_____

_____

3.2 Are any of the above-named children step-children? <u>Yes / No</u>

3.3 Are provisions needed for after-born children? <u>Yes / No</u>

4.   Payment of Death Taxes (if provision needed)

4.1 Are taxes on probate and nonprobate assets, including apportionment property, to be paid from the trust principal? (Option 1)

Yes / No

4.2 Are taxes to be paid by beneficiary and taxes collected on apportionment property? (Option 2)

Yes / No

4.3 Are taxes on probate and nonprobate assets to be paid from trust principal, but taxes on apportionment property to be collected? (Option 3)

Yes / No

4.4 Other tax provisions _____

_____

5.   Allocations at Death

5.1 Separate trust for lifetime of beneficiaries? (Option 1) <u>Yes / No</u>

    A. Provision for educational incentive? <u>Yes / No</u>
       (See 5.c)

    B. Provision for distribution to descendants? <u>Yes / No</u>
       (See 5.d)

    C. Provision for trustee authority to withhold? <u>Yes / No</u>
       (See 5.e)

    D. Power of appointment:

       Limited to descendants/charities? (Option 1) <u>Yes / No</u>

       Broad? (Option 2) <u>Yes / No</u>

Limited and age restricted? (Option 3) <u>Yes / No</u>

Broad and age restricted? (Option 4) <u>Yes / No</u>
(See 5.f)

If no power of appointment or not exercised and a child is deceased:

Deceased child's share distributed
to such child's estate? (Option 1) <u>Yes / No</u>

or Deceased child's share per stirpes
to lineal descendants? (Option 2) <u>Yes / No</u>
(See 5.g)

5.2 Separate trusts until minimum age of beneficiaries? (Option 2) <u>Yes / No</u>

    A. Provision for educational incentive? <u>Yes / No</u>
    (See 5.c)

    B. Provide for distribution one-half at each of two ages? <u>Yes / No</u>

       If yes: Initial age to inherit: _____

                          Final age to inherit: _____
    (See 5.d)

    C. Provision for trustee authority to withhold? <u>Yes / No</u>
    (See 5.e)

    D. If a child is deceased:

    Deceased child's share distributed
    to such child's estate? (Option 1) <u>Yes / No</u>

    or Deceased child's share per stirpes
    to lineal descendants? (Option 2) <u>Yes / No</u>
    (See 5.f)

5.3 Single testamentary trust for children? (Option 3) <u>Yes / No</u>

    A. Final age to inherit: _____
    (See 5.c)

    B. If a child is deceased:

    Deceased child's share distributed
    to such child's estate? (Option 1) <u>Yes / No</u>

    or Deceased child's share per stirpes
    to lineal descendants? (Option 2) <u>Yes / No</u>
    (See 5.c)

    C. Provision for trustee authority to withhold? <u>Yes / No</u>
    (See 5.b)

6.   **Special Provisions**:

Residential Real Estate? <u>Yes / No</u>

Rule against Perpetuities? <u>Yes / No</u>

Subchapter S Stock? <u>Yes / No</u>

Reliance on Will? <u>Yes / No</u>

Method of Payment? <u>Yes / No</u>

Accrued Income and Termination:

    Distributed to such interested person's estate? (Option 1) <u>Yes / No</u>

    Remain an asset of the trust (not distributed)? (Option 2) <u>Yes / No</u>

Life Insurance Policies? <u>Yes / No</u>

7.   **Default Provisions (if needed), if All Named Beneficiaries are Deceased**:

_____

_____

_____

8.   **Definition of "Child" and "Descendant"**

Include children adopted prior to age _____ (18, 21, etc.).

Include provision for illegitimate children (treated same, etc.)? <u>Yes / No</u>

9.   **Powers**

    Environmental Powers? <u>Yes / No</u> (See Paragraph 11)

    Farm Powers? <u>Yes / No</u> (See Paragraph 12)

    Limitation on Trustee Powers? <u>Yes / No</u>

10. **Trustees**

    Name of first successor trustee: _____

    Name of second successor trustee: _____

    Corporate trustee compensation? (Option 1) <u>Yes / No</u>

    Individual reimbursed for expenses but no compensation? (Option 2) <u>Yes / No</u>

    Individual receives compensation? (Option 3) <u>Yes / No</u>

        Amount of compensation: $_____

    Provision needed for children to act as trustee of own trust? <u>Yes / No</u>

11. **Incompetency**

One physician decides? (Option 1) <u>Yes / No</u>

Two physicians decide and one board certified? (Option 2) <u>Yes / No</u>

12   **No-Contest**

Is No-Contest provision needed? <u>Yes / No</u>

SINGLE PERSON INTER VIVOS TRUST

This trust is an inter vivos trust used when the grantor desires to establish a trust for him or herself and then make provisions for the distribution of the trust assets upon the grantor's death. This trust can be modified to be used in multiple situations involving a single person, or can be used for a couple when they each desire to create a separate trust. If used in this situation, then modifications will need to be made for provisions for the survivor of the couple, as this instrument is drafted assuming a single individual. In most situations, the joint trust will be more appropriate for a couple.

I, [Grantor], currently of [Grantor's city], [Grantor's state], acting as grantor and trustee hereby transfer to myself, as trustee, the property described in Schedule A. This property and all investments, reinvestments and additions which may sometimes be referred to in this instrument as the "trust property" or "trust assets" are to be held subject to the following provisions:

COMMENT: In this trust the grantor will also act as trustee during his or her lifetime. The trust may be funded at the time it is created or the grantor may choose to fund the trust at a later date. Also, this trust has the benefit of being a so-called living trust, which is intended to simplify estate settlement, as well as, providing for the benefit of children.

1. Name of Trust. This instrument and the initial trust hereby established may be named the "[Name of trust] Trust."

COMMENT: The trust may have any name the grantor desires. Often times, the grantor will simply name the trust after him or herself.

2. Family Information.

OPTION 1: Naming of all children My [child is or children are], [names of children], and all references in this will to "my [child is or children are]" only to [him her or them].

OPTION 2: Inclusion of step-children Even though some of the above named children are step-children it is my intent that each of the above-named children be treated for purposes of this instrument as if they and their lineal descendants are my natural born children.

OPTION 3: After-born children If subsequent to the execution of this instrument there shall be an additional child or children born to me, then such child or children shall share in the benefits of the trusts established in this instrument to the same extent as my above named children and their descendants; and the provisions of this instrument shall be deemed modified to the extent necessary to carry out this intent.

COMMENT: The full name of the children should be inserted. In most situations of a single person, there will not be step-children, thus Option 2 will not be needed. The same may also be true for Option 3.

3. Provisions During My Lifetime. During my lifetime, I shall be paid the net trust income and the principal of the trust property as I direct. If my successor trustee determines that I am unable to manage my financial affairs based on the criteria in paragraph 20 below, the trustee shall pay to or use all, part or none, of the income and principal of the trust property as the trustee

believes appropriate for my reasonable maintenance, support, and health. If any net income remains undistributed at the end of each calendar year (excluding income distributed during the sixty-five (65) day period under Internal Revenue Code Section 663), the trustee shall add it to the principal of the trust.

COMMENT: These are basic provisions to provide that, during the lifetime of the grantor, all income and principal is for the sole benefit of the grantor. In order to maintain privacy, the grantor may elect to transfer brokerage accounts and other assets to the trust. In this way, those assets need not be reported to the probate court in settlement of the grantor's estate. Throughout the grantor's lifetime, he or she acts as trustee in making distributions to him or herself with a successor trustee making distributions in the event of disability. Please note that this form cross-references paragraph 20 which defines incompetency. Care must be taken to insert the correct paragraph number, as if any of the ensuing paragraphs are deleted, this will change the paragraph numbers.

---

4. <u>Payment of Debts, Death Taxes and Funeral Expenses.</u> **OPTION 1: Death taxes paid from trust** On my death the trustee shall pay all of my just debts, my funeral expenses, costs of estate administration, and death taxes, if any, from trust principal and the trustee shall not seek contribution toward or recovery of any such payments; provided, however, such obligations and death taxes shall be paid by the trustee only to the extent the personal representative of my probate estate certifies in writing to the trustee that the residue of my probate estate is insufficient to pay such obligations and death taxes. Death taxes means any estate or inheritance taxes, but not generation-skipping transfer taxes, imposed under the laws of any jurisdiction due to my death on any property passing by reason of my death. Any generation-skipping transfer taxes shall be paid from the property that incurred such tax.

OPTION 2: Death taxes paid by beneficiary and collecting taxes on apportionment property On my death the trustee shall pay all of my just debts, my funeral expenses and costs of estate administration from trust principal as soon as possible after my death. Any death taxes owed shall be charged against the trust share passing to the person whose share generated such tax. Death taxes means any estate or inheritance taxes, but not generation-skipping transfer taxes, imposed under the laws of any jurisdiction due to my death on any property passing by reason of my death. With regard to apportionment property, my trustee shall take such actions as are necessary to obtain reimbursement with respect to apportionment property, including withholding distribution. Apportionment property means (a) any property with respect to which my trustee may be entitled to recover federal estate tax under Internal Revenue Code Section 2207, 2207A, or 2207B and (b) any policies of insurance, or the proceeds of policies of insurance, on my life which are not owned by me at my death. Any generation-skipping transfer taxes shall be paid from the property that incurred such tax.

OPTION 3: Death taxes paid from residue but collecting taxes on apportionment property On my death the trustee shall pay all of my just debts, my funeral expenses and costs of estate administration from trust principal as soon as possible after my death.

I further direct that my death taxes, if any, be paid out of trust principal, other than apportionment property, without proration and my trustee shall not seek contribution toward or recovery of any such payments. Death taxes means any estate or inheritance taxes, but not generation-skipping transfer taxes, imposed under the laws of any jurisdiction due to my death on any property passing by reason of my death whether or not such property passes under this will. With regard to apportionment property, my trustee shall take such actions as are necessary to obtain reimbursement with respect to apportionment property, including withholding distribution. Apportionment property means (a) any property with respect to which my trustee may be entitled to recover federal estate tax under Internal Revenue Code Section 2207, 2207A, or 2207B and (b) any policies of insurance, or the proceeds of policies of insurance, on my life which are not owned by me at my death. Any generation-skipping transfer taxes shall be paid from the property that incurred such tax.

COMMENT: If the person owns sufficient assets in his or her individual name, rather than all assets being titled in the trust, then this provision is not needed to pay final expenses. The concern giving rise to this provision is that all assets will be owned in the trust and there are not sufficient estate assets with which to pay final expenses. The more difficult question becomes the payment of death taxes. In many situations, there will be no death taxes anticipated, thus in some situations, these provisions can be deleted. Otherwise, a decision must be made as to who bears the burden of paying these taxes. An excellent ABA resource discussing tax payment clauses, apportionment property and the GST tax is Thomas M. Featherston, Jr. et al., *Drafting for Tax and Administrative Issues*, American Bar Association (Chicago: 2000).

---

5. <u>Allocations at my Death.</u> Following my death, the trustee shall hold and administer the trust property, including property which the trustee receives under my will or from any other source, as follows:

OPTION 1: Separate trust for lifetime of beneficiaries

a. The trust property shall be divided and allocated into equal shares for my children. If a child is deceased, that deceased child's share shall be divided and allocated per stirpes among that deceased child's then living lineal descendants. Property allocated to a child or more remote lineal descendant of mine shall be retained in trust as a separate trust which shall be named for that person subject to the following provisions.

COMMENT: Option 1 creates a separate trust for each child of the grantor; and if a child is deceased, then a separate trust is created for each of that deceased child's then living children.

---

b. The trustee may pay to or use all, part or none, of the income and principal of such person's trust as the trustee believes appropriate for the reasonable maintenance, support, health and education (including college or graduate, professional or vocational school education) of such person, considering such person's income or assets and all other circumstances and factors the trustee believes pertinent. It is my desire that distributions of income and principal not impair such person's motivation to be productive and self-supporting, thus my trustee shall not make distributions of income and principal from such person's trust if such person is not productive, mature, and responsible. If any net income remains undistributed at the end of each calendar year (excluding income distributed during the sixty-five [65] day period under Internal Revenue Code Section 663), the trustee shall add it to the principal of the trust.

COMMENT: The first sentence provides broad discretion to the trustee in making distributions for the child or more remote descendant. The second sentence is not essential, but is provided to illustrate a possible restriction that the grantor may desire. The third sentence can be eliminated, but is provided to cover situations in which income is not distributed before year end; and to set the time at which accumulated income is added to trust principal.

---

c. Notwithstanding the above paragraphs, following high school graduation, if a person for whom a trust is held hereunder fails to pursue post-secondary education leading to a bachelor's degree from an accredited college or university, all trust distributions, except for health care needs, shall cease until such person reaches the age of twenty-three (23) years. A person pursuing post-secondary education must annually maintain a 2.50 GPA based on a 4.0 grading scale in order to receive trust distributions, except for health care needs, prior to the age of twenty-three (23) years. If a person for whom a trust is named earns a bachelor's degree from an accredited college or university before such person reaches the age of twenty-three (23) years, the trustee shall within ninety (90) days of such person's graduation distribute [enter number] percent ([enter number]%) of the trust assets to such person free of trust.

COMMENT: This provision is intended to provide a model for the lawyer to consider in addressing an incentive for a child or more remote descendant to pursue post-secondary education and to maintain an adequate grade point average. This paragraph may need to be moved to become part of paragraph a or as a separate paragraph b. In this form, the decision was made to place it in this location as it and the following paragraphs are offered as supplemental provisions that some clients will want and others will not. Be certain to modify the reference in the first sentence to the phrase "nothwithstanding . . . paragraphs" if it is moved elsewhere in the document.

d. In addition, the trustee may pay to or use for the benefit of any one or more of the descendants of a person for whom a trust is held hereunder such part or all of the principal of such person's trust at such time or times and in such equal or unequal proportions among them as the trustee believes appropriate for the reasonable maintenance, support, health and education (including college or graduate, professional or vocational school education) of such descendants as a group, considering their respective incomes or assets and all other circumstances and factors the trustee believes pertinent.

COMMENT: In some situations, the grantor may desire for the trust beneficiary's own descendants to receive distributions from the trust. This provision permits such distributions, but such distributions are limited to trust principal and not both income and principal. If that flexibility is desired, then a minor modification may be made to this paragraph.

e. In addition to the restrictions provided in the above paragraphs and as a condition precedent to distributions under those paragraphs, my trustee shall withhold or postpone any or all distributions of income or principal from a person's trust if my trustee believes a distribution to such person could result in the loss of some part or all of the distribution due to any possible civil or criminal legal action involving such person or such person's spouse, or due to such person or such person's spouse being addicted to alcohol or any legal or illegal controlled substance. The decision of my trustee shall be final and binding and shall not be subject to question by any person or in any court.

COMMENT: If the client is faced with a child or more remote descendant who has substance abuse or other serious problems making distributions from the trust unwise, or if the client is concerned about such possibility, then paragraph e or a variation of it may be helpful. It is designed to give the trustee full authority to withhold all distributions of income and principal when a child or more remote descendant is facing substance abuse or other significant personal problems.

f. **OPTION 1: Power of Appointment Limited** Upon the death of a person for whom a trust held under this paragraph is named, any part or all of the principal of such person's trust and any accrued or undistributed income shall be distributed to or for the benefit of my descendants and public charities in such proportions and subject to such trusts, powers and conditions as such person may provide and appoint by will specifically referring to this power to appoint.

f. **OPTION 2: Power of Appointment Broad** Upon the death of a person for whom a trust held under this paragraph is named, any part or all of the principal of such person's trust and any accrued or undistributed income shall be distributed to or for the benefit of such individual or individuals and entities other than such person's own estate or the creditors of such person's estate in such proportions and subject to such trusts, powers and conditions as such person may provide and appoint by will specifically referring to this power to appoint.

f. **OPTION 3: Power of Appointment Limited and Age Restricted** Upon the death of a person who is at least [insert age] years of age and for whom a trust held under this paragraph is named, any part or all of the principal of such person's trust and any accrued or undistributed income thereof shall be distributed to or for the benefit of my descendants and public charities in such proportions and subject to such trusts, powers and conditions as such person may provide and appoint by will specifically referring to this power to appoint.

f. **OPTION 4: Power of Appointment Broad and Age Restricted** Upon the death of a person who is at least [insert age] years of age and for whom a trust held under this paragraph is named, any part or all of the principal of such person's trust and any accrued or undistributed income thereof shall be distributed to or for the benefit of such individual or individuals and entities other than such person's own estate or the creditors of such person's estate in such proportions and subject to such trusts, powers and conditions as such person may provide and appoint by will specifically referring to this power to appoint.

COMMENT: In many situations, the grantor will want the trust beneficiary to have the right to designate how and to whom the trust property is to be distributed upon the death of the beneficiary. Option 1 limits distributions to the grantor's descendants and provides a contingent possibility to public charities. Option 2 is an extremely broad power of appointment that includes virtually anyone or any entity to whom the beneficiary might desire to give the property at death. Options 3 and 4 are similar to Options 1 and 2 with the exception of adding the requirement that the trust beneficiary be a certain minimum age before exercising the power of appointment.

---

g. Upon the death of a person for whom a trust held under this paragraph is named, any principal of such person's trust (not effectively disposed of by any other provisions of this paragraph 5) shall be divided and allocated per stirpes among the then living lineal descendants of such person, if any, otherwise per stirpes among the then living lineal descendants of the nearest lineal ancestor of such person who also is a descendant of mine and of whom one or more descendants then are living, or, if none, per stirpes among my then living lineal descendants.

COMMENT: If the trust beneficiary does not exercise the power of appointment granted above, or if no power of appointment is given to the beneficiary, then the trust must direct to whom the trust property will be distributed upon the death of the beneficiary. Care must be taken to be certain that the per stirpes distribution provided in this form is adequate. This provision should not be used routinely without an analysis of its effect under the facts of the particular estate plan. For example, in many situations the phrase "per stirpes among the then living lineal descendants of the nearest lineal ancestor of such person who was also a descendant of mine and of whom one or more descendants then are living" may need to be omitted.

Distribution shall be made outright to such descendant or descendants unless: (i) distribution is to be made to a descendant for whom a trust then held under this trust instrument is named in which event such distribution shall be added to that trust, or (ii) distribution is to be made to a descendant who has not reached the age of [Age of remote descendants] years and for whom no trust is then held in which event, the trustee shall retain any property otherwise distributable to such descendant as a separate trust named for such descendant to be distributed to such descendant when he or she reaches the age of [Age for remote descendants] years. If such descendant is already [Age for remote descendants] years of age, then such descendant shall receive his or her share outright. Until such descendant reaches [Age for remote descendants] years of age, the trustee shall distribute the income and principal of a trust so retained in such amounts, if any, and at such times as the trustee believes appropriate for the reasonable maintenance, support, health and education (including college or graduate, professional or vocational school education) of the descendant for whom the trust is named, considering such descendant's income or assets and all other circumstances and factors the trustee believes pertinent. It is my desire that distributions of income and principal not impair a descendant's motivation to be productive and self-supporting, thus my trustee shall not make distributions of income and principal from a descendant's trust if my descendant is not productive, mature, and responsible. If any net income remains undistributed at the end of each calendar year (excluding income distributed during the sixty-five (65) day period under Internal Revenue Code Section 663), the trustee shall add it to the principal of the trust.

OPTION 1: If a descendant for whom a trust held under this paragraph is named dies prior to termination of such descendant's trust, then such descendant's trust shall terminate and the trust property shall be distributed to such descendant's own estate.

OPTION 2: On the death of a descendant for whom a trust held under this paragraph is named, any principal and undistributed income of such descendant's trust shall be divided and allocated per stirpes among the then living lineal descendants of such descendant, if any, otherwise such descendant's trust shall be divided and allocated per stirpes among the then living lineal descendants of the nearest lineal ancestor of such person who also is a descendant of mine and of whom one or more descendants then are living, or, if none, such person's trust shall be divided and allocated per stirpes among my then living lineal descendants.

COMMENT: The above provisions permit a distribution to a more remote descendant to be distributed to that person's own trust if he or she is a recipient of a trust under this instrument, or if not and the remote descendant is under a specified minimum age, then the trustee may hold that person's share in trust until that person reaches the minimum age with the trust property to be used for that person until distribution. If this option is used, then Option 1 or 2 above should be selected to determine to whom the trust property is distributed should that remote descendant die before termination of the trust. Also, see the Comment above following 5.g.

OPTION 2: Separate trust until minimum age of beneficiaries

a. The trust property shall be divided and allocated into equal shares for my children. If a child is deceased, that deceased child's share shall be divided and allocated per stirpes among that deceased child's then living lineal descendants. Property allocated to a child or more remote lineal descendant of mine shall be retained in trust as a separate trust which shall be named for that person subject to the following provisions.

COMMENT: Option 2 is the same as Option 1 except that the trust terminates upon the beneficiary reaching certain ages as provided in paragraph d below.

---

b. The trustee may pay to or use all, part or none, of the income and principal of such person's trust as the trustee believes appropriate for the reasonable maintenance, support, health, and education (including college or graduate, professional or vocational school education) of such person, considering such person's income or assets and all other circumstances and factors the trustee believes pertinent. It is my desire that distributions of income and principal not impair such person's motivation to be productive and self-supporting, thus my trustee shall not make distributions of income and principal from such person's trust if such person is not productive, mature, and responsible. If any net income remains undistributed at the end of each calendar year (excluding income distributed during the sixty-five (65) day period under Internal Revenue Code Section 663), the trustee shall add it to the principal of the trust.

COMMENT: The first sentence provides broad discretion to the trustee in making distributions for the child or more remote descendant. The second sentence is not essential, but is provided to illustrate a possible restriction that the grantor may desire. The third sentence can be eliminated, but is provided to cover situations in which income is not distributed before year end; and to set the time at which accumulated income is added to trust principal.

c. Notwithstanding the above paragraphs, following high school graduation, if a person for whom a trust is held hereunder fails to pursue post-secondary education leading to a bachelor's degree from an accredited college or university, all trust distributions, except for health care needs, shall cease until such person reaches the age of twenty-three (23) years. A person pursuing post-secondary education must annually maintain a 2.50 GPA based on a 4.0 grading scale in order to receive trust distributions, except for health care needs, prior to the age of twenty-three (23) years. If a person for whom a trust is named earns a bachelor's degree from an accredited college or university before such person reaches the age of twenty-three (23) years, the trustee shall within ninety (90) days of such person's graduation distribute [enter number] percent ([enter number]%) of the trust assets to such person free of trust.

COMMENT: This provision is intended to provide a model for the lawyer to consider in addressing an incentive for a child or more remote descendant to pursue post-secondary education and to maintain an adequate grade point average. This paragraph may need to be moved to become part of paragraph a or as a separate paragraph b. In this form, the decision was made to place it in this location as it and the following paragraphs are offered as supplemental provisions that some clients will want and others will not. Be certain to modify the reference in the first sentence to the phrase "nothwithstanding . . . paragraphs" if it is moved elsewhere in the document.

d. When a person for whom a trust held under this paragraph is named reaches the age of [initial age to inherit] years or such person has already reached such age, the trustee shall distribute to such person one-half (1/2) of the then principal of that person's trust; and when such person reaches the age of [final age to inherit] years, the person's trust shall terminate and the balance of such person's trust shall be distributed outright to such person.

COMMENT: This trust terminates for the beneficiary upon that person reaching a specified age. This form has distributions at two ages with the trust terminating upon distribution at the second age.

e. In addition to the restrictions provided in the above paragraphs and as a condition precedent to distributions under those paragraphs, my trustee shall withhold or postpone any or all distributions of income or principal from a person's trust if my trustee believes a distribution to such person could result in the loss of some part or all of the distribution due to any possible civil or criminal legal action involving such person or such person's spouse, or due to such person or such person's spouse being addicted to alcohol or any legal or illegal controlled substance. The decision of my trustee shall be final and binding and shall not be subject to question by any person or in any court.

COMMENT: If the client is faced with a child or more remote descendant who has substance abuse or other serious problems making distributions from the trust unwise, or if the client is concerned about such possibility, then paragraph e or a variation of it may be helpful. It is designed to give the trustee full authority to withhold all distributions of income and principal when a child or more remote descendant is facing substance abuse or other significant personal problems.

f. **OPTION 1**: If a person for whom a trust held under this paragraph is named dies prior to termination of such person's trust, then such person's trust shall terminate and shall be distributed to such person's own estate.

f. **OPTION 2**: Upon the death of a person for whom a trust held under this paragraph is named, any principal and undistributed income of such person's trust shall be divided and allocated per stirpes among the then living lineal descendants of such person, if any, otherwise such person's trust shall be divided and allocated per stirpes among the then living lineal descendants of the nearest lineal ancestor of such person who also is a descendant of mine and of whom one or more descendants then are living, or, if none, such person's trust shall be divided and allocated per stirpes among my then living lineal descendants.

COMMENT: Options 1 and 2 do not grant to the trust beneficiary a power of appointment. Thus, the trust instrument must direct to whom the trust property will be distributed upon the death of the beneficiary. Care must be taken to be certain that the per stirpes distribution provided in this form is adequate. This provision should not be used routinely without an analysis of its effect under the facts of the particular estate plan. For example, in many situations the phrase "per stirpes among the then living lineal descendants of the nearest lineal ancestor of such person who was also a descendant of mine and of whom one or more descendants then are living" may need to be omitted.

Distribution shall be made outright to such descendant or descendants unless: (i) distribution is to be made to a descendant for whom a trust then held under this trust instrument is named in which event such distribution shall be added to that trust, or (ii) distribution is to be made to a descendant who has not reached the age of [Age of remote descendants] years and for whom no trust is then held in which event, the trustee shall retain any property otherwise distributable to such descendant as a separate trust named for such descendant to be distributed to such descendant when he or she reaches the age of [Age for remote descendants] years. If such descendant is already [Age for remote descendants] years of age, then such descendant shall receive his or her share outright. Until such descendant reaches [Age for remote descendants] years of age, the trustee shall distribute the income and principal of a trust so retained in such amounts, if any, and at such times as the trustee believes appropriate for the reasonable maintenance, support, health and education (including college or graduate, professional or vocational school education) of the descendant for whom the trust is named, considering such descendant's income or assets and all other circumstances and factors the trustee believes pertinent. It is my desire that distributions of income and principal not impair a descendant's motivation to be productive and self-supporting, thus my trustee shall not make distributions of income and principal from a descendant's trust if my descendant is not productive, mature, and responsible. If any net income remains undistributed at the end of each calendar year (excluding income distributed during the sixty-five (65) day period under Internal Revenue Code Section 663), the trustee shall add it to the principal of the trust.

OPTION 1: If a descendant for whom a trust held under this paragraph is named dies prior to termination of such descendant's trust, then such descendant's trust shall terminate and the trust property shall be distributed to such descendant's own estate.

OPTION 2: On the death of a descendant for whom a trust held under this paragraph is named, any principal and undistributed income of such descendant's trust shall be divided and allocated per stirpes among the then living lineal descendants of such descendant, if any, otherwise such descendant's trust shall be divided and allocated per stirpes among the then living lineal descendants of the nearest lineal ancestor of such person who also is a descendant of mine and of whom one or more descendants then are living, or, if none, such person's trust shall be divided and allocated per stirpes among my then living lineal descendants.

COMMENT: The above provisions permit a distribution to a more remote descendant to be distributed to that person's own trust if he or she is a recipient of a trust under this instrument, or if not and the remote descendant is under a specified minimum age, then the trustee may hold that person's share in trust until that person reaches the minimum age with the trust property to be used for that person until distribution. If this option is used, then Option 1 or 2 above should be selected to determine to whom the trust property is distributed should that remote descendant die before termination of the trust. Care must be taken to be certain that the per stirpes distribution provided in this form is adequate. This provision should not be used routinely without an analysis of its effect under the facts of the particular estate plan. For example, in many situations the phrase "per stirpes among the then living lineal descendants of the nearest lineal ancestor of such person who was also a descendant of mine and of whom one or more descendants then are living" may need to be omitted.

OPTION 3: Single trust for children

a. Until my youngest child becomes [final age to inherit] years old, my trustee shall pay or use all, part or none of the income and principal of the trust, without regard to equality of distribution, to or for the benefit of my children as the trustee believes appropriate for the reasonable maintenance, support, health, and education (including college or graduate, professional or vocational school education) of my children, considering each child's income or assets and all other circumstances and factors the trustee believes pertinent. It is my desire that distributions of income and principal not impair such person's motivation to be productive and self-supporting, thus my trustee shall not make distributions of income and principal from such person's trust if such person is not productive, mature, and responsible. If any net income remains undistributed at the end of each calendar year (excluding income distributed during the sixty-five (65) day period under Internal Revenue Code Section 663), the trustee shall add it to the principal of the trust. Disbursements of income and principal shall not be taken into account when my trustee makes final distribution of the trust property upon termination of the trust.

COMMENT: This trust allows the trustee to make distributions among all the grantor's children without regard to equality. This gives the trustee broad discretion to make distributions among the children based upon their then current needs. Because of the broadness of the discretion granted to the trustee, paragraph d from Option 1 has not been included but can be modified and added if the lawyer so desires. The second sentence above is not essential, but is provided to illustrate a possible restriction that the grantor may desire. The third sentence can be eliminated, but is provided for situations in which income is not distributed before year end; and to set the time at which accumulated income is added to trust principal.

b. In addition to the restrictions provided in the above paragraphs and as a condition precedent to distributions under those paragraphs, my trustee shall withhold or postpone any or all distributions of income or principal from a person's trust if my trustee believes a distribution to such person could result in the loss of some part or all of the distribution due to any possible civil or criminal legal action involving such person or such person's spouse, or due to such person or such person's spouse being addicted to alcohol or any legal or illegal controlled substance. The decision of my trustee shall be final and binding and shall not be subject to question by any person or in any court.

COMMENT: If the client is faced with a child who has substance abuse or other serious problems making distributions from the trust unwise, or if the client is concerned about such possibility, then this paragraph or a variation of it may be helpful. It is designed to give the trustee full authority to withhold all distributions of income and principal when a child is facing substance abuse or other significant personal problems.

c. Upon my youngest child reaching [final age to inherit] years of age, the trust shall terminate and my trustee shall distribute the trust property to my children in equal shares. If a child is deceased, my deceased child's share shall be distributed to that child's then living lineal descendants per stirpes if any, otherwise such child's trust shall be divided and allocated per stirpes among the then living lineal descendants of the nearest lineal ancestor of such child who also is a descendant of mine and of whom one or more descendants then are living, or, if none, such child's trust shall be divided and allocated per stirpes among my then living lineal descendants.

COMMENT: The trust terminates upon the youngest child reaching a particular age, at which time the trust terminates and each child receives an equal share. This form does not grant the trust beneficiaries a power of appointment. Thus, the trust instrument directs to whom the trust property will be distributed upon the death of the beneficiary prior to termination of the trust. This form provides a basic per stirpes distribution. Care must be taken to be certain the per stirpes distribution provided in this form is adequate. This provision should not be used routinely without an analysis of its effect under the facts of the particular estate plan. For example, in many situations the phrase "per stirpes among the then living lineal descendants of the nearest lineal ancestor of such person who was also a descendant of mine and of whom one or more descendants then are living" may need to be omitted.

Distribution shall be made outright to such descendant or descendants unless: (i) distribution is to be made to a descendant for whom a trust then held under this trust instrument is named in which event such distribution shall be added to that trust, or (ii) distribution is to be made to a descendant who has not reached the age of [Age of remote descendants] years and for whom no trust is then held in which event, the trustee shall retain any property otherwise distributable to such descendant as a separate trust named for such descendant to be distributed to such descendant when he or she reaches the age of [Age for remote descendants] years. If such descendant is already [Age for remote descendants] years of age, then such descendant shall receive his or her share outright. Until such descendant reaches [Age for remote descendants] years of age, the trustee shall distribute the income and principal of a trust so retained in such amounts, if any, and at such times as the trustee believes appropriate for the reasonable maintenance, support, health and education (including college or graduate, professional or vocational school education) of the descendant for whom the trust is named, considering such descendant's income or assets and all other circumstances and factors the trustee believes pertinent. It is my desire that distributions of income and principal not impair a descendant's motivation to be productive and self-supporting, thus my trustee shall not make distributions of income and principal from a descendant's trust if my descendant is not productive, mature, and responsible. If any net income remains undistributed at the end of each calendar year (excluding income distributed during the sixty-five (65) day period under Internal Revenue Code Section 663), the trustee shall add it to the principal of the trust.

OPTION 1: If a descendant for whom a trust held under this paragraph is named dies prior to termination of such descendant's trust, then such descendant's trust shall terminate and the trust property shall be distributed to such descendant's own estate.

OPTION 2: On the death of a descendant for whom a trust held under this paragraph is named, any principal and undistributed income of such descendant's trust shall be divided and allocated per stirpes among the then living lineal descendants of such descendant, if any, otherwise such descendant's trust shall be divided and allocated per stirpes among the then living lineal descendants of the nearest lineal ancestor of such person who also is a descendant of mine and of whom one or more descendants then are living, or, if none, such person's trust shall be divided and allocated per stirpes among my then living lineal descendants.

COMMENT: The above provisions permit a distribution to a more remote descendant to be distributed to that person's own trust if he or she is a recipient of a trust under this instrument, or if not and the remote descendant is under a specified minimum age, then the trustee may hold that person's share in trust until that person reaches the minimum age with the trust property to be used for that person until distribution. If this option is used, then Option 1 or 2 above should be selected to determine to whom the trust property is distributed should that remote descendant die before termination of the trust. Care must be taken to be certain that the per stirpes distribution provided in this form is adequate. This provision should not be used routinely without an analysis of its effect under the facts of the particular estate plan. For example, in many situations the phrase "per stirpes among the then living lineal descendants of the nearest lineal ancestor of such person who was also a descendant of mine and of whom one or more descendants then are living" may need to be omitted.

---

6. <u>Special Provisions.</u> In addition to the other provisions of this trust agreement:

COMMENT: The following are various provisions that may be needed in a given situation, but rarely will all of these paragraphs be needed.

---

a. <u>Residential Real Estate.</u> In the event any residential real estate is included among the trust assets and [person's name] is then living, [he or she] may occupy such residence rent-free during [his or her] lifetime. [Person's name] shall pay all property taxes, insurance premiums, and the expenses of ordinary maintenance and repair. Further, [person's name] may purchase any such residential real estate at its then appraised value as determined by a professional real estate appraiser.

COMMENT: In the event the grantor desires for his or her personal residence to be available for a trust beneficiary, then this paragraph, or a modification of it, may be appropriate.

---

b. <u>Rule Against Perpetuities.</u> If not sooner terminated, twenty-one years after the death of the last to die of my descendants who are living at the time of my death, my trustee shall distribute the trust property to each person for whom a trust is held under this trust agreement.

COMMENT: The lawyer will need to determine if there is any concern over the rule against perpetuities, and if so, the above provision, or a modification of it, will be necessary. In most drafting situations, there will not be the possibility of violating this rule, thus the lawyer may want to omit this paragraph.

---

c. <u>Subchapter S Stock.</u> In the event a trust under this agreement holds Subchapter S stock, then the terms of this trust are hereby modified so that this trust qualifies as a Qualified Subchapter S Trust ("QSST") under section 1361(d) of the Internal Revenue Code. Therefore, any trust that has more than one permissible beneficiary shall be divided on a prorata basis into separate trusts for those beneficiaries, resulting in each trust having only one beneficiary who shall be the only recipient of trust income and principal until the earlier of the beneficiary's death or the termination of the trust. This provision shall not preclude the limitations on distributions of income and principal as required in paragraph 5.

COMMENT: One of the general tax law requirements for a corporation being taxed as a Subchapter S corporation, which allows the corporate income to flow to the owners and be taxed to them rather than facing the possible double-taxation of the traditional corporate tax law, is that a trust cannot be an owner. Of course, with the tax law there are always exceptions. There are several situations in which a trust can be a stockholder of a Subchapter S corporation. This paragraph is intended to ensure that the corporation will maintain its status as a Subchapter S corporation, even though some of its stock is held in trust. This is a technical and somewhat tricky tax trap. An excellent ABA resource addressing this issue is Thomas M. Featherston, Jr. et al., *Drafting for Tax and Administrative Issues*, American Bar Association (Chicago: 2000). Be sure to change the number in the last sentence if any paragraphs prior to paragraph 5 are deleted.

---

d. <u>Reliance on Will.</u> The trustee may rely on a will admitted to probate in any jurisdiction as the last will and testament of such person, or may assume (absent actual knowledge to the contrary) the person had no will if a will has not been admitted to probate within three months after such person's death.

COMMENT: This is a "boilerplate" provision that is helpful, but this provision must be reviewed to be certain that it is needed, and to make any modifications that are required.

---

e. <u>Method of Payment.</u> If a person entitled to receive income or principal distributions is unable to manage his or her financial affairs due to any type of mental or physical incapacity, then distributions may be made to or for such person's benefit, including making distributions to such person's guardian, conservator, committee, or a custodian under a Uniform Gift or Transfer to Minors Act.

COMMENT: This is a "boilerplate" provision that is usually inserted in a trust instrument.

---

f. Accrued Income and Termination. Income accrued and undistributed at the termination of a person's interest in trust property **OPTION 1** shall be distributed to such person's estate. **OPTION 2** shall remain an asset of the trust and shall not be distributed to such person's estate.

***

COMMENT: This is a helpful provision for administrative reasons to clarify for the trustee whether accumulated but undistributed income should remain in the trust after the beneficiary's death or if it should be distributed to that beneficiary's estate. One of the two options should be selected.

***

g. Rights and Duties Relating to Life Insurance Policies. After my death when life insurance policies become payable to the trust, my trustee shall promptly furnish proof of loss to the life insurance companies, and shall collect and receive the proceeds of the policies. My trustee shall have power to execute and deliver receipts and other instruments and to take such action as is appropriate for this collection. If my trustee deems it necessary to institute legal action for the collection of any policies, [he, she or it] shall be indemnified for all costs, including attorney's fees.

My trustee, in [his, her or its] sole discretion, may accept any of the optional modes of payment provided in any of such policies where such modes of payment are permitted to the trustee by the life insurance company. No life insurance company under any policy of insurance deposited with my trustee shall be responsible for the application or disposition of the proceeds of such policy by my trustee. Payment to my trustee of such life insurance proceeds shall be a full discharge of the liability of the life insurance company under such policy.

***

COMMENT: This paragraph is needed only if life insurance is made payable to the trust. The provisions are customary and are intended to avoid liability for the life insurance company and the trustee over receipt of life insurance death proceeds and the selection of the mode of payment. While these are routine provisions, the lawyer should review them to be certain that they are appropriate.

***

7. Default Provisions. Any trust property not disposed of by any of the above provisions shall be distributed on the date of such failure of disposition to [default provisions].

***

COMMENT: If there are a limited number of beneficiaries, then it may be wise to insert a default provision providing for the ultimate recipient should all the beneficiaries in paragraph 5 and their descendants be deceased. If this is too remote of a possibility, some clients may direct that this paragraph be deleted.

***

8. Protection from Creditors. No trust beneficiary shall have the right to sell, transfer, assign, alienate, pledge, or in any way encumber trust assets, including income and principal, nor shall trust assets be subject to execution, levy, sale, garnishment, attachment, bankruptcy, or other legal proceedings. Any such actions by a trust beneficiary or a third party seeking to enforce a claim against the trust assets shall not be recognized under any circumstances by the trustee. These provisions do not prevent the trustee from making distributions for the benefit of a trust beneficiary in such amounts and at such times as the trustee determines necessary for the trust beneficiary's maintenance, support, health and education.

COMMENT: This is a standard paragraph that precludes the trust assets from being attached by claims of creditors.

9. Definitions. For all purposes of this instrument, the following shall apply:

a. The words "child," "children," "descendant" or "descendants" shall exclude adopted persons unless they are adopted prior to [insert age] years; and shall include only persons legitimately born unless a decree of adoption terminates the parental rights of the natural mother during her lifetime, or the natural father signs a written notarized instrument during his lifetime in which he irrevocably states that the child is to be considered legitimately born for purposes of inheriting under this will.

COMMENT: Some clients will want to restrict distribution for an adopted child to preclude a child adopted as an adult. Thus, many will use the age 18 or perhaps a slightly older age such as 20 or 21. Other clients may wish to restrict the age to a younger adopted child, such as under the age of 10. The issue of illegitimate children should also be addressed. In many situations, a child or more remote descendant should be treated the same as any other child, in which case the portion of this paragraph that deals with illegitimate children can be deleted. In other situations there may be a limited or no relationship with the child, in which event no distribution should be made to that child. This form gives the father the right to allow the child to inherit by the father signing a written document allowing inheritance.

b. Whenever assets are to be divided and allocated per stirpes, the assets to be divided or allocated shall be divided into as many equal shares as are necessary to divide or allocate one share to each then living child of such person and to provide one share collectively for the then living descendants of each child of such person who then is deceased leaving one or more descendants then living. Any collective share shall be divided and allocated per stirpes among the descendants of such deceased person in accordance with the preceding sentence.

COMMENT: Since the term per stirpes is used often in this document, a definition is provided of that term. The lawyer should modify this definition to conform with his or her own state law should it differ any from this definition. Of course, a definition is not essential, since the term will be defined under state law. But since it is a term that clients are not familiar with, it is often helpful to define it for them in the document. An excellent ABA resource that explains the term per stirpes and its variations is Jeffrey N. Penell and Alan Newman, *Estate and Trust Planning*, American Bar Association (Chicago, 2005) pp. 19–26.

10. Trustee Powers. In the administration of the trusts, the trustee shall have the following powers and rights and all others granted by law:

a. To sell publicly or privately any trust property, for cash or on time, without an order of court and upon such terms and conditions as my trustee deems proper; and no person dealing with my trustee shall have any obligation to look to the application of the purchase money.

b. To invest and reinvest all or any part of the principal of the trust in any stocks, bonds, mortgages, shares or interests in common trust funds, mutual funds, or other securities or property, real, personal, or mixed, and of any kind or nature whatsoever, as the trustee deems proper, and without diversification if the trustee deems it advisable, irrespective of whether or not such securities or property are eligible for trust investment under state or any other law, and may change any investment received or made by the trustee, and may hold cash if the trustee deems it advisable.

c. To exercise broad discretion as to diversification of trust property, and shall not be required to reduce any concentrated holdings merely because of such concentration, and shall have full discretion as to the percentage to be invested in fixed income securities, and is specifically relieved from any requirements, legal or otherwise, as to the percentage of the trust assets to be invested in fixed income securities, and may invest or retain invested any trust estates wholly in common stocks.

d. To sell, convey, lease or mortgage, repair and improve, and take any and all other steps with regard to any real estate that may at any time be a part of the principal of the trust; and any lease of such real property or contract with regard thereto made by the trustee shall be binding for the full period of the lease or contract, even though the period shall extend beyond the termination of the trust.

e. To vote shares of stock held in the trust at stockholders' meetings in person or by special, limited, or general proxy, with or without power of substitution, as seems best to the trustee.

f. To participate in the liquidation, reorganization, consolidation, incorporation and reincorporation, or any other financial readjustment of any corporation, limited liability company or business in which the trust is, or shall be financially interested.

g. To borrow money from any source for any purpose connected with the protection, preservation, improvement or development of the trust hereunder, whenever in the trustee's judgment the trustee deems it advisable, and as security to mortgage or pledge any real estate or personal property forming a part of the trust upon such terms and conditions as the trustee may deem advisable.

h. To hold any and all securities in bearer form, in the trustee's own name, or the name of some other person, partnership, or corporation, or in the name of a duly appointed nominee, with or without disclosing the fiduciary ownership.

i. To divide the principal of the trust property into parts or shares and to distribute or allot same, and to make such division in cash or in kind or both. For the purpose of such division or allotment, the judgment of the trustee concerning the propriety thereof and relative value of property so distributed or allotted shall be binding and conclusive with respect to all interested persons.

j. To merge and consolidate the trust property of any separate trust held hereunder with other trusts and then to administer such trust property as a single trust provided the separate trust is for the benefit of the same persons with substantially the same terms, conditions and federal tax consequences.

k. To pay such income and principal during the minority or incapacity of any beneficiary for whose benefit income and principal may be expended, in any one or more of the following ways: (1) directly to the beneficiary; (2) to the legal guardian or committee of the beneficiary; (3) to a relative of the beneficiary to be expended by the relative for the maintenance, health, and education of the beneficiary; or (4) by expending the same directly for the maintenance, health, and education of the beneficiary. The trustee shall not be obliged to see to the application of the funds so expended, but the receipt of such person shall be full acquittance to the trustee.

l. To continue and operate any business owned by me at my death and to do any and all things deemed appropriate by the trustee, including the power to form a limited liability company or incorporate the business and to put additional capital into the business, for such time as the trustee deems advisable, without liability for loss resulting from the continuance or operation of the business except for the trustee's own negligence; and to close out, liquidate, or sell the business at such time and upon such terms as the trustee deems proper, and in this connection a sale may be made (pursuant to an agreement entered into by me during my lifetime, or otherwise) to a partner, officer, member, employee or beneficiary under this trust. I am aware of the fact that certain risks are inherent in the operation of any business and, therefore, my trustee shall not be liable for any loss resulting from the retention and operation of any business unless such loss results directly from my trustee's gross negligence or willful misconduct.

m. To have the same powers, authorities, and discretions in the management of the trust as I would have in the management and control of my own personal assets. The trustee may continue to exercise any powers and discretions granted in this instrument for a reasonable period after the termination of any trust under this instrument.

COMMENT: The above powers are a set of standard powers that appear throughout this book. The powers should be reviewed to be certain that you the lawyer understand each power, the client is in agreement with each of the powers granted and that the powers granted are needed. Because this is a generic and broad statement of powers, some of these powers may not be necessary. For example, powers to sell or lease real estate are not needed if the grantor knows the trust will consist only of cash and other intangible investments.

---

11. <u>Environmental Interests.</u> In the administration of this trust, my trustee shall have the power and authority to inspect, assess and evaluate any assets held in this trust, or proposed to be added to this trust, to determine if any environmental concerns exist with such asset or assets, and if so, my trustee may take any remedial action my trustee believes necessary to prevent, abate or remedy any environmental concerns whether or not my trustee is required to do so by any governmental agency. Further, my trustee may refuse to accept or may disclaim any asset or assets proposed to be added to the trust if my trustee believes there are possible environmental concerns that could result in liability to the trust or the trustee. Also, my trustee may settle or compromise any claims or lawsuits alleging environmental concerns which have been asserted by a private party or governmental agency. The decisions of my trustee regarding environmental concerns shall be final and binding on all parties and shall not be subject to question by anyone or in any court.

COMMENT: In many situations, it will be appropriate to address concerns of the trustee if the trust holds, or is expected to receive by will or other transfer, an asset that may have environmental concerns. This paragraph, or a variation of it, is helpful to the trustee in addressing this oftentimes difficult fiduciary problem. If there is any possibility the trust may hold assets that have environmental concerns, then the lawyer should address those issues fully with the client and with the trustee, including successor trustees, to avoid the situation in which a named trustee refuses to serve due to concerns over personal liability of the fiduciary for environmental cleanup costs.

---

12. <u>Trustee Powers as to Farms and Farm Real Estate.</u> In the administration of any farms and farmland held in this trust, the trustee shall have the following powers and rights:

a. To formulate and carry out a general farm plan of operation.

b. To make leases and enter into contracts with tenants, either on shares or for stated compensation, or to employ and pay such labor as might be employed.

c. To buy, breed, raise, and sell all kinds of livestock, either on shares with a tenant or solely on behalf of the trust estate.

d. To plant, cultivate, fertilize, produce, and market all crops raised on the farm, and to collect, receive and receipt for all shares, rent, and other income from the farm.

e. To ditch and drain so much of the land as might be considered desirable, and to make such repairs and improvements to building, land, and other items of property as may be consistent with good farm management.

f. To enter into contracts with the United States Department of Agriculture, or other Federal or State governmental agencies, for crop reductions or soil conservation practices.

g. To pay all taxes and assessments against the farm property and insure the improvements against loss by fire, windstorm, and other casualties.

h. To credit receipts and charge expenditures to and against the income account or the principal account as may be appropriate under applicable rules of trust accounting. In this regard, it is especially provided that any capital improvements made by the trustee in the exercise of prudent trust management shall be allocated between the income account and the principal account on the basis of the ratio of the life expectancy of the income beneficiary at that time to the normally expected useful life of the capital improvement.

i. To employ farm management services to the extent that this may be considered desirable for the proper formulation of farming plans and the active management of farm properties under the supervision and responsibility of the trustee.

j. To borrow monies which may be required from time to time to finance the farm operations, and to encumber trust assets to secure such loans.

k. To do any and all other things consistent with the provisions of this trust to facilitate an orderly distribution of our assets calculated to accomplish the purposes herein set out in an economically feasible manner.

COMMENT: In the event the trust will include a farm that will continue to be owned in trust, then these additional trust provisions should be considered. The general trustee powers should be sufficient, but when drafting for a farming client these more specific trustee powers are usually helpful.

---

13. <u>Limitation on Powers of Individual Trustee.</u> Notwithstanding any other powers granted to my trustee in this instrument, an individual trustee (a) shall have no power to make payments or distributions that would discharge the trustee's legal obligation to support the trust beneficiary, (b) shall not exercise any power or discretion in any manner that would be deemed to be a general power of appointment under Internal Revenue Code Section 2041, (c) shall be limited by the ascertainable standard of "maintenance, support, health and education" when making payments or distributions to the trustee personally or to anyone for whom the trustee has a beneficial interest, and (d) shall possess no incidence of ownership or powers with respect to life insurance in which the trustee is the insured and has fiduciary power over such life insurance.

COMMENT: There are some situations in which an individual trustee may have adverse estate or income tax consequences when given broad powers as trustee. If a corporate trustee is used, then this paragraph is not needed. But an individual trustee must be certain that acting as trustee does not result in any adverse estate or income tax consequences. This paragraph is intended to ensure that adverse tax consequences are avoided if overly broad powers are granted in the trust instrument. The lawyer is urged to exercise caution when using individual trustees coupled with broad discretionary powers of income and principal distribution to a trust beneficiary because of possible adverse tax consequences. An ABA resource to acquaint oneself with these issues is L. Rush Hunt and Lara Rae Hunt, *A Lawyer's Guide to Estate Planning*, American Bar Association (Chicago: 2004) §14.4.

14. <u>Trustee Resignation.</u> My trustee may resign at any time by giving written notice to my successor trustee named below, if any, and if none, then written notice shall be given to each current adult income beneficiary who is then living.

COMMENT: If a trustee resigns, there must be some method of notice and appointment of a successor trustee. This paragraph provides a method of notification. It is not an essential trust provision, but is a helpful one.

15. <u>Trustee Succession and Appointment.</u> If I cease to act as trustee due to death, incompetency, resignation or cease to serve for any reason, then [Name of successor trustee] shall serve as successor trustee. If [Name of successor trustee] dies, becomes incompetent, resigns or ceases to serve for any reason, then [Name of second successor trustee] shall serve as successor trustee. The last serving successor trustee may name his or her own successor trustee by a written instrument delivered to the successor trustee or by will. The successor trustee may be an individual or a financial institution possessing trust powers under state or federal law. Any further vacancy in the office of trustee shall be filled by decision of the probate court where I resided at the time of my death.

COMMENT: A decision must be made as to succession of trustees and the method of appointing a successor trustee if all of those named successor trustees are unable to serve. It is also essential to clarify whether successor trustees must only be financial institutions or if individuals may also be considered. Once a decision is made as to the succession of trustees, then the last three sentences should be reviewed to be certain to what extent each of those are needed.

Following my death, each of my children shall serve as the sole trustee of his or her own trust. Each child in a written instrument delivered to the successor trustee or by will may name his or her own successor trustee. The successor trustee may be an individual or a financial institution possessing trust powers under state or federal law. Any further vacancy in the office of trustee shall be filled by decision of the probate court where I resided at the time of my death.

COMMENT: If the trust continues during the lifetime of the grantor's children, then in many situations it will be appropriate for each child to act as trustee of his or her own trust. Thus, the above paragraph is needed in those situations. If the child is not to act as his or her own trustee, then this paragraph should be deleted.

In the event a trustee named in this instrument is also a trust beneficiary and claims are filed against the trust or threatened to be filed against the trust, litigation is filed against or threatened to be filed against a beneficiary, a voluntary or involuntary petition is filed in bankruptcy court, or a receivership is ordered by a state court, then and in such event the trustee who is also a beneficiary hereunder shall cease to act as trustee. In this event, such beneficiary shall name an independent trustee to serve as a successor trustee. In the event it becomes necessary to name an independent trustee, I name [Name of trustee remover] to serve as trustee remover having the power to remove a successor trustee and to name another successor trustee, or to name a successor trustee in the event an acting trustee resigns. Any successor trustee so named by my trustee remover may be an individual or a financial institution possessing trust powers under state or federal law. My trustee remover may name [his or her] own successor trustee remover.

COMMENT: In the event the child acts as his or her own trustee and a claim is made against the trust by a creditor of that child, then it may be wise practice for the child to resign as trustee and name an independent trustee who can then assert the "Protection from Creditor" provisions in the trust instrument on behalf of the child. If the lawyer elects to use this approach in drafting, then a method of naming an independent trustee is needed and there should be someone named as a trustee remover, having the power to remove the named independent trustee and name another trustee. Even if this paragraph is needed, it may require some modifications to fit the particular situation.

---

16. <u>Powers of Successor Trustee.</u> Each successor trustee shall have the same rights, titles, powers, duties, discretions, and immunities and otherwise be in the same position as if originally named trustee. No successor trustee shall be personally liable for any act or failure to act of a predecessor trustee. Further, a successor trustee may accept the account furnished and the property delivered by or for a predecessor trustee without liability for so doing, and such acceptance shall be a full and complete discharge to the predecessor trustee.

COMMENT: This paragraph clarifies that a successor trustee has the same powers as the initial trustee. Further, the paragraph relieves the successor trustee from liability for the prior acts of the resigning trustee and waives any requirements of audit or inquiry into the activities of the prior trustee. This is essential for any successor trustee.

---

17. <u>Compensation of Trustee.</u> **OPTION 1: Corporate trustee compensation** A corporate trustee shall receive compensation in accordance with its regular schedule of fees in effect at the time such services are rendered.

OPTION 2: Individual does not receive compensation An individual trustee shall not be paid any compensation, but shall be reimbursed for out-of-pocket expenses.

OPTION 3: Individual does receive compensation An individual trustee shall be paid [insert amount of compensation] as compensation for such services and shall be reimbursed for out-of-pocket expenses.

COMMENT: Three options are provided, but the actual drafting of this paragraph may be different than each of these options. If the only trustee to be used is a corporate trustee, then Option 1 is a standard trust provision. If there is a possibility of individual trustees, then care should be given to the method for setting this fee. If no fee is to be paid because the trustee is a close family member, then it is suggested that Option 2 be used. If the grantor expects a fee to be charged, then an amount or a formula, such as a percentage of income or principal, must be set. It is unwise to simply provide for compensation to be a reasonable fee, as that leaves an individual trustee with great uncertainty as to the fee to be charged. Without the grantor clarifying compensation, the trustee could find him or herself in litigation with the beneficiary.

18. <u>Court Accountings.</u> To the extent such requirements can be waived, the trustee shall not be required (a) to file any inventory of trust property or accounts or reports of the administration of the trusts, or to register the trusts, in any court, (b) to furnish any bond or other security for the proper performance of the trustee's duties or (c) to obtain authority from a court for the exercise of any power conferred on the trustee by this instrument. This waiver does not preclude the trustee from registering any trust created in this instrument and petitioning a court having jurisdiction over registered trusts for a judicial ruling on any matter relating to administration of any trust created in this instrument.

COMMENT: The first sentence is to clarify the normal situation that an inter vivos trust is not subject to judicial oversight. The second sentence may be omitted, but is suggested as a potential benefit in some states. In a state in which a trust can be registered, it may be possible to have minor trust matters resolved by the court in which the trust is registered. This creates a simplified process for dealing with minor administrative matters. Without this provision, a court might be reluctant to decide matters for a trust which is not required to be registered under state law.

19. <u>Severability.</u> If any provisions of this trust shall be unenforceable, the remaining provisions shall nevertheless be carried into effect.

COMMENT: This is the same type of standard provision often seen in contracts that is intended to save the document if a particular provision is found to be invalid or void. It is doubtful this provision will have any practical effect in most trust situations, but it is a "boilerplate" provision that is frequently found in trust instruments and for which there is no disadvantage.

20. <u>Certification of Incompetency.</u> **OPTION 1: Decided by treating physician** Any person acting or named to act as a trustee in this instrument is considered to be unable to serve or to continue serving when a physician whom such person has consulted within the prior three years has certified as to such consultation and the certification states that the person is incapable of managing the affairs of the trusts I have established in this instrument, regardless of cause and regardless of whether there is an adjudication of incompetency. No person shall be liable to anyone for actions taken in reliance on the physician's certification or for dealing with a trustee other than the one removed for incompetency based on such certification.

OPTION 2: Decided by two physicians Any person acting or named to act as a trustee in this instrument is considered to be unable to serve or to continue serving when a written certification is received from two (2) physicians, both of whom have personally examined the person and at least one (1) of whom is board-certified in the specialty most closely associated with the health condition alleged to cause such incompetency. The certification must state that the person is incapable of managing the affairs of this trust, regardless of cause and regardless of whether there is an adjudication of incompetence. No person is liable to anyone for actions taken in reliance on these certifications, or for dealing with a trustee other than the one removed for incompetency based on these certifications.

COMMENT: This provision relates back to paragraph 15 concerning the succession of trustees. It defines incompetency, which is one of those events requiring a successor trustee. The first option involves consultation with the trustee's personal physician, whereas Option 2 involves a panel of two physicians, one of whom is board certified in the speciality most closely associated with the health condition of the trustee. Clients differ as to which provision they prefer and are more concerned about the provision when the grantor is also the initial trustee. Absent a strong preference by the grantor, Option 1 is the provision most frequently used.

---

21. <u>Titles and References.</u> The underscored titles of paragraphs in this instrument are for information purposes only and shall be given no legal effect.

COMMENT: This is another common "boilerplate" provision that is perhaps not essential, but for which there is no disadvantage.

---

22. <u>Governing Law.</u> The laws of the State of [insert state] shall govern the interpretation and validity of the provisions of this instrument and all questions relating to the management, administration, investment, and distribution of the trusts hereby created.

COMMENT: It is a standard provision in both trust instruments and in contracts to specify the state law that applies in interpretation of the instrument. This will usually be the grantor's state of residency but also the state in which the lawyer is licensed to practice.

Notwithstanding the foregoing, my trustee shall have the power, exercisable in the trustee's sole and absolute discretion, to declare, by written instrument that the forum for this trust and all trusts established herein shall be another state in which event the laws of that state shall govern the interpretation and validity of the provisions of this instrument and all questions relating to the management, administration, investment, and distribution of the trusts hereby created.

COMMENT: In those situations in which the trust is drafted to provide asset protection for the grantor's children, it may be wise to include power for the trustee to change the situs of the trust to another state whose laws are more favorable to the protection of the trust assets should the trustee find that the laws of the home state are less favorable to asset protection.

---

23. <u>No-Contest.</u> If any beneficiary of this trust, or the guardian or legal representative of such beneficiary, contests the validity of this trust or of any of its provisions or shall institute or join in (except as a party defendant) any proceeding to contest the validity of this trust or to prevent any provision of it from being carried out in accordance with its terms (regardless of whether or not such proceedings are instituted in good faith and with probable cause), then all benefits provided for such beneficiary hereunder are revoked and such benefits shall pass as if such beneficiary and such beneficiary's descendants all had predeceased me.

COMMENT: This provision or some variation of it should be considered if there is any concern that a beneficiary or heir-at-law may challenge the trust. The lawyer may need to modify this provision to meet any requirements of state law.

---

24. <u>Power To Amend or Revoke.</u> I reserve the right from time to time by written instrument delivered to the trustee to amend or revoke this instrument and the trusts hereby evidenced, in whole or in part.

COMMENT: This instrument is revocable thus permitting the grantor to make any amendments he or she chooses or to revoke the trust in its entirety.

    The undersigned has signed this instrument and has established the foregoing trusts on this the _____ day of _____, [Current year].

GRANTOR AND TRUSTEE:

_____

[Grantor]

STATE OF [State of notary]   )

) SCT.

COUNTY OF [County of notary])

    The undersigned, a Notary Public within and for the state and county aforesaid, does hereby certify that the foregoing trust agreement executed by [Grantor], as grantor and trustee, was on this day produced to me in my county by [Grantor], who executed, acknowledged and swore the same before me to be [his or her] act and deed in due form of law.

    Given under my hand and notarial seal on this the _____ day of _____, [Current year].

_____

Notary Public, State at Large

My commission expires:_____

PREPARED BY:

_____

[Name of Attorney
[Name of Law Firm]
Attorneys at Law
[Street Address]
[City], [State] [Zip Code]
[Telephone Number]

SCHEDULE A

[NAME OF TRUST] TRUST

Cash. . . . . $ 10.00

The lawyer will note a deposit of $10 in the trust. State law will determine the necessity of an initial deposit. An unfunded trust that contains no principal may be deemed a "dry" trust under state law, meaning that it is not a valid document. Some lawyers go to the added step of affixing a $10 bill to schedule A, while others are satisfied with a cash deposit which does have the disadvantage of not being traceable. If there is the possibility of a contest of the trust, the cautious practice would be to affix a $10 bill to schedule A.

JOINT TRUST WORKSHEET

1. **Grantor and Trustee Information**

    Grantor 1 Name _____

    Grantor 2 Name _____

    Grantors' City and State _____

2. **Name of Trust**

    "_____ Trust"

3. **Children**

    3.1 Names of Children _____

    _____

    _____

    3.2 Are any of the above-named children step-children? Yes / No

    3.3 Are provisions needed for after-born children? Yes / No

4. **Payment of Death Taxes (if provision needed)**

    4.1 Are taxes on probate and nonprobate assets, including apportionment property, to be paid from the trust principal? (Option 1) | Yes / No |

    4.2 Are taxes to be paid by beneficiary and taxes collected on apportionment property? (Option 2) | Yes / No |

    4.3 Are taxes on probate and nonprobate assets to be paid from trust principal, but taxes on apportionment property to be collected? (Option 3) | Yes / No |

    4.4 Other tax provisions _____

    _____

5. **Allocations at Death**

    5.1 Separate trust for lifetime of beneficiaries? (Option 1) Yes / No

    A. Provision for educational incentive? Yes / No
       (See 5.c)

    B. Provision for distribution to descendants? Yes / No
       (See 5.d)

    C. Provision for trustee authority to withhold? Yes / No
       (See 5.e)

    D. Power of appointment:

       Limited to descendants/charities? (Option 1) Yes / No

       Broad? (Option 2) Yes / No

       Limited and age restricted? (Option 3) Yes / No

       Broad and age restricted? (Option 4) Yes / No
       (See 5.f)

If no power of appointment or not exercised and a child is deceased:

Deceased child's share distributed
to such child's estate? (Option 1) <u>Yes / No</u>

or Deceased child's share per stirpes
to lineal descendants? (Option 2) <u>Yes / No</u>
(See 5.g)

5.2 Separate trusts until minimum age of beneficiaries? (Option 2) <u>Yes / No</u>

    A. Provision for educational incentive? <u>Yes / No</u>
    (See 5.c)

    B. Provide for distribution one-half at each of two ages? <u>Yes / No</u>

        If yes: Initial age to inherit: _____

                        Final age to inherit: _____
    (See 5.d)

    C. Provision for trustee authority to withhold? <u>Yes / No</u>
    (See 5.e)

    D. If a child is deceased:

    Deceased child's share distributed
    to such child's estate? (Option 1) <u>Yes / No</u>

    or Deceased child's share per stirpes
    to lineal descendants? (Option 2) <u>Yes / No</u>
    (See 5.f)

5.3 Single testamentary trust for children? (Option 3) <u>Yes / No</u>

    A. Final age to inherit: _____
    (See 5.c)

    B. If a child is deceased:

    Deceased child's share distributed
    to such child's estate? (Option 1) <u>Yes / No</u>

    or Deceased child's share per stirpes
    to lineal descendants? (Option 2) <u>Yes / No</u>
    (See 5.c)

    C. Provision for trustee authority to withhold? <u>Yes / No</u>
    (See 5.b)

6.   **Special Provisions**:

Residential Real Estate? <u>Yes / No</u>

Rule against Perpetuities? <u>Yes / No</u>

Subchapter S Stock? <u>Yes / No</u>

Reliance on Will? <u>Yes / No</u>

Method of Payment? <u>Yes / No</u>

Accrued Income and Termination:

Distributed to such interested person's estate? (Option 1) <u>Yes / No</u>

Remain an asset of the trust (not distributed)? (Option 2) <u>Yes / No</u>

Life Insurance Policies? <u>Yes / No</u>

7.   Default Provisions (if needed), if All Named Beneficiaries are Deceased:

_____

_____

_____

8.   Definition of "Child" and "Descendant"

Include children adopted prior to age _____ (18, 21, etc.).

Include provision for illegitimate children (treated same, etc.)? <u>Yes / No</u>

9.   Powers

Environmental Powers? <u>Yes / No</u> (See Paragraph 11)

Farm Powers? <u>Yes / No</u> (See Paragraph 12)

Limitation on Trustee Powers? <u>Yes / No</u>

10.   Trustees

Name of first successor trustee: _____

Name of second successor trustee: _____

Corporate trustee compensation? (Option 1) <u>Yes / No</u>

Individual reimbursed for expenses but no compensation? (Option 2) <u>Yes / No</u>

Individual receives compensation? (Option 3) <u>Yes / No</u>

Amount of compensation: $_____

Provision needed for children to act as trustee of own trust? <u>Yes / No</u>

11.   Incompetency

One physician decides? (Option 1) <u>Yes / No</u>

Two physicians decide and one board certified? (Option 2) <u>Yes / No</u>

12.   No-Contest

Is No-Contest provision needed? <u>Yes / No</u>

13.   Revocation

Both spouses? (Option 1) <u>Yes / No</u>

Survivor with limits (Option 2) <u>Yes / No</u>

Survivor without limits (Option 3) <u>Yes / No</u>

JOINT TRUST

This trust is a joint inter vivos trust used when a couple desires to establish a trust for themselves and then make provisions for the distribution of the trust assets for the survivor of them and then to the ultimate beneficiaries upon the death of the survivor of the couple. This trust can serve as a convenient tool for asset management and to simplify the estate settlement process. All that is necessary is for the couple's assets to be transferred to the trust while the couple is living, or such transfer can be made by the survivor. This trust is not appropriate for situations in which federal estate tax planning is necessary. Thus, it should be not be used when the anticipated taxable estate of the couple exceeds the amount of the federal estate tax exemption, which is $3,500,000 in 2009. Also, the trust should not be used if there is any anticipation that the estate may grow in amount in excess of the estate tax exempt amount in the years following the lawyer drafting the trust. However, this trust becomes a very convenient planning tool for those estates that do not present estate tax planning needs.

We, [Grantor 1] and [Grantor 2], currently of [Grantors' city], [Grantors' state], acting as grantors and trustees hereby transfer to ourselves, as co-trustees the property described in Schedule A. This property and all investments, reinvestments and additions which may sometimes be referred to in this instrument as the "trust property" or "trust assets" are to be held subject to the following provisions:

COMMENT: In this trust the grantors will also act as trustee during their lifetime. The trust may be funded at the time it is created or the grantors may choose to fund the trust at a later date. Also, this trust has the benefit of being a so-called living trust, which is intended to simplify estate settlement, as well as, providing for the benefit of children.

---

1. <u>Name of Trust.</u> This instrument and the initial trust hereby established may be named the "[Name of trust] Trust."

COMMENT: The trust may have any name the grantors desire. Often times, the grantors will simply name the trust after themselves.

---

2. <u>Family Information.</u>

OPTION 1: Naming of all children Our [child is or children are], [names of children], and all references in this will to "our [child is or children are]" only to [him her or them].

OPTION 2: Inclusion of step-children Even though some of the above named children are step-children it is our intent that each of the above-named children be treated for purposes of this instrument as if they and their lineal descendants are our natural born children.

OPTION 3: After-born children If subsequent to the execution of this instrument there shall be an additional child or children born to us, then such child or children shall share in the benefits of the trusts established in this instrument to the same extent as our above named children and their descendants; and the provisions of this instrument shall be deemed modified to the extent necessary to carry out this intent.

COMMENT: The full names of the children should be inserted. If step-children are involved, Option 2 should be considered. Also, Option 3 may be appropriate if there is the possibility of additional children. The lawyer's state law should provide for this contingency, but it still may be appropriate to add this provision to the will. Concerns about adopted or illegitimate children inheriting and the extent to that inheritance are considered in paragraph 9. If there is the need to disinherit a child, then Option 5 of the master will can be used with only minor modifications.

3. <u>Provisions During Our Lifetime.</u> During the lifetime of both of us and during the lifetime of the survivor of us, the trustee shall pay the net trust income and the principal of the trust property as we, or the survivor of us, directs. If our successor trustee determines that both of us are unable, or the survivor of us is unable to manage our (or the survivor's) financial affairs based on the criteria in paragraph 20 below, the trustee shall pay to or use all, part or none, of the income and principal of the trust property as the trustee believes appropriate for our (or the survivor's) reasonable maintenance, support, and health. If any net income remains undistributed at the end of each calendar year (excluding income distributed during the sixty-five (65) day period under Internal Revenue Code Section 663), the trustee shall add it to the principal of the trust.

COMMENT: These are basic provisions to provide that, during the lifetime of the grantors, all income and principal is for the sole benefit of the grantors. In order to maintain privacy, the grantors may elect to transfer brokerage accounts and other assets to the trust. In this way, those assets need not be reported to the probate court in settlement of the grantors' estate. Throughout the grantors' lifetime, they jointly act as co-trustees in making distributions to themselves with a successor trustee making distributions in the event of disability. Please note that this form cross-references paragraph 20 which defines incompetency. Care must be taken to insert the correct paragraph number, as if any of the ensuing paragraphs are deleted, this will change the paragraph numbers.

4. <u>Payment of Debts, Death Taxes and Funeral Expenses</u>. **OPTION 1: Death taxes paid from trust** On the death of each of us the trustee shall pay all of our just debts, our funeral expenses, costs of estate administration, and death taxes, if any, from trust principal and the trustee shall not seek contribution toward or recovery of any such payments; provided, however, such obligations and death taxes shall be paid by the trustee only to the extent the personal representative of our respective probate estates certifies in writing to the trustee that the residue of our probate estates are insufficient to pay such obligations and death taxes. Death taxes means any estate or inheritance taxes, but not generation-skipping transfer taxes, imposed under the laws of any jurisdiction due to each of our deaths on any property passing by reason of our deaths. Any generation-skipping transfer taxes shall be paid from the property that incurred such tax.

OPTION 2: Death taxes paid by beneficiary and collecting taxes on apportionment property On the death of each of us the trustee shall pay each of our just debts, our funeral expenses and costs of estate administration from trust principal as soon as possible after each of our deaths. Any death taxes owed shall be charged against the trust share passing to the person whose share generated such tax. Death taxes means any estate or inheritance taxes, but not generation-skipping transfer taxes, imposed under the laws of any jurisdiction due to each of our deaths on any property passing by reason of our deaths. Additionally, our trustee shall take such actions as are necessary to obtain reimbursement with respect to apportionment property, including withholding distribution. Apportionment property means (a) any property with respect to which our trustee may be entitled to recover federal estate tax under Internal Revenue Code Section 2207, 2207A, or 2207B and (b) any policies of insurance, or the proceeds of policies of insurance, on our respective lives which were not owned by us at our respective deaths. Any generation-skipping transfer taxes shall be paid from the property that incurred such tax.

OPTION 3: Death taxes paid from residue but collecting taxes on apportionment property On the death of each of us the trustee shall pay our just debts, our funeral expenses and costs of estate administration from trust principal as soon as possible after each of our deaths.

We further direct that our death taxes, if any, be paid out of trust principal, other than apportionment property, without proration and our trustee shall not seek contribution toward or recovery of any such payments. Death taxes means any estate or inheritance taxes, but not generation-skipping transfer taxes, imposed under the laws of any jurisdiction due to each of our deaths on any property passing by reason of our deaths whether or not such property passes under this will. With regard to apportionment property, our trustee shall take such actions as are necessary to obtain reimbursement with respect to apportionment property, including withholding distribution. Apportionment property means (a) any property with respect to which our trustee may be entitled to recover federal estate tax under Internal Revenue Code Section 2207, 2207A, or 2207B and (b) any policies of insurance, or the proceeds of policies of insurance, on our respective lives which are not owned by us at our respective deaths. Any generation-skipping transfer taxes shall be paid from the property that incurred such tax.

COMMENT: If the couple owns sufficient assets in their individual or joint names, rather than all assets being titled in the trust, then this provision is not needed to pay final expenses. The concern giving rise to this provision is that all assets will be owned in the trust and there are not sufficient estate assets with which to pay final expenses. The more difficult question becomes the payment of death taxes. In many situations, there will be no death taxes anticipated, thus in some situations, these provisions can be deleted. Otherwise, a decision must be made as to who bears the burden of paying these taxes. An excellent ABA resource discussing tax payment clauses, apportionment property and the GST tax is Thomas M. Featherston, Jr. et al., *Drafting for Tax and Administrative Issues*, American Bar Association (Chicago: 2000).

---

5. <u>Allocations at Our Deaths.</u> Following the death of the last of us to die, the trustee shall hold and administer the trust property, including property which the trustee receives under either of our wills or from any other source, as follows:

OPTION 1: Separate trust for lifetime of beneficiaries

a. The trust property shall be divided and allocated into equal shares for our children. If a child is deceased, that deceased child's share shall be divided and allocated per stirpes among that deceased child's then living lineal descendants. Property allocated to a child or more remote lineal descendant of ours shall be retained in trust as a separate trust which shall be named for that person subject to the following provisions.

COMMENT: Option 1 creates a separate trust for each child of the grantors; and if a child is deceased, then a separate trust is created for each of that deceased child's then living children.

---

b. The trustee may pay to or use all, part or none, of the income and principal of such person's trust as the trustee believes appropriate for the reasonable maintenance, support, health, and education (including college or graduate, professional or vocational school education) of such person, considering such person's income or assets and all other circumstances and factors the trustee believes pertinent. It is our desire that distributions of income and principal not impair such person's motivation to be productive and self-supporting, thus our trustee shall not make distributions of income and principal from such person's trust if such person is not productive, mature, and responsible. If any net income remains undistributed at the end of each calendar year (excluding income distributed during the sixty-five (65) day period under Internal Revenue Code Section 663), the trustee shall add it to the principal of the trust.

COMMENT: The first sentence provides broad discretion to the trustee in making distributions for the child or more remote descendant. The second sentence is not essential, but is provided to illustrate a possible restriction that the grantors may desire. The third sentence can be eliminated, but is provided to cover situations in which income is not distributed before year end; and to set the time at which accumulated income is added to trust principal.

---

c. Notwithstanding the above paragraphs, following high school graduation, if a person for whom a trust is held hereunder fails to pursue post-secondary education leading to a bachelor's degree from an accredited college or university, all trust distributions, except for health care needs, shall cease until such person reaches the age of twenty-three (23) years. A person pursuing post-secondary education must annually maintain a 2.50 GPA based on a 4.0 grading scale in order to receive trust distributions, except for health care needs, prior to the age of twenty-three (23) years. If a person for whom a trust is named earns a bachelor's degree from an accredited college or university before such person reaches the age of twenty-three (23) years, the trustee shall within ninety (90) days of such person's graduation distribute [enter number] percent ([enter number]%) of the trust assets to such person free of trust.

COMMENT: This provision is intended to provide a model for the lawyer to consider in addressing an incentive for a child or more remote descendant to pursue post-secondary education and to maintain an adequate grade point average. This paragraph may need to be moved to become part of paragraph a or as a separate paragraph b. In this form, the decision was made to place it in this location as it and the following paragraphs are offered as supplemental provisions that some clients will want and others will not. Be certain to modify the reference in the first sentence to the phrase "nothwithstanding . . . paragraphs" if it is moved elsewhere in the document.

---

d. In addition, the trustee may pay to or use for the benefit of any one or more of the descendants of a person for whom a trust is held hereunder such part or all of the principal of such person's trust at such time or times and in such equal or unequal proportions among them as the trustee believes appropriate for the reasonable maintenance, support, health and education (including college or graduate, professional or vocational school education) of such descendants as a group, considering their respective incomes or assets and all other circumstances and factors the trustee believes pertinent.

COMMENT: In some situations, the grantors may desire for the trust beneficiary's own descendants to receive distributions from the trust. This provision permits such distributions, but such distributions are limited to trust principal and not both income and principal. If that flexibility is desired, then a minor modification may be made to this paragraph.

---

e. In addition to the restrictions provided in the above paragraphs and as a condition precedent to distributions under those paragraphs, our trustee shall withhold or postpone any or all distributions of income or principal from a person's trust if our trustee believes a distribution to such person could result in the loss of some part or all of the distribution due to any possible civil or criminal legal action involving such person or such person's spouse, or due to such person or such person's spouse being addicted to alcohol or any legal or illegal controlled substance.

The decision of our trustee shall be final and binding and shall not be subject to question by any person or in any court.

COMMENT: If the clients are faced with a child or more remote descendant who has substance abuse or other serious problems making distributions from the trust unwise, or if the clients are concerned about such possibility, then paragraph e or a variation of it may be helpful. It is designed to give the trustee full authority to withhold all distributions of income and principal when a child or more remote descendant is facing substance abuse or other significant personal problems.

---

f. **OPTION 1: Power of Appointment Limited** Upon the death of a person for whom a trust held under this paragraph is named, any part or all of the principal of such person's trust and any accrued or undistributed income shall be distributed to or for the benefit of our descendants and public charities in such proportions and subject to such trusts, powers and conditions as such person may provide and appoint by will specifically referring to this power to appoint.

f. **OPTION 2: Power of Appointment Broad** Upon the death of a person for whom a trust held under this paragraph is named, any part or all of the principal of such person's trust and any accrued or undistributed income shall be distributed to or for the benefit of such individual or individuals and entities other than such person's own estate or the creditors of such person's estate in such proportions and subject to such trusts, powers and conditions as such person may provide and appoint by will specifically referring to this power to appoint.

f. **OPTION 3: Power of Appointment Limited and Age Restricted** Upon the death of a person who is at least [insert age] years of age and for whom a trust held under this paragraph is named, any part or all of the principal of such person's trust and any accrued or undistributed income thereof shall be distributed to or for the benefit of our descendants and public charities in such proportions and subject to such trusts, powers and conditions as such person may provide and appoint by will specifically referring to this power to appoint.

f. **OPTION 4: Power of Appointment Broad and Age Restricted** Upon the death of a person who is at least [insert age] years of age and for whom a trust held under this paragraph is named, any part or all of the principal of such person's trust and any accrued or undistributed income thereof shall be distributed to or for the benefit of such individual or individuals and entities other than such person's own estate or the creditors of such person's estate in such proportions and subject to such trusts, powers and conditions as such person may provide and appoint by will specifically referring to this power to appoint.

COMMENT: In many situations, the grantors will want the trust beneficiary to have the right to designate how and to whom the trust property is to be distributed upon the death of the beneficiary. Option 1 limits distributions to the grantors' descendants and provides a contingent possibility to public charities. Option 2 is an extremely broad power of appointment that includes virtually anyone or any entity to whom the beneficiary might desire to give the property at death. Options 3 and 4 are similar to Options 1 and 2 with the exception of adding the requirement that the trust beneficiary be a certain minimum age before exercising the power of appointment.

---

g. Upon the death of a person for whom a trust held under this paragraph is named, any principal of such person's trust (not effectively disposed of by any other provisions of this paragraph 5) shall be divided and allocated per stirpes among the then living lineal descendants of such person, if any, otherwise per stirpes among the then living lineal descendants of the nearest lineal ancestor of such person who also was a descendant of ours and of whom one or more descendants then are living, or, if none, per stirpes among our then living lineal descendants.

COMMENT: If the trust beneficiary does not exercise the power of appointment granted above, or if no power of appointment is given to the beneficiary, then the trust must direct to whom the trust property will be distributed upon the death of the beneficiary. Care must be taken to be certain that the per stirpes distribution provided in this form is adequate. This provision should not be used routinely without an analysis of its effect under the facts of the particular estate plan. For example, in many situations the phrase "per stirpes among the then living lineal descendants of the nearest lineal ancestor of such person who was also a descendant of ours and of whom one or more descendants then are living" may need to be omitted.

Distribution shall be made outright to such descendant or descendants unless: (i) distribution is to be made to a descendant for whom a trust then held under this trust instrument is named in which event such distribution shall be added to that trust, or (ii) distribution is to be made to a descendant who has not reached the age of [Age of remote descendants] years and for whom no trust is then held in which event, the trustee shall retain any property otherwise distributable to such descendant as a separate trust named for such descendant to be distributed to such descendant when he or she reaches the age of [Age for remote descendants] years. If such descendant is already [Age for remote descendants] years of age, then such descendant shall receive his or her share outright. Until such descendant reaches [Age for remote descendants] years of age, the trustee shall distribute the income and principal of a trust so retained in such amounts, if any, and at such times as the trustee believes appropriate for the reasonable maintenance, support, health and education (including college or graduate, professional or vocational school education) of the descendant for whom the trust is named, considering such descendant's income or assets and all other circumstances and factors the trustee believes pertinent. It is our desire that distributions of income and principal not impair a descendant's motivation to be productive and self-supporting, thus our trustee shall not make distributions of income and principal from a descendant's trust if our descendant is not productive, mature, and responsible. If any net income remains undistributed at the end of each calendar year (excluding income distributed during the sixty-five (65) day period under Internal Revenue Code Section 663), the trustee shall add it to the principal of the trust.

OPTION 1: If a descendant for whom a trust held under this paragraph is named dies prior to termination of such descendant's trust, then such descendant's trust shall terminate and shall be distributed to such descendant's own estate.

OPTION 2: On the death of a descendant for whom a trust held under this paragraph is named, any principal and undistributed income of such descendant's trust shall be divided and allocated per stirpes among the then living lineal descendants of such descendant, if any, otherwise such descendant's trust shall be divided and allocated per stirpes among the then living lineal descendants of the nearest lineal ancestor of such person who also was a descendant of ours and of whom one or more descendants then are living, or, if none, such person's trust shall be divided and allocated per stirpes among our then living lineal descendants.

COMMENT: The above provisions permit a distribution to a more remote descendant to be distributed to that person's own trust if he or she is a recipient of a trust under this instrument, or if not and the remote descendant is under a specified minimum age, then the trustee may hold that person's share in trust until that person reaches the minimum age with the trust property to be used for that person until distribution. If this option is used, then Option 1 or 2 above should be selected to determine to whom the trust property is distributed should that remote descendant die before termination of the trust. Also, see the Comment above following Option 1, 5.g.

OPTION 2: Separate trust until minimum age of beneficiaries

a. The trust property shall be divided and allocated into equal shares for our children. If a child is deceased, that deceased child's share shall be divided and allocated per stirpes among that deceased child's then-living lineal descendants. Property allocated to a child or more remote lineal descendant of ours shall be retained in trust as a separate trust which shall be named for that person subject to the following provisions.

COMMENT: Option 2 is the same as Option 1 except that the trust terminates upon the beneficiary reaching certain ages as provided in paragraph d below.

---

b. The trustee may pay to or use all, part or none, of the income and principal of such person's trust as the trustee believes appropriate for the reasonable maintenance, support, health, and education (including college or graduate, professional or vocational school education) of such person, considering such person's income or assets and all other circumstances and factors the trustee believes pertinent. It is our desire that distributions of income and principal not impair such person's motivation to be productive and self-supporting, thus our trustee shall not make distributions of income and principal from such person's trust if such person is not productive, mature, and responsible. If any net income remains undistributed at the end of each calendar year (excluding income distributed during the sixty-five (65) day period under Internal Revenue Code Section 663), the trustee shall add it to the principal of the trust.

COMMENT: The first sentence provides broad discretion to the trustee in making distributions for the child or more remote descendant. The second sentence is not essential, but is provided to illustrate a possible restriction that the grantor may desire. The third sentence can be eliminated, but is provided to cover situations in which income is not distributed before year end; and to set the time at which accumulated income is added to trust principal.

---

c. Notwithstanding the above paragraphs, following high school graduation, if a person for whom a trust is held hereunder fails to pursue post-secondary education leading to a bachelor's degree from an accredited college or university, all trust distributions, except for health care needs, shall cease until such person reaches the age of twenty-three (23) years. A person pursuing post-secondary education must annually maintain a 2.50 GPA based on a 4.0 grading scale in order to receive trust distributions, except for health care needs, prior to the age of twenty-three (23) years. If a person for whom a trust is named earns a bachelor's degree from an accredited college or university before such person reaches the age of twenty-three (23) years, the trustee shall within ninety (90) days of such person's graduation distribute [enter number] percent ([enter number]%) of the trust assets to such person free of trust.

COMMENT: This provision is intended to provide a model for the lawyer to consider in addressing an incentive for a child or more remote descendant to pursue post-secondary education and to maintain an adequate grade point average. This paragraph may need to be moved to become part of paragraph a or as a separate paragraph b. In this form, the decision was made to place it in this location as it and the following paragraphs are offered as supplemental provisions that some clients will want and others will not. Be certain to modify the reference in the first sentence to the phrase "nothwithstanding . . . paragraphs" if it is moved elsewhere in the document.

d. When a person for whom a trust held under this paragraph is named reaches the age of [initial age to inherit] years, the trustee shall distribute to such person one-half ($^1/_2$) of the then principal of that person's trust; and when such person reaches the age of [final age to inherit] years, the person's trust shall terminate and the balance of such person's trust shall be distributed outright to such person.

COMMENT: This trust terminates for the beneficiary upon that person reaching a specified age. This form has distributions at two ages with the trust terminating upon distribution at the second age.

e. In addition to the restrictions provided in the above paragraphs and as a condition precedent to distributions under those paragraphs, our trustee shall withhold or postpone any or all distributions of income or principal from a person's trust if our trustee believes a distribution to such person could result in the loss of some part or all of the distribution due to any possible civil or criminal legal action involving such person or such person's spouse, or due to such person or such person's spouse being addicted to alcohol or any legal or illegal controlled substance. The decision of our trustee shall be final and binding and shall not be subject to question by any person or in any court.

COMMENT: If the clients are faced with a child or more remote descendant who has substance abuse or other serious problems making distributions from the trust unwise, or if the clients are concerned about such possibility, then paragraph e or a variation of it may be helpful. It is designed to give the trustee full authority to withhold all distributions of income and principal when a child or more remote descendant is facing substance abuse or other significant personal problems.

f. **OPTION 1**: If a person for whom a trust held under this paragraph is named dies prior to termination of such person's trust, then such person's trust shall terminate and shall be distributed to such person's own estate.

f. **OPTION 2**: On the death of a person for whom a trust held under this paragraph is named, any principal and undistributed income of such person's trust shall be divided and allocated per stirpes among the then living lineal descendants of such person, if any, otherwise such person's trust shall be divided and allocated per stirpes among the then living lineal descendants of the nearest lineal ancestor of such person who also was a descendant of ours and of whom one or more descendants then are living, or, if none, such person's trust shall be divided and allocated per stirpes among our then living lineal descendants.

COMMENT: Options 1 and 2 do not grant to the trust beneficiary a power of appointment. Thus, the trust instrument must direct to whom the trust property will be distributed upon the death of the beneficiary. Care must be taken to be certain that the per stirpes distribution provided in Option 2 is adequate. This provision should not be used without an analysis of its effect under the facts of the particular estate plan. For example, in many situations the phrase "per stirpes among the then living lineal descendants of the nearest lineal ancestor of such person who was also a descendant of mine and of whom one or more descendants then are living" may need to be omitted.

Distribution shall be made outright to such descendant or descendants unless: (i) distribution is to be made to a descendant for whom a trust then held under this trust instrument is named in which event such distribution shall be added to that trust, or (ii) distribution is to be made to a descendant who has not reached the age of [Age of remote descendants] years and for whom no trust is then held in which event, the trustee shall retain any property otherwise distributable to such descendant as a separate trust named for such descendant to be distributed to such descendant when he or she reaches the age of [Age for remote descendants] years. If such descendant is already [Age for remote descendants] years of age, then such descendant shall receive his or her share outright. Until such descendant reaches [Age for remote descendants] years of age, the trustee shall distribute the income and principal of a trust so retained in such amounts, if any, and at such times as the trustee believes appropriate for the reasonable maintenance, support, health and education (including college or graduate, professional or vocational school education) of the descendant for whom the trust is named, considering such descendant's income or assets and all other circumstances and factors the trustee believes pertinent. It is our desire that distributions of income and principal not impair a descendant's motivation to be productive and self-supporting, thus our trustee shall not make distributions of income and principal from a descendant's trust if such descendant is not productive, mature, and responsible. If any net income remains undistributed at the end of each calendar year (excluding income distributed during the sixty-five (65) day period under Internal Revenue Code Section 663), the trustee shall add it to the principal of the trust.

OPTION 1: If a descendant for whom a trust held under this paragraph is named dies prior to termination of such descendant's trust, then such descendant's trust shall terminate and the trust property shall be distributed to such descendant's own estate.

OPTION 2: On the death of a descendant for whom a trust held under this paragraph is named, any principal and undistributed income of such descendant's trust shall be divided and allocated per stirpes among the then living lineal descendants of such descendant, if any, otherwise such descendant's trust shall be divided and allocated per stirpes among the then living lineal descendants of the nearest lineal ancestor of such person who also is a descendant of ours and of whom one or more descendants then are living, or, if none, such person's trust shall be divided and allocated per stirpes among our then-living lineal descendants.

COMMENT: The above provisions permit a distribution to a more remote descendant to be distributed to that person's own trust if he or she is a recipient of a trust under this instrument, or if not and the remote descendant is under a specified minimum age, then the trustee may hold that person's share in trust until that person reaches the minimum age with the trust property to be used for that person until distribution. If this option is used, then Option 1 or 2 above should be selected to determine to whom the trust property is distributed should that remote descendant die before termination of the trust. Care must be taken to be certain that the per stirpes distribution provided in this form is adequate. This provision should not be used routinely without an analysis of its effect under the facts of the particular estate plan. For example, in many situations the phrase "per stirpes among the then living lineal descendants of the nearest lineal ancestor of such person who was also a descendant of mine and of whom one or more descendants then are living" may need to be omitted.

OPTION 3: Single trust for children

a. Until our youngest child becomes [final age to inherit] years old, our trustee shall pay or use all, part or none of the income and principal of the trust, without regard to equality of distribution, to or for the benefit of our children as the trustee believes appropriate for the reasonable maintenance, support, health, and education (including college or graduate, professional or vocational school education) of our children, considering each child's income or assets and all other circumstances and factors the trustee believes pertinent. It is our desire that distributions of income and principal not impair such person's motivation to be productive and self-supporting, thus our trustee shall not make distributions of income and principal from such person's trust if such person is not productive, mature, and responsible. If any net income remains undistributed at the end of each calendar year (excluding income distributed during the sixty-five (65) day period under Internal Revenue Code Section 663), the trustee shall add it to the principal of the trust. Disbursements of income and principal shall not be taken into account when our trustee makes final distribution of the trust property upon termination of the trust.

COMMENT: This trust allows the trustee to make distributions among all the grantors' children without regard to equality. This gives the trustee broad discretion to make distributions among the children based upon their then current needs. Because of the broadness of the discretion granted to the trustee, paragraph d from Option 1 has not been included but can be modified and added if the lawyer so desires. The second sentence above is not essential, but is provided to illustrate a possible restriction that the grantor may desire. The third sentence can be eliminated, but is provided for situations in which income is not distributed before year end; and to set the time at which accumulated income is added to trust principal.

---

b. In addition to the restrictions provided in the above paragraphs and as a condition precedent to distributions under those paragraphs, our trustee shall withhold or postpone any or all distributions of income or principal from a person's trust if our trustee believes a distribution to such person could result in the loss of some part or all of the distribution due to any possible civil or criminal legal action involving such person or such person's spouse, or due to such person or such person's spouse being addicted to alcohol or any legal or illegal controlled substance. The decision of our trustee shall be final and binding and shall not be subject to question by any person or in any court.

COMMENT: If the clients are faced with a child who has substance abuse or other serious problems making distributions from the trust unwise, or if the clients are concerned about such possibility, then this paragraph or a variation of it may be helpful. It is designed to give the trustee full authority to withhold all distributions of income and principal when a child is facing substance abuse or other significant personal problems.

---

c. Upon our youngest child reaching [final age to inherit] years of age, the trust shall terminate and our trustee shall distribute the trust property to our children in equal shares. If a child is deceased our deceased child's share shall be distributed to that child's then living lineal descendants per stirpes if any, otherwise such child's trust shall be divided and allocated per stirpes among the then living lineal descendants of the nearest lineal ancestor of such child who also was a descendant of ours and of whom one or more descendants then are living, or, if none, such child's trust shall be divided and allocated per stirpes among our then living lineal descendants.

COMMENT: The trust terminates upon the youngest child reaching a particular age, at which time the trust terminates and each child receives an equal share. This form does not grant the trust beneficiaries a power of appointment. Thus, the trust instrument directs to whom the trust property will be distributed upon the death of the beneficiary prior to the termination of the trust. This form provides a basic per stirpes distribution. Care must be taken to be certain the per stirpes distribution provided in this form is adequate. This provision should not be used routinely without an analysis of its effect under the facts of the particular estate plan. For example, in many situations the phrase "per stirpes among the then living lineal descendants of the nearest lineal ancestor of such person who was also a descendant of mine and of whom one or more descendants then are living" may need to be omitted.

Distribution shall be made outright to such descendant or descendants unless: (i) distribution is to be made to a descendant for whom a trust then held under this trust instrument is named in which event such distribution shall be added to that trust, or (ii) distribution is to be made to a descendant who has not reached the age of [Age of remote descendants] years and for whom no trust is then held in which event, the trustee shall retain any property otherwise distributable to such descendant as a separate trust named for such descendant to be distributed to such descendant when he or she reaches the age of [Age for remote descendants] years. If such descendant is already [Age for remote descendants] years of age, then such descendant shall receive his or her share outright. Until such descendant reaches [Age for remote descendants] years of age, the trustee shall distribute the income and principal of a trust so retained in such amounts, if any, and at such times as the trustee believes appropriate for the reasonable maintenance, support, health and education (including college or graduate, professional or vocational school education) of the descendant for whom the trust is named, considering such descendant's income or assets and all other circumstances and factors the trustee believes pertinent. It is our desire that distributions of income and principal not impair a descendant's motivation to be productive and self-supporting, thus our trustee shall not make distributions of income and principal from a descendant's trust if such descendant is not productive, mature, and responsible. If any net income remains undistributed at the end of each calendar year (excluding income distributed during the sixty-five (65) day period under Internal Revenue Code Section 663), the trustee shall add it to the principal of the trust.

OPTION 1: If a descendant for whom a trust held under this paragraph is named dies prior to termination of such descendant's trust, then such descendant's trust shall terminate and the trust property shall be distributed to such descendant's own estate.

OPTION 2: On the death of a descendant for whom a trust held under this paragraph is named, any principal and undistributed income of such descendant's trust shall be divided and allocated per stirpes among the then living lineal descendants of such descendant, if any, otherwise such descendant's trust shall be divided and allocated per stirpes among the then living lineal descendants of the nearest lineal ancestor of such person who also is a descendant of ours and of whom one or more descendants then are living, or, if none, such person's trust shall be divided and allocated per stirpes among our then living lineal descendants.

COMMENT: The above provisions permit a distribution to a more remote descendant to be distributed to that person's own trust if he or she is a recipient of a trust under this instrument, or if not and the remote descendant is under a specified minimum age, then the trustee may hold that person's share in trust until that person reaches the minimum age with the trust property to be used for that person until distribution. If this option is used, then Option 1 or 2 above should be selected to determine to whom the trust property is distributed should that remote descendant die before termination of the trust. Care must be taken to be certain that the per stirpes distribution provided in this form is adequate. This provision should not be used routinely without an analysis of its effect under the facts of the particular estate plan. For example, in many situations the phrase "per stirpes among the then living lineal descendants of the nearest lineal ancestor of such person who was also a descendant of mine and of whom one or more descendants then are living" may need to be omitted.

---

6. Special Provisions. In addition to the other provisions of this trust agreement:

COMMENT: The following are various provisions that may be needed in a given situation, but rarely will all of these paragraphs be needed.

---

a. <u>Residential Real Estate.</u> In the event any residential real estate is included among the trust assets and my [husband or wife] is then living, [he or she] may occupy such residence rent-free during [his or her] lifetime. My [husband or wife] shall pay all property taxes, insurance premiums, and the expenses of ordinary maintenance and repair. Further, my [husband or wife] may purchase any such residential real estate at its then appraised value as determined by a professional real estate appraiser.

COMMENT: In the event the grantors desire for their personal residence to be available for the survivor of them or for some other trust beneficiary, then this paragraph, or a modification of it, may be appropriate.

b. <u>Rule Against Perpetuities.</u> If not sooner terminated, twenty-one years after the death of the last to die of us and our descendants who are living at the time of the death of the first to die of us, our trustee shall distribute the trust property to each person for whom a trust is held under this trust agreement.

COMMENT: The lawyer will need to determine if there is any concern over the rule against perpetuities, and if so, the above provision, or a modification of it, will be necessary. In most drafting situations, there will not be the possibility of violating this rule, thus the lawyer may want to omit this paragraph.

c. <u>Subchapter S Stock.</u> In the event a trust under this agreement holds Subchapter S stock, then the terms of this trust are hereby modified so that this trust qualifies as a Qualified Subchapter S Trust ("QSST") under section 1361(d) of the Internal Revenue Code. Therefore, any trust that has more than one permissible beneficiary shall be divided on a prorata basis into separate trusts for those beneficiaries, resulting in each trust having only one beneficiary who shall be the only recipient of trust income and principal until the earlier of the beneficiary's death or the termination of the trust. This provision shall not preclude the limitations on distributions of income and principal as required in paragraph 5.

COMMENT: One of the general tax law requirements for a corporation being taxed as a Subchapter S corporation, which allows the corporate income to flow to the owners and be taxed to them rather than facing the possible double-taxation of the traditional corporate tax law, is that a trust cannot be an owner. Of course, with the tax law there are always exceptions. There are several situations in which a trust can be a stockholder of a Subchapter S corporation. This paragraph is intended to ensure that the corporation will maintain its status as a Subchapter S corporation, even though some of its stock is held in trust. This is a technical and somewhat tricky tax trap. An excellent ABA resource addressing this issue is Thomas M. Featherston, Jr. et al., *Drafting for Tax and Administrative Issues*, American Bar Association (Chicago: 2000). Be sure to change the number in the last sentence if any paragraphs prior to paragraph 5 are deleted.

d. <u>Reliance on Will.</u> The trustee may rely on a will admitted to probate in any jurisdiction as the last will and testament of such person, or may assume (absent actual knowledge to the contrary) the person had no will if a will has not been admitted to probate within three months after such person's death.

COMMENT: This is a "boilerplate" provision that is helpful, but this provision must be reviewed to be certain that it is needed, and to make any modifications that are required.

e. <u>Method of Payment.</u> If a person entitled to receive income or principal distributions is unable to manage his or her financial affairs due to any type of mental or physical incapacity, then distributions may be made to or for such person's benefit, including making distributions to such person's guardian, conservator, committee, or a custodian under a Uniform Gift or Transfer to Minors Act.

COMMENT: This is a "boilerplate" provision that is usually inserted in a trust instrument.

---

f. <u>Accrued Income and Termination.</u> Income accrued and undistributed at the termination of a person's interest in trust property **OPTION 1** shall be distributed to such person's estate. **OPTION 2** shall remain an asset of the trust and shall not be distributed to such person's estate.

COMMENT: This is a helpful provision for administrative reasons to clarify for the trustee whether accumulated but undistributed income should remain in the trust after the beneficiary's death or if it should be distributed to that beneficiary's estate. One of the two options should be selected.

---

g. <u>Rights and Duties Relating to Life Insurance Policies.</u> After each of our deaths when life insurance policies become payable to the trust, our trustee shall promptly furnish proof of loss to the life insurance companies, and shall collect and receive the proceeds of the policies. Our trustee shall have power to execute and deliver receipts and other instruments and to take such action as is appropriate for this collection. If our trustee deems it necessary to institute legal action for the collection of any policies, [he, she or it] shall be indemnified for all costs, including attorney's fees.

Our trustee, in [his, her or its] sole discretion, may accept any of the optional modes of payment provided in any of such policies where such modes of payment are permitted to the trustee by the life insurance company. No life insurance company under any policy of insurance deposited with our trustee shall be responsible for the application or disposition of the proceeds of such policy by our trustee. Payment to our trustee of such life insurance proceeds shall be a full discharge of the liability of the life insurance company under such policy.

COMMENT: This paragraph is needed only if life insurance is made payable to the trust. The provisions are customary and are intended to avoid liability for the life insurance company and the trustee over receipt of life insurance death proceeds and the selection of the mode of payment. While these are routine provisions, the lawyer should review them to be certain that they are appropriate.

---

7. <u>Default Provisions.</u> Any trust property not disposed of by any of the above provisions shall be distributed on the date of such failure of disposition to [default provisions].

COMMENT: If there are a limited number of beneficiaries, then it may be wise to insert a default provision providing for the ultimate recipient should all the beneficiaries in paragraph 5 and their descendants be deceased. If this is too remote of a possibility, some clients may direct that this paragraph be deleted.

---

8. <u>Protection from Creditors.</u> No trust beneficiary shall have the right to sell, transfer, assign, alienate, pledge, or in any way encumber trust assets, including income and principal, nor shall

trust assets be subject to execution, levy, sale, garnishment, attachment, bankruptcy, or other legal proceedings. Any such actions by a trust beneficiary or a third party seeking to enforce a claim against the trust assets shall not be recognized under any circumstances by the trustee. These provisions do not prevent the trustee from making distributions for the benefit of a trust beneficiary in such amounts and at such times as the trustee determines necessary for the trust beneficiary's maintenance, support, health and education.

COMMENT: This is a standard paragraph that precludes the trust assets from being attached by claims of creditors.

9. <u>Definitions.</u> For all purposes of this instrument, the following shall apply:

a. The words "child," "children," "descendant" or "descendants" shall exclude adopted persons unless they are adopted prior to [insert age] years; and shall include only persons legitimately born unless a decree of adoption terminates the parental rights of the natural mother during her lifetime, or the natural father signs a written notarized instrument during his lifetime in which he irrevocably states that the child is to be considered legitimately born for purposes of inheriting under this will.

COMMENT: Some clients will want to restrict distribution for an adopted child to preclude a child adopted as an adult. Thus, many will use the age 18 or perhaps a slightly older age such as 20 or 21. Other clients may wish to restrict the age to a younger adopted child, such as under the age of 10. The issue of illegitimate children should also be addressed. In many situations, a child or more remote descendant should be treated the same as any other child, in which case the portion of this paragraph that deals with illegitimate children can be deleted. In other situations there may be a limited or no relationship with the child, in which event no distribution should be made to that child. This form gives the father of the child the right to allow the child to inherit by the father signing a written document allowing inheritance.

b. Whenever assets are to be divided and allocated per stirpes, the assets to be divided or allocated shall be divided into as many equal shares as are necessary to divide or allocate one share to each then living child of such person and to provide one share collectively for the then living descendants of each child of such person who then is deceased leaving one or more descendants then living. Any collective share shall be divided and allocated per stirpes among the descendants of such deceased person in accordance with the preceding sentence.

COMMENT: Since the term per stirpes is used often in this document, a definition is provided of that term. The lawyer should modify this definition to conform with his or her own state law should it differ any from this definition. Of course, a definition is not essential, since the term will be defined under state law. But since it is a term that clients are not familiar with, it is often helpful to define it for them in the document. An excellent ABA resource that explains the term per stirpes and its variations is Jeffrey N. Penell and Alan Newman, *Estate and Trust Planning*, American Bar Association (Chicago, 2005) pp. 19–26.

10. <u>Trustee Powers.</u> In the administration of the trusts, the trustee shall have the following powers and rights and all others granted by law:

a. To sell publicly or privately any trust property, for cash or on time, without an order of court and upon such terms and conditions as our trustee deems proper; and no person dealing with our trustee shall have any obligation to look to the application of the purchase money.

b. To invest and reinvest all or any part of the principal of the trust in any stocks, bonds, mortgages, shares or interests in common trust funds, mutual funds, or other securities or property, real, personal, or mixed, and of any kind or nature whatsoever, as the trustee deems proper, and without diversification if the trustee deems it advisable, irrespective of whether or not such securities or property are eligible for trust investment under state or any other law, and may change any investment received or made by the trustee, and may hold cash if the trustee deems it advisable.

c. To exercise broad discretion as to diversification of trust property, and shall not be required to reduce any concentrated holdings merely because of such concentration, and shall have full discretion as to the percentage to be invested in fixed income securities, and is specifically relieved from any requirements, legal or otherwise, as to the percentage of the trust assets to be invested in fixed income securities, and may invest or retain invested any trust estates wholly in common stocks.

d. To sell, convey, lease or mortgage, repair and improve, and take any and all other steps with regard to any real estate that may at any time be a part of the principal of the trust; and any lease of such real property or contract with regard thereto made by the trustee shall be binding for the full period of the lease or contract, even though the period shall extend beyond the termination of the trust.

e. To vote shares of stock held in the trust at stockholders' meetings in person or by special, limited, or general proxy, with or without power of substitution, as seems best to the trustee.

f. To participate in the liquidation, reorganization, consolidation, incorporation and reincorporation, or any other financial readjustment of any corporation, limited liability company or business in which the trust is, or shall be financially interested.

g. To borrow money from any source for any purpose connected with the protection, preservation, improvement or development of the trust hereunder, whenever in the trustee's judgment the trustee deems it advisable, and as security to mortgage or pledge any real estate or personal property forming a part of the trust upon such terms and conditions as the trustee may deem advisable.

h. To hold any and all securities in bearer form, in the trustee's own name, or the name of some other person, partnership, or corporation, or in the name of a duly appointed nominee, with or without disclosing the fiduciary ownership.

i. To divide the principal of the trust property into parts or shares and to distribute or allot same, and to make such division in cash or in kind or both. For the purpose of such division or allotment, the judgment of the trustee concerning the propriety thereof and relative value of property so distributed or allotted shall be binding and conclusive with respect to all interested persons.

j. To merge and consolidate the trust property of any separate trust held hereunder with other trusts and then to administer such trust property as a single trust provided the separate trust is for the benefit of the same persons with substantially the same terms, conditions and federal tax consequences.

k. To pay such income and principal during the minority or incapacity of any beneficiary for whose benefit income and principal may be expended, in any one or more of the following ways: (1) directly to the beneficiary; (2) to the legal guardian or committee of the beneficiary; (3) to a relative of the beneficiary to be expended by the relative for the maintenance, health, and education of the beneficiary; or (4) by expending the same directly for the maintenance, health, and education of the beneficiary. The trustee shall not be obliged to see to the application of the funds so expended, but the receipt of such person shall be full acquittance to the trustee.

l. To continue and operate any business owned by us at our respective deaths and to do any and all things deemed appropriate by the trustee, including the power to form a limited liability company or incorporate the business and to put additional capital into the business, for such time as the trustee deems advisable, without liability for loss resulting from the continuance or operation of the business except for the trustee's own negligence; and to close out, liquidate, or sell the business at such time and upon such terms as the trustee deems proper, and in this connection a sale may be made (pursuant to an agreement entered into by us during our lifetime, or otherwise) to a partner, officer, member, employee or beneficiary under this trust. We are aware of the fact that certain risks are inherent in the operation of any business and, therefore, our trustee shall not be liable for any loss resulting from the retention and operation of any business unless such loss results directly from our trustee's gross negligence or willful misconduct.

m. To have the same powers, authorities, and discretions in the management of the trust as we would have in the management and control of our own personal assets. The trustee may continue to exercise any powers and discretions granted in this instrument for a reasonable period after the termination of any trust under this instrument.

COMMENT: The above powers are a set of standard powers that appear throughout this book. The powers should be reviewed to be certain that you the lawyer understand each power, the client is in agreement with each of the powers granted and that the powers granted are needed. Because this is a generic and broad statement of powers, some of these powers may not be necessary. For example, powers to sell or lease real estate are not needed if the grantors know the trust will consist only of cash and other intangible investments.

---

11. Environmental Interests. In the administration of this trust, our trustee shall have the power and authority to inspect, assess and evaluate any assets held in this trust, or proposed to be added to this trust, to determine if any environmental concerns exist with such asset or assets, and if so, our trustee may take any remedial action our trustee believes necessary to prevent, abate or remedy any environmental concerns whether or not our trustee is required to do so by any governmental agency. Further, our trustee may refuse to accept or may disclaim any asset or assets proposed to be added to the trust if our trustee believes there are possible environmental concerns that could result in liability to the trust or the trustee. Also, our trustee may settle or compromise any claims or lawsuits alleging environmental concerns which have been asserted by a private party or governmental agency. The decisions of our trustee regarding environmental concerns shall be final and binding on all parties and shall not be subject to question by anyone or in any court.

COMMENT: In many situations, it will be appropriate to address concerns of the trustee if the trust holds, or is expected to receive by will or other transfer, an asset that may have environmental concerns. This paragraph, or a variation of it, is helpful to the trustee in addressing this oftentimes difficult fiduciary problem. If there is any possibility the trust may hold assets that have environmental concerns, then the lawyer should address those issues fully with the client and with the trustee, including successor trustees, to avoid the situation in which a named trustee refuses to serve due to concerns over personal liability of the fiduciary for environmental cleanup costs.

---

12. <u>Trustee Powers as to Farms and Farm Real Estate.</u> In the administration of any farms and farmland held in this trust, the trustee shall have the following powers and rights:

a. To formulate and carry out a general farm plan of operation.

b. To make leases and enter into contracts with tenants, either on shares or for stated compensation, or to employ and pay such labor as might be employed.

c. To buy, breed, raise, and sell all kinds of livestock, either on shares with a tenant or solely on behalf of the trust estate.

d. To plant, cultivate, fertilize, produce, and market all crops raised on the farm, and to collect, receive and receipt for all shares, rent, and other income from the farm.

e. To ditch and drain so much of the land as might be considered desirable, and to make such repairs and improvements to building, land, and other items of property as may be consistent with good farm management.

f. To enter into contracts with the United States Department of Agriculture, or other Federal or State governmental agencies, for crop reductions or soil conservation practices.

g. To pay all taxes and assessments against the farm property and insure the improvements against loss by fire, windstorm, and other casualties.

h. To credit receipts and charge expenditures to and against the income account or the principal account as may be appropriate under applicable rules of trust accounting. In this regard, it is especially provided that any capital improvements made by the trustee in the exercise of prudent trust management shall be allocated between the income account and the principal account on the basis of the ratio of the life expectancy of the income beneficiary at that time to the normally expected useful life of the capital improvement.

i. To employ farm management services to the extent that this may be considered desirable for the proper formulation of farming plans and the active management of farm properties under the supervision and responsibility of the trustee.

j. To borrow monies which may be required from time to time to finance the farm operations, and to encumber trust assets to secure such loans.

k. To do any and all other things consistent with the provisions of this trust to facilitate an orderly distribution of our assets calculated to accomplish the purposes herein set out in an economically feasible manner.

COMMENT: In the event the trust will include a farm that will continue to be owned in trust, then these additional trust provisions should be considered. The general trustee powers should be sufficient, but when drafting for a farming client these more specific trustee powers are usually helpful.

---

13. <u>Limitation on Powers of Individual Trustee.</u> Notwithstanding any other powers granted to our trustee in this instrument, an individual trustee (a) shall have no power to make payments or distributions that would discharge the trustee's legal obligation to support the trust beneficiary, (b) shall not exercise any power or discretion in any manner that would be deemed to be a general power of appointment under Internal Revenue Code Section 2041, (c) shall be limited by the ascertainable standard of "maintenance, support, health and education" when making payments or distributions to the trustee personally or to anyone for whom the trustee has a beneficial interest, and (d) shall possess no incidence of ownership or powers with respect to life insurance in which the trustee is the insured and has fiduciary power over such life insurance.

COMMENT: There are some situations in which an individual trustee may have adverse estate or income tax consequences when given broad powers as trustee. If a corporate trustee is used, then this paragraph is not needed. But an individual trustee must be certain that acting as trustee does not result in any adverse estate or income tax consequences. This paragraph is intended to ensure that adverse tax consequences are avoided if overly broad powers are granted in the trust instrument. The lawyer is urged to exercise caution when using individual trustees coupled with broad discretionary powers of income and principal distribution to a trust beneficiary because of possible adverse tax consequences. An ABA resource to acquaint oneself with these issues is L. Rush Hunt and Lara Rae Hunt, *A Lawyer's Guide to Estate Planning*, American Bar Association (Chicago: 2004) §14.4.

14. <u>Trustee Resignation.</u> Our trustee may resign at any time by giving written notice to our successor trustee named below, if any, and if none, then written notice shall be given to each current adult income beneficiary who is then living.

COMMENT: If a trustee resigns, there must be some method of notice and appointment of a successor trustee. This paragraph provides a method of notification. It is not an essential trust provision, but is a helpful one.

15. <u>Trustee Succession and Appointment.</u> If one of us ceases to act as trustee due to death, incompetency, resignation or ceases to serve for any reason, then the other of us shall serve as sole trustee. If both of us die, become incompetent, resign or cease to serve for any reason, then [Name of successor trustee] shall serve as successor trustee. If [Name of successor trustee] dies, becomes incompetent, resigns or ceases to serve for any reason, then [Name of second successor trustee] shall serve as successor trustee. The last serving successor trustee may name his or her own successor trustee by a written instrument delivered to the successor trustee or by will. The successor trustee may be an individual or a financial institution possessing trust powers under state or federal law. Any further vacancy in the office of trustee shall be filled by decision of the probate court where the last of us to die resided at the time of his or her death.

COMMENT: A decision must be made as to succession of trustees and the method of appointing a successor trustee if all of those named successor trustees are unable to serve. It is also essential to clarify whether successor trustees must only be financial institutions or if individuals may also be considered. Once a decision is made as to the succession of trustees, then the last three sentences should be reviewed to be certain to what extent each of those are needed.

Following the death of the last of us to die, each of our children shall serve as the sole trustee of his or her own trust. Each child in a written instrument delivered to the successor trustee or by will may name his or her own successor trustee. The successor trustee may be an individual or a financial institution possessing trust powers under state or federal law. Any further vacancy in the office of trustee shall be filled by decision of the probate court where the last of us to die resided at the time of his or her death.

COMMENT: If the trust continues during the lifetime of the grantor's children, then in many situations it will be appropriate for each child to act as trustee of his or her own trust. Thus, the above paragraph is needed in those situations. If the child is not to act as his or her own trustee, then this paragraph should be deleted.

In the event a trustee named in this instrument is also a trust beneficiary and claims are filed against the trust or threatened to be filed against the trust, litigation is filed against or threatened to be filed against a beneficiary, a voluntary or involuntary petition is filed in bankruptcy court, or a receivership is ordered by a state court, then and in such event the trustee who is also a beneficiary hereunder shall cease to act as trustee. In this event, such beneficiary shall name an independent trustee to serve as a successor trustee. In the event it becomes necessary to name an independent trustee, we name [Name of trustee remover] to serve as trustee remover having the power to remove a successor trustee and to name another successor trustee, or to name a successor trustee in the event an acting trustee resigns. Any successor trustee so named by our trustee remover may be an individual or a financial institution possessing trust powers under state or federal law. Our trustee remover may name [his or her] own successor trustee remover.

COMMENT: In the event the child acts as his or her own trustee and a claim is made against the trust by a creditor of that child, then it may be wise practice for the child to resign as trustee and name an independent trustee who can then assert the "Protection from Creditor" provisions in the trust instrument on behalf of the child. If the lawyer elects to use this approach in drafting, then a method of naming an independent trustee is needed and there should be someone named as a trustee remover, having the power to remove the named independent trustee and name another trustee. Even if this paragraph is needed, it may require some modifications to fit the particular situation.

16. <u>Powers of Successor Trustee.</u> Each successor trustee shall have the same rights, titles, powers, duties, discretions, and immunities and otherwise be in the same position as if originally named trustee. No successor trustee shall be personally liable for any act or failure to act of a predecessor trustee. Further, a successor trustee may accept the account furnished and the property delivered by or for a predecessor trustee without liability for so doing, and such acceptance shall be a full and complete discharge to the predecessor trustee.

COMMENT: This paragraph clarifies that a successor trustee has the same powers as the initial trustee. Further, the paragraph relieves the successor trustee from liability for the prior acts of the resigning trustee and waives any requirements of audit or inquiry into the activities of the prior trustee. This is essential for any successor trustee.

17. <u>Compensation of Trustee.</u> **OPTION 1: Corporate trustee compensation** A corporate trustee shall receive compensation in accordance with its regular schedule of fees in effect at the time such services are rendered.

OPTION 2: Individual does not receive compensation An individual trustee shall not be paid any compensation, but shall be reimbursed for out-of-pocket expenses.

OPTION 3: Individual does receive compensation An individual trustee shall be paid [insert amount of compensation] as compensation for such services and shall be reimbursed for out-of-pocket expenses.

COMMENT: Three options are provided, but the actual drafting of this paragraph may be different than each of these options. If the only trustee to be used is a corporate trustee, then Option 1 is a standard trust provision. If there is a possibility of individual trustees, then care should be given to the method for setting this fee. If no fee is to be paid because the trustee is a close family member, then it is suggested that Option 2 be used. If the grantor expects a fee to be charged, then an amount or a formula, such as a percentage of income or principal, must be set. It is unwise to simply provide for compensation to be a reasonable fee, as that leaves an individual trustee with great uncertainty as to the fee to be charged. Without the grantors clarifying compensation, the trustee could find him or herself in litigation with the beneficiary.

18. <u>Court Accountings.</u> To the extent such requirements can be waived, the trustee shall not be required (a) to file any inventory of trust property or accounts or reports of the administration of the trusts, or to register the trusts, in any court, (b) to furnish any bond or other security for the proper performance of the trustee's duties or (c) to obtain authority from a court for the exercise of any power conferred on the trustee by this instrument. This waiver does not preclude the trustee from registering any trust created in this instrument and petitioning a court having jurisdiction over registered trusts for a judicial ruling on any matter relating to administration of any trust created in this instrument.

COMMENT: The first sentence is to clarify the normal situation that an inter vivos trust is not subject to judicial oversight. The second sentence may be omitted, but is suggested as a potential benefit in some states. In a state in which a trust can be registered, it may be possible to have minor trust matters resolved by the court in which the trust is registered. This creates a simplified process for dealing with minor administrative matters. Without this provision, a court might be reluctant to decide matters for a trust which is not required to be registered under state law.

19. <u>Severability.</u> If any provisions of this trust shall be unenforceable, the remaining provisions shall nevertheless be carried into effect.

COMMENT: This is the same type of standard provision often seen in contracts that is intended to save the document if a particular provision is found to be invalid or void. It is doubtful this provision will have any practical effect in most trust situations, but it is a "boilerplate" provision that is frequently found in trust instruments and for which there is no disadvantage.

20. <u>Certification of Incompetency.</u> **OPTION 1: Decided by treating physician** Any person acting or named to act as a trustee in this instrument is considered to be unable to serve or to continue serving when a physician whom such person has consulted within the prior three years has certified as to such consultation and the certification states that the person is incapable of managing the affairs of the trusts we have established in this instrument, regardless of cause and regardless of whether there is an adjudication of incompetency. No person shall be liable to anyone for actions taken in reliance on the physician's certification or for dealing with a trustee other than the one removed for incompetency based on such certification.

OPTION 2: Decided by two physicians Any person acting or named to act as a trustee in this instrument is considered to be unable to serve or to continue serving when a written certification is received from two (2) physicians, both of whom have personally examined the person and at least one (1) of whom is board-certified in the specialty most closely associated with the health condition alleged to cause such incompetency. The certification must state that the person is incapable of managing the affairs of this trust, regardless of cause and regardless of whether there is an adjudication of incompetence. No person is liable to anyone for actions taken in reliance on these certifications, or for dealing with a trustee other than the one removed for incompetency based on these certifications.

COMMENT: This provision relates back to paragraph 15 concerning the succession of trustees. It defines incompetency, which is one of those events requiring a successor trustee. The first option involves consultation with the trustee's personal physician, whereas Option 2 involves a panel of two physicians, one of whom is board certified in the speciality most closely associated with the health condition of the trustee. Clients differ as to which provision they prefer and are more concerned about the provision when the grantor is also the initial trustee. Absent a strong preference by the grantor, Option 1 is the provision most frequently used.

21. <u>Titles and References.</u> The underscored titles of paragraphs in this instrument are for information purposes only and shall be given no legal effect.

COMMENT: This is another common "boilerplate" provision that is perhaps not essential, but for which there is no disadvantage.

22. <u>Governing Law.</u> The laws of the State of [insert state] shall govern the interpretation and validity of the provisions of this instrument and all questions relating to the management, administration, investment, and distribution of the trusts hereby created.

COMMENT: It is a standard provision in both trust instruments and in contracts to specify the state law that applies in interpretation of the instrument. This will usually be the grantors' state of residency but also the state in which the lawyer is licensed to practice.

Notwithstanding the foregoing, our trustee shall have the power, exercisable in the trustee's sole and absolute discretion, to declare, by written instrument that the forum for this trust and all trusts established herein shall be another state in which event the laws of that state shall govern the interpretation and validity of the provisions of this instrument and all questions relating to the management, administration, investment, and distribution of the trusts hereby created.

COMMENT: In those situations in which the trust is drafted to provide asset protection for the grantors' children, it may be wise to include power for the trustee to change the situs of the trust to another state whose laws are more favorable to the protection of the trust assets should the trustee find that the laws of the home state are less favorable to asset protection.

23. <u>No-Contest.</u> If any beneficiary of this trust, or the guardian or legal representative of such beneficiary, contests the validity of this trust or of any of its provisions or shall institute or join in (except as a party defendant) any proceeding to contest the validity of this trust or to prevent any provision of it from being carried out in accordance with its terms (regardless of whether or not such proceedings are instituted in good faith and with probable cause), then all benefits provided for such beneficiary hereunder are revoked and such benefits shall pass as if such beneficiary and such beneficiary's descendants all had predeceased me.

COMMENT: This provision or some variation of it should be considered if there is any concern that a beneficiary or heir-at-law may challenge the trust. The lawyer may need to modify this provision to meet any requirements of state law.

24. Power to Amend or Revoke. **OPTION 1: Only by both spouses** We reserve the right from time to time by written instrument delivered to the trustee, while we are both living, to amend or revoke this instrument and the trusts hereby evidenced, in whole or in part. After one of us is deceased or becomes incompetent, the trust shall become irrevocable as to all property held under this instrument and the trusts established in this instrument. It is our expressed intent by this trust to enter into a contract to preclude the right of the survivor of us to dispose of any property held in this trust or that is payable to this trust either during the lifetime of the survivor of us, or at the death of the survivor of us except as is provided in this trust instrument.

OPTION 1a: Add to Option 1 if survivor is granted a limited power of appointment Notwithstanding the above restriction, the survivor of us shall have the right at death to direct any part or all of the trust property to or for the benefit of our descendants and public charities in such proportions and subject to such trusts, powers and conditions as the survivor of us may provide and appoint by will specifically referring to this power to appoint.

OPTION 2: Survivor can amend or revoke We reserve the right from time to time by written instrument delivered to the trustee, while we are both living and by the survivor of us after one of us dies, to amend or revoke this instrument and the trusts hereby evidenced, in whole or in part.

COMMENT: A decision needs to be made as to the extent to which the joint trust can be amended after the death, or possibly after the disability, of one of the two grantors. In many situations, the clients will want the survivor to have full rights to amend or revoke the document, in which case Option 2 should be used. In other situations, the couple will be concerned that the survivor may remarry and make imprudent decisions that will reduce the estate assets available for the ultimate estate beneficiaries. If this is the situation, Option 1 should be used, and the possibility of Option 1.a added granting a limited power of appointment should be considered.

The undersigned have signed this instrument and have established the foregoing trusts on this the _____ day of _____, [Current year].

GRANTORS AND TRUSTEES:

_____
[Grantor 1]

_____
[Grantor 2]

STATE OF [State of notary]   )

) SCT.

COUNTY OF [County of notary])

The undersigned, a Notary Public within and for the state and county aforesaid, does hereby certify that the foregoing trust agreement executed by [Grantor 1] and [Grantor 2], as grantors and trustees, was on this day produced to me in our county by [Grantor 1] and [Grantor 2], both of whom executed, acknowledged and swore the same before me to be their act and deed in due form of law.

Given under my hand and notarial seal on this the _____ day of _____, [Current year].

_____

Notary Public, State at Large

My commission expires:_____

PREPARED BY:

_____

[Name of Attorney]
[Name of Law Firm]
Attorneys at Law
[Street Address]
[City], [State] [Zip Code]
[Telephone Number]

SCHEDULE A

[NAME OF TRUST] TRUST

Cash. . . . . $ 10.00

The lawyer will note a deposit of $10 in the trust. State law will determine the necessity of an initial deposit. An unfunded trust that contains no principal may be deemed a "dry" trust under state law, meaning that it is not a valid document. Some lawyers go to the added step of affixing a $10 bill to schedule A, while others are satisfied with a cash deposit which does have the disadvantage of not being traceable. If there is the possibility of a contest of the trust, the cautious practice would be to affix a $10 bill to schedule A.

GENERAL DURABLE POWER OF ATTORNEY AND
HEALTH CARE POWER OF ATTORNEY WORKSHEET

Client's Name _____

Client's City and State _____

1.   Durable General Power of Attorney

	Name	**Address**
1.1 First choice for client		
1.2 Second choice for client		
1.3 First choice for spouse/partner		
1.4 Second choice for spouse/partner		

1.5 Are provisions needed to permit decisions being made concerning IRAs, 401Ks, and other retirement plans, including changing beneficiaries? (See 1.g)	Yes / No
1.6 Are provisions needed for gift giving? If so, is option 1, option 2, or a variation required? (See 1.j) _____	Yes / No
1.7 Are each of the other powers granted in paragraph 1 needed? If no, which ones are omitted?	Yes / No
1.8 Are provisions needed for a business? (See 1.m)	Yes / No
1.9 Is compensation to be paid? (See 2) If so, option 1 or option 2?	Yes / No
1.10 Is the power of attorney effective immediately? (Option 1) If no (Option 2), is incompetency determined under option 1, option 2 or a variation? (See 4 and 5)	Yes / No
1.11 If more than one person is to act as power of attorney or successor power of attorney, may the powers be exercised by either of the persons or must the powers be exercised jointly? (See 7) If single, modify paragraph.	Single / Joint

2.   Health Care Power of Attorney

	Name	**Address**
2.1 First choice for client		
2.2 Second choice for client		
2.3 First choice for spouse/partner		
2.4 Second choice for spouse/partner		

	Client	Spouse/ Partner
2.5 Is your life to be artificially prolonged by machine, such as a respirator? (See introductory paragraph and 2.a)	Yes / No	Yes / No
2.6 Are you to receive nutrition and hydration (including water) by tube? (See introductory paragraph and 2.a)	Yes / No	Yes / No
2.7 On your death, do you wish to donate your organs? (See 2.g)	Yes / No	Yes / No
2.8 On your death, do you wish to donate your body for science or medical research? (See 2.g)	Yes / No	Yes / No
2.9 Is the statement of desires in paragraph 3 satisfactory?	Yes / No	Yes / No
2.10 If there are joint decision makers, may they act individually or must they act jointly?	Single / Joint	Single / Joint

DURABLE GENERAL POWER OF ATTORNEY

The form that follows is a general power of attorney that includes multiple provisions that will need to be modified to meet the needs of the particular client and the requirements of state law.

I, [Name of client], currently a resident of [Client's city of residence], [Client's state of residence], do hereby make, constitute and appoint [Relation of POA if any], [Name of POA], currently a resident of [POA's city of residence], [POA's state of residence], my true and lawful attorney-in-fact for me and in my name, place, and stead, and on my behalf, and for my use and benefit:

COMMENT: The full name of the client, person acting as power of attorney, and their respective current city and state of residence should be included.

1. <u>Powers of Attorney-in-Fact.</u> This instrument is to be construed and interpreted as a general power of attorney. My attorney-in-fact shall have the following rights and powers; however, the enumeration of these rights and powers is not intended to, nor does it, limit or restrict, and is not to be construed or interpreted as limiting or restricting, the general powers of my attorney-in-fact.

COMMENT: Caution should be exercised to determine which powers are desired by the client. In many situations, all of the powers will be desired. However, there will be some situations in which the client desires to limit the power to sell real estate (1.a) or the type of investments that can be made by the person acting as power of attorney. In some situations, the client will prefer to eliminate the powers over commodity transactions (1.l), and many times there will be no business interest (1.m), thus that paragraph will not be needed.

In some situations, the client will want to grant powers of gift giving (1.j). If so, Option 1, which is an unlimited grant of gift-giving power but is limited to the other spouse and descendants, may be appropriate. In other situations, Option 2, which limits the power to gifts not to exceed the annual gift tax exclusion and the tuition and medical exclusion, will be desired. Care must be given to be certain of the potential recipients of the gifts, that is, meaning whether the power is limited just to the other spouse, or does it include all descendants; and if so should the descendants' spouses be included. In other situations, a variation of the two options will be required.

a. <u>Real estate transactions.</u> To buy, sell, exchange, rent and lease real estate; to collect all rent, sale proceeds and earnings from real estate; to convey, assign and accept title to real estate; to grant easements, create conditions and release rights of homestead with respect to real estate; to create land trusts and exercise all powers under land trusts; to hold, possess, maintain, repair, improve, subdivide, manage, operate and insure real estate; to pay, contest, protest and compromise real estate taxes and assessments; and, in general, to exercise all powers with respect to real estate which I could if present and under no disability.

b. <u>Financial institution transactions</u>. To open, close, continue and control all accounts and deposits in any type of financial institution (which term includes, without limitation, banks, trust companies, savings and building and loan associations, credit unions and brokerage firms); to deposit in and withdraw from and write checks on any financial institution account or deposit; and, in general, to exercise all powers with respect to financial institution transactions which I could if present and under no disability.

c. <u>Stock and bond transactions.</u> **To buy and sell** all types of securities (which term includes, without limitation, stocks, bonds, mutual funds and all other types of investment securities and financial instruments); to collect, hold and safekeep all dividends, interest, earnings, proceeds of sale, distributions, shares, certificates and other evidences of ownership paid or distributed with respect to securities; to exercise all voting rights with respect to securities in person or by proxy, enter into voting trusts and consent to limitations on the right to vote; and, in general, to exercise all powers with respect to securities which I could if present and under no disability.

d. <u>Tangible personal property transactions.</u> To buy and sell, lease, exchange, collect, possess and take title to all tangible personal property; to move, store, ship, restore, maintain, repair, improve, manage, preserve, insure and safekeep tangible personal property; and, in general, to exercise all powers with respect to tangible personal property which I could if present and under no disability.

e. <u>Safe deposit box transactions.</u> To open, continue and have access to all safe deposit boxes; sign, renew, release or terminate any safe deposit contract; to drill or surrender any safe deposit box; and, in general, to exercise all powers with respect to safe deposit matters which I could if present and under no disability.

f. <u>Insurance and annuity transactions.</u> To procure, acquire, continue, renew, terminate or otherwise deal with any type of insurance or annuity contract (which terms include, without limitation, life, accident, health, disability, automobile casualty, property or liability insurance); to pay premiums or assessments on or surrender and collect all distributions, proceeds or benefits payable under any insurance or annuity contract; and, in general, to exercise all powers with respect to insurance and annuity contracts which I could if present and under no disability.

g. <u>Retirement plan transactions.</u> To contribute to, withdraw from and deposit funds in any type of retirement plan (which term includes, without limitation, any tax qualified or nonqualified pension, profit sharing, stock bonus, 401(k) plan, employee savings and other retirement plan, individual retirement account, deferred compensation plan and any other type of employee benefit plan); to select and change payment options for me under any retirement plan; to make rollover contributions from any retirement plan to other retirement plans or individual retirement accounts; to exercise all investment powers available under any type of self-directed retirement plan; and, in general, to exercise all powers with respect to retirement plans and retirement plan account balances which I could if present and under no disability.

h. <u>Social Security, unemployment and military service benefits.</u> To prepare, sign and file any claim or application for Social Security, unemployment or military service benefits; to sue for, settle or abandon any claims to any benefit or assistance under any federal, state, local or foreign statute or regulation; to control, deposit to any account, collect, receipt for, and take title to and hold all benefits under any Social Security, unemployment, military service or other state, federal, local or foreign statute or regulation; and, in general, to exercise all powers with respect to Social Security, unemployment, military service and governmental benefits which I could if present and under no disability.

i. <u>Tax matters.</u> To sign, verify and file all my federal, state and local income, gift, estate, property and other tax returns, including joint returns and declarations of estimated tax; to pay all taxes; to claim, sue for and receive all tax refunds; to examine and copy all of my tax returns and records; to represent me before any federal, state or local revenue agency or taxing body and sign and deliver all tax powers of attorney on my behalf that may be necessary for such purposes; to waive rights and sign all documents on my behalf as required to settle, pay and determine all tax liabilities; and, in general, to exercise all powers with respect to tax matters which I could if present and under no disability.

j. **OPTION 1**: <u>Gift giving.</u> To give my [husband or wife], [insert spouse's name], and to any one or more of my lawful lineal descendants so much of my property, including (but not limited to) any cash, securities, life insurance policies, and real property in such amounts as my attorney-in-fact considers appropriate for their comfort and care. All such gifts may be made outright, in trust, or to any legal guardian or custodian under any applicable Uniform Transfers or Gifts to Minors Act, as my attorney-in-fact deems appropriate, even if my attorney-in-fact is such trustee, guardian, or custodian;

OPTION 2: To make annual exclusion gifts under Internal Revenue Code §2503(b) and to make tuition and medical exclusion gifts under Internal Revenue Code §2503(e) to any one or more of my lawful lineal descendants in such amounts as my attorney-in-fact considers appropriate. All such gifts may be made outright, in trust, or to any legal guardian or custodian under any applicable Uniform Transfers or Gifts to Minors Act, as my attorney-in-fact deems appropriate, even if my attorney-in-fact is such trustee, guardian, or custodian;

k. <u>Claims and litigation.</u> To institute, prosecute, defend, abandon, compromise, arbitrate, settle and dispose of any claim in favor of or against me or any property interests of mine; to collect and receipt for any claim or settlement proceeds and waive or release all rights of mine; to employ attorneys and others and enter into contingency agreements and other contracts as necessary in connection with litigation; and, in general, to exercise all powers with respect to claims and litigation which I could if present and under no disability.

l. <u>Commodity and option transactions.</u> To buy, sell, exchange, assign, convey, settle and exercise commodities futures contracts and call and put options on stocks and stock indices traded on a regulated options exchange and collect and receipt for all proceeds of any such transactions; to establish or continue option accounts for me with any securities or futures broker; and, in general, to exercise all powers with respect to commodities and options which I could if present and under no disability.

m. <u>Business operations.</u> To organize or continue and conduct any business (which term includes, without limitation, any farming, manufacturing, service, mining, retailing or other type of business operation) in any form, whether as a proprietorship, joint venture, partnership, corporation, limited liability company, trust or other legal entity; to operate, buy, sell, expand, contract, terminate or liquidate any business; to direct, control, supervise, manage or participate in the operation of any business and engage, compensate and discharge business managers, employees, agents, attorneys, accountants and consultants; and, in general, to exercise all powers with respect to business interests and operations which I could if present and under no disability.

n. <u>Borrowing transactions.</u> To borrow money; to mortgage or pledge any real estate or tangible or intangible personal property as security for such purposes; to sign, renew, extend, pay and satisfy any notes or other forms of obligation; and, in general, to exercise all powers with respect to secured and unsecured borrowing which I could if present and under no disability.

o. <u>Estate transactions.</u> To accept, receipt for, exercise, release, reject, renounce, assign, disclaim, demand, sue for, claim and recover any legacy, bequest, devise, gift or other property interest or payment due or payable to or for me; to assert any interest in and exercise any power over any trust, estate or property subject to fiduciary control; to establish a revocable trust solely for my benefit that terminates at my death and is then distributable to the personal representative of my estate; and, in general, to exercise all powers with respect to estates and trusts which I could if present and under no disability; provided, however, that my attorney-in-fact may not make or change a will and may not revoke or amend a trust revocable or amendable by me or require the trustee of any trust for my benefit to pay income or principal to my attorney-in-fact unless specific written authority to that end is given by me, and specific reference is made to the trust.

p. <u>HIPAA authorization.</u> To request any physician, health care professional, health care provider, and medical care facility to provide to my attorney-in-fact information relating to my physical and mental condition and the diagnosis, prognosis, care and treatment thereof upon the request of my attorney-in-fact. It is my intent by this authorization for my attorney-in-fact to be considered personal representatives under privacy regulations related to protected health information and for my attorney-in-fact to be entitled to all health information in the same manner as if I personally were making the request. This authorization and request shall also be considered a consent to the release of such information under current laws, rules, regulations as well as under future laws, rules, and regulations and amendments to such laws, rules, and regulations to include but not be limited to the express grant of authority to personal representatives as provided by Regulation Section 164.502(g) of Title 45 of the Code of Federal Regulations and the medical information privacy law and regulations generally referred to as HIPAA;

2. <u>Compensation.</u> **OPTION 1**: My attorney-in-fact shall be entitled to reasonable compensation for services rendered as attorney-in-fact under this power of attorney.

OPTION 2: My attorney-in-fact shall not be entitled to compensation for services rendered as attorney-in-fact under this power of attorney, but may be reimbursed for out-of-pocket expenses.

COMMENT: A decision should be made as to whether or not the person acting as power of attorney is to be paid compensation. Oftentimes, no compensation will be appropriate, as a family member will be acting in this capacity and will not want to be paid, but should be reimbursed for out of pocket expenses as provided in Option 2. Otherwise, if compensation is appropriate, then Option 1 will be used.

---

3. <u>Durability.</u> This instrument shall not be affected by my disability as it is my intent that the authority hereby conferred shall be exercisable notwithstanding my disability or incapacity.

COMMENT: The lawyer should refer to his or her own state law to be certain that the wording used to continue the power of attorney during disability is consistent with state law.

---

4. <u>Effective Date and Revocation.</u> **OPTION 1**: The rights, powers and authority of my attorney-in-fact granted in this instrument shall commence and be in full force and effect on this date, and such rights, powers, and authority shall remain in full force and effect until I give notice in writing that such power is terminated.

OPTION 2: The rights, powers and authority of my attorney-in-fact granted in this instrument shall commence and be in full force and effect upon my incompetency as determined below, and such rights, powers, and authority shall remain in full force and effect until I regain my competency and give notice in writing that such power is terminated.

COMMENT: Option 1 provides that the power of attorney is effective upon execution, whereas Option 2 provides that it is only effective upon incompetency. The advantage of Option 1 is that there is no necessity to establish incompetency before acting as power of attorney. The disadvantage is obvious, as one could act under the document even though the client had not expected the power to be exercised until disability. If Option 2 is desired, then paragraph 5 should be considered, as it defines incompetency.

---

5. <u>Incompetency.</u> **OPTION 1**: I shall be deemed to be incompetent when a physician whom I have consulted within the prior three years has certified as to such consultation and the physician's certification states that I am incapable of managing my affairs, regardless of cause and regardless of whether there is an adjudication of incompetency.

OPTION 2: I shall be deemed to be incompetent when a written certification is received from two (2) physicians, both of whom have personally examined me and at least one (1) of whom is board-certified in the specialty most closely associated with the health condition alleged to cause my incompetency. The certification must state that I am incapable of managing my affairs, regardless of cause and regardless of whether there is an adjudication of incompetence.

COMMENT: When the power of attorney only becomes effective upon incompetency (Option 2 in paragraph 4 above), then the client must determine how incompetency is to be determined. Many clients are comfortable with their then-treating physician or one with whom they have consulted during the prior three years making the decision. Others prefer the more restrictive approach of Option 2, with two physicians making the decision, one of whom is board-certified in the specialty most closely associated with the cause of incompetency.

6. <u>Successor.</u> In the event my aforenamed attorney-in-fact shall predecease me, be disabled or otherwise fail to serve, I appoint [Relation of Successor POA], [Name of Successor POA], to serve as my successor attorney-in-fact to have all powers and authority as are granted herein.

COMMENT: The full name and relationship of the successor should be inserted in this paragraph.

7. <u>Joint Successor Attorneys-in-Fact.</u> My successor attorneys-in-fact may exercise all powers conferred upon them herein by their individual or joint signatures. Any party may rely upon the individual signature of any one of my successor attorneys-in-fact and need not require both signatures.

COMMENT: In some situations, two individuals are named as successor co-powers of attorney. If this is done, then a decision must be made as to whether those two individuals may act independently of each other, or if all action requires a joint decision. This paragraph permits a decision to be made by either of the two individuals. Obviously, when only one individual is named, this paragraph should be deleted. If the client names two individuals as the initial attorneys-in-fact, then paragraph 7 can be modified, removing reference to the "successor" and redrafting the paragraph to apply to that situation.

IN TESTIMONY WHEREOF, I have signed this document on this the _____ day of _____ _____, [Current year].

_____
[Name of client]

STATE OF KENTUCKY)

) SCT.

COUNTY OF HOPKINS)

The undersigned, a Notary Public within and for the State and County aforesaid, does hereby certify that the foregoing Power of Attorney was this day executed by [Name of client], who executed and acknowledged the same before me to be [his or her] act and deed in due form of law.

Given under my hand and notarial seal on this the _____ day of _____, [Current year].

_____
Notary Public, State at Large

My commission expires: _____

PREPARED BY:

_____
[Name of Attorney]
[Name of Law Firm]
Attorneys at Law
[Street Address]
[City], [State] [Zip Code]
[Telephone Number]

HEALTH CARE POWER OF ATTORNEY

This health care power of attorney is intended to be a broad form that can be used in any state. Obviously, it must be modified to meet the requirements of state law should it be restrictive and not permit the broad grant of power that is contained in this instrument. For an excellent ABA resource on advanced directives, the reader is referred to Carol Krohm and Scott Summers, *Advance Health Care Directives*, American Bar Association (Chicago: 2002).

I, [Name of Client], currently a resident of [Client's city of residence], [Client's state of residence], hereby appoint [Relation of HCPOA], [Name of HCPOA], currently a resident of [HCPOA's city of residence], [HCPOA's state of residence], as my health care power of attorney, to act for me and in my name (in any way I could act in person) to make any and all decisions for me concerning my personal care, medical treatment, hospitalization, health care, the use of life-sustaining treatment, and to require, withhold or withdraw any type of medical treatment or procedure, even though my death may ensue, all as authorized more specifically in this document. The definition of a life-sustaining treatment is any medical procedure, treatment or intervention that utilizes mechanical or other artificial means to sustain, restore, or supplant a spontaneous vital function and is of such a nature as to afford me no reasonable expectation of recovery from a terminal condition, persistent vegetative state, or end-stage condition.

COMMENT: The introductory paragraph simply requires the full names of the client and the health care decision maker, as well as their respective current city and state of residence. Care should be taken to be sure that the grant of power and the definition of life-sustaining treatment is satisfactory with the client.

1. <u>Effective Date and Durability.</u> By this document I intend to create a durable power of attorney which is valid under [insert state] law pursuant to [insert state statute if applicable] (or any subsequent statute) and which is effective upon, and only during any period of incapacity in which, in the opinion of my health care power of attorney with the advice of my attending physician, I am unable to make or communicate a choice regarding a particular health care decision.

COMMENT: The client's state of residence for which the health care power of attorney is to apply should be inserted, as should any applicable state statute or administrative regulation.

2. <u>Powers of Health Care Power of Attorney.</u> I grant to my health care power of attorney full authority to make decisions for me regarding my health care after consultation with my attending physician. In exercising this authority, my health care power of attorney shall follow my desires as stated in this document or otherwise known to my health care power of attorney. In making any decision, my health care power of attorney shall attempt to discuss the proposed decision with me to determine my desires if I am able to communicate in any way. If my health care power of attorney cannot determine the choice I would want made, then my health care power of attorney shall make a choice for me based upon what my health care power of attorney believes to be in my best interest. My health care power of attorney's authority to interpret my desires is intended to be as broad as possible. Accordingly, my health care power of attorney is authorized as follows:

COMMENT: The following listing of powers granted to the health care power of attorney are broad and should cover most all situations. The lawyer will want to be certain that the grant of powers is consistent with the client's wishes.

a. To consent, refuse, or withdraw consent to any and all types of medical care, treatment, surgical procedures, diagnostic procedures, medication, and the use of mechanical or other procedures that affect any bodily function, including (but not limited to) artificial respiration, cardiopulmonary resuscitation, and nutritional support and hydration, including the use of a nasogastric tube or tube into the stomach, intestines, or veins;

b. To have access to medical records and information to the same extent that I am entitled to, including the right to disclose the contents to others;

c. To authorize my admission to or discharge (even against medical advice) from any hospital, nursing home, residential care, assisted living or similar facility or service;

d. To contract on my behalf for any health care related service or facility on my behalf, without my health care power of attorney incurring personal financial liability for such contracts;

e. To hire and fire medical, social service, and other support personnel responsible for my care;

f. To authorize, or refuse to authorize, any medication or procedure intended to relieve pain, even though such use may lead to physical damage, addiction, or hasten the moment of (but not intentionally cause) my death;

g. To make anatomical gifts of part or all of my body for medical purposes, authorize an autopsy, and direct the disposition of my remains including, donating my body for science or medical research, to the extent permitted by law;

h. To take any other action necessary to do what I authorize here, including (but not limited to) granting any waiver or release from liability required by any hospital, physician, or other health care provider; signing any documents relating to refusals of treatment or the leaving of a facility against medical advice, and pursuing any legal action in my name, and at the expense of my estate to force compliance with my wishes as determined by my health care power of attorney, or to seek actual or punitive damages for the failure to comply.

3. <u>Statement of Desires.</u> Although I greatly value life, I also believe that at some point life has such diminished value that my medical treatment should be stopped, and I should be allowed to die. Therefore, I do not want my life to be prolonged and I do not want life-sustaining treatment:

a. If I have a condition that is incurable or irreversible and, without the administration of life-sustaining treatment my attending physician believes, in accordance with reasonable medical standards, my death is expected to result within a relatively short period of time; or

b. If I am in a coma or persistent vegetative state which my attending physician believes, in accordance with reasonable medical standards, to be irreversible.

COMMENT: The statement of desires should be reviewed with the client to be certain that these statements are consistent with the client's own desires. Obviously, the lawyer can modify these statements as is necessary.

4. <u>Successor.</u> If my health care power of attorney dies, becomes legally disabled, resigns, or refuses to act, I name [Relation of Successor HCPOA], [Name of Successor HCPOA], to act as successor to my health care power of attorney.

COMMENT: The full name and relationship, if any, of the successor health care power of attorney should be inserted.

---

5. <u>Joint Successor Health Care Powers of Attorney.</u> My successor health care power of attorneys may exercise all powers conferred upon them herein by their individual or joint signatures. Any party may rely upon the individual signature of any one of my successor health care powers of attorney and need not require both signatures.

COMMENT: This paragraph is needed only if there are joint successor health care powers of attorney, or it can be modified if the client names two individuals as the initial health care decision makers. In either event, the document should address whether that decision-making power requires agreement by the two named individuals, or if either one of them may make the decision. This form permits either person to make these decisions. If the decision is to be made jointly, then some minor modification to paragraph 5 may be required.

---

6. <u>Protection of Third Parties Who Rely on My Health Care Power of Attorney.</u> No person or institution who relies in good faith upon any representations by my health care power of attorney or successor health care power of attorney shall be liable to me, my estate, my heirs or assigns, for recognizing the health care power of attorney's authority. Further, I hereby adopt and ratify all of the acts of my health care power of attorney done in pursuance of the powers herein granted, as fully as if I were acting in my own proper person.

7. <u>HIPAA Authorization.</u> Effective immediately and continuously until my death or revocation by a writing signed by me or someone authorized to make health care treatment decisions for me, I authorize all health care providers or other covered entities to disclose to my health care power of attorney, including any successor health care power of attorney, upon my health care power of attorney's request, any information, oral or written, regarding my physical or mental health, including, but not limited to, medical and hospital records, including what is otherwise private, privileged, protected or personal health information, including but not limited to, health information as defined and described in the Health Insurance Portability and Accountability Act of 1996 (Public Law 104-191, 110 Stat. 2024), the regulations promulgated thereunder and any other state or local laws and rules. Information disclosed by a health care provider or other covered entity may be redisclosed and may no longer be subject to the privacy rules provided by 45 CFR § 164.

8. <u>Nomination of Guardian.</u> If a guardian of my person should for any reason need to be appointed, I nominate my health care power of attorneys in the order named above to serve as my guardian without the necessity of posting a surety bond.

9. <u>Administrative Provisions.</u> With respect to this health care power of attorney, I provide as follows:

a. I revoke any prior living will, health care surrogate or power of attorney for health care.

b. This health care power of attorney is intended to be valid in any jurisdiction in which it is presented.

    c. My health care power of attorney shall not be entitled to compensation for services performed under this health care power of attorney, but such person shall be entitled to reimbursement for all reasonable expenses incurred as a result of carrying out any provision of this health care power of attorney.

    d. The powers delegated under this health care power of attorney are separable, so that the invalidity of one or more powers shall not affect any others.

BY SIGNING HERE I INDICATE THAT I UNDERSTAND THE CONTENTS OF THIS DOCUMENT AND THE EFFECT OF THIS GRANT OF POWERS TO MY HEALTH CARE POWER OF ATTORNEY.

    IN TESTIMONY WHEREOF, I have signed my name on this the _____ day of _____ _____, [Current year].

                                                      _____
                                                      [Name of Client]

COMMONWEALTH OF [State of Notary]

COUNTY OF [County of Notary]

    Before me, the undersigned authority, came [Name of Client] who is of sound mind and 18 years of age, or older, and acknowledged that [he or she] voluntarily dated and signed this writing or directed it to be signed and dated as above.

    WITNESS my hand this _____ day of _____, [Current year].

                                                         _____

                                                      Notary Public, State at Large

                                                      My commission expires _____

PREPARED BY:

_____
[Name of Attorney]
[Name of Law Firm]
Attorneys at Law
[Street Address]
[City], [State] [Zip Code]
[Telephone Number]

PRE-MARITAL AGREEMENT WORKSHEET

1. Name of Wife _____

2. Name of Husband_____

3. Which Spouse do You Represent (Client)? _____

4. Other Spouse Represented by Separate Counsel? (Option 1) <u>Yes / No</u>

    Other Spouse Elects Not to be Represented? (Option 2) <u>Yes / No</u>

5. Wife's Asset/Liability Information to be Included in Schedule A:

A. Cash Equivalents
Checking accounts and/or any other bank accounts or certificates of deposit?

	Name of Institution, Address, Account Number	Approx. Balance
Checking Accounts	1.	
	2.	
	3.	
	4.	
Certificates of Deposit, Savings Accounts	1.	
	2.	
	3.	
	4.	
	TOTAL:	$

B. Stocks

Number of Shares	Company	Current Market Value
	TOTAL:	$

C. Bonds

Maturity Value	Description	Current Market Value
	TOTAL:	$

D. Mutual Funds

Number of Units	Company	Current Market Value
	TOTAL:	$

E. Real Estate (please bring deeds)

Do you own a home or any other real estate? Indicate which is your residence.

Description and Location	Current Market Value	Mortgage Amount
TOTAL:	$	$

F. Business

Do you own an interest in any business?

Description of Business	Percentage of Ownership	Name of Co-owners	Market Value
		TOTAL:	$

Is there an existing buy-sell agreement? <u>Yes / No</u>

G. Retirement Benefits

Do you have any IRAs, 401Ks, or other retirement benefits?

Description	Beneficiary	Approximate Value
	TOTAL:	$

H. Life Insurance

Do you have any life insurance policies and/or annuities?

Insurance Company	First Beneficiary	Second Beneficiary	Death Benefit

I. Other - Trusts, Anticipated Inheritance, Etc.

_____

_____

_____

J. Personal Property

Do you own any other titled property such as a car, boat, etc?

Description	Approximate Value	Amount of Lien
TOTAL:	$	$

Do you own any other personal property that is not titled?

Description	Approximate Value
Home Furnishings	
Jewelry	
Collections	
Other	
Other	
TOTAL:	$

K. Liabilities

Description	Lender/Debtor	Approximate Value
Home mortgage		
Other mortgages		
Other debts		

L. Continuation of Assets

Type of Asset	Description of Asset	Current Market Value

M. Income Tax Return

Please provide a copy of your most recent personal income tax return to be included in Schedule B.

6.   Husband's Asset/Liability Information to be Included in Schedule C:

A. Cash Equivalents

Checking accounts and/or any other bank accounts or certificates of deposit?

	Name of Institution, Address, Account Number	Approx. Balance
Checking Accounts	1.	
	2.	
	3.	
	4.	
Certificates of Deposit, Savings Accounts	1.	
	2.	
	3.	
	4.	
	TOTAL:	$

B. Stocks

Number of Shares	Company	Current Market Value
	TOTAL:	$

C. Bonds

Maturity Value	Description	Current Market Value
	TOTAL:	$

D. Mutual Funds

Number of Units	Company	Current Market Value
	TOTAL:	$

E. Real Estate (please bring deeds)

Do you own a home or any other real estate? Indicate which is your residence.

Description and Location	Current Market Value	Mortgage Amount
TOTAL:	$	$

F. Business

Do you own an interest in any business?

Description of Business	Percentage of Ownership	Name of Co-owners	Market Value
		TOTAL:	$

Is there an existing buy-sell agreement? Yes / No

G. Retirement Benefits

Do you have any IRAs, 401Ks, or other retirement benefits?

Description	Beneficiary	Approximate Value
	TOTAL:	$

H. Life Insurance

Do you have any life insurance policies and/or annuities?

Insurance Company	First Beneficiary	Second Beneficiary	Death Benefit

I. Other - Trusts, Anticipated Inheritance, Etc.

_____

_____

_____

J. Personal Property

Do you own any other titled property such as a car, boat, etc.?

Description	Approximate Value	Amount of Lien
TOTAL:	$	$

Do you own any other personal property that is not titled?

Description	Approximate Value
Home Furnishings	
Jewelry	
Collections	
Other	
Other	
TOTAL:	$

K. Liabilities

Description	Lender/Debtor	Approximate Value
Home mortgage		
Other mortgages		
Other debts		

L. Continuation of Assets

Type of Asset	Description of Asset	Current Market Value

M. Income Tax Return

Please provide a copy of your most recent personal income tax return to be included in Schedule D.

PRE-MARITAL AGREEMENT

Pre-marital agreements are often the source of much litigation. The lawyer drafting such an agreement must be aware of the requirements of state law and should modify this document accordingly. The essence of most pre-marital agreements is that there must be full disclosure of all assets in order for there to be a clear waiver, and the party with the lesser sized estate must not be unduly influenced or manipulated into executing the document. Separate independent legal representation is highly desirable, although oftentimes only one of the spouses chooses to be represented. The lawyer must be careful to clarify that he or she only represents one of the parties and for there to be clear disclosure of such fact in the document. The document that follows includes provisions as to waivers in the event of the death of the first spouse and provisions in the event of divorce. In some states, provisions in regard to divorce (rather than death) will not be enforceable as they are deemed to be contrary to public policy. In other states, even though the divorce provisions may be allowed, there will be greater judicial scrutiny over such provisions than those that apply in the event of death. The form offered should be edited for use in the lawyer's own state.

This Pre-marital Agreement is entered into by [wife's name], herein referred to as the wife, and [husband's name], herein referred to as the husband.

WITNESSETH:

WHEREAS, the wife and the husband plan to marry and have entered into an oral agreement as to how the property which each of them currently own should be disposed of in the event of either the death of a spouse or divorce, and

WHEREAS, the wife and the husband now desire to enter into a written agreement to set forth how all property they now own and will own in the future are to be owned and the extent to which their property is subject to rights of the other spouse in the event of either the death of a spouse or divorce, and

WHEREAS, the wife and the husband each understand that pursuant to this agreement they are each foregoing legal rights they have in the event of either the death of a spouse or divorce;

NOW THEREFORE, in consideration of the mutual promises of the wife and the husband which are made by each of them in consideration of their marriage, in consideration of the recitals set forth above, and in consideration of the covenants and conditions contained hereinbelow, all of which the wife and the husband acknowledge have a good and valuable consideration, it is mutually agreed as follows:

1. Wife's Property. The wife shall keep and retain sole ownership and control of all property which is currently titled in her sole name or is titled in her sole name in the future and shall have the right to dispose of such property either during her lifetime or at her death either by her last will and testament or by intestate succession without interference by the husband, his heirs, personal representative, and assigns, as if she had remained unmarried. In an effort to provide full disclosure by the wife, schedule A is attached which sets forth the property which is now titled in the name of the wife and schedule B provides the wife's most recent income tax return.

2. Husband's Property. The husband shall keep and retain sole ownership and control of all property which is currently titled in his sole name or is titled in his sole name in the future and shall have the right to dispose of such property either during his lifetime or at his death either by his last will and testament or by intestate succession without interference by the wife, her heirs, personal representative and assigns, as if he had remained unmarried. In an effort to provide full disclosure by the husband, schedule C is attached which sets forth the property which is now

titled in the name of the husband and schedule D provides the husband's most recent income tax return.

3. Gifts and Inheritances. In the event either or both the wife and the husband should inherit property or be given property from any source whatsoever then such property shall be treated as the sole property of the party who inherited or was given such property and shall be disposed of by the party who inherited or was given such property without interference or claim from the other party in the same manner as set forth above in paragraphs 1 and 2.

4. Jointly Owned Property. The wife and the husband agree that in the event of the death of the first of them to die, any property they acquire during their marriage that is titled in joint owner-ship with right of survivorship shall be the sole property of the survivor of them. In the event property is titled jointly without right of survivorship, or as a tenancy in common, then such property shall be deemed to be owned one-half ($^1/_2$) by the wife and one-half ($^1/_2$) by the husband unless the document of title provides for a different ownership percentage in which event such document of title shall resolve the question of the percentage of ownership owned by each of the parties. Each party shall retain sole ownership and control of his or her fractional property interest and shall have the right to dispose of such property without interference or claim from the other party as is provided above in paragraphs 1 and 2.

5. Community Property. No property owned by the wife and the husband shall be deemed to be community property and no property shall be subject to division in the event of death or divorce based upon laws related to community property. All property owned by the wife and the husband shall be deemed to be their separate property or co-owned property in accordance with the provi-sions set forth above.

6. Annuities and Retirement Benefits. In the event either the wife or the husband own annui-ties, retirement benefits, or retirement plan assets that are deemed to be qualified retirement plan assets under any section of the Internal Revenue Code, the wife and the husband do hereby release and waive any and all rights granted to them under state or federal law, thus permitting the spouse who owns the annuity, retirement benefit or qualified retirement plan to name the beneficiary of such annuity, retirement benefit or qualified retirement plan without claim from the other spouse. Each spouse agrees to sign all other documents that may be required to carry out this agreement.

7. Mutual Waiver in Event of Death. The wife and the husband each hereby expressly waive and release the right to take against any last will and testament of the other spouse or to claim a statutory, dower or courtesy interest in the property of the spouse who is first to die pursuant to the provisions of any statute or rule of law granting dower, courtesy, marital portion, homestead, or other rights, of, in, and to the estate of the other, and further agree that in no event and in no circumstances shall either the wife or the husband have any right of election to take against the estate of the other party.

8. Mutual Waiver of Support. The wife and the husband each acknowledge that they have suf-ficient financial resources, education, and ability to be self supporting and waive any right of support from the other spouse due to either the death of a spouse or divorce.

9. Mutual Waiver in Event of Divorce. The wife and the husband agree that in the event of divorce they each shall receive the property titled in their sole name, any property titled jointly with right of survivorship, or as a tenancy in common, shall be divided one-half ($^1/_2$) to each of them, and any property titled jointly without right of survivorship shall be divided between the parties based upon their respective percentage ownership in such asset as reflected in the docu-ment of title; and the parties hereby waive any right they may have to a different division of

property as is otherwise granted in the event of divorce under the laws of [state]. Further, each party waives the right to receive alimony or maintenance from the other.

10. <u>Waiver as to Future Growth and Later Acquired Property.</u> Whether due to death or divorce, the wife and the husband agree and hereby waive all rights they each have as to the property owned by the other spouse, including not only the current value of such property, but all future income earned from such property and all future gains, losses, and appreciation in value in such property. In addition the wife and the husband waive all rights they each have as to all property acquired in the future by the other spouse, including the income earned from such property and all future gains, losses, and appreciation in value of such property, except as modified in paragraph 4.

11. <u>Good Faith Disclosure.</u> Each party recognizes that the descriptions of the property owned by each of the parties as reflected in schedules A and C are intended only as a general description and that the values inserted in these schedules are intended only as good faith estimates of value. The wife and the husband each covenant to the other that the attached schedules are a good faith effort to provide full disclosure to the other party of all property they currently own and the value of that property. Each party has agreed to provide the other party with any additional information they request as to such property and their respective incomes, as each party intends to provide as full a disclosure to the other as is possible. The wife and the husband each agree that no further information or disclosure is needed.

12. <u>Legal Representation.</u> **OPTION 1:** Each party has been represented by separate independent legal counsel and each party has been fully advised of their respective rights and do hereby waive all rights other than those provided for in this agreement. **OPTION 2:** The [insert spouse represented] is represented by [his or her] counsel, [insert attorney name]. The [insert spouse not represented] is not represented by separate counsel, but has been fully advised of [his or her] right to be represented by separate legal counsel. Also, the [insert spouse not represented] has been advised and understands that the [insert spouse represented]'s counsel, [insert attorney name], does not represent [him or her]; and [he or she] has declined to have legal representation.

COMMENT: The agreement should clearly disclose if each party is represented by separate legal counsel, in which event Option 1 should be used, or if only one of the parties is represented by legal counsel, then the lawyer should undertake to only represent one of the parties and use Option 2, or a variation of it.

---

13. <u>Binding Effect.</u> All the terms, covenants, and conditions of this agreement shall be binding upon the parties hereto and their respective estates, personal representatives, heirs and assigns.

14. <u>Governing Law.</u> This agreement shall be regulated and construed under the laws of the [state or commonwealth] of [name of state].

    IN TESTIMONY WHEREOF, the parties have hereunto set their hands on this the _____ day of _____, [current year].

_____
Wife

_____
Husband

STATE OF [State of Notary]   )

) SCT.

COUNTY OF [County of Notary])

    Subscribed, sworn to, and acknowledged before me by [wife's name], this the _____ day of _____, [current year].

                                               _____

                                               Notary Public, State at Large

                                               My Commission Expires:_____

STATE OF [State of Notary]   )

) SCT.

COUNTY OF [County of Notary])

    Subscribed, sworn to, and acknowledged before me by [husband's name], this the _____ day of _____, [current year].

                                                 _____

                                               Notary Public, State at Large

                                               My Commission Expires:_____

SCHEDULE A

WIFE'S PROPERTY

SCHEDULE B

WIFE'S MOST RECENTLY AVAILABLE INCOME TAX RETURN

SCHEDULE C

HUSBAND'S PROPERTY

SCHEDULE D

HUSBAND'S MOST RECENTLY AVAILABLE INCOME TAX RETURN

POST-MARITAL AGREEMENT WORKSHEET

1.   Name of Wife _____

2.   Name of Husband_____

3.   Which Spouse do You Represent (Client)? _____

4.   Other Spouse Represented by Separate Counsel? (Option 1) Yes / No

      Other Spouse Elects Not to be Represented? (Option 2) Yes / No

5.   Wife's Asset/Liability Information to be Included in Schedule A:

A. Cash Equivalents

Checking accounts and/or any other bank accounts or certificates of deposit?

	Name of Institution, Address, Account Number	Approx. Balance
Checking Accounts	1.	
	2.	
	3.	
	4.	
Certificates of Deposit, Savings Accounts	1.	
	2.	
	3.	
	4.	
		$

B. Stocks

Number of Shares	Company	Current Market Value
	TOTAL:	$

C. Bonds

Maturity Value	Description	Current Market Value
	TOTAL:	$

D. Mutual Funds

Number of Units	Company	Current Market Value
	TOTAL:	$

E. Real Estate (please bring deeds)

Do you own a home or any other real estate? Indicate which is your residence.

Description and Location	Current Market Value	Mortgage Amount
TOTAL:	$	$

F. Business

Do you own an interest in any business?

Description of Business	Percentage of Ownership	Name of Co-owners	Market Value
		TOTAL:	$

Is there an existing buy-sell agreement? <u>Yes / No</u>

G. Retirement Benefits

Do you have any IRAs, 401Ks, or other retirement benefits?

Description	Beneficiary	Approximate Value
	TOTAL:	$

H. Life Insurance

Do you have any life insurance policies and/or annuities?

Insurance Company	First Beneficiary	Second Beneficiary	Death Benefit

I. Other - Trusts, Anticipated Inheritance, Etc.

_____

_____

_____

J. Personal Property

Do you own any other titled property such as a car, boat, etc.?

Description	Approximate Value	Amount of Lien
TOTAL:	$	$

Do you own any other personal property that is not titled?

Description	Approximate Value
Home Furnishings	
Jewelry	
Collections	
Other	
Other	
TOTAL:	$

K. Liabilities

Description	Lender/Debtor	Approximate Value
Home mortgage		
Other mortgages		
Other debts		

L. Continuation of Assets

Type of Asset	Description of Asset	Current Market Value

6.   Husband's Asset/Liability Information to be Included in Schedule B:

A. Cash Equivalents

Checking accounts and/or any other bank accounts or certificates of deposit?

	Name of Institution, Address, Account Number	Approx. Balance
Checking Accounts	1.	
	2.	
	3.	
	4.	
Certificates of Deposit, Savings Accounts	1.	
	2.	
	3.	
	4.	
	TOTAL:	$

B. Stocks

Number of Shares	Company	Current Market Value
	TOTAL:	$

C. Bonds

Maturity Value	Description	Current Market Value
	TOTAL:	$

D. Mutual Funds

Number of Units	Company	Current Market Value
	TOTAL:	$

E. Real Estate (please bring deeds)

Do you own a home or any other real estate? Indicate which is your residence.

Description and Location	Current Market Value	Mortgage Amount
TOTAL:	$	$

F. Business

Do you own an interest in any business?

Description of Business	Percentage of Ownership	Name of Co-owners	Market Value
		TOTAL:	$

Is there an existing buy-sell agreement? Yes / No

G. Retirement Benefits

Do you have any IRAs, 401Ks, or other retirement benefits?

Description	Beneficiary	Approximate Value
	TOTAL:	$

H. Life Insurance

Do you have any life insurance policies and/or annuities?

Insurance Company	First Beneficiary	Second Beneficiary	Death Benefit

I. Other - Trusts, Anticipated Inheritance, Etc.

_____

_____

_____

J. Personal Property

Do you own any other titled property such as a car, boat, etc.?

Description	Approximate Value	Amount of Lien
TOTAL:	$	$

Do you own any other personal property that is not titled?

Description	Approximate Value
Home Furnishings	
Jewelry	
Collections	
Other	
Other	
TOTAL:	$

K. Liabilities

Description	Lender/Debtor	Approximate Value
Home mortgage		
Other mortgages		
Other debts		

L. Continuation of Assets

Type of Asset	Description of Asset	Current Market Value

7. Jointly Owned Property

Description of Property	How Titled?	Approximate Value

POST-MARITAL AGREEMENT

Prior to using this post-nuptial agreement, the lawyer needs to be certain his or her state law permits such an agreement. State law may permit such an agreement in the event of death, but not in the event of divorce. In other states, the agreement may be enforceable in both events, but the criteria for enforceability in the event of divorce may be different than in the event of death. The lawyer will need to make appropriate changes when using this form to comply with requirements of state law. As drafted it is more restrictive than many clients will want. It is only intended to be a template to assist in preparation of a post-nuptial agreement. With these caveats in mind, a post-nuptial agreement can be particularly effective when trying to draft estate planning documents through the minefield of problems presented by clients with children from prior marriages. In larger estates, consideration must also be given as to what impact, if any, such agreement may have on estate taxes on each spouse's estate and the availability of the federal estate tax marital deduction.

This Post-marital Agreement is entered into by [wife's name], herein referred to as the wife, and [husband's name], herein referred to as the husband.

WITNESSETH:

WHEREAS, the wife and the husband are married and did not enter into a pre-marital agreement, but have now entered into an oral agreement as to how the property which each of them currently own should be disposed of in the event of either the death of a spouse or divorce, and

WHEREAS, the wife and the husband now desire to enter into a written agreement to set forth how all property they now own and will own in the future are to be owned and the extent to which their property is subject to rights of the other spouse in the event of either the death of a spouse or divorce, and

WHEREAS, the wife and the husband each understand that pursuant to this agreement they are each forgoing legal rights they have in the event of either the death of a spouse or divorce;

NOW THEREFORE, in consideration of the recitals set forth above, and in consideration of the covenants and conditions contained herein below, all of which the wife and the husband acknowledge have a good and valuable consideration, it is mutually agreed as follows:

1. Wife's Property. The wife shall keep and retain sole ownership and control of all property which is currently titled in her sole name or is titled in her sole name in the future and shall have the right to dispose of such property either during her lifetime or at her death either by her last will and testament or by intestate succession without interference by the husband, his heirs, personal representative, and assigns. In an effort to provide full disclosure by the wife, schedule A is attached which sets forth the property which is now titled in the name of the wife.

2. Husband's Property. The husband shall keep and retain sole ownership and control of all property which is currently titled in his sole name or is titled in his sole name in the future and shall have the right to dispose of such property either during his lifetime or at his death either by his last will and testament or by intestate succession without interference by the wife, her heirs, personal representative and assigns. In an effort to provide full disclosure by the husband, schedule B is attached which sets forth the property which is now titled in the name of the husband.

3. Gifts and Inheritances. In the event either or both the wife and the husband should inherit property or be given property from any source whatsoever then such property shall be treated as the sole property of the party who inherited or was given such property and shall be disposed of by the party who inherited or was given such property without interference or claim from the other party in the same manner as set forth above in paragraphs 1 and 2.

4. <u>Jointly Owned Property.</u> The wife and the husband agree that in the event of the death of the first of them to die, any property they own that is titled in joint ownership with right of survivorship shall be deemed to be the sole property of the survivor of them. In the event such property is titled jointly without right of survivorship, or as a tenancy in common, then such property shall be deemed to be owned one-half ($^1/_2$) by the wife and one-half ($^1/_2$) by the husband unless the document of title provides for a different ownership percentage in which event such document of title shall resolve the question of the percentage of ownership owned by each of the parties. Each party shall retain sole ownership and control of his or her fractional property interest and shall have the right to dispose of such property without interference or claim from the other party as is provided above in paragraphs 1 and 2.

5. <u>Community Property.</u> No property owned by the wife and the husband shall be deemed to be community property and no property shall be subject to division in the event of death or divorce based upon laws related to community property. All property owned by the wife and the husband shall be deemed to be their separate property or co-owned property in accordance with the provisions set forth above.

6. <u>Annuities and Retirement Benefits.</u> In the event either the wife or the husband own annuities, retirement benefits, or retirement plan assets that are deemed to be qualified retirement plan assets under any section of the Internal Revenue Code, the wife and the husband do hereby release and waive any and all rights granted to them under state or federal law, thus permitting the spouse who owns the annuity, retirement benefits, or qualified retirement plan to name the beneficiary of such qualified retirement plan without claim from the other spouse. Each spouse agrees to sign all other documents that may be required to carry out this agreement.

7. <u>Mutual Waiver in Event of Death.</u> The wife and the husband each hereby expressly waive and release the right to take against any last will and testament of the other spouse or to claim a statutory, dower or courtesy interest in the property of the spouse who is first to die pursuant to the provisions of any statute or rule of law granting dower, courtesy, marital portion, homestead, or other rights, of, in, and to the estate of the other, and further agree that in no event and in no circumstances shall either the wife or the husband have any right of election to take against the estate of the other party.

8. <u>Mutual Waiver of Support.</u> The wife and the husband each acknowledge that they have sufficient financial resources, education, and ability to be self supporting and waive any right of support from the other spouse due to either the death of a spouse or divorce.

9. <u>Mutual Waiver in Event of Divorce.</u> The wife and the husband agree that in the event of divorce they each shall receive the property titled in their sole name, any property titled jointly with right of survivorship shall be divided one-half ($^1/_2$) to each of them, and any property titled jointly without right of survivorship, or as a tenancy in common, shall be divided between the parties based upon their respective percentage ownership in such asset as reflected in the document of title; and the parties hereby waive any right they may have to a different division of property as is otherwise granted in the event of divorce under the laws of [state]. Further, each party waives the right to receive alimony or maintenance from the other.

10. <u>Waiver as to Future Growth and Later Acquired Property.</u> Whether due to death or divorce, the wife and the husband agree and hereby waive all rights they each have as to the property owned by the other spouse, including not only the current value of such assets, but all future income earned from such property, and all future gains, losses, and appreciation in value in such property. In addition the wife and the husband waive all rights they each have as to all property acquired in the future by the other spouse, including the income earned from such property and

all the future gains, losses, and appreciation in value of such property, except as modified in paragraph 4.

11. <u>Good Faith Disclosure.</u> Each party recognizes that the descriptions of the property owned by each of the parties as reflected in schedules A and B are intended only as a general description and that the values inserted in these schedules are intended only as good faith estimates of value. The wife and the husband each covenant to the other that the attached schedules are a good faith effort to provide full disclosure to the other party of all property they currently own and the value of that property. Each party has agreed to provide the other party with any additional information they request as to such property, as each party intends to provide as full a disclosure to the other as is possible. The wife and the husband each agree that no further information or disclosure is needed.

12. <u>Legal Representation.</u> **OPTION 1:** Each party has been represented by separate indepen-dent legal counsel and each party has been fully advised of their respective rights and do hereby waive all rights other than those provided for in this agreement. **OPTION 2:** The parties have been explained their right to separate legal representation and the conflict of interest in [insert attorney name] representing both of them. The [insert spouse not represented] recognizes that [insert attorney name] represents the [insert spouse represented] in the preparation of this Agree-ment and that [he or she, spouse not represented] is not represented by [insert attorney name]. The [insert spouse not represented] has been fully advised of [his or her, spouse not represented] right to seek an attorney, has had ample opportunity to seek the advice of another attorney, and does hereby waive such right.

COMMENT: The agreement should clearly disclose if each party is represented by separate legal counsel, in which event Option 1 should be used, or if only one of the parties is represented by legal counsel, then the lawyer should undertake to only represent one of the parties and use Option 2, or a variation of it. The ethical dilemma is more difficult in a post-marital agreement as the clients often consider the lawyer to be their joint lawyer. If joint representation is undertaken then the document should reflect that fact and that the clients have been advised of the conflict and waive it. Much care should be taken in this situation.

---

13. <u>Binding Effect.</u> All the terms, covenants, and conditions of this agreement shall be binding upon the parties hereto and their respective personal representatives, heirs and assigns.

14. <u>Governing Law.</u> This agreement shall be regulated and construed under the laws of the [state or commonwealth] of [name of state].

IN TESTIMONY WHEREOF, the parties have hereunto set their hands on this the _____ day of _____, [current year].

_____
Wife

_____
Husband

STATE OF [State of Notary]   )

)SCT.

COUNTY OF [County of Notary])

    Subscribed, sworn to, and acknowledged before me by [wife's name], this the _____ day of _____, [current year].

_____

Notary Public, State at Large

My Commission Expires:_____

STATE OF [State of Notary]   )

)SCT.

COUNTY OF [County of Notary])

    Subscribed, sworn to, and acknowledged before me by [husband's name], this the _____ day of _____, [current year].

_____

Notary Public, State at Large

My Commission Expires:_____

SCHEDULE A

WIFE'S PROPERTY

SCHEDULE B

HUSBAND'S PROPERTY

MEMORANDUM OF AGREEMENT

In some estate planning situations, clients are told to retitle assets between the husband and the wife. This is sometimes done for tax planning reasons, or to ensure sufficient assets in a spouse's sole name in order to fund a trust. In any situation in which assets are retitled between husband and wife, it may be wise to have them execute this memorandum or a variation of it. The concern is that, after transfers have been made between the spouses, they will subsequently divorce. A spouse may claim that the property transferred to him or her was a gift during marriage and not subject to division by the courts in the event of divorce. The lawyer will need to be familiar with his or her own state law as to how such transfers will be treated. If there is a possibility of a problem of a transfer being treated as non-marital property then this document or a variation of it is important.

We, [name of husband] and [name of wife], by this memorandum acknowledge our understanding from our attorney, [name of attorney], that certain transfers of assets, and re-titling of assets is required in order to either obtain a federal estate tax savings for our estate, or to ensure other non-tax estate planning objectives.

We acknowledge our attorney has advised us that such transfers may be deemed to be gifts to the other spouse or to otherwise change the marital or non-marital character of the assets so transferred in the event of a dissolution of our marriage. We hereby agree that in making any transfer of assets and/or re-titling of assets now and those we may make in the future that it is not our intent to re-characterize the nature of the property we have acquired during our marriage whether purchased by one, the other, or both of us, or obtained by gift or inheritance by either of us. Our intention is not to re-characterize marital property as non-marital property, or to re-characterize non-marital property as marital property as those terms are used in domestic relations law of the state of [name of state], or any other existing or hereinafter enacted laws or judicial decisions relating to dissolution of marriage.

We further acknowledge that our attorney has cautioned each of us that there is a risk that in spite of this agreement such transfers may change the character of the assets so transferred, but each of us desires to go forward with such transfers recognizing and understanding these risks and understanding that this agreement may not be enforced by the courts.

Finally, we agree that neither of us will maintain in any subsequent divorce proceeding that any such transfers modified in any way the character of such transferred property including any earnings or appreciation to such property during our marriage.

IN TESTIMONY WHEREOF, the parties have hereunto set their hands on this the _____ day of _____, [current year].

_____

[name of husband]

_____

[name of wife]

STATE OF [State of Notary]   )

)SCT.

COUNTY OF [County of Notary])

    Subscribed and sworn to before me by [name of husband], on this the _____ day of [current month], [current year].

_____

Notary Public, State at Large

My Commission Expires:_____

STATE OF [State of Notary]   )

)SCT.

COUNTY OF [County of Notary])

    Subscribed and sworn to before me by [name of wife], on this the _____ day of [current month], [current year].

_____

Notary Public, State at Large

My Commission Expires:_____

PREPARED BY:

_____

[Name of Attorney]
[Name of Law Firm]
Attorneys at Law
[Street Address]
[City], [State] [Zip Code]
[Telephone Number]

PART III–DRAFTING FOR CLIENTS WITH CHILDREN

Will with Testamentary Trust for Young Children

Inter Vivos Trust for Single Parent with Young Children

Child's Educational Trust with Withdrawal Rights

Minor's Trust—Internal Revenue Code 2503(c) Trust

WILL WITH TESTAMENTARY TRUST FOR YOUNG CHILDREN WORKSHEET

1. **Testator and Family Information**

    1.1 Name of Testator _____

    1.2 Testator City and State _____

    1.3 Name of Spouse _____

    1.4 Names of Children _____

    _____

    _____

    1.5 Are any of the above-named children step-children? <u>Yes / No</u>
    (See This Will Paragraph 1, Option 2)

    1.6 Are provisions needed for after-born children? <u>Yes / No</u>
    (See This Will Paragraph 1, Option 3)

    1.7 Are provisions needed for adopted and/or illegitimately born children? <u>Yes / No</u>
    (See Master Will Paragraph 1, Option 4 at page 25)

    1.8 Are any children to be disinherited? <u>Yes / No</u>
    (See Master Will Paragraph 1, Option 5 at page 26)

    Name of disinherited child: _____

    1.9 Are any loans or gifts/advancements to be considered for any child? <u>Yes / No</u>

    Name of Child: _____

    Is loan or gift/advancement to be considered in making distribution? <u>Yes / No</u>

    _____

    (See Master Will Paragraphs 4 and 5, Options 1 and 2 at page 28)

2. Specific Bequests and Legacies

2.1 Specific Gifts (See Master Will Paragraph 3 at pages 27 and 28)

  a. Description _____

  b. Primary Beneficiary _____

  c. Contingent Beneficiary_____

  d. Survivorship Period _____

2.2 Tangible Personal Property (spouse, and if not surviving, to children)

  If no agreement among children as to division:
  (See Master Will Paragraph 6 at page 29)

  Personal Representative Decides? <u>Yes / No</u>

  Sell and Distribute Proceeds to Residue? <u>Yes / No</u>

3. Residuary Estate if No Surviving Spouse

3.1 Separate testamentary trusts for children? (Option 1) <u>Yes / No</u>

  A. Provide for distribution one-half at each of two ages? <u>Yes / No</u>

      If yes: Initial age to inherit: _____

                   Final age to inherit: _____

  B. If a child is deceased:

      Deceased child's share
      distributed to such child's estate? (Option 1) <u>Yes / No</u>

      Or Deceased child's share
      distributed per stirpes to lineal descendants? (Option 2) <u>Yes / No</u>

  C. Provision for educational incentive? <u>Yes / No</u>

  D. Provision for trustee authority to withhold? <u>Yes / No</u>

3.2 Single testamentary trust for children? (Option 2) <u>Yes / No</u>

  A. Final age to inherit: _____

  B. Deceased child's share:

      Allocated per stirpes to lineal descendants? <u>Yes / No</u>

      If no, what distribution _____
      (See Option 1, Paragraph 4.c)

  C. Provision for trustee authority to withhold? <u>Yes / No</u>

4. Default Provisions, if all named beneficiaries are deceased:

_____

_____

_____

5. **Powers**

    Environmental Powers? <u>Yes / No</u> (See Master Will Paragraph 15 beginning at page 38)

    Farm Powers? <u>Yes / No</u> (See Master Will Paragraph 16 beginning at page 39)

    Limitation on Trustee Powers? <u>Yes / No</u>

6. **Trustees**

    Name of initial trustee: _____

    Name of successor trustee: _____

    Corporate trustee compensation? (Option 1) <u>Yes / No</u>

    Individual reimbursed for expenses but no compensation? (Option 2) <u>Yes / No</u>

    Individual receives compensation? (Option 3) <u>Yes / No</u>

        Amount of compensation: $_____

7. **Personal Representative**

    7.1 Spouse named initial personal representative? <u>Yes / No</u>

    7.2 If spouse not initial personal representative:

        Name_____ Address _____

    7.3 Successor Personal Representative:

        Name _____

        Relationship _____

        Address_____

    7.4 Surety Bond Waived? <u>Yes / No</u>

8. **Incompetency**

    One physician decides? (Option 1) <u>Yes / No</u>

    Two physicians decide and one board certified? (Option 2) <u>Yes / No</u>

9. **Guardian, if spouse not surviving:**

        Name _____

        Relationship _____

        Address _____

        Successor _____

        Relationship _____

        Address _____

        Surety Bond Waived? <u>Yes / No</u>

        Special provisions or bequests for guardian?_____

        _____

10. **Miscellaneous**

    Is no contest provision needed? <u>Yes / No</u>

    Is employment of law firm needed? <u>Yes / No</u>

11. **Survivorship** (See Master Will Paragraph 29 at page 44)

    1. Simultaneous Death <u>Yes / No</u>

      If yes, which spouse is presumed to die first? _____

    2. General Survivorship _____ days

      Does this apply to spouse? <u>Yes / No</u>

WILL WITH TESTAMENTARY TRUST FOR YOUNG CHILDREN

The will that follows is intended for a couple with young children. The will can easily be modified for a single parent. This is a basic will that provides for the estate passing to surviving spouse outright, then at the survivor's death, or upon the death of the couple in the event of a simultaneous death, the estate passes into a trust for their young children.

OF

[FULL NAME OF CLIENT]

I, [Full Name of Client], currently of [Client's City], [Client's State], make this my last will and testament, hereby revoking all wills and codicils previously made by me.

1. <u>Family Information.</u> My [husband or wife]'s name is [husband or wife's name], and all references in this will to "my [husband or wife]" are only to [him or her].

OPTION 1: Naming of all children My [child is or children are], [names of children], and all references in this will to "my [child is or children are]" only to [him her or them].

OPTION 2: Inclusion of step-children Even though some of these children are step-children it is my intent that each of the above-named children be treated for purposes of inheriting under this will as if they and their lineal descendants are my natural born children and descendants.

OPTION 3: After-born children If subsequent to the execution of this will there shall be an additional child or children born to me, then such child or children shall share in the benefits of my estate to the same extent as my above named children and their descendants; and the provisions of this will shall be deemed modified to the extent necessary to carry out this intent.

COMMENT: The full name of the other spouse and children should be inserted. If step-children are involved, Option 2 should be considered. Also, Option 3 may be appropriate if there is the possibility of additional children. The lawyer's state law should provide for this contingency, but it still may be appropriate to add this provision to the will. If there are concerns about adopted or illegitimate children inheriting and the extent to that inheritance, or the need to disinherit a child, then Options 4 and 5 of master will should be considered.

---

2. <u>Payment of Debts, Death Taxes and Funeral Expenses.</u> I direct that all of my just debts, my funeral expenses, costs of estate administration, and death taxes, if any, be paid from the residue of my estate as soon as possible after my death. I further direct that any real property that is subject to a mortgage or lien shall pass under my will subject to such mortgage or lien, rather than such indebtedness being paid from my estate. Death taxes means any estate or inheritance taxes imposed under the laws of any jurisdiction due to my death on any property passing by reason of my death whether or not such property passes under this will.

COMMENT: This is a basic clause providing for the payment of final expenses and death taxes with property subject to a mortgage indebtedness not being required to be paid, but rather the real estate passes to the beneficiary subject to the mortgage. Obviously, modifications can be made to this paragraph if needed. Also, if there is the need to consider more detailed provisions dealing with the payment of death taxes, such as those taxes being paid by the persons who inherit the property, or those receiving non-probate property being required to pay the estate taxes owed on that property, then the other options in paragraph 2 of the master will beginning at page 26 should be considered.

3. <u>Residuary Estate.</u> I give the residue of my estate to my [husband or wife], if [he or she] survives me, and if not, I give the residue of my estate **OPTION 1: Separate trusts for children** in equal shares to my children, subject to the trust provisions below. If a child is deceased my deceased child's share shall be distributed to that child's then living lineal descendants per stirpes, if any, otherwise such share shall be distributed to my then living lineal descendants, per stirpes. The share of a descendant shall be held in a separate trust named for that descendant and shall be administered and distributed for that descendant subject to the same trust provisions below for my children. **OPTION 2: Single trust for children** to my children, subject to the trust provisions below.

COMMENT: The entire estate is distributed to the surviving spouse, or if there is no surviving spouse then the entire estate passes into trust. The options are Option 1 for there to be a separate trust for each of the children or Option 2 for one trust for all of the children. This will is designed for parents with young children. If there are adult children, then paragraph 7 of the master will at page 30 should be considered, as it deals with the distribution of a deceased child's share. Also, no special provisions are made in this will for the distribution of personal property, as all of the property passes outright to the surviving spouse or else into a trust for the young children. Provisions for personal property are in paragraph 6 of the master will at page 29.

4. **OPTION 1: Separate trusts for children** <u>Child's Trust.</u> If a child entitled to a share under this will is below the age of [final age to inherit] years that child's share shall be retained in trust as a separate trust which shall be named for that child. If a child is already [final age to inherit] years old, then such child shall receive his or her share outright.

COMMENT: Option 1 creates separate trusts for each child. Paragraph 4.b provides for a distribution of principal one-half at each of two ages. If that method is followed, then the final age to inherit is inserted into the two places above.

a. Subject to the limitations in paragraph 9, the trustee may pay to or use all, part or none, of the income and principal of a child's trust as the trustee believes appropriate for the reasonable maintenance, support, health, and education (including college or graduate, professional or vocational school education) of such child, considering such child's income or assets and all other circumstances and factors the trustee believes pertinent. It is my desire that distributions of income and principal not impair my child's motivation to be productive and self-supporting, thus my trustee shall not make distributions of income and principal from a child's trust if my child is not productive, mature, and responsible. If any net income remains undistributed at the end of each calendar year (excluding income distributed during the sixty-five (65) day period under Internal Revenue Code Section 663), the trustee shall add it to the principal of my child's trust.

COMMENT: The first sentence provides broad discretion to the trustee in making distributions for the child, but is limited to avoid adverse tax consequences that may befall an individual trustee. The second sentence is not essential, but is provided to illustrate a possible restriction that the testator may desire. The third sentence can be eliminated, but is provided for situations in which income is not distributed before year end; and to set the time at which accumulated income is added to trust principal.

b. When a child for whom a trust held under this paragraph is named reaches the age of [initial age to inherit] years, the trustee shall distribute to such child one-half ($^1/_2$) of the then principal of that child's trust; and when such child reaches the age of [final age to inherit] years, the child's trust shall terminate and the balance of such child's trust shall be distributed outright to such child.

COMMENT: The trust can terminate and be distributed outright at one age, or in any number of other increments. This instrument provides for distribution at two ages with one-half at an age such as 25 and the remaining one-half at an age such as 30. Clients differ as to the proper ages.

---

c. **OPTION 1: Default to child's estate** If a child for whom a trust held under this paragraph is named dies prior to termination of such child's trust, then such child's trust shall terminate and shall be distributed to such child's own estate.

c. **OPTION 2: Default to descendants** On the death of a child for whom a trust held under this paragraph is named, any principal and undistributed income of such child's trust shall be divided and allocated per stirpes among the then living lineal descendants of such child, if any, and if none, such child's trust shall be divided and allocated per stirpes among my then living lineal descendants.

COMMENT: A decision must be made as to the distribution of the trust should the child die before termination of the trust. Option 1 is the simplest, as it permits the trust assets to be distributed to that child's own estate for distribution pursuant to the child's will if the child is old enough to have written a will, or pursuant to intestate laws. That result may be appropriate or it could be a disaster. The lawyer must determine if Option 1 is appropriate. Option 2 is designed to maintain a per stirpes distribution, which is more complicated than one might assume. A review of this form and its applicability and possible modification is essential. This gets a bit confusing to explain to a client, but it should be considered. An excellent ABA resource that explains this issue in detail is Jeffrey N. Penell and Alan Newman, *Estate and Trust Planning,* American Bar Association (Chicago, 2005) pp. 19–26.

---

d. Notwithstanding paragraphs 4.a and 4.b, following high school graduation, if a child for whom a trust is held hereunder fails to pursue post-secondary education leading to a bachelor's degree from an accredited college or university, all trust distributions, except for health care needs, shall cease until such child reaches the age of twenty-three (23) years. A child pursuing post-secondary education must annually maintain a 2.50 GPA based on a 4.0 grading scale in order to receive trust distributions, except for health care needs, prior to the age of twenty-three (23) years. If a child for whom a trust is named earns a bachelor's degree from an accredited college or university before such child reaches the age of twenty-three (23) years, the trustee shall within ninety (90) days of my child's graduation distribute [enter number] percent ([enter number]%) of the trust assets to my child free of trust.

COMMENT: This provision is intended to provide a model for the lawyer to consider in addressing an incentive for a child to pursue post-secondary education and to maintain an adequate grade point average. This paragraph may need to be moved to become part of paragraph a or as a separate paragraph b. In this form, the decision was made to place it in this location as it and the following paragraph are both offered as supplemental provisions that some clients will want and others will not. Be certain to modify the reference in the first sentence to the correct paragraph numbers.

---

e. In addition to the restrictions provided above in paragraphs 4.a through 4.d and as a condition precedent to distributions under those paragraphs, my trustee shall withhold or postpone any or all distributions of income or principal from a child's trust if my trustee believes a distribution to such child could result in the loss of some part or all of the distribution due to any possible civil or criminal legal action involving my child or my child's spouse, or due to my child or my child's spouse being addicted to alcohol or any legal or illegal controlled substance. The decision of my trustee shall be final and binding and shall not be subject to question by any person or in any court.

COMMENT: If the client is faced with a child who has substance abuse or other serious problems making distributions from the trust unwise, or if the client is concerned about such possibility, then paragraph e or a variation of it may be helpful. It is designed to give the trustee full authority to withhold all distributions of income and principal when a child is facing substance abuse or other significant personal problems.

OPTION 2: Single trust for children   Children's Trust. If my youngest child is below the age of [final age to inherit] years my entire residuary estate shall be retained in trust for my afore-named children, and shall be held, administered and distributed for their benefit according to the following provisions. If my youngest child is already [final age to inherit] years old, then the trust shall terminate and the trust assets shall be distributed to my children as provided below.

COMMENT: This trust provides one single trust for all of the testator's children. Therefore, trust distributions can be made among all children and the trust does not terminate until the youngest child reaches a particular age. That age will be inserted at the appropriate places above.

---

a. Until my youngest child becomes [final age to inherit] years old, my trustee shall pay to or use all, part or none of the income and principal of the trust, without regard to quality of distribution, to or for the benefit of my children as the trustee believes appropriate for the reasonable maintenance, support, health, and education (including college or graduate, professional or vocational school education) of my children, considering each child's income or assets and all other circumstances and factors the trustee believes pertinent. It is my desire that distributions of income and principal not impair a child's motivation to be productive and self-supporting, thus my trustee shall not make distributions of income and principal to a child who is not productive, mature, and responsible. If any net income remains undistributed at the end of each calendar year (excluding income distributed during the sixty-five (65) day period under Internal Revenue Code Section 663), the trustee shall add it to the principal of the trust. Disbursements of income and principal shall not be taken into account when my trustee makes final distribution of the trust property upon termination of the trust.

COMMENT: This trust allows the trustee to make distributions among all the testator's children without regard to equality in distributions among the children. This gives the trustee broad discretion to make distributions among the children based upon their then current needs, but is limited to avoid adverse tax consequences that may befall an individual trustee. Because of the broadness of the discretion granted to the trustee, paragraph d from Option 1 has not been included but can be modified and added if the lawyer so desires. The second sentence above is not essential, but is provided to illustrate a possible restriction that the testator may desire. The third sentence can be eliminated, but is provided for situations in which income is not distributed before year end; and to set the time at which accumulated income is added to trust principal.

b. Upon my youngest child reaching [final age to inherit] years of age, the trust shall terminate and my trustee shall distribute the trust property to my children in equal shares. If a child is deceased my deceased child's share shall be distributed to that child's then living lineal descendants per stirpes, if any, otherwise such share shall be distributed to my then living lineal descendants, per stirpes.

COMMENT: The trust terminates upon the youngest child reaching a particular age, at which time the trust terminates and each child receives an equal share. If a child is deceased, that child's share is distributed equally to his or her descendants. Otherwise distribution is equal among the testator's descendants per stirpes. Also, see Option 1 paragraph 4.c and the comment that follows.

---

c. In addition to the restrictions provided above and as a condition precedent to the trustee making any distributions to my children, my trustee shall withhold or postpone any or all distributions of income or principal to a child if my trustee believes a distribution to such child could result in the loss of some part or all of the distribution due to any possible civil or criminal legal action involving my child or my child's spouse, or due to my child or my child's spouse being addicted to alcohol or any legal or illegal controlled substance. The decision of my trustee shall be final and binding and shall not be subject to question by any person or in any court.

COMMENT: Paragraph c is offered as an alternative should there be the possibility that one or more children have substance abuse or other serious problems. It is provided out of sequence as many clients may not desire this provision. If it is needed, this writer suggests that it be placed as either part of 4.a or a separate paragraph 4.b followed by a renumbering of 4.b and 4.c.

---

5. <u>Default Provisions.</u> If all beneficiaries under this instrument are deceased, my estate or trust assets shall be distributed to [default provisions].

COMMENT: If there are a limited number of beneficiaries, then it may be wise to insert a default provision providing for the ultimate recipient should all the beneficiaries in paragraph 4 and their descendants be deceased. If this is too remote of a possibility, some clients may direct that this paragraph be deleted.

---

6. <u>Protection from Creditors.</u> No trust beneficiary shall have the right to sell, transfer, assign, alienate, pledge, or in any way encumber trust assets, including income and principal, nor shall trust assets be subject to execution, levy, sale, garnishment, attachment, bankruptcy, or other legal proceedings. Any such actions by a trust beneficiary or a third party seeking to enforce a claim against the trust assets shall not be recognized under any circumstances by the trustee. These provisions do not prevent the trustee from making distributions for the benefit of a trust beneficiary in such amounts and at such times as the trustee determines necessary for the trust beneficiary's maintenance, support, health and education.

COMMENT: This is a standard paragraph that precludes the trust assets from being attached by claims of creditors. The lawyer should check state law before advising a client of the effect of this provision.

---

7. <u>Definition of Per Stirpes.</u> Whenever assets are to be divided and allocated per stirpes, the assets to be divided or allocated shall be divided into as many equal shares as are necessary to divide or allocate one share to each then living child of such person and to provide one share collectively for the then living descendants of each child of such person who then is deceased leaving one or more descendants then living. Any collective share shall be divided and allocated per stirpes among the descendants of such deceased person in accordance with the preceding sentence.

COMMENT: Since the term per stirpes is used often in this document, a definition is provided of that term. The lawyer should modify this definition to conform with his or her own state law should it differ from this definition. Of course, a definition is not essential, since the term will be defined under state law. But since it is a term that clients are not familiar with, it is often helpful to define it for them in the document. An excellent ABA resource that explains the term per stirpes and its variations is Jeffrey N. Penell and Alan Newman, *Estate and Trust Planning,* American Bar Association (Chicago, 2005) pp. 19–26.

---

8. <u>Trustee Powers.</u> In the administration of the trusts, the trustee shall have the following powers and rights and all others granted by law:

a. To sell publicly or privately any trust property, for cash or on time, without an order of court and upon such terms and conditions as my trustee deems proper; and no person dealing with my trustee shall have any obligation to look to the application of the purchase money.

b. To invest and reinvest all or any part of the principal of the trust in any stocks, bonds, mortgages, shares or interests in common trust funds, mutual funds, or other securities or property, real, personal, or mixed, and of any kind or nature whatsoever, as the trustee deems proper, and without diversification if the trustee deems it advisable, irrespective of whether or not such securities or property are eligible for trust investment under state or any other law, and may change any investment received or made by the trustee, and may hold cash if the trustee deems it advisable.

c. To exercise broad discretion as to diversification of trust property, and shall not be required to reduce any concentrated holdings merely because of such concentration, and shall have full discretion as to the percentage to be invested in fixed income securities, and is specifically relieved from any requirements, legal or otherwise, as to the percentage of the trust assets to be invested in fixed income securities, and may invest or retain invested any trust estates wholly in common stocks.

d. To sell, convey, lease or mortgage, repair and improve, and take any and all other steps with regard to any real estate that may at any time be a part of the principal of the trust; and any lease of such real property or contract with regard thereto made by the trustee shall be binding for the full period of the lease or contract, even though the period shall extend beyond the termination of the trust.

e. To vote shares of stock held in the trust at stockholders' meetings in person or by special, limited, or general proxy, with or without power of substitution, as seems best to the trustee.

f. To participate in the liquidation, reorganization, consolidation, incorporation and reincorporation, or any other financial readjustment of any corporation, limited liability company or business in which the trust is, or shall be financially interested.

g. To borrow money from any source for any purpose connected with the protection, preservation, improvement or development of the trust hereunder, whenever in the trustee's judgment the trustee deems it advisable, and as security to mortgage or pledge any real estate or personal property forming a part of the trust upon such terms and conditions as the trustee may deem advisable.

h. To hold any and all securities in bearer form, in the trustee's own name, or the name of some other person, partnership, or corporation, or in the name of a duly appointed nominee, with or without disclosing the fiduciary ownership.

i. To divide the principal of the trust property into parts or shares and to distribute or allot same, and to make such division in cash or in kind or both. For the purpose of such division or allotment, the judgment of the trustee concerning the propriety thereof and relative value of property so distributed or allotted shall be binding and conclusive with respect to all interested persons.

j. To merge and consolidate the trust property of any separate trust held hereunder with other trusts and then to administer such trust property as a single trust provided the separate trust is for the benefit of the same persons with substantially the same terms, conditions and federal tax consequences.

k. To pay such income and principal during the minority or incapacity of any beneficiary for whose benefit income and principal may be expended, in any one or more of the following ways: (1) directly to the beneficiary; (2) to the legal guardian or committee of the beneficiary; (3) to a relative of the beneficiary to be expended by the relative for the maintenance, health, and education of the beneficiary; or (4) by expending the same directly for the maintenance, health, and education of the beneficiary. The trustee shall not be obliged to see to the application of the funds so expended, but the receipt of such person shall be full acquittance to the trustee.

l. To continue and operate any business owned by me at my death and to do any and all things deemed appropriate by the trustee, including the power to form a limited liability company or incorporate the business and to put additional capital into the business, for such time as the trustee deems advisable, without liability for loss resulting from the continuance or operation of the business except for the trustee's own negligence; and to close out, liquidate, or sell the business at such time and upon such terms as the trustee deems proper, and in this connection a sale may be made (pursuant to an agreement entered into by me during my lifetime, or otherwise) to a partner, officer, member, employee or beneficiary under this trust. I am aware of the fact that certain risks are inherent in the operation of any business and, therefore, my trustee shall not be liable for any loss resulting from the retention and operation of any business unless such loss results directly from my trustee's gross negligence or willful misconduct.

m. To have the same powers, authorities, and discretions in the management of the trust as I would have in the management and control of my own personal assets. The trustee may continue to exercise any powers and discretions granted in this instrument for a reasonable period after the termination of any trust under this instrument.

COMMENT: The above powers are a set of standard powers that appear throughout this book. The powers should be reviewed to be certain that you the lawyer understand each power, the client is in agreement with each of the powers granted and that the powers granted are needed. Because this is a generic and broad statement of powers, some of these powers may not be necessary. For example, powers to sell or lease real estate are not needed if the grantor knows the trust will consist only of cash and other intangible investments.

---

9. Limitation on Powers of Individual Trustee. Notwithstanding any other powers granted to my trustee in this instrument, an individual trustee (a) shall have no power to make payments or distributions that would discharge the trustee's legal obligation to support the trust beneficiary, (b) shall not exercise any power or discretion in any manner that would be deemed to be a general power of appointment under Internal Revenue Code Section 2041, (c) shall be limited by the ascertainable standard of "maintenance, support, health and education" when making payments or distributions to the trustee personally or to anyone for whom the trustee has a beneficial interest,

and (d) shall possess no incidence of ownership or powers with respect to life insurance in which the trustee is the insured and has fiduciary power over such life insurance.

COMMENT: There are some situations in which an individual trustee may have adverse estate or income tax consequences when given broad powers as trustee. If a corporate trustee is used, then this paragraph is not needed. But an individual trustee must be certain that acting as trustee does not result in any adverse estate or income tax consequences. This paragraph is intended to ensure that adverse tax consequences are avoided if overly broad powers are granted in the trust instrument. The lawyer is urged to exercise caution when using individual trustees coupled with broad discretionary powers of income and principal distribution to a trust beneficiary because of possible adverse tax consequences. An ABA resource to acquaint oneself with these issues is L. Rush Hunt and Lara Rae Hunt, *A Lawyer's Guide to Estate Planning*, American Bar Association (Chicago: 2004) §14.4.

10. <u>Trustee Resignation.</u> My trustee may resign at any time by giving written notice to my successor trustee named below, if any, and if none, then written notice shall be given to each current adult income beneficiary who is then living.

COMMENT: If a trustee resigns, there must be some method of notice and appointment of a successor trustee. This paragraph provides a method of notification. It is not an essential trust provision, but is a helpful one.

11. <u>Trustee Appointment and Succession.</u> The initial trustee shall be [trustee name]. If my initial trustee ceases to act as trustee due to death, incompetency, resignation or any other reason, then [successor trustee's name] shall be successor trustee. My successor trustee may name [his or her] own successor trustee by a written instrument delivered to the successor trustee, or by will. The successor trustee shall be an individual or a financial institution possessing trust powers under state or federal law. Any further vacancy in the office of trustee shall be filled by decision of the probate court where I resided at the time of my death. No trustee or successor trustee shall be required to post a surety bond for serving as trustee or successor trustee.

COMMENT: A decision must be made as to succession of trustees and the method of appointing a successor trustee if all of those named successor trustees are unable to serve. It is also essential to clarify whether successor trustees must only be financial institutions or if individuals may also be considered. Once a decision is made as to the succession of trustees, then the last three sentences should be reviewed to be certain to what extent each of those are needed.

12. <u>Powers of Successor Trustee.</u> Each successor trustee shall have the same rights, titles, powers, duties, discretions, and immunities and otherwise be in the same position as if originally named trustee. No successor trustee shall be personally liable for any act or failure to act of a predecessor trustee. Further, a successor trustee may accept the account furnished and the property delivered by or for a predecessor trustee without liability for so doing, and such acceptance shall be a full and complete discharge to the predecessor trustee.

COMMENT: This paragraph clarifies that a successor trustee has the same powers as the initial trustee. Further, the paragraph relieves the successor trustee from liability for the prior acts of the resigning trustee and waives any requirements of audit or inquiry into the activities of the prior trustee. This is essential for any successor trustee.

13. Compensation of Trustee. **OPTION 1: Corporate trustee compensation** A corporate trustee shall receive compensation in accordance with its regular schedule of fees in effect at the time such services are rendered.

OPTION 2: Individual does not receive compensation An individual trustee shall not be paid any compensation, but shall be reimbursed for out-of-pocket expenses.

OPTION 3: Individual does receive compensation An individual trustee shall be paid [insert amount of compensation] as compensation for such services and shall be reimbursed for out-of-pocket expenses.

COMMENT: Three options are provided, but the actual drafting of this paragraph may be different than each of these options. If the only trustee to be used is a corporate trustee, then Option 1 is a standard trust provision. If there is a possibility of individual trustees, then care should be given to the method for setting this fee. If no fee is to be paid because the trustee is a close family member, then it is suggested that Option 2 be used. If the testator expects a fee to be charged, then an amount or a formula, such as a percentage of income or principal, must be set. It is unwise to simply provide for compensation to be a reasonable fee, as that leaves an individual trustee with great uncertainty as to the fee to be charged. Without the testator clarifying compensation, the trustee could find him or herself in litigation with the beneficiary.

14. Appointment of Personal Representative. My [husband or wife], shall be the personal representative of my estate. If my [husband or wife] fails to qualify as personal representative, or having qualified, dies, becomes incompetent, resigns, or declines to continue to serve, then my [relationship of successor PR] [name of successor PR] shall serve as my successor personal representative. Neither my [husband or wife] nor my successor personal representative shall be required to furnish any surety bond for serving as my personal representative.

COMMENT: The full names of the personal representative and successor personal representative are required as is a decision concerning the waiver of a surety bond. The form, as drafted, assumes the intent to waive such bond.

15. Powers of Personal Representative. I hereby grant to my personal representative (including my successor personal representative) the absolute power to deal with any property, real or personal, held in my estate, as freely as I might in the handling of my own affairs. This power may be exercised independently and without the approval of any court, and no person dealing with my personal representative shall be required to inquire into the propriety of the actions of my personal representative. Without in any way limiting the generality of the foregoing provisions, I grant to my personal representative in addition to those powers specified under state law the following powers:

a. To sell, exchange, assign, transfer and convey any security or property, real or personal, held in my estate at public or private sale, at such time and at such reasonable price and upon such reasonable terms and conditions (including credit) as my personal representative may determine; and without regard to whether or not such sale is necessary in order to settle my estate.

b. To lease any real estate for such term, or terms, and upon such reasonable conditions and rentals and in such manner as my personal representative deems proper, and any lease so made shall be valid and binding for its full term even though such lease term extends beyond the duration of the administration of my estate; to make repairs, replacements and improvements, structural or otherwise, to any such real estate; to subdivide real estate, dedicate real estate to public use and grant easements as my personal representative deems proper.

c. To employ accountants, attorneys and such other agents as my personal representative deems necessary; to pay reasonable compensation for such services and to charge same to (or apportion same between) income and principal as my personal representative deems proper.

d. To join with my [husband or wife] on my behalf in filing income tax returns, or to consent for gift tax purposes to having gifts made by either of us during my life considered as made one-half by each of us, and any resulting tax liability shall be paid by my estate, except such portion as my personal representative and my [husband or wife] agree should be paid by my [husband or wife].

COMMENT: A statement of the powers of the personal representative is not essential, as those powers are specified by state law; however, those state laws may not be sufficiently broad. Often state laws do not include power over real estate. Paragraph 15.c may not be essential, but this writer prefers to clarify that the personal representative may hire at the expense of the estate professionals to assist in estate settlement. Paragraph 15.d deals with the signing of tax returns and, while not essential, still is appropriate in most situations.

---

16. Certification of Incompetency. **OPTION 1: Decided by treating physician** Any person acting or named to act in a fiduciary capacity in this will is considered to be unable to serve or to continue serving when a physician whom such person has consulted within the prior three years has certified as to such consultation and the certification states that the person is incapable of managing the affairs of my estate or any trust I have established, regardless of cause and regardless of whether there is an adjudication of incompetency. No person is liable to anyone for actions taken in reliance on the physician's certification or for dealing with a personal representative or trustee other than the one removed for incompetency based on these certifications.

OPTION 2: Decided by two physicians Any person acting or named to act in a fiduciary capacity in this will is considered to be unable to serve or to continue serving when a written certification is received from two (2) physicians, both of whom have personally examined the person and at least one (1) of whom is board-certified in the specialty most closely associated with the health condition alleged to cause such incompetency. The certification must state that the person is incapable of managing his or her own finances, regardless of cause and regardless of whether there is an adjudication of incompetence, or need for a conservator, guardian, or other personal representative. No person is liable to anyone for actions taken in reliance on these certifications, or for dealing with a personal representative or trustee other than the one removed for incompetency based on these certifications.

COMMENT: This provision relates both to paragraph 11 concerning the succession of trustees, paragraph 14 regarding the successor personal representative, and paragraph 17 concerning the appointment of an alternate guardian. It defines incompetency, which is one of those events requiring a successor trustee, personal representative or an alternate guardian. The first option involves consultation with the person's personal physician, whereas Option 2 involves a panel of two physicians, one of whom is board certified in the speciality most closely associated with the health condition of the person acting in a fiduciary capacity. Clients differ as to which provision they prefer. Absent a strong preference by the testator, Option 1 is the provision most frequently used.

17. <u>Appointment of Guardian.</u> If my [husband or wife] does not survive me, my [relationship], [Name of Guardian], shall be guardian of each child for whom it is necessary to appoint a guardian. If [Name of Guardian] does not act as guardian, or having qualified dies, becomes incompetent, resigns, or declines to continue to serve, then my [relationship], [Alternate guardian] shall be guardian of each child for whom it is necessary to appoint a guardian. No surety bond shall be required of my guardians.

COMMENT: This is a standard paragraph naming a guardian for any children for whom a guardian is necessary. If there is only one possible guardian and no alternate guardian, then the second sentence can be omitted. This paragraph omits the requirement of a surety bond.

18. <u>No-Contest Provision.</u> If any beneficiary contests the probate or validity of my will or any of its provisions, including the provisions of any testamentary trust, or if any beneficiary joins in any such action, then all provisions in this instrument for the benefit of such beneficiary are revoked and his or her share shall be distributed as if such beneficiary predeceased me dying without any lineal descendants.

COMMENT: This provision or some variation of it should be considered if there is any concern that a beneficiary or heir-at-law may challenge the will or testamentary trust. The lawyer may need to modify this provision to meet any requirements of state law.

19. <u>Employment of Attorney.</u> I request but do not require that my personal representative employ the law firm of [insert name of law firm], [city], [state] to be my estate's attorney as the attorneys in that law firm are the most familiar with my intentions expressed in this will.

COMMENT: This paragraph may be appropriate when the client is expecting the lawyer who drafted the will to be available to settle the estate. Often the children do not know the parent's preference for a lawyer, thus the provision is inserted. The employment of the testator's lawyer is made permissive to avoid any appearance of self-dealing by the lawyer preparing the will. There will be situations in which the client insists the wording be made mandatory. If so, the lawyer may wish to document this fact by memo to the file, signed by the client.

IN TESTIMONY WHEREOF, I, [Name of Client], sign my name to this instrument this _____ day of _____, [current year], and being first duly sworn, do hereby declare to the undersigned authority that I sign and execute this instrument as my last will and that I sign it willingly, that I execute it as my free and voluntary act for the purposes therein expressed, and that I am 18 years of age or older, of sound mind, and under no constraint or undue influence.

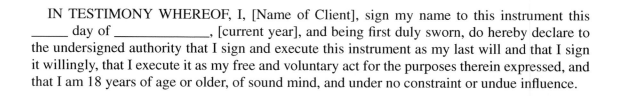

[Name of Client], Testator

We _____ and _____, the witnesses, sign our names to this instrument, being first duly sworn, and do hereby declare to the undersigned authority that [Name of Client] signs and executes this instrument as [his or her] Last Will and Testament dated _____, [current year], and that [he or she] signs it willingly and that each of us, in the presence and hearing of [Name of Client] and in the presence of the other subscribing witness, hereby signs this Last Will and Testament as witness to the [Name of Client]'s signing, and that to the best of their knowledge, [Name of Client] is eighteen (18) years of age or older, of sound mind and under no constraint or undue influence, all on this _____ day of _____, [current year].

_____   _____
Witness   Address

_____   _____
Witness   Address

STATE OF [State of Notary]   )
)SCT.
COUNTY OF [County of Notary])

    Subscribed, sworn to, and acknowledged before me by [Name of Client], and subscribed and sworn to before me by _____ and _____, witnesses, this the _____ day of _____, [current year].

                                        _____

                                        Notary Public, State at Large

                                        My Commission Expires:_____

COMMENT: The above provisions are in compliance with the writer's own state law to avoid the necessity of locating witnesses to the will at a later date. This provision should be modified to meet the requirement of the lawyer's own state law.

PREPARED BY:

_____
[Name of Attorney]
[Name of Law Firm]
Attorneys at Law
[Street Address]
[City], [State] [Zip Code]
[Telephone Number]

INTER VIVOS TRUST FOR SINGLE PARENT WITH YOUNG CHILDREN WORKSHEET

1. Grantor and Trustee Information

Name _____

City and State _____

2. Name of Trust

"_____ Trust"

3. Children

3.1 Names of Children _____

_____

_____

3.2 Are any of the above-named children step-children? <u>Yes / No</u>
(See Single Trust Paragraph 2, Option 2 at page 58)

3.3 Are provisions needed for after-born children? <u>Yes / No</u>
(See Single Trust Paragraph 2, Option 3 at page 58)

4. Allocations at Death

4.1 Separate trusts for children? (Option 1) <u>Yes / No</u>

A. Provide for distribution one-half at each of two ages? <u>Yes / No</u>

If yes: Initial age to inherit: _____

Final age to inherit:_____

B. If a child is deceased:

Deceased child's share distributed
to such child's estate? (Option 1) <u>Yes / No</u>

or Deceased child's share per stirpes
to lineal descendants? (Option 2) <u>Yes / No</u>

C. Provision for educational incentive? <u>Yes / No</u>

D. Provision for trustee authority to withhold? <u>Yes / No</u>

4.2 Single trust for children? (Option 2) <u>Yes / No</u>

A. Final age to inherit: _____

B. Deceased Child's Share:

Allocated per stirpes to lineal descendants? <u>Yes / No</u>

If no, what distribution _____
(See Option 1, Paragraph 4.c)

C. Provision for trustee authority to withhold? <u>Yes / No</u>

5.   **Default Provisions (if needed), if All Named Beneficiaries are Deceased**:

_____

_____

_____

6.   **Definition of "Child" and "Descendant"**

Include children adopted prior to age _____ (18, 21, etc.).

Include provision for illegitimate children (treated same, etc.)? Yes / No

7.   **Powers**

Environmental Powers? Yes / No (See Single Trust, Paragraph 11 at page 73)

Farm Powers? Yes / No (See Single Trust, Paragraph 12 beginning at page 73)

Limitation on Trustee Powers? Yes / No

8.   **Trustees**

Name of first successor trustee: _____

Name of second successor trustee: _____

Corporate trustee compensation? (Option 1) Yes / No

Individual reimbursed for expenses but no compensation? (Option 2) Yes / No

Individual receives compensation? (Option 3) Yes / No

Amount of compensation: $_____

9.   **Incompetency**

One physician decides? (Option 1) Yes / No

Two physicians decide and one board certified? (Option 2) Yes / No

10.   **No Contest**

Is No Contest provision needed? Yes / No

INTER VIVOS TRUST FOR SINGLE PARENT WITH YOUNG CHILDREN

This is an inter vivos trust where a single person establishes a trust for him or herself and then makes provision for young children. With modifications it can be used for a couple. If the person has older children, then modifications will need to be made to the trust. This trust is similar in format to the will with testamentary trust for young children, but will be a better solution in those situations in which the client seeks the privacy of assets held in a trust rather than passing those assets under a will through the probate process. In some situations the use of a trust may simplify estate settlement and reduce estate settlement expenses.

I, [Grantor], currently of [Grantor's city], [Grantor's state], acting as grantor and trustee hereby transfer to myself, as trustee, the property described in Schedule A. This property and all investments, reinvestments and additions which may sometimes be referred to in this instrument as the "trust property" or "trust assets" are to be held subject to the following provisions:

COMMENT: In this trust the grantor will also act as trustee during his or her lifetime. The trust may be funded at the time it is created or the grantor may choose to fund the trust at a later date. Thus, this trust has the benefit of being a so-called living trust, which is intended to simplify estate settlement, as well as, providing for the benefit of children.

1. <u>Name of Trust.</u> This instrument and the initial trust hereby established may be named the "[Name of trust] Trust."

COMMENT: The trust may have any name the grantor desires. Often times, the grantor will simply name the trust after him or herself.

2. <u>Children Named.</u> My [child is or children are] [Names of child or children] and all references in this instrument to "my [child is or children are]" only to [him, her or them].

COMMENT: This trust as drafted is designed for a single person with children. The full name of each of the children will be inserted. If there is a need to consider step-children or after-born children, those provisions are in paragraph 2 of the single trust at page 58.

3. <u>Provisions During My Lifetime.</u> During my lifetime, I shall be paid the net trust income and the principal of the trust property as I direct. If my successor trustee determines that I am unable to manage my financial affairs, the trustee shall pay to or use all, part or none, of the income and principal of the trust property as the trustee believes appropriate for my reasonable maintenance, support, and health. If any net income remains undistributed at the end of each calendar year (excluding income distributed during the sixty-five (65) day period under Internal Revenue Code Section 663), the trustee shall add it to the principal of the trust.

COMMENT: These are basic provisions to provide that, during the lifetime of the grantor, all income and principal is for the sole benefit of the grantor. In order to maintain privacy, the grantor will elect to transfer brokerage accounts and other assets to the trust. In this way, those assets need not be reported to the probate court in settlement of the grantor's estate. Throughout the grantor's lifetime, he or she acts as trustee in making distributions to him or herself with a successor trustee making distributions in the event of disability.

4. Allocations at My Death. **OPTION 1: Separate trusts for children** Following my death, the trustee shall divide the trust property into separate equal shares for my children. If a child is deceased, my deceased child's share shall be distributed to that child's then living lineal descendants, per stirpes, if any, otherwise such share shall be distributed to my then living lineal descendants, per stirpes. If a child entitled to a share under this will is below the age of [final age to inherit] years that child's share shall be retained in trust as a separate trust which shall be named for that child. If a child is already [final age to inherit] years old, then such child shall receive his or her share outright. The share of a descendant shall be held in a separate trust named for that descendant and shall be administered and distributed for that descendant subject to the same trust provisions below for my children.

COMMENT: Option 1 creates separate trusts for each child. Paragraph 4.b provides for a distribution of principal one-half at each of two ages. If that method is followed, then the final age to inherit is inserted into the two places above.

---

a. The trustee may pay to or use all, part or none, of the income and principal of a child's trust as the trustee believes appropriate for the reasonable maintenance, support, health, and education (including college or graduate, professional or vocational school education) of such child, considering such child's income or assets and all other circumstances and factors the trustee believes pertinent. It is my desire that distributions of income and principal not impair my child's motivation to be productive and self-supporting, thus my trustee shall not make distributions of income and principal from a child's trust if my child is not productive, mature, and responsible. If any net income remains undistributed at the end of each calendar year (excluding income distributed during the sixty-five (65) day period under Internal Revenue Code Section 663), the trustee shall add it to the principal of my child's trust.

COMMENT: The first sentence provides broad discretion to the trustee in making distributions for the child. The second sentence is not essential, but is provided to illustrate a possible restriction that the grantor may desire. The third sentence can be eliminated, but is provided to cover situations in which income is not distributed before year end; and to set the time at which accumulated income is added to trust principal.

---

b. When a child for whom a trust held under this paragraph is named reaches the age of [initial age to inherit] years, the trustee shall distribute to such child one-half ($^1/_2$) of the then principal of that child's trust; and when such child reaches the age of [final age to inherit] years, the child's trust shall terminate and the balance of such child's trust shall be distributed outright to such child.

COMMENT: The trust can terminate and be distributed outright at one age, or in any number of other increments. This instrument provides for distribution at two ages with one-half at an age such as 25 and the remaining one-half at an age such as 30. Clients differ as to the proper ages.

---

c. **OPTION 1: Default to child's estate** If a child for whom a trust held under this paragraph is named dies prior to termination of such child's trust, then such child's trust shall terminate and shall be distributed to such child's own estate.

c. **OPTION 2: Default to descendants** On the death of a child for whom a trust held under this paragraph is named, any principal and undistributed income of such child's trust shall be divided and allocated per stirpes among the then living lineal descendants of such child, if any, and if none, such child's trust shall be divided and allocated per stirpes among my then living lineal descendants.

COMMENT: A decision must be made as to the distribution of the trust should the child die before termination of the trust. Option 1 is the simplest, as it permits the trust assets to be distributed to that child's own estate for distribution pursuant to the child's will if the child is old enough to have written a will, or pursuant to intestate laws. That result may be appropriate or it could be a disaster. The lawyer must determine if Option 1 is appropriate. Option 2 is designed to maintain a per stirpes distribution first to the child's own children, or if there are none, then to the grantor's descendants on a per stirpes basis. A review of this form and its applicability and possible modifications is essential. This gets a bit confusing to explain to a client, but it should be considered. An excellent ABA resource that explains this issue in detail is Jeffrey N. Penell and Alan Newman, *Estate and Trust Planning,* American Bar Association (Chicago, 2005) pp. 19–26.

---

d. Notwithstanding the provisions in the above paragraphs, following high school graduation, if a child for whom a trust is held hereunder fails to pursue post-secondary education leading to a bachelor's degree from an accredited college or university, all trust distributions, except for health care needs, shall cease until such child reaches the age of twenty-three (23) years. A child pursuing post-secondary education must annually maintain a 2.50 GPA based on a 4.0 grading scale in order to receive trust distributions, except for health care needs, prior to the age of twenty-three (23) years. If a child for whom a trust is named earns a bachelor's degree from an accredited college or university before such child reaches the age of twenty-three (23) years, the trustee shall within ninety (90) days of my child's graduation distribute [enter number] percent ([enter number]%) of the trust assets to my child free of trust.

COMMENT: This provision is intended to provide a model for the lawyer to consider in addressing an incentive for a child to pursue post-secondary education and to maintain an adequate grade point average. This paragraph may need to be moved to become part of paragraph a or as a separate paragraph b. In this form, the decision was made to place it in this location as it and the following paragraph are both offered as supplemental provisions that some clients will want and others will not. Be certain to modify the reference in the first sentence to the phrase "notwithstanding . . . paragraphs" if it is moved elsewhere in the document.

---

e. In addition to the restrictions provided in the above paragraphs and as a condition precedent to distributions under those paragraphs, my trustee shall withhold or postpone any or all distributions of income or principal from a child's trust if my trustee believes a distribution to such child could result in the loss of some part or all of the distribution due to any possible civil or criminal legal action involving my child or my child's spouse, or due to my child or my child's spouse being addicted to alcohol or any legal or illegal controlled substance. The decision of my trustee shall be final and binding and shall not be subject to question by any person or in any court.

COMMENT: If the client is faced with a child who has substance abuse or other serious problems making distributions from the trust unwise, or if the client is concerned about such possibility, then paragraph e or a variation of it may be helpful. It is designed to give the trustee full authority to withhold all distributions of income and principal when a child is facing substance abuse or other significant personal problems.

OPTION 2: Single trust for children If my youngest child is below the age of [final age to inherit] years the trust property shall be retained in trust for my aforenamed children, and shall be held, administered and distributed for their benefit according to the following provisions. If my youngest child is already [final age to inherit] years old, then the trust shall terminate and the trust assets shall be distributed to my children as provided below.

COMMENT: This trust provides one single trust for all of the grantor's children. Therefore, trust distributions can be made among all children and the trust does not terminate until the youngest child reaches a particular age. That age will be inserted at the appropriate places above.

a. Until my youngest child becomes [final age to inherit] years old, my trustee shall pay to or use all, part or none of the income and principal of the trust, without regard to quality of distribution, to or for the benefit of my children as the trustee believes appropriate for the reasonable maintenance, support, health, and education (including college or graduate, professional or vocational school education) of my children, considering each child's income or assets and all other circumstances and factors the trustee believes pertinent. It is my desire that distributions of income and principal not impair a child's motivation to be productive and self-supporting, thus my trustee shall not make distributions of income and principal to a child who is not productive, mature, and responsible. If any net income remains undistributed at the end of each calendar year (excluding income distributed during the sixty-five (65) day period under Internal Revenue Code Section 663), the trustee shall add it to the principal of the trust. Disbursements of income and principal shall not be taken into account when my trustee makes final distribution of the trust property upon termination of the trust.

COMMENT: This trust allows the trustee to make distributions among all the grantor's children without regard to equality. This gives the trustee broad discretion to make distributions among the children based upon their then current needs. Because of the broadness of the discretion granted to the trustee, paragraph d from Option 1 has not been included but can be modified and added if the lawyer so desires. The second sentence above is not essential, but is provided to illustrate a possible restriction that the grantor may desire. The third sentence can be eliminated, but is provided for situations in which income is not distributed before year end; and to set the time at which accumulated income is added to trust principal.

b. Upon my youngest child reaching [final age to inherit] years of age, the trust shall terminate and my trustee shall distribute the trust property to my children in equal shares. If a child is deceased my deceased child's share shall be distributed to that child's then living lineal descendants per stirpes, if any, otherwise such share shall be distributed to my then living lineal descendants, per stirpes.

COMMENT: The trust terminates upon the youngest child reaching a particular age, at which time the trust terminates and each child receives an equal share. If a child is deceased, that child's share is distributed equally to his or her descendants. Otherwise distribution is equal among the grantor's descendants per stirpes. Also, see Option 1 Paragraph 4.c and the comment that follows.

c. In addition to the restrictions provided above and as a condition precedent to the trustee making any distributions to my children, my trustee shall withhold or postpone any or all distributions of income or principal to a child if my trustee believes a distribution to such child could result in the loss of some part or all of the distribution due to any possible civil or criminal legal action involving my child or my child's spouse, or due to my child or my child's spouse being addicted to alcohol or any legal or illegal controlled substance. The decision of my trustee shall be final and binding and shall not be subject to question by any person or in any court.

COMMENT: Paragraph c is offered as an alternative should there be the possibility that one or more children have substance abuse or other serious problems. It is provided out of sequence as many clients may not desire this provision. If it is needed, this writer suggests that it be placed as either part of 4.a or a separate paragraph 4.b followed by a renumbering of 4.b and 4.c.

---

5. <u>Default Provisions.</u> Any trust property not disposed of by any of the above provisions shall be distributed on the date of such failure of disposition to [default provisions].

COMMENT: If there are a limited number of beneficiaries, then it may be wise to insert a default provision providing for the ultimate recipient should all the beneficiaries in paragraph 4 and their descendants be deceased. If this is too remote of a possibility, some clients may direct that this paragraph be deleted.

---

6. <u>Protection from Creditors.</u> No trust beneficiary shall have the right to sell, transfer, assign, alienate, pledge, or in any way encumber trust assets, including income and principal, nor shall trust assets be subject to execution, levy, sale, garnishment, attachment, bankruptcy, or other legal proceedings. Any such actions by a trust beneficiary or a third party seeking to enforce a claim against the trust assets shall not be recognized under any circumstances by the trustee. These provisions do not prevent the trustee from making distributions for the benefit of a trust beneficiary in such amounts and at such times as the trustee determines necessary for the trust beneficiary's maintenance, support, health and education.

COMMENT: This is a standard paragraph that precludes the trust assets from being attached by claims of creditors. The lawyer should check state law before advising a client of the effect of this provision.

---

7. <u>Definitions.</u> For all purposes of this instrument, the following shall apply:

a. The words "child," "children," "descendant" or "descendants" shall exclude adopted persons unless they are adopted prior to [insert age] years; and shall include only persons legitimately born unless a decree of adoption terminates the parental rights of the natural mother during her lifetime, or the natural father signs a written notarized instrument during his lifetime in which he irrevocably states that the child is to be considered legitimately born for purposes of inheriting under this will.

COMMENT: Some clients will want to restrict distribution for an adopted child to preclude a child adopted as an adult. Thus, many will use the age 18 or perhaps a slightly older age such as 20 or 21. Other clients may wish to restrict the age to a younger adopted child, such as under the age of 10. The issue of illegitimate children should also be addressed. In many situations, a child or more remote descendant should be treated the same as any other child, in which case the portion of this paragraph that deals with illegitimate children can be deleted. In other situations there may be a limited or no relationship with the child, in which event no distribution should be made to that child. This form gives the parent of the child the right to allow them to inherit by the father signing a written document allowing inheritance.

b. Whenever assets are to be divided and allocated per stirpes, the assets to be divided or allocated shall be divided into as many equal shares as are necessary to divide or allocate one share to each then living child of such person and to provide one share collectively for the then living descendants of each child of such person who then is deceased leaving one or more descendants then living. Any collective share shall be divided and allocated per stirpes among the descendants of such deceased person in accordance with the preceding sentence.

COMMENT: Since the term per stirpes is used often in this document, a definition is provided of that term. The lawyer should modify this definition to conform with his or her own state law should it differ any from this definition. Of course, a definition is not essential, since the term will be defined under state law. But since it is a term that clients are not familiar with, it is often helpful to define it for them in the document. An excellent ABA resource that explains the term per stirpes and its variations is Jeffrey N. Penell and Alan Newman, *Estate and Trust Planning,* American Bar Association (Chicago, 2005) pp. 19–26.

---

8. Trustee Powers. In the administration of the trusts, the trustee shall have the following powers and rights and all others granted by law:

a. To sell publicly or privately any trust property, for cash or on time, without an order of court and upon such terms and conditions as my trustee deems proper; and no person dealing with my trustee shall have any obligation to look to the application of the purchase money.

b. To invest and reinvest all or any part of the principal of the trust in any stocks, bonds, mortgages, shares or interests in common trust funds, mutual funds, or other securities or property, real, personal, or mixed, and of any kind or nature whatsoever, as the trustee deems proper, and without diversification if the trustee deems it advisable, irrespective of whether or not such securities or property are eligible for trust investment under state or any other law, and may change any investment received or made by the trustee, and may hold cash if the trustee deems it advisable.

c. To exercise broad discretion as to diversification of trust property, and shall not be required to reduce any concentrated holdings merely because of such concentration, and shall have full discretion as to the percentage to be invested in fixed income securities, and is specifically relieved from any requirements, legal or otherwise, as to the percentage of the trust assets to be invested in fixed income securities, and may invest or retain invested any trust estates wholly in common stocks.

d. To sell, convey, lease or mortgage, repair and improve, and take any and all other steps with regard to any real estate that may at any time be a part of the principal of the trust; and any lease of such real property or contract with regard thereto made by the trustee shall be binding for the full period of the lease or contract, even though the period shall extend beyond the termination of the trust.

e. To vote shares of stock held in the trust at stockholders' meetings in person or by special, limited, or general proxy, with or without power of substitution, as seems best to the trustee.

f. To participate in the liquidation, reorganization, consolidation, incorporation and reincorporation, or any other financial readjustment of any corporation, limited liability company or business in which the trust is, or shall be financially interested.

g. To borrow money from any source for any purpose connected with the protection, preservation, improvement or development of the trust hereunder, whenever in the trustee's judgment the trustee deems it advisable, and as security to mortgage or pledge any real estate or personal property forming a part of the trust upon such terms and conditions as the trustee may deem advisable.

h. To hold any and all securities in bearer form, in the trustee's own name, or the name of some other person, partnership, or corporation, or in the name of a duly appointed nominee, with or without disclosing the fiduciary ownership.

i. To divide the principal of the trust property into parts or shares and to distribute or allot same, and to make such division in cash or in kind or both. For the purpose of such division or allotment, the judgment of the trustee concerning the propriety thereof and relative value of property so distributed or allotted shall be binding and conclusive with respect to all interested persons.

j. To merge and consolidate the trust property of any separate trust held hereunder with other trusts and then to administer such trust property as a single trust provided the separate trust is for the benefit of the same persons with substantially the same terms, conditions and federal tax consequences.

k. To pay such income and principal during the minority or incapacity of any beneficiary for whose benefit income and principal may be expended, in any one or more of the following ways: (1) directly to the beneficiary; (2) to the legal guardian or committee of the beneficiary; (3) to a relative of the beneficiary to be expended by the relative for the maintenance, health, and education of the beneficiary; or (4) by expending the same directly for the maintenance, health, and education of the beneficiary. The trustee shall not be obliged to see to the application of the funds so expended, but the receipt of such person shall be full acquittance to the trustee.

l. To continue and operate any business owned by me at my death and to do any and all things deemed appropriate by the trustee, including the power to form a limited liability company or incorporate the business and to put additional capital into the business, for such time as the trustee deems advisable, without liability for loss resulting from the continuance or operation of the business except for the trustee's own negligence; and to close out, liquidate, or sell the business at such time and upon such terms as the trustee deems proper, and in this connection a sale may be made (pursuant to an agreement entered into by me during my lifetime, or otherwise) to a partner, officer, member, employee or beneficiary under this trust. I am aware of the fact that certain risks are inherent in the operation of any business and, therefore, my trustee shall not be liable for any loss resulting from the retention and operation of any business unless such loss results directly from my trustee's gross negligence or willful misconduct.

m. To have the same powers, authorities, and discretions in the management of the trust as I would have in the management and control of my own personal assets. The trustee may continue to exercise any powers and discretions granted in this instrument for a reasonable period after the termination of any trust under this instrument.

COMMENT: The above powers are a set of standard powers that appear throughout this book. The powers should be reviewed to be certain that you the lawyer understand each power, the client is in agreement with each of the powers granted and that the powers granted are needed. Because this is a generic and broad statement of powers, some of these powers may not be necessary. For example, powers to sell or lease real estate are not needed if the grantor knows the trust will consist only of cash and other intangible investments.

---

9. <u>Limitations on Powers of Individual Trustee.</u> Notwithstanding any other powers granted to my trustee in this instrument, an individual trustee (a) shall have no power to make payments or distributions that would discharge the trustee's legal obligation to support the trust beneficiary, (b) shall not exercise any power or discretion in any manner that would be deemed to be a general power of appointment under Internal Revenue Code Section 2041, (c) shall be limited by the ascertainable standard of "maintenance, support, health and education" when making payments

or distributions to the trustee personally or to anyone for whom the trustee has a beneficial interest, and (d) shall possess no incidence of ownership or powers with respect to life insurance in which the trustee is the insured and has fiduciary power over such life insurance.

COMMENT: There are some situations in which an individual trustee may have adverse estate or income tax consequences when given broad powers as trustee. If a corporate trustee is used, then this paragraph is not needed. But an individual trustee must be certain that acting as trustee does not result in any adverse estate or income tax consequences. This paragraph is intended to ensure that adverse tax consequences are avoided if overly broad powers are granted in the trust instrument. The lawyer is urged to exercise caution when using individual trustees coupled with broad discretionary powers of income and principal distribution to a trust beneficiary because of possible adverse tax consequences. An ABA resource to acquaint oneself with these issues is L. Rush Hunt and Lara Rae Hunt, *A Lawyer's Guide to Estate Planning,* American Bar Association (Chicago: 2004) §14.4.

---

10. <u>Trustee Resignation.</u> My trustee may resign at any time by giving written notice to my successor trustee named below, if any, and if none, then written notice shall be given to each current adult income beneficiary who is then living.

COMMENT: If a trustee resigns, there must be some method of notice and appointment of a successor trustee. This paragraph provides a method of notification. It is not an essential trust provision, but is a helpful one.

---

11. <u>Trustee Succession and Appointment.</u> If I cease to act as trustee due to death, incompetency, resignation or cease to serve for any reason, then [Name of successor trustee] shall serve as successor trustee. If [Name of successor trustee] dies, becomes incompetent, resigns or ceases to serve for any reason, then [Name of second successor trustee] shall serve as successor trustee. The last serving successor trustee may name [his or her] own successor trustee by a written instrument delivered to the successor trustee or by will. The successor trustee may be an individual or a financial institution possessing trust powers under state or federal law. Any further vacancy in the office of trustee shall be filled by decision of the probate court where I resided at the time of my death.

COMMENT: A decision must be made as to succession of trustees and the method of appointing a successor trustee if all of those named successor trustees are unable to serve. It is also essential to clarify whether successor trustees must only be financial institutions or if individuals may also be considered. Once a decision is made as to the succession of trustees, then the last three sentences should be reviewed to be certain to what extent each of those are needed.

---

12. <u>Powers of Successor Trustee.</u> Each successor trustee shall have the same rights, titles, powers, duties, discretions, and immunities and otherwise be in the same position as if originally named trustee. No successor trustee shall be personally liable for any act or failure to act of a predecessor trustee. Further, a successor trustee may accept the account furnished and the property delivered by or for a predecessor trustee without liability for so doing, and such acceptance shall be a full and complete discharge to the predecessor trustee.

COMMENT: This paragraph clarifies that a successor trustee has the same powers as the initial trustee. Further, the paragraph relieves the successor trustee from liability for the prior acts of the resigning trustee and waives any requirements of audit or inquiry into the activities of the prior trustee. This is essential for any successor trustee.

13. <u>Compensation of Trustee.</u> **OPTION 1: Corporate trustee compensation** A corporate trustee shall receive compensation in accordance with its regular schedule of fees in effect at the time such services are rendered.

OPTION 2: Individual does not receive compensation An individual trustee shall not be paid any compensation, but shall be reimbursed for out-of-pocket expenses.

OPTION 3: Individual does receive compensation An individual trustee shall be paid [insert amount of compensation] as compensation for such services and shall be reimbursed for out-of-pocket expenses.

COMMENT: Three options are provided, but the actual drafting of this paragraph may be different than each of these options. If the only trustee to be used is a corporate trustee, then Option 1 is a standard trust provision. If there is a possibility of individual trustees, then care should be given to the method for setting this fee. If no fee is to be paid because the trustee is a close family member, then it is suggested that Option 2 be used. If the grantor expects a fee to be charged, then an amount or a formula, such as a percentage of income or principal, must be set. It is unwise to simply provide for compensation to be a reasonable fee, as that leaves an individual trustee with great uncertainty as to the fee to be charged. Without the grantor clarifying compensation, the trustee could find him or herself in litigation with the beneficiary.

14. <u>Court Accountings.</u> To the extent such requirements can be waived, the trustee shall not be required (a) to file any inventory of trust property or accounts or reports of the administration of the trusts, or to register the trusts, in any court, (b) to furnish any bond or other security for the proper performance of the trustee's duties or (c) to obtain authority from a court for the exercise of any power conferred on the trustee by this instrument. This waiver does not preclude the trustee from registering any trust created in this instrument and petitioning a court having jurisdiction over registered trusts for a judicial ruling on any matter relating to administration of any trust created in this instrument.

COMMENT: The first sentence is to clarify the normal situation that an inter vivos trust is not subject to judicial oversight. The second sentence may be omitted, but is suggested as a potential benefit in some states. In a state in which a trust can be registered, it may be possible to have minor trust matters resolved by the court in which the trust is registered. This creates a simplified process for dealing with minor administrative matters. Without this provision, a court might be reluctant to decide matters for a trust which is not required to be registered under state law.

15. <u>Severability.</u> If any provisions of this trust shall be unenforceable, the remaining provisions shall nevertheless be carried into effect.

COMMENT: This is the same type of standard provision often seen in contracts that is intended to save the document if a particular provision is found to be invalid or void. It is doubtful this provision will have any practical effect in most trust situations, but it is a "boilerplate" provision that is frequently found in trust instruments and for which there is no disadvantage.

16. <u>Certification of Incompetency.</u> **OPTION 1: Decided by treating physician** Any person acting or named to act as a trustee in this instrument is considered to be unable to serve or to continue serving when a physician whom such person has consulted within the prior three years has certified as to such consultation and the certification states that the person is incapable of managing the affairs of the trusts I have established in this instrument, regardless of cause and regardless of whether there is an adjudication of incompetency. No person shall be liable to anyone for actions taken in reliance on the physician's certification or for dealing with a trustee other than the one removed for incompetency based on such certification.

OPTION 2: Decided by two physicians Any person acting or named to act as a trustee in this instrument is considered to be unable to serve or to continue serving when a written certification is received from two (2) physicians, both of whom have personally examined the person and at least one (1) of whom is board-certified in the specialty most closely associated with the health condition alleged to cause such incompetency. The certification must state that the person is incapable of managing the affairs of this trust, regardless of cause and regardless of whether there is an adjudication of incompetence. No person is liable to anyone for actions taken in reliance on these certifications, or for dealing with a trustee other than the one removed for incompetency based on these certifications.

COMMENT: This provision relates back to paragraph 11 concerning the succession of trustees. It defines incompetency, which is one of those events requiring a successor trustee. The first option involves consultation with the trustee's personal physician, whereas Option 2 involves a panel of two physicians, one of whom is board certified in the speciality most closely associated with the health condition of the trustee. Clients differ as to which provision they prefer and are more concerned about the provision when the grantor is also the initial trustee. Absent a strong preference by the grantor, Option 1 is the provision most frequently used.

17. <u>Titles and References.</u> The underscored titles of paragraphs in this instrument are for information purposes only and shall be given no legal effect.

COMMENT: This is another common "boilerplate" provision that is perhaps not essential, but for which there is no disadvantage.

18. <u>Governing Law.</u> The laws of the State of [insert state] shall govern the interpretation and validity of the provisions of this instrument and all questions relating to the management, administration, investment, and distribution of the trusts hereby created.

COMMENT: It is a standard provision in both trust instruments and in contracts to specify the state law that applies in interpretation of the instrument. This will usually be the grantor's state of residency but also the state in which the lawyer is licensed to practice.

19. <u>No-Contest.</u> If any beneficiary of this trust, or the guardian or legal representative of such beneficiary, contests the validity of this trust or of any of its provisions or shall institute or join in (except as a party defendant) any proceeding to contest the validity of this trust or to prevent any provision of it from being carried out in accordance with its terms (regardless of whether or not such proceedings are instituted in good faith and with probable cause), then all benefits provided for such beneficiary hereunder are revoked and such benefits shall pass as if such beneficiary and such beneficiary's descendants all had predeceased me.

COMMENT: This provision or some variation of it should be considered if there is any concern that a beneficiary or heir-at-law may challenge the trust. The lawyer may need to modify this provision to meet any requirements of state law.

20. <u>Power To Amend or Revoke.</u> I reserve the right from time to time by written instrument delivered to the trustee to amend or revoke this instrument and the trusts hereby evidenced, in whole or in part.

COMMENT: This instrument is revocable thus permitting the grantor to make any amendments he or she chooses or to revoke the trust in its entirety.

The undersigned has signed this instrument and has established the foregoing trust on this the _____ day of _____, [Current year].

GRANTOR AND TRUSTEE:

_____
[Grantor]

STATE OF [State of notary])
) SCT.
COUNTY OF [County of notary])

The undersigned, a Notary Public within and for the state and county aforesaid, does hereby certify that the foregoing trust agreement executed by [Grantor], as grantor and trustee, was on this day produced to me in my county by [Grantor], who executed, acknowledged and swore the same before me to be [his or her] act and deed in due form of law.

Given under my hand and notarial seal on this the _____ day of _____, [Current year].

_____

Notary Public, State at Large

My commission expires:_____

PREPARED BY:

_____
[Name of Attorney]
[Name of Law Firm]
Attorneys at Law
[Street Address]
[City], [State] [Zip Code]
[Telephone Number]

SCHEDULE A

[NAME OF TRUST] TRUST

Cash. . . . . $ 10.00

The lawyer will note a deposit of $10 in the trust. State law will determine the necessity of an initial deposit. An unfunded trust that contains no principal may be deemed a "dry" trust under state law, meaning that it is not a valid document. Some lawyers go to the added step of affixing a $10 bill to schedule A, while others are satisfied with a cash deposit which does have the disadvantage of not being traceable. If there is the possibility of a contest of the trust, the cautious practice would be to affix a $10 bill to schedule A.

CHILD'S EDUCATIONAL TRUST WITH WITHDRAWAL RIGHTS WORKSHEET

1. **Grantor Information**

    1.1 Grantor Name_____

    1.2 Grantor City and State _____

2. **Trustee Information**

    2.1 Trustee Name _____

    2.2 Trustee City and State _____

3. **Name of Trust**

    "_____ Trust"

4. **Beneficiary Information**

    4.1 Name of Child _____

    4.2 Child's Date of Birth _____

    4.3 If Beneficiary not Child, describe _____

5. **Child's Trust**

    5.1 If child dies, distribute to child's estate? (Option 1) <u>Yes / No</u>
       or per stirpes to lineal descendants? (Option 2) <u>Yes / No</u>

    5.2 Is trust to terminate prior to child's death? <u>Yes / No</u>
       (If yes, see Single Trust Paragraph 5, Option 2 at page 63)

6. **Withdrawal Rights for Beneficiary**

    Greater of $5,000 or 5% of principal value? (Option 1) <u>Yes / No</u>

    Amount of annual federal gift tax exclusion? (Option 2) <u>Yes / No</u>

7. **Default Provisions (if needed) if All Named Beneficiaries Deceased:**

    _____

    _____

    _____

8. **Definition of "Child" and "Descendant"**

    Include child adopted prior to age _____ (18, 21, etc.)

    Include provision for illegitimate children (treated same, etc.)? <u>Yes / No</u>
       (If no, modify paragraph 7.a)

9. **Powers**

    Environmental Powers? <u>Yes / No</u> (See Single Trust Paragraph 11 at page 73)

    Farm Powers? <u>Yes / No</u> (See Single Trust Paragraph 12 beginning at page 73)

    Limitation on Trustee Powers? <u>Yes / No</u>

10. **Trustees**

    Name of initial trustee: _____

    Name of first successor trustee: _____

    Name of second successor trustee: _____

    Corporate trustee compensation? (Option 1) <u>Yes / No</u>

    Individual reimbursed for expenses but no compensation? (Option 2) <u>Yes / No</u>

    Individual receives compensation? (Option 3) <u>Yes / No</u>

        Amount of compensation: $_____

11. **Incompetency**

    One physician decides? (Option 1) <u>Yes / No</u>

    Two physicians decide and one board certified? (Option 2) <u>Yes / No</u>

12. **No Contest Provision**

    Is No Contest Provision needed? <u>Yes / No</u>

CHILD'S EDUCATIONAL TRUST WITH WITHDRAWAL RIGHTS

There are a number of options for creating an educational fund for a child. This trust represents one of these options and is designed to permit regular gifts to the trust that qualify for the annual gift tax exclusion in order to create over a term of years, a trust fund that will provide for a child's education. This trust is designed to take advantage of the so called "Crummey" withdrawal rights. At this writing, the current annual gift tax exclusion is $13,000 per year or twice that amount if gift-splitting is used by a married couple. Thus, over a term of years, a large trust fund can be created for a child. A disadvantage is that to receive the gift tax exclusion, the child must have a limited right of withdrawal of the amount contributed by the grantor. This is not a significant disadvantage and will be discussed subsequently. An excellent ABA resource is Carmina Y. D'Aversa, *Tax, Estate, and Lifetime Planning for Minors,* American Bar Association (Chicago: 2006).

I, [grantor's name], currently of [grantor's city], [grantor's state], as grantor and [trustee's name], currently of [trustee's city], [trustee's state], as trustee hereby enter into this trust agreement, and I transfer to my trustee the property described in Schedule A. This property and all investments, reinvestments and additions which may sometimes be referred to in this instrument as the "trust property" or "trust assets" are to be held subject to the following provisions:

COMMENT: The grantor cannot be the trustee of this trust. To do so will result in the trust being a taxable asset of the grantor's estate. This trust was drafted assuming a separate trustee who is an independent third party—either an individual or a financial institution. If the grantor intends to use his or her spouse or another family member, consideration should be given as to whether or not a fiduciary power as trustee could be deemed a power that would result in inclusion of the trust assets in the trustee's own estate for estate tax purposes, or result in an income tax liability to the trustee. For a discussion of the issues involved in naming an individual trustee, see L. Rush Hunt and Lara Rae Hunt, *A Lawyer's Guide to Estate Planning,* American Bar Association (Chicago: 2004) §14.4.

---

1. <u>Name of Trust.</u> This instrument and the initial trust hereby established may be named the "[Name of trust] Trust."

COMMENT: Typically, the trust name will be the name of the child, but another name may be used.

---

2. <u>Beneficiary Information.</u> My child [name of child] whose date of birth is [insert date of birth] is the beneficiary of this trust and references to "my child" or "the beneficiary" are only to [him or her].

COMMENT: This paragraph is drafted for a beneficiary who is the child of the grantor. If the beneficiary is not a child, then the relationship should be inserted in lieu of the word "child" followed by the full name of the person who is the beneficiary. If the beneficiary is someone other than a child, then appropriate changes should also be made to change the reference to "my child" in paragraph 3 to the appropriate relationship. It is not essential to include the beneficiary's date of birth. This can be retained or deleted as deemed appropriate.

---

3. <u>Trust Provisions for Child.</u> The trustee shall hold and administer the trust property, including property which the trustee receives under my will or from any other source as follows:

a. The trustee may pay to or use all, part or none, of the income and principal of my child's trust as the trustee believes appropriate for the reasonable maintenance, support, health and education (including college or graduate, professional or vocational school education) of my child, considering my child's income or assets and all other circumstances and factors the trustee believes pertinent. It is my desire that distributions of income and principal not impair my child's motivation to be productive and self-supporting, thus my trustee shall not make distributions of income and principal from my child's trust if my child is not productive, mature, and responsible. If any net income remains undistributed at the end of each calendar year (excluding income distributed during the sixty-five [65] day period under Internal Revenue Code Section 663), the trustee shall add it to the principal of my child's trust.

COMMENT: The first sentence provides broad discretion to the trustee in making distributions for the child, but is limited to avoid adverse tax consequences that may befall an individual trustee. The second sentence is not essential, but is provided to illustrate a possible restriction that the grantor may desire. The third sentence can be eliminated, but is provided for situations in which income is not distributed before year end; and to set the time at which accumulated income is added to trust principal.

b. Upon the death of my child, the trustee shall distribute the trust assets in such proportions and in such manner, outright or in trust or otherwise, to or for the benefit of any one or more persons or entities as my child may appoint by specific reference to the power of appointment in my child's last will and testament admitted to probate, including the power of my child to appoint the trust property or any part of it to my child's own estate, my child's creditors or the creditors of my child's estate. If my child fails to exercise this power of appointment, then the trust principal and undistributed income of my child's trust shall be divided and allocated per stirpes among the then living lineal descendants of my child, if any, or, if none, such child's trust shall be divided and allocated per stirpes among my then living lineal descendants.

COMMENT: There is a gift tax problem associated with a gift to a person who does not exercise the withdrawal right in paragraph 5 below. The problem exists due to the annual gift tax exclusion ($13,000 per donee, or $26,000 with gift-splitting) exceeding the $5,000 or 5% of the value of the trust assets requirement under the power of appointment rules in IRC Section 2514(e). The problem arises because the demand power is a general power of appointment, and to the extent it exceeds the greater of $5,000 or 5% of the trust assets, the failure to exercise the power (which should not be exercised) by the beneficiary results in a taxable gift to the contingent remainder beneficiaries. Option 1 in the withdrawal power in paragraph 5 limits the withdrawal to the "5 and 5" requirement which eliminates the gift tax problem. Until the trust principal exceeds $100,000, this solution limits the annual gift to $5,000. If this option is selected, paragraph 3.b above can be modified as desired as the requirement of a general appointment is not needed. If Option 2 in paragraph 5 is used in order to increase the annual gift to the trust to the $13,000 annual gift to the trust or $26,000 with gift-splitting, then paragraph 3.b should be used. An excellent ABA resource that provides a further discussion of this tax problem and its various solutions is Louis A. Mezzullo, *An Estate Planner's Guide to Life Insurance,* American Bar Association (Chicago, 2000).

COMMENT: The per stirpes distribution is a default if the power is not exercised, and in some situations is more complicated than one might assume. Care should be taken in drafting this provision. A good ABA resource that reviews this issue in detail is Jeffrey N. Penell and Alan Newman, *Estate and Trust Planning,* American Bar Association (Chicago, 2005) pp. 19-26.

Distribution shall be made outright to such descendant or descendants unless: (i) distribution is to be made to a descendant for whom a trust then held under this trust instrument is named in which event such distribution shall be added to that trust, or (ii) distribution is to be made to a descendant who has not reached the age of [Age of remote descendants] years in which event, the trustee shall retain any property otherwise distributable to such descendant as a separate trust named for such descendant to be distributed to such descendant when he or she reaches the age of [Age for remote descendants] years. If such descendant is already [Age for remote descendants] years of age, then such descendant shall receive his or her share outright. Until such descendant reaches [Age for remote descendants] years of age, the trustee shall distribute the income and principal of a trust so retained in such amounts, if any, and at such times as the trustee believes appropriate for the reasonable maintenance, support, health and education (including college or graduate, professional or vocational school education) of the descendant for whom the trust is named, considering such descendant's income or assets and all other circumstances and factors the trustee believes pertinent. It is my desire that distributions of income and principal not impair a descendant's motivation to be productive and self-supporting, thus my trustee shall not make distributions of income and principal from a descendant's trust if my descendant is not productive, mature, and responsible. If any net income remains undistributed at the end of each calendar year (excluding income distributed during the sixty-five (65) day period under Internal Revenue Code Section 663), the trustee shall add it to the principal of the trust.

OPTION 1: If a descendant for whom a trust held under this paragraph is named dies prior to termination of such descendant's trust, then such descendant's trust shall terminate and the trust property shall be distributed to such descendant's own estate.

OPTION 2: On the death of a descendant for whom a trust held under this paragraph is named, any principal and undistributed income of such descendant's trust shall be divided and allocated per stirpes among the then living lineal descendants of such descendant, if any, or, if none, such person's trust shall be divided and allocated per stirpes among my then living lineal descendants.

COMMENT: The above provisions permit a distribution to a more remote descendant to be distributed to that person's own trust if he or she is a recipient of a trust under this instrument, or if not and the remote descendant is under a specified minimum age, then the trustee shall hold that person's share in trust until that person reaches the minimum age with the trust property to be used for that person until termination of the trust. If this option is used, then Option 1 or 2 above should be selected to determine to whom the trust property is distributed should that remote descendant die before termination of the trust. Care must be taken to be certain that the per stirpes distribution provided in this form is adequate. This provision should not be used routinely without an analysis of its effect under the facts of the particular estate plan.

4. <u>Default Provisions.</u> Any trust property not disposed of by any of the above provisions shall be distributed on the date of such failure of disposition to [default provisions].

COMMENT: If there are a limited number of beneficiaries, then it may be wise to insert a default provision naming the ultimate recipient should all named beneficiaries and their descendants be deceased. If that is too remote of a possibility, some clients will choose that this paragraph be deleted.

5. <u>Withdrawal Rights.</u> Following any addition to the trust, my child shall have the unrestricted right to withdraw an amount equal to **OPTION 1:** the greater of five thousand dollars ($5,000) or five percent (5%) of the value of the principal of the trust. **OPTION 2:** the annual per-donee federal gift tax exclusion, including the amount of the gift tax exclusion if gift-splitting is elected by the donor of the gift. This right of withdrawal is non-cumulative and shall lapse thirty (30) calendar days following the date of the addition, but in no event later than December 31 in the year of the addition. In the event my child is under the age of eighteen (18) years or under any legal disability, this right of withdrawal may be exercised by my child's legal guardian, if any, and if none, the trustee shall designate an appropriate adult individual (other than myself) who may make the demand on behalf of my child. My trustee shall provide written notice to my child, or to my child's guardian or the adult designated by my trustee, as soon as it is reasonably possible to do so after the trustee receives the addition to the trust.

COMMENT: A gift to a trust does not normally qualify for the annual gift tax exclusion as it is a gift of a future interest. The annual gift tax exclusion is only available for a present interest gift. In order to create a trust in which a gift to the trust qualifies as a present interest, the trust beneficiary must be given a right of withdrawal of the gift. That is the purpose of this withdrawal right. There are several alternatives for the withdrawal right. Option 1 is the safest, as it only permits a withdrawal of the greater of $5,000 or 5% of the trust principal. Until the trust principal exceeds $100,000, $5,000 will be the greater amount. A withdrawal right limited in this manner results in no adverse gift tax consequences to the child as discussed above in the comment to paragraph 3. Option 2 permits a larger gift that still results in no adverse gift tax consequences to the child due to the power of appointment in paragraph 3.b above. If paragraph 3.b is not appropriate, then Option 1 is the better option.

COMMENT: To ensure that the child has the opportunity to exercise the right of withdrawal, the trustee must send a letter to the child, the child's guardian, or the person designated by the trustee to receive notice and make demand on behalf of the child of the gift to the trust. This should be a letter from the trustee to that person stating the amount of the gift, the date of the gift, and the period of time during which the person may exercise this right. This requirement must be adhered to and no effort should be made to have the right waived. A letter must be given each time a gift is made to the trust. Wise practice is for the trustee to retain copies of all letters.

6. <u>Protection from Creditors.</u> No trust beneficiary shall have the right to sell, transfer, assign, alienate, pledge, or in any way encumber trust assets, including income and principal, nor shall trust assets be subject to execution, levy, sale, garnishment, attachment, bankruptcy, or other legal proceedings. Any such actions by a trust beneficiary or a third party seeking to enforce a claim against the trust assets shall not be recognized under any circumstances by the trustee. These provisions do not prevent the trustee from making distributions for the benefit of a trust beneficiary in such amounts and at such times as the trustee determines necessary for the trust beneficiary's maintenance, support, health and education.

COMMENT: This is a standard paragraph that precludes the trust assets from being attached by claims of creditors.

7. Definitions. For all purposes of this instrument, the following shall apply:

a. The words "child," "descendant" or "descendants" shall exclude adopted persons unless they are adopted prior to [insert age] years; and shall include only persons legitimately born unless a decree of adoption terminates the parental rights of the natural mother during her lifetime, or the natural father signs a written notarized instrument during his lifetime in which he irrevocably states that the child is to be considered legitimately born for purposes of inheriting under this will.

COMMENT: Some clients will want to restrict distribution for an adopted descendant to preclude a child adopted as an adult. Thus, many clients will use the age 18 or perhaps a slightly older age such as 20 or 21. Other clients may wish to restrict the age to a younger adopted child, such as one under the age of 10. The issue of illegitimate descendants should also be considered. In many situations, a child or more remote descendant should be treated the same as any other child, in which case the portion of this paragraph that deals with illegitimate children can be deleted. In other situations there may be a limited or no relationship with the child, in which event no distribution should be made to that child. This form gives the father of the child the right to allow the child to inherit if the father signs a written document allowing the inheritance.

b. Whenever assets are to be divided and allocated per stirpes, the assets to be divided or allocated shall be divided into as many equal shares as are necessary to divide or allocate one share to each then living child of such person and to provide one share collectively for the then living descendants of each child of such person who then is deceased leaving one or more descendants then living. Any collective share shall be divided and allocated per stirpes among the descendants of such deceased person in accordance with the preceding sentence.

COMMENT: Since the term per stirpes is used often in this document, a definition is provided of that term. The lawyer should modify this definition to conform with his or her own state law should it differ any from this definition. Of course, a definition is not essential, since the term will be defined under state law. But since it is a term that clients are not familiar with, it is often helpful to define it for them in the document. An excellent ABA resource that discusses this issue in detail is Jeffrey N. Penell and Alan Newman, *Estate and Trust Planning,* American Bar Association (Chicago, 2005) pp. 19–26.

8. Trustee Powers. In the administration of the trusts, the trustee shall have the following powers and rights and all others granted by law:

a. To sell publicly or privately any trust property, for cash or on time, without an order of court, upon such terms and conditions as my trustee deems proper; and no person dealing with my trustee shall have any obligation to look to the application of the purchase money.

b. To invest and reinvest all or any part of the principal of the trust in any stocks, bonds, mortgages, shares, or interests in common trust funds, mutual funds, or other securities or property, real, personal, or mixed, and of any kind or nature whatsoever, as the trustee deems proper, and without diversification if the trustee deems it advisable, irrespective of whether or not such securities or property are eligible for trust investment under state or any other law, and may change any investment received or made by the trustee, and may hold cash if the trustee deems it advisable.

c. To exercise broad discretion as to diversification of trust property, and shall not be required to reduce any concentrated holdings merely because of such concentration, and shall have full discretion as to the percentage to be invested in fixed income securities, and is specifically relieved from any requirements, legal or otherwise, as to the percentage of the trust assets to be invested in fixed income securities, and may invest or retain invested any trust estates wholly in common stocks.

d. To sell, convey, lease or mortgage, repair and improve, and take any and all other steps with regard to any real estate that may at any time be a part of the principal of the trust; and any lease of such real property or contract with regard thereto made by the trustee shall be binding for the full period of the lease or contract, even though said period shall extend beyond the termination of the trust.

e. To vote shares of stock held in the trust at stockholders' meetings in person or by special, limited, or general proxy, with or without power of substitution, as seems best to the trustee.

f. To participate in the liquidation, reorganization, consolidation, incorporation and reincorporation, or any other financial readjustment of any limited liability company, corporation or business in which the trust is or shall be financially interested.

g. To borrow money from any source for any purpose connected with the protection, preservation, improvement or development of the trust hereunder, whenever in the trustee's judgment the trustee deems it advisable, and as security to mortgage or pledge any real estate or personal property forming a part of the trust upon such terms and conditions as the trustee may deem advisable.

h. To hold any and all securities in bearer form, in the trustee's own name, or the name of some other person, partnership, or corporation, or in the name of a duly appointed nominee, with or without disclosing the fiduciary ownership thereof.

i. To divide the principal of the trust property into parts or shares and to distribute or allot same, and to make such division in cash or in kind or both. For the purpose of such division or allotment, the judgment of the trustee concerning the propriety thereof and relative value of property so distributed or allotted shall be binding and conclusive with respect to all interested persons.

j. To merge and consolidate the trust property of any separate trust held hereunder with other trusts and then to administer such trust property as a single trust provided the separate trust is for the benefit of the same persons with substantially the same terms, conditions and federal tax consequences.

k. To pay such income and principal during the minority or incapacity of any beneficiary for whose benefit income and principal may be expended, in any one or more of the following ways: (1) directly to the beneficiary; (2) to the legal guardian or committee of the beneficiary; (3) to a relative of the beneficiary to be expended by the relative for the maintenance, health, and education of the beneficiary; or (4) by expending the same directly for the maintenance, health, and education of the beneficiary. The trustee shall not be obliged to see to the application of the funds so paid, but the receipt of such person shall be full acquittance to the trustee.

l. To continue and operate any business owned by me at my death and to do any and all things deemed appropriate by the trustee, including the power to form a limited liability company or incorporate the business and to put additional capital into the business, for such time as the trustee deems advisable, without liability for loss resulting from the continuance or operation of the business except for the trustee's own negligence; and to close out, liquidate, or sell the business at such time and upon such terms as the trustee deems proper, and in this connection a sale may be made (pursuant to an agreement entered into by me during my lifetime, or otherwise) to a partner, officer, member, employee or beneficiary under this trust. I am aware of the fact that certain risks are inherent in the operation of any business and, therefore, my trustee shall not be liable for any loss resulting from the retention and operation of any business unless such loss results directly from my trustee's gross negligence or willful misconduct.

m. To have the same powers, authorities, and discretions in the management of the trust as I would have in the management and control of my own personal assets. The trustee may continue to exercise any powers and discretions granted in this instrument for a reasonable period after the termination of any trust under this instrument.

COMMENT: The above powers are a set of standard powers that appear throughout this book. The powers should be reviewed to be certain that you the lawyer understand each power, the client is in agreement with each of the powers granted and that the powers granted are needed. Because this is a generic and broad statement of powers, some of these powers may not be necessary. For example, powers to sell or lease real estate are not needed if the grantor knows the trust will consist only of cash and other intangible investments.

---

9. <u>Limitation on Powers of Individual Trustee.</u> Notwithstanding any other powers granted to my trustee in this instrument, an individual trustee (a) shall have no power to make payments or distributions that would discharge the trustee's legal obligation to support the trust beneficiary, (b) shall not exercise any power or discretion in any manner that would be deemed to be a general power of appointment under Internal Revenue Code Section 2041, (c) shall be limited by the ascertainable standard of "maintenance, support, health and education" when making payments or distributions to the trustee personally or to anyone for whom the trustee has a beneficial interest, and (d) shall possess no incidence of ownership or powers with respect to life insurance in which the trustee is the insured and has fiduciary power over such life insurance.

COMMENT: There are some situations in which an individual trustee may have adverse estate or income tax consequences when given broad powers as trustee. If a corporate trustee is used, then this paragraph is not needed. But an individual trustee must be certain that acting as trustee does not result in any adverse estate or income tax consequences. This paragraph is intended to ensure that adverse tax consequences are avoided if overly broad powers are granted in the trust instrument. The lawyer is urged to exercise caution when using individual trustees coupled with broad discretionary powers of income and principal distribution to a trust beneficiary because of possible adverse tax consequences. An ABA resource to acquaint oneself with these issues is L. Rush Hunt and Lara Rae Hunt, *A Lawyer's Guide to Estate Planning,* American Bar Association (Chicago: 2004) §14.4.

---

10. <u>Trustee Resignation.</u> My trustee may resign at any time by giving written notice to my successor trustee named below, if any, and if none, then written notice shall be given to each current adult income beneficiary who is then living.

COMMENT: If a trustee resigns, there must be some method of notice and appointment of a successor trustee. This paragraph provides a method of notification. It is not an essential trust provision, but is a helpful one.

---

11. <u>Trustee Succession and Appointment.</u> If [trustee's name] dies, becomes incompetent, resigns or ceases to serve for any reason, then [insert name of first successor trustee] shall serve as successor trustee. If [insert name of first successor trustee] dies, becomes incompetent, resigns or ceases to serve for any reason, then [insert name of second successor trustee] shall serve as successor trustee. The last serving successor trustee may name [his or her] own successor trustee by a written instrument delivered to the successor trustee or by will. The successor trustee may be an individual or a financial institution possessing trust powers under state or federal law. Any further vacancy in the office of trustee shall be filled by decision of the probate court where I resided at the time of my death.

COMMENT: A decision must be made as to succession of trustees and the method of appointing a successor trustee if those named successor trustees are unable to serve. It is also essential to clarify whether successor trustees must only be financial institutions or if individuals may also be considered. Once a decision is made as to the succession of trustees, then the last three sentences should be reviewed to be certain to what extent each of those are needed.

---

12. <u>Powers of Successor Trustee.</u> Each successor trustee shall have the same rights, titles, powers, duties, discretions, and immunities and otherwise be in the same position as if originally named trustee. No successor trustee shall be personally liable for any act or failure to act of a predecessor trustee. Further, a successor trustee may accept the account furnished and the property delivered by or for a predecessor trustee without liability for so doing, and such acceptance shall be a full and complete discharge to the predecessor trustee.

COMMENT: This paragraph clarifies that a successor trustee has the same powers as the initial trustee. Further, the paragraph relieves the successor trustee from liability for the prior acts of the resigning trustee and waives any requirements of audit or inquiry into the activities of the prior trustee. This is essential for any successor trustee.

---

13. <u>Compensation of Trustee.</u> **OPTION 1: Corporate trustee compensation** A corporate trustee shall receive compensation in accordance with its regular schedule of fees in effect at the time such services are rendered.

OPTION 2: Individual does not receive compensation An individual trustee shall not be paid any compensation, but shall be reimbursed for out-of-pocket expenses.

OPTION 3: Individual does receive compensation An individual trustee shall be paid [insert amount of compensation] as compensation for such services and shall be reimbursed for out-of-pocket expenses.

COMMENT: Three options are provided, but the actual drafting of this paragraph may be different than each of these options. If the only trustee to be used is a corporate trustee, then Option 1 is a standard trust provision. If there is a possibility of individual trustees, then care should be given to the method for setting this fee. If no fee is to be paid because the trustee is a close family member, then it is suggested that Option 2 be used. If the grantor expects a fee to be charged, then an amount or a formula, such as a percentage of income or principal, must be set. It is unwise to simply provide for compensation to be a reasonable fee, as that leaves an individual trustee with great uncertainty as to the fee to be charged. Without the grantor clarifying compensation, the trustee could find him or herself in litigation with the beneficiary.

---

14. <u>Court Accountings.</u> To the extent such requirements can be waived, the trustee shall not be required (a) to file any inventory of trust property or accounts or reports of the administration of the trusts, or to register the trusts, in any court, (b) to furnish any bond or other security for the proper performance of the trustee's duties or (c) to obtain authority from a court for the exercise of any power conferred on the trustee by this instrument. This waiver does not preclude the trustee from registering any trust created in this instrument and petitioning a court having jurisdiction over registered trusts for a judicial ruling on any matter relating to administration of any trust created by this instrument.

COMMENT: The first sentence is to clarify the normal situation that an inter vivos trust is not subject to judicial oversight. The second sentence may be omitted, but is suggested as a potential benefit in some states. In a state in which a trust may be registered, it may be possible to have minor trust matters resolved by the court in which the trust is registered. This creates a simplified process for dealing with minor administrative matters. Without this provision, a court might be reluctant to decide matters for a trust which is not required to be registered under state law.

15. <u>Severability.</u> If any provisions of this trust shall be unenforceable, the remaining provisions shall nevertheless be carried into effect.

COMMENT: This is the same type of standard provision often seen in contracts that is intended to save the document if a particular provision is found to be invalid or void. It is doubtful this provision will have any practical effect in most trust situations, but it is a "boilerplate" provision that is frequently found in trust instruments and for which there is no disadvantage.

16. **OPTION 1: Decided by treating physician** <u>Certification of Incompetency.</u> Any person acting or named to act as a trustee in this instrument is considered to be unable to serve or to continue serving when a physician whom such person has consulted within the prior three years has certified as to such consultation and the certification states that the person is incapable of managing the affairs of the trusts I have established in this instrument, regardless of cause and regardless of whether there is an adjudication of incompetency. No person shall be liable to anyone for actions taken in reliance on the physician's certification, or for dealing with a trustee other than the one removed for incompetency based on such certification.

OPTION 2: Decided by two physicians <u>Certification of Incompetency.</u> Any person acting or named to act as a trustee in this instrument is considered to be unable to serve or to continue serving when a written certification is received from two (2) physicians, both of whom have personally examined the person and at least one (1) of whom is board-certified in the specialty most closely associated with the health condition alleged to cause such incompetency. The certification must state that the person is incapable of managing the affairs of this trust, regardless of cause and regardless of whether there is an adjudication of incompetence. No person is liable to anyone for actions taken in reliance on these physician's certifications, or for dealing with a trustee other than the one removed for incompetency based on these certifications.

COMMENT: This provision relates back to paragraph 11 concerning the succession of trustees. It defines incompetency, which is one of those events requiring a successor trustee. The first option involves consultation with the trustee's personal physician, whereas Option 2 involves a panel of two physicians, one of whom is board certified in the speciality most closely associated with the health condition of the trustee. Clients differ as to which provision they prefer and are more concerned about the provision when the grantor is also the initial trustee. Absent a strong preference by the grantor, Option 1 is the provision most frequently used.

17. Titles and References. The underscored titles of paragraphs in this instrument are for information purposes only and shall be given no legal effect.

COMMENT: This is another common "boilerplate" provision that is perhaps not essential, but for which there is no disadvantage.

18. Governing Law. The laws of the State of [insert state] shall govern the interpretation and validity of the provisions of this instrument and all questions relating to the management, administration, investment, and distribution of the trusts hereby created.

COMMENT: It is a standard provision in both trust instruments and in contracts to specify the state law that applies in interpretation of the instrument. This will usually be the grantor's state of residency but also should be the state in which the lawyer is licensed to practice.

19. No-Contest. If any beneficiary of this trust, or the guardian or legal representative of such beneficiary, contests the validity of this trust or of any of its provisions or shall institute or join in (except as a party defendant) any proceeding to contest the validity of this trust or to prevent any provision of it from being carried out in accordance with its terms (regardless of whether or not such proceedings are instituted in good faith and with probable cause), then all benefits provided for such beneficiary hereunder are revoked and such benefits shall pass as if such beneficiary and such beneficiary's descendants all had predeceased me.

COMMENT: This provision or some variation of it should be considered if there is any concern that a beneficiary or heir-at-law may challenge the trust. The lawyer may need to modify this provision to meet any requirements of state law.

20. Irrevocability. This trust agreement shall be absolutely irrevocable, and I have no right whatsoever to withdraw any property from the trust, to modify the trust in any manner, or to exercise any control over the trust property.

COMMENT: These trusts are irrevocable as they are most often used by grantors who desire to have the gifted assets excluded from their estate. Therefore the utility of this trust is limited to grantors with larger estates that may result in federal estate taxes.

The undersigned have signed this instrument and have established the foregoing trusts on this the _____ day of _____, [Current Year].

GRANTOR:

_____

[grantor's name]

TRUSTEE:

_____

[trustee's name]

STATE OF [State of Notary]   )

) SCT.

COUNTY OF [County of Notary])

    The undersigned, a Notary Public within and for the state and county aforesaid, does hereby certify that the foregoing trust agreement executed by [grantor's name], as grantor, was on this day produced to me in my county by [grantor's name], who executed, acknowledged and swore the same before me to be [his or her] act and deed in due form of law.

    Given under my hand and notarial seal on this the ___ day of _____, [Current Year].

                                                 _____

                                               Notary Public, State at Large

                                               My commission expires:_____

STATE OF [State of Notary]   )

) SCT.

COUNTY OF [County of Notary])

    The undersigned, a Notary Public within and for the state and county aforesaid, does hereby certify that the foregoing trust agreement executed by [trustee's name], as trustee, was on this day produced to me in my county by [trustee's name], who executed, acknowledged and swore the same before me to be [his or her] act and deed in due form of law.

    Given under my hand and notarial seal on this the ___ day of _____, [Current Year].

                                                 _____

                                               Notary Public, State at Large

                                               My commission expires:_____

PREPARED BY:

_____

[Name of Attorney]
[Name of Law Firm]
Attorneys at Law
[Street Address]
[City], [State] [Zip Code]
[Telephone Number]

SCHEDULE A

[NAME OF TRUST] TRUST

Cash. . . . . $ 10.00

The lawyer will note on schedule A, a deposit of $10 in the trust. State law will determine the necessity of an initial deposit. An unfunded trust that contains no principal may be deemed a "dry" trust under state law, meaning that it is not a valid document. Some lawyers go to the added step of affixing a $10 bill to schedule A, while others are satisfied with a cash deposit which does have the disadvantage of not being traceable. If there is the possibility of a contest of the trust, the cautious practice is to affix a $10 bill to schedule A.

MINOR'S TRUST—INTERNAL REVENUE CODE SECTION 2503(C) TRUST WORKSHEET

1. **Grantor Information**

   Name _____

   City and State _____

2. **Trustee Information**

   Name _____

   City and State _____

3. **Name of Trust**

   "_____ Trust"

4. **Child/ Beneficiary Information**

   Name of Child _____

   Child's Date of Birth _____

5. **Age Trust Terminates:** _____ years of age

6. **Default Provisions (if needed), if All Named Beneficiaries are Deceased:**

   _____

   _____

   _____

   _____

7. **Definition of "Child" and "Descendant"**

   Include children adopted prior to age _____ (18, 21, etc.).

   Include provision for illegitimate children (treated same, etc.)? Yes / No

8. **Powers**

   Environmental Powers? Yes / No (See Single Trust Paragraph 11 at page 73)

   Farm Powers? Yes / No (See Single Trust Paragraph 12 beginning at page 73)

   Limitation on Trustee Powers? Yes / No

9. **Trustees**

   Name of first successor trustee: _____

   Name of second successor trustee: _____

   Corporate trustee compensation? (Option 1) Yes / No

   Individual reimbursed for expenses but no compensation? (Option 2) Yes / No

   Individual receives compensation? (Option 3) Yes / No

   Amount of compensation: $_____

10. **Incompetency**

    One physician decides? (Option 1) Yes / No

    Two physicians decide and one board certified? (Option 2) Yes / No

MINOR'S TRUST—INTERNAL REVENUE CODE SECTION 2503(C) TRUST

This is a trust specifically permitted under the Internal Revenue Code that permits transfers into the trust to qualify for the annual gift tax exclusion, even though a transfer into a trust is a future interest gift that otherwise would not qualify for the annual gift tax exclusion. Since this is a statutory trust, the pertinent provisions of the Internal Revenue Code Section 2503(c) must be followed. An excellent ABA resource for estate planning issues involving minors is Carmina Y. D'Aversa, *Tax, Estate, and Lifetime Planning for Minors,* American Bar Association (Chicago: 2006).

I, [grantor's name], currently of [grantor's city], [grantor's state], as grantor and [trustee's name], currently of [trustee's city], [trustee's state], as trustee hereby enter into this trust agreement, and I transfer to my trustee the property described in Schedule A. This property and all investments, reinvestments and additions which may sometimes be referred to in this instrument as the "trust property" or "trust assets" are to be held subject to the following provisions:

COMMENT: The grantor's full name and city and state of residence should be included. The same information is required for the trustee. The grantor must not be the trustee. If the grantor were to die prior to termination of the trust, the trust powers would cause the income and principal of the trust to be included in the grantor's estate under Internal Revenue Code Sections 2036 and 2038. It is also advisable that the spouse not act as the trustee, as a trustee who may make trust distributions for a person for whom they are legally obligated to support results in inclusion of the assets under that spouse/trustee's own estate should that spouse die prior to termination of the trust. Thus, a third party trustee should be utilized.

1. <u>Name of Trust.</u> This instrument and the initial trust hereby established may be named the "[Name of trust] Trust."

COMMENT: While a trust may have any name, it should be named after the child who is the beneficiary of the trust.

2. <u>Beneficiary Information.</u> My child [name of child] whose date of birth is [insert date of birth] is the beneficiary of this trust and references to "my child" or "the beneficiary" are only to [him or her].

COMMENT: The child's full name should be inserted, including the child's date of birth as that information is needed due to the requirements in paragraphs 3 through 5 below.

3. <u>Trust Provisions Until Age Twenty-One.</u> Until my child reaches twenty-one (21) years of age, the trustee may pay to my child, or pay for the benefit of my child, as much of the net income and principal of my child's trust as the trustee deems to be proper. If any net income remains undistributed at the end of each calendar year (excluding income distributed during the sixty-five [65] day period under Internal Revenue Code Section 663), the trustee shall add it to the principal of the trust.

If my child dies before reaching twenty-one [21] years of age, my child's trust shall terminate. My child shall have a general power of appointment over this trust and the trustee shall pay the entire principal and all accumulated income to such persons or entities, either outright or in further trust, and subject to such conditions as my child appoints by will, provided the will must specifically refer to this general power of appointment in order for the power to be validly exercised. If my child does not validly exercise this general power of appointment, the trust property shall be paid to my child's surviving lineal descendants, per stirpes. If my child has no surviving lineal descendants, the trust property shall be distributed to my living lineal descendants, per stirpes. If I have no living lineal descendants, the trust property shall be distributed to [insert default beneficiaries].

COMMENT: To qualify for the annual gift tax exclusion, the trust must permit income and principal to be paid to the child prior to age 21, although it is not necessary that any distributions be made to the child prior to age 21. Any restrictions on the trustee's discretion to distribute income or principal should be avoided so as not to run afoul of this requirement. An additional requirement for the annual gift tax exclusion is that the trust must be payable to the child's estate, or pursuant to a general power of appointment granted to the child should the child die prior to reaching 21 years of age. This trust uses the option of the general power of appointment rather than the trust assets being payable to the estate. Either option is permissible.

---

4. <u>Trust Provisions After Age Twenty-One.</u> If my child does not make a timely written demand as required in paragraph 5 below, the trust shall continue after age twenty-one on the following terms:

a. The trustee shall pay to my child, or pay for my child's benefit, the entire net income in quarterly or more frequent installments.

b. The trustee may pay to my child, or apply for my child's benefit, so much or all of the principal of my child's trust as the trustee believes proper to provide for the maintenance, support, health and education of my child. Without limiting the discretion of the trustee, proper uses may include educational or medical needs, the cost of acquiring a home, and the cost of starting or continuing a business.

c. When my child reaches [insert age] [age in numbers] years of age, the trust shall terminate and the entire remaining principal and all accumulated income shall be paid outright to my child.

d. If my child dies before reaching [insert age] [(age in numbers)] years of age, my child's trust shall terminate and the trustee shall pay the remaining principal, plus all accumulated income to such persons or entities, either outright or in further trust, and subject to such conditions as my child appoints by will, provided the will must specifically refer to this power of appointment in order for the power to be validly exercised. If my child does not validly exercise this power of appointment, the trust property shall be paid to my child's surviving lineal descendants, per stirpes. If my child has no surviving lineal descendants, the trust property shall be distributed to my living lineal descendants, per stirpes, if any, and if none, then the trust property shall be distributed to [insert default beneficiary].

COMMENT: The trust must terminate at age 21 and be distributed to the child. It is permissible for the trust to continue after age 21 as long as the child has the right to withdraw the entire trust at age 21 and elects not to do so. This trust grants the child a general power of appointment should the child die prior to the termination of the trust, just as was done in the case of the trust prior to age 21 in paragraph 3 above.

---

5. <u>Power to Compel Distribution.</u> For six months beginning on my child's twenty-first [21st] birthday, after which this power shall lapse, my child may demand in writing payment from the trustee of the entire principal and all accumulated income of the trust. If my child makes a timely written demand, my child's trust shall terminate and the entire principal and all accumulated income shall be paid to my child.

COMMENT: As stated above the child must have the right to receive all trust property at age 21. This paragraph ensures that the child has that right. Care must be taken to provide the child notice of the termination of the trust and his or her right to receive all trust property. A proper waiver by the child will allow the trust to continue as discussed above.

6. <u>Separate Trusts for Descendants of Beneficiary.</u> If a person other than my child who is entitled to receive distribution under this instrument due to my child's death and such person has not reached the age of twenty-one (21) years, the trustee shall hold the trust assets that would otherwise be distributable to such person in a separate trust named for that person. Until such person reaches the age of twenty-one (21) years, the trustee may pay to or apply for the benefit of such person the income and principal of such person's trust in such amounts, if any, and at such times as the trustee believes appropriate for the reasonable maintenance, support, health, and education (including college or graduate, professional or vocational school education) of such person, considering such person's income or assets and all other circumstances and factors the trustee believes pertinent. If the person dies before reaching the age of twenty-one (21) years, the trustee shall distribute the then remaining trust assets of such person's trust to the then living intestate heirs at law of such person under the [state of grantor/other] laws of intestate succession then in force, excluding me as a recipient of any intestate share.

COMMENT: This provision avoids the result of a child who is survived by one or more young descendants from dying without exercising the general power of appointment, thus requiring the inheritance to be subject to state guardianship laws. This provision allows that descendant's share of the trust property to be retained in trust until the descendant reaches 21 years of age, with the trustee using that person's share for his or her benefit or reasonable maintenance, support, health and educational needs, with the trust terminating at age 21 and being distributed to that descendant. The provisions in this paragraph are merely one option. The lawyer should customize this paragraph to the client's own desires.

7. <u>Default Provisions.</u> Any trust property not disposed of by any of the above provisions shall be distributed on the date of such failure of disposition to [insert default provisions].

COMMENT: The lawyer will need to make the decision as to whether or not a default provision is needed in light of the prior provisions of this trust.

8. <u>Definitions.</u> For all purposes of this instrument, the following shall apply:

a. The words "child," "descendant" or "descendants" shall exclude adopted persons unless they are adopted prior to [insert age] [(age in numbers)] years; and shall include only persons legitimately born unless a decree of adoption terminates the parental rights of the natural mother during her lifetime, or the natural father signs a written notarized instrument during his lifetime in which he irrevocably states that the child is to be considered legitimately born for purposes of inheriting under this will.

COMMENT: Some clients will want to restrict distribution for an adopted child to preclude a child adopted as an adult. Thus, many will use the age 18 or perhaps a slightly older age such as 20 or 21. Other clients may wish to restrict the age to a younger adopted child, such as under the age of 10. The issue of illegitimate children should also be addressed. In many situations, a child or more remote descendant should be treated the same as any other child, in which case the portion of this paragraph that deals with illegitimate children can be deleted. In other situations there may be a limited or no relationship with the child, in which event no distribution should be made to that child. This provision will require modification to meet the client's particular situation.

---

b. Whenever assets are to be divided and allocated per stirpes, the assets to be divided or allocated shall be divided into as many equal shares as are necessary to divide or allocate one share to each then living child of such person and to provide one share collectively for the then living descendants of each child of such person who then is deceased leaving one or more descendants then living. Any collective share shall be divided and allocated per stirpes among the descendants of such deceased person in accordance with the preceding sentence.

COMMENT: Since the term per stirpes is used often in this document, a definition is provided of that term. The lawyer should modify this definition to conform with his or her own state law should it differ any from this definition. Of course, a definition is not essential, since the term will be defined under state law. But since it is a term that clients are not familiar with, it is often helpful to define it for them in the document. An excellent ABA resource that explains the term per stirpes and its variations is Jeffrey N. Penell and Alan Newman, *Estate and Trust Planning,* American Bar Association (Chicago, 2005) pp. 19–26.

---

9. <u>Protection from Creditors.</u> No trust beneficiary shall have the right to sell, transfer, assign, alienate, pledge, or in any way encumber trust assets, including income and principal, nor shall trust assets be subject to execution, levy, sale, garnishment, attachment, bankruptcy, or other legal proceedings. Any such actions by a trust beneficiary or a third party seeking to enforce a claim against the trust assets shall not be recognized under any circumstances by the trustee. These provisions do not prevent the trustee from making distributions for the benefit of a trust beneficiary in such amounts and at such times as the trustee determines necessary for the trust beneficiary's maintenance, support, health and education.

COMMENT: This is a standard paragraph that precludes the trust assets from being attached by claims of creditors. The lawyer should check state law before advising a client of the effect of this provision.

---

10. <u>Trustee Powers.</u> In the administration of the trusts, the trustee shall have the following powers and rights and all others granted by law:

a. To sell publicly or privately any trust property, for cash or on time, without an order of court, upon such terms and conditions as shall seem best to the trustee; and no person dealing with the trustee shall have any obligation to look to the application of the purchase money therefor.

b. To invest and reinvest all or any part of the principal of the trust assets in any stocks, bonds, mortgages, shares, or interests in common trust funds, mutual funds, or other securities or property, real, personal, or mixed, and of any kind or nature whatsoever, as the trustee deems advisable, and without diversification if the trustee deems it advisable, irrespective of whether or not such securities or property are eligible for trust investment under state or any other law, and may change any investment received or made by the trustee, and may hold cash if the trustee deems it advisable.

c. To exercise broad discretion as to diversification of trust property, and shall not be required to reduce any concentrated holdings merely because of such concentration, and shall have full discretion as to the percentage to be invested in fixed income securities, and is specifically relieved from any requirements, legal or otherwise, as to the percentage of the trust assets to be invested in fixed income securities, and may invest and retain invested any trust estate wholly in common stocks.

d. To sell, convey, lease or mortgage, repair and improve, and take any and all other steps with regard to any real estate that may at any time be a part of the principal of the trust; and any lease of such real property or contract with regard thereto made by the trustee shall be binding for the full period of the lease or contract, though said period shall extend beyond the termination of the trust.

e. To vote shares of stock held in the trust at stockholders' meetings in person or by special, limited, or general proxy, with or without power of substitution, as to the trustee seems best.

f. To participate in the liquidation, reorganization, consolidation, incorporation and reincorporation, or any other financial readjustment of any limited liability company, corporation or business in which the trust is or shall be financially interested.

g. To borrow money from any source for any purpose connected with the protection, preservation, improvement or development of the trust hereunder, whenever in the trustee's judgment the trustee deems it advisable, and as security to mortgage or pledge any real estate or personal property forming a part of the trust upon such terms and conditions as the trustee may deem advisable.

h. To hold any and all securities in bearer form, in the trustee's own name, or the name of some other person, partnership, or corporation, or in the name of a duly appointed nominee, with or without disclosing the fiduciary ownership thereof.

i. To divide the principal of the trust property into parts or shares and to distribute or allot same, the trustee is authorized to make such division in cash or in kind or both; and for the purpose of such division or allotment, the judgment of the trustee concerning the propriety thereof and relative value of property so distributed or allotted shall be binding and conclusive with respect to all persons interested herein.

j. To merge and consolidate the trust property of any separate trust held hereunder with other trusts and then to administer such trust property as a single trust provided the separate trust is for the benefit of the same persons with substantially the same terms, conditions and federal tax consequences.

k. To pay such income and principal during the minority or incapacity of any beneficiary to whom income is herein directed to be paid, or for whose benefit income and principal may be expended, in any one or more of the following ways: (1) directly to said beneficiary; (2) to the legal guardian or committee of said beneficiary; (3) to a relative of said beneficiary to be expended by such relative for the maintenance, health, and education of said beneficiary; or (4) by expending the same directly for the maintenance, health, and education of said beneficiary. The trustee shall not be obliged to see to the application of the funds so paid, but the receipt of such person shall be full acquittance to the trustee.

l. To continue and operate any business owned by me at my death and to do any and all things deemed appropriate by the trustee, including the power to form a limited liability company or incorporate the business and to put additional capital into the business, for such time as the trustee deems advisable, without liability for loss resulting from the continuance or operation of the business except for the trustee's own negligence; and to close out, liquidate, or sell the business at such time and upon such terms as the trustee deems proper, and in this connection a sale may be made (pursuant to an agreement entered into by me during my lifetime, or otherwise) to a partner, officer, member, employee or beneficiary under this trust. I am aware of the fact that certain risks are inherent in the operation of any business and, therefore, my trustee shall not be liable for any loss resulting from the retention and operation of any business unless such loss results directly from my trustee's gross negligence or willful misconduct.

m. To have the same powers, authorities, and discretions in the management of the trust as I would have in the management and control of my own personal assets. The trustee may continue to exercise any powers and discretions hereunder for a reasonable period after the termination of any trust under this instrument.

COMMENT: The above powers are a set of standard powers that appear throughout this book. The powers should be reviewed to be certain that you the lawyer understand each power, the client is in agreement with each of the powers granted and that the powers granted are needed. Because this is a generic and broad statement of powers, some of these powers may not be necessary. For example, powers to sell or lease real estate are not needed if the grantor knows the trust will consist only of cash and other intangible investments.

11. <u>Limitation on Powers of Individual Trustee.</u> Notwithstanding any other powers granted to my trustee in this instrument, an individual trustee (a) shall have no power to make payments or distributions that would discharge the trustee's legal obligation to support the trust beneficiary, (b) shall not exercise any power or discretion in any manner that would be deemed to be a general power of appointment under Internal Revenue Code Section 2041, (c) shall be limited by the ascertainable standard of "maintenance, support, health and education" when making payments or distributions to the trustee personally or to anyone for whom the trustee has a beneficial interest, and (d) shall possess no incidence of ownership or powers with respect to life insurance in which the trustee is the insured and has fiduciary power over such life insurance.

COMMENT: There are some situations in which an individual trustee may have adverse estate or income tax consequences when given broad powers as trustee. If a corporate trustee is used, then this paragraph is not needed. But an individual trustee must be certain that acting as trustee does not result in any adverse estate or income tax consequences. This paragraph is intended to ensure that adverse tax consequences are avoided if overly broad powers are granted in the trust instrument. The lawyer is urged to exercise caution when using individual trustees coupled with broad discretionary powers of income and principal distribution to a trust beneficiary because of possible adverse tax consequences. An ABA resource to acquaint oneself with these issues is L. Rush Hunt and Lara Rae Hunt, *A Lawyer's Guide to Estate Planning,* American Bar Association (Chicago: 2004) §14.4.

12. <u>Trustee Resignation.</u> My trustee may resign at any time by giving written notice to my successor trustee named below, if any, and if none, then written notice shall be given to each current adult income beneficiary who is then living.

COMMENT: If a trustee resigns, there must be some method of notice and appointment of a successor trustee. This paragraph provides a method of notification. It is not an essential trust provision, but is a helpful one.

---

13. <u>Trustee Succession and Appointment.</u> If [trustee's name] dies, becomes incompetent, resigns or ceases to serve for any reason, then [insert name of first successor trustee] shall serve as successor trustee. If [insert name of first successor trustee] dies, becomes incompetent, resigns or ceases to serve for any reason, then [insert name of second successor trustee] shall serve as successor trustee. The last serving successor trustee may name [his or her] own successor trustee by a written instrument delivered to the successor trustee or by will. The successor trustee may be an individual or a financial institution possessing trust powers under state or federal law. Any further vacancy in the office of trustee shall be filled by decision of the probate court where I resided at the time of my death.

COMMENT: A decision must be made as to succession of trustees and the method of appointing a successor trustee if all of those named successor trustees are unable to serve. It is also essential to clarify whether successor trustees must only be financial institutions or if individuals may also be considered. Once a decision is made as to the succession of trustees, then the last three sentences should be reviewed to be certain to what extent each of those are needed.

---

14. <u>Powers of Successor Trustee.</u> Each successor trustee shall have the same rights, titles, powers, duties, discretions, and immunities and otherwise be in the same position as if originally named trustee. No successor trustee shall be personally liable for any act or failure to act of a predecessor trustee. Further, a successor trustee may accept the account furnished and the property delivered by or for a predecessor trustee without liability for so doing, and such acceptance shall be a full and complete discharge to the predecessor trustee.

COMMENT: This paragraph clarifies that a successor trustee has the same powers as the initial trustee. Further, the paragraph relieves the successor trustee from liability for the prior acts of the resigning trustee and waives any requirements of audit or inquiry into the activities of the prior trustee. This is essential for any successor trustee.

---

15. <u>Compensation of Trustee.</u> **OPTION 1: Corporate trustee compensation** A corporate trustee shall receive compensation in accordance with its regular schedule of fees in effect at the time such services are rendered.

OPTION 2: Individual does not receive compensation An individual trustee shall not be paid any compensation, but shall be reimbursed for out-of-pocket expenses.

OPTION 3: Individual does receive compensation An individual trustee shall be paid [insert amount of compensation] as compensation for such services and shall be reimbursed for out-of-pocket expenses.

COMMENT: Three options are provided, but the actual drafting of this paragraph may be different than each of these options. If the only trustee to be used is a corporate trustee, then Option 1 is a standard trust provision. If there is a possibility of individual trustees, then care should be given to the method for setting this fee. If no fee is to be paid because the trustee is a close family member, then it is suggested that Option 2 be used. If the grantor expects a fee to be charged, then an amount or a formula, such as a percentage of income or principal, must be set. It is unwise to simply provide for compensation to be a reasonable fee, as that leaves an individual trustee with great uncertainty as to the fee to be charged. Without the grantor clarifying compensation, the trustee could find him or herself in litigation with the beneficiary.

16. <u>Court Accountings.</u> To the extent such requirements can be waived, the trustee shall not be required (a) to file any inventory of trust property or accounts or reports of the administration of the trusts, or to register the trusts, in any court, (b) to furnish any bond or other security for the proper performance of the trustee's duties or (c) to obtain authority from a court for the exercise of any power conferred on the trustee by this instrument. This waiver does not preclude the trustee from registering any trust created in this instrument and petitioning a court having jurisdiction over registered trusts for a judicial ruling on any matter relating to administration of any trust created by this instrument.

COMMENT: The first sentence is to clarify the normal situation that an inter vivos trust is not subject to judicial oversight. The second sentence may be omitted, but is suggested as a potential benefit in some states. In a state in which a trust can be registered, it may be possible to have minor trust matters resolved by the court in which the trust is registered. This creates a simplified process for dealing with minor administrative matters. Without this provision, a court might be reluctant to decide matters for a trust which is not required to be registered under state law.

17. <u>Severability.</u> If any provisions of this trust shall be unenforceable, the remaining provisions shall nevertheless be carried into effect.

COMMENT: This is the same type of standard provision often seen in contracts that is intended to save the document if a particular provision is found to be invalid or void. It is doubtful this provision will have any practical effect in most trust situations, but it is a "boilerplate" provision that is frequently found in trust instruments and for which there is no disadvantage.

18. <u>Certification of Incompetency.</u> **OPTION 1: Decided by treating physician** Any person acting or named to act as a trustee in this instrument is considered to be unable to serve or to continue serving when a physician whom such person has consulted within the prior three years has certified as to such consultation and the certification states that the person is incapable of managing the affairs of the trusts I have established in this instrument, regardless of cause and regardless of whether there is an adjudication of incompetency. No person shall be liable to anyone for actions taken in reliance on the physician's certification, or for dealing with a trustee other than the one removed for incompetency based on such certification.

OPTION 2: Decided by two physicians Any person acting or named to act as a trustee in this instrument is considered to be unable to serve or to continue serving when a written certification is received from two (2) physicians, both of whom have personally examined the person and at least one (1) of whom is board-certified in the specialty most closely associated with the health condition alleged to cause such incompetency. The certification must state that the person is incapable of managing the affairs of this trust, regardless of cause and regardless of whether there is an adjudication of incompetence. No person is liable to anyone for actions taken in reliance on these physician's certifications, or for dealing with a trustee other than the one removed for incompetency based on these certifications.

COMMENT: This provision relates back to paragraph 13 concerning the succession of trustees. It defines incompetency, which is one of those events requiring a successor trustee. The first option involves consultation with the trustee's personal physician, whereas Option 2 involves a panel of two physicians, one of whom is board certified in the speciality most closely associated with the health condition of the trustee. Clients differ as to which provision they prefer and are more concerned about the provision when the grantor is also the initial trustee. Absent a strong preference by the grantor, Option 1 is the provision most frequently used.

---

19. <u>Titles and References.</u> The underscored titles of paragraphs in this instrument are for information purposes only and shall be given no legal effect.

COMMENT: This is another common "boilerplate" provision that is perhaps not essential, but for which there is no disadvantage.

---

20. <u>Governing Law.</u> The laws of the State of [insert state] shall govern the interpretation and validity of the provisions of this instrument and all questions relating to the management, administration, investment, and distribution of the trusts hereby created.

COMMENT: It is a standard provision in both trust instruments and in contracts to specify the state law that applies in interpretation of the instrument. This will usually be the grantor's state or residency but also the state in which the lawyer is licensed to practice.

---

21. <u>Irrevocability.</u> This trust agreement shall be absolutely irrevocable, and I have no right whatsoever to withdraw any property from the trust, to modify the trust in any manner, or to exercise any control over the trust property.

COMMENT: This trust must be irrevocable.

The undersigned have signed this instrument and have established the foregoing trusts on this the _____ day of _____, [Current Year].

GRANTOR:

_____

[grantor's name]

TRUSTEE:

_____

[trustee's name]

STATE OF [State of Notary]   )

) SCT.

COUNTY OF [County of Notary])

　　The undersigned, a Notary Public within and for the state and county aforesaid, does hereby certify that the foregoing trust agreement executed by [grantor's name], as grantor, was on this day produced to me in my county by [grantor's name], who executed, acknowledged and swore the same before me to be [his or her] act and deed in due form of law.

　　Given under my hand and notarial seal on this the ____ day of_____, [Current Year].

_____

Notary Public, State at Large

My commission expires:_____

STATE OF [State of Notary]   )

) SCT.

COUNTY OF [County of Notary])

　　The undersigned, a Notary Public within and for the state and county aforesaid, does hereby certify that the foregoing trust agreement executed by [trustee's name], as trustee, was on this day produced to me in my county by [trustee's name], who executed, acknowledged and swore the same before me to be [his or her] act and deed in due form of law.

　　Given under my hand and notarial seal on this the ____ day of_____, [Current Year].

_____

Notary Public, State at Large

My commission expires:_____

PREPARED BY:

_____

[Name of Attorney]
[Name of Law Firm]
Attorneys at Law
[Street Address]
[City], [State] [Zip Code]
[Telephone Number]

SCHEDULE A

[NAME OF TRUST] TRUST

Cash. . . . . $ 10.00

The lawyer will note on schedule A, a deposit of $10 in the trust. State law will determine the necessity of an initial deposit. An unfunded trust that contains no principal may be deemed a "dry" trust under state law, meaning that it is not a valid document. Some lawyers go to the added step of affixing a $10 bill to schedule A, while others are satisfied with a cash deposit which does have the disadvantage of not being traceable. If there is the possibility of a contest of the trust, the cautious practice is to affix a $10 bill to schedule A.

PART IV–DRAFTING FOR BENEFICIARIES WITH SPECIAL NEEDS

Will with Testamentary Trust for Couple with Handicapped Child/Person

Inter Vivos Trust for Handicapped Child or Person/Special Needs Trust/Supplemental Care Trust

Qualifying Income Trust

Spendthrift Trust

4

WILL WITH TESTAMENTARY TRUST FOR COUPLE
WITH HANDICAPPED CHILD/PERSON WORKSHEET

1. **Testator and Family Information**

    1.1 Name of Testator _____

    1.2 Testator City and State _____

    1.3 Name of Spouse _____

    1.4 Name of Handicapped Child _____

    Names of Other Children _____

    _____

    _____

    1.5 Are any of the above-named children step-children? <u>Yes / No</u>
    (See Master Will Paragraph 1, Option 2 at page 25)

    1.6 Are provisions needed for after-born children? <u>Yes / No</u>
    (See Master Will Paragraphs 1, Option 3 at page 25)

    1.7 Are provisions needed for adopted and/or illegitimately born children? <u>Yes / No</u>
    (See Master Will Paragraph 1, Option 4 at page 25)

    1.8 Are any children to be disinherited? <u>Yes / No</u>
    (See Master Will Paragraph 1, Option 5 at page 25)

    Name of disinherited child: _____

    1.9 Is loan or gift/advancement to be considered in making distribution? <u>Yes / No</u>
    (See Master Will Paragraphs 4 and 5, Options 1 and 2 at page 28)

    Name of Person: _____

2. **Specific Bequests and Legacies** (See Master Will paragraph 3 at page 27)

    2.1 Specific Gifts

      a. Description _____

      b. Primary Beneficiary _____

      c. Contingent Beneficiary_____

      d. Survivorship Period _____

    2.2 Tangible Personal Property (spouse, and if not surviving, to children)

    If no agreement among children as to division:

    Personal Representative Decides? (Option 1) Yes / No

    Sell and Distribute Proceeds to Residue? (Option 2) Yes / No

3. **Payment of Death Taxes**

    3.1 Are taxes on probate and nonprobate assets, including
        apportionment property, to be paid from the residue?
        (This is option in Will) | Yes / No |

    3.2 If death taxes are to be paid by beneficiary but taxes collected
        on apportionment property, see Master Will Paragraph 2, Option 2
        at page 26 | Yes / No |

    3.3 If death taxes are to be paid from the residue but taxes collected
        on apportionment property, see Master Will Paragraph 2, Option 3
        at page 27 | Yes / No |

    3.4 Other tax provisions _____

    _____

4. **Residuary Estate if No Surviving Spouse**

    If a child is deceased:

    Deceased child's share distributed to such child's estate? Yes / No

    or Deceased child's share per stirpes to lineal descendants? Yes / No

    (See Master Will Paragraphs 8 and 9 beginning at page 31, or Will with Testamentary
    Trust for Young Children Paragraphs 3 and 4 beginning at page 154.)

5. **Distribution, upon the Death of the Handicapped Child or Person:**

    _____

    _____

    _____

6. **Powers**

    Environmental Powers? Yes / No (See Master Will Paragraph 15 at page 38)

    Farm Powers? Yes / No (See Master Will Paragraph 16 at page 39)

    Limitation on Trustee Powers? Yes / No

7.   Trustees

Name of initial trustee:_____

Name of successor trustee:_____

Corporate trustee compensation? (Option 1) <u>Yes / No</u>

Individual reimbursed for expenses but no compensation? (Option 2) <u>Yes / No</u>

Individual receives compensation? (Option 3) <u>Yes / No</u>

    Amount of compensation: $_____

8.   Personal Representative

8.1 Spouse named initial personal representative? <u>Yes / No</u>

8.2 If spouse not initial personal representative:

    Name_____ Address _____

8.3 Successor Personal Representative:

    Name _____

    Relationship _____

    Address _____

8.4 Surety Bond Waived? <u>Yes / No</u>

8.5 Special Provisions needed to operate business? <u>Yes / No</u>
(See Master Will Paragraph 24 at page 42)

9.   Incompetency

One physician decides? (Option 1) <u>Yes / No</u>

Two physicians decide and one board certified? (Option 2) <u>Yes / No</u>

10.   Miscellaneous

Is no contest provision needed? <u>Yes / No</u> (See Master Will Paragraph 26 at page 43)

Is employment of law firm needed? <u>Yes / No</u>

11.   Guardian, if spouse not surviving:

    Name _____

    Relationship _____

    Address_____

    Surety Bond Waived? <u>Yes / No</u>

    Special provisions or bequests for guardian?_____

    _____

12.   Survivorship (See Master Will Paragraph 29 at page 44)

1.   Simultaneous Death <u>Yes / No</u>

    If yes, which spouse is presumed to die first? _____

2.   General Survivorship _____ days

    Does this apply to spouse? <u>Yes / No</u>

WILL WITH TESTAMENTARY TRUST FOR COUPLE
WITH HANDICAPPED CHILD/PERSON

COMMENT: This will is similar to the inter vivos trust for a handicapped person. It contains the same trust provisions as the inter vivos trust to ensure eligibility for SSI and Medicaid. Unlike the inter vivos trust, this will has traditional provisions for a will and creates a testamentary trust for the handicapped person. The will is drafted for a handicapped child, but the word "child" may be changed to the appropriate relationship or the word "individual" can be inserted. An excellent ABA resource is Clifton B. Kruse, Jr., *Third Party and Self-Created Trusts*, 3rd edition, American Bar Association (Chicago, 2002).

I, [full name of client], currently of [client's city], [client's state], make this my last will and testament, hereby revoking all wills and codicils previously made by me.

1. <u>Family Information.</u> My [husband or wife]'s name is [husband or wife's full name], and all references in this will to "my [husband or wife]" are only to [him or her].

My [son or daughter], [handicapped child's full name], is handicapped to such a degree as to require special care and due to [his or her] condition, no outright distribution is made to my [son or daughter]. My other [child is or children are], [full names of children], and all references in this will to "my [child is or children are]" only to [him her or them].

COMMENT: The full name of the spouse should be inserted, then the full name of each of the children is also inserted. As can be seen, the handicapped child is treated differently than the other children to make it clear that the handicapped child has no outright distribution under the will. If there are step-children or the concern to include after-born children, adopted or illegitimately born children or the disinheritance of a child, then reference should be made to paragraph 1 in the Master Will at page 25.

2. <u>Payment of Debts, Death Taxes and Funeral Expenses.</u> I direct that all of my just debts, my funeral expenses, costs of estate administration, and death taxes, if any, be paid from the residue of my estate as soon as possible after my death. I further direct that any real property that is subject to a mortgage or lien shall pass under my will subject to such mortgage or lien, rather than such indebtedness being paid from my estate. Death taxes means any estate or inheritance taxes, but not generation-skipping transfer taxes, imposed under the laws of any jurisdiction due to my death on any property passing by reason of my death whether or not such property passes under this will. Any generation-skipping transfer taxes resulting from a transfer occurring under my will shall be paid from the property that incurred such tax and shall not be paid from my other estate assets.

COMMENT: This is a standard paragraph requiring payment of final expenses. If there is real estate subject to a mortgage, the second sentence of the paragraph makes the distribution of that real estate subject to the mortgage rather than the mortgage being paid from the residue of the estate. If there is no such encumbered real estate, the sentence can be deleted. Of course, if the mortgage is to be paid from the residue, then the sentence should be deleted; or to avoid any confusion, the sentence should be redrafted to clarify that mortgage indebtednesses on real estate are to be paid from the estate. Any state or federal death taxes are to be paid from the residue. If any part of those taxes are to be paid otherwise, then specific provisions should be made for those payments. Several options for the payment of death taxes are found in paragraph 2 of the Master Will at page 26, to which reference should be made. In most situations, there will not be any concern with generation-skipping transfer taxes. In that situation, the final sentence can be deleted, as can the phrase concerning "generation-skipping transfer taxes" in the third sentence.

3. <u>Disposition of Tangible Personal Property.</u> I give to my [husband or wife], all of my personal and household effects, including but not limited to furniture, furnishings, appliances, clothing, jewelry, automobiles and any other similar tangible personal property. If my [husband or wife] does not survive me, I give all such tangible personal property to my [child or children], in as nearly equal shares as is possible.

OPTION 1: If no agreement personal representative decides If my children cannot agree upon this division within ninety (90) days after the appointment of my personal representative, then the division made by my personal representative shall be final and binding upon my children and shall not be subject to question by anyone or in any court.

OPTION 2: If no agreement sell and pass to residue If my children cannot agree upon this division within ninety (90) days after the appointment of my personal representative, then my personal representative shall sell all property with respect to which my children have not reached an agreement and the net sales proceeds shall be distributed as part of the residue of my estate.

COMMENT: Gifts of personal property can be the source of family disagreements and even litigation. While the initial gift of such property to the surviving spouse is not a problem, the problem arises when the personal property passes to the children. Options 1 and 2 provide two different approaches for handling distribution in the event of a disagreement. The lawyer may choose either of those options, write his/her own method of resolving the conflict or leave out these options and hope for the best. This writer has found that going to court over grandmother's clock is something most clients don't want. Thus, Option 1, Option 2 or some variation may be helpful.

I may leave with my will or among my papers a handwritten letter or handwritten memorandum concerning the distribution of certain items of my tangible personal property. If so, I direct my personal representative to distribute those items of my tangible personal property as I have provided in that letter or memorandum.

COMMENT: Some clients have items of personal property that they want to give to particular family members or friends. Rather than having a lengthy will naming these items and then having to document their transfer to the court, some lawyers prefer the use of a handwritten letter that is dated and signed at the bottom of the page by the testator as a preferable option. This approach allows the ease of changing the document over the years. It has the disadvantage of possibly not being an enforceable document depending upon state law. If the document qualifies under state law as a holographic codicil or due to enactment of Section 2-513 of the Uniform Probate Code, then it is enforceable and the personal representative is required to account for those items named in the letter and to ensure their distribution to the correct beneficiary. A problem with the handwritten letter is that it is unlikely that it will be written in a way to address the lapse of a gift if a beneficiary predeceases the testator or the applicability of the rule of ademption in the event the gift is no longer in existence at the testator's death. The lawyer must refer to his or her own state law as to these two issues.

4. <u>Residuary Estate.</u> I give the residue of my estate to my [husband or wife], if [he or she] survives me. If my [husband or wife] does not survive me, I give the residue of my estate one-half (¹/₂) to my children, [full names of children who receive outright], in equal shares. If a child is deceased, such child's share shall be distributed to [describe alternate distribution plan]. I give the remaining one-half (¹/₂) of the residue of my estate to my trustee for [full name of handicapped child] to be held in trust for [him or her] to be administered and distributed according to the following terms:

COMMENT: This residuary clause gives the entire residue to the surviving spouse. Obviously, if there is no surviving spouse then appropriate changes must be made. The estate then passes outright to those children other than the handicapped child. The handicapped child's share then passes into the testamentary trust in the will. If a child who is to receive a distribution outright is deceased, the will must address the alternate distribution, such as per stirpes among that child's own descendants, or whatever other plan of distribution is desired. Also, a decision must be made as to what percentage of the estate is to be distributed to each child and then appropriate changes must be made to this paragraph.

---

a. Throughout the lifetime of my [son or daughter], [full name of handicapped child], unless this trust is sooner terminated, the trustee shall pay or use all, part, or none of the income and principal of the trust to or for the benefit of my [son or daughter], [full name of handicapped child], to provide for [his or her] extra and supplemental care, maintenance, support and education, in addition to the benefits [he or she] otherwise receives as a result of [his or her] handicap or disability from any local, state or federal government, or from any public or private agencies, any of which provide services or benefits to persons who are handicapped.

COMMENT: This is a typical wording for a special needs trust. The intent is to give the trustee sole discretion in making distributions and to clarify that all distributions are supplemental to other benefits the beneficiary receives.

---

b. It is the express purpose of this trust to supplement other benefits which my [son or daughter] is entitled to receive. This trust is not intended to provide basic support, but rather is to be a discretionary trust to provide for supplemental needs of my [son or daughter] which are not otherwise provided for by various public and private assistance. To this end, the trustee may provide benefits for my [son or daughter] which the trustee considers necessary for [his or her] care, maintenance, support and education that cannot, in the trustee's opinion, be provided by the aforementioned public and private assistance programs. This includes but is not limited to such items as vacation, entertainment and recreational trips and the expenses of a traveling companion to accompany my [son or daughter] on such trips; personal items such as radios, televisions and other electronic entertainment devices; healthcare services, supplies, and special equipment; training programs; and rehabilitation supplemental to those my [son or daughter] is entitled to receive under any public or private assistance program. The trustee's obligation to make such payments is entirely discretionary; provided, however, the trustee may not exercise any discretion in making distributions from this trust that would make my [son or daughter] ineligible for any public or private benefits otherwise available to my [son or daughter] from any agency, private or public, including state or federal social service agencies.

COMMENT: This paragraph continues to clarify that the trust is supplemental to basic needs that are provided by state or federal programs, such as SSI or Medicaid. The third and fourth sentences are not essential and may be omitted. The final sentence in the paragraph makes it clear that the trustee is not permitted to make any distributions that would cause ineligibility for assistance benefits, such as SSI and Medicaid.

c. Any payments from this trust shall be paid directly to the person or business which supplies such services or benefits.

COMMENT: This paragraph may not be essential in some states. It is inserted to avoid the result of a distribution being treated as a resource for the beneficiary if it is paid to an account such as a guardianship account held for the benefit of the beneficiary from which payments are made for services or benefits received by the beneficiary. Some states take the position that such a distribution is a resource, which will then create partial or total ineligibility for government benefits. Making direct distributions to the provider of the services or benefits should avoid this unintended result.

d. This trust shall terminate upon the death of my [son or daughter] and shall be distributed to [describe distribution plan]. In the event of a determination by any agency or court of competent jurisdiction that the income or principal of this trust is liable for the basic maintenance, support and medical care of my [son or daughter] which would otherwise be provided for [him or her] by local, state, or federal government agencies or programs, or from any public or private agencies, then and in such event this trust shall terminate and the then remaining trust assets shall be distributed to [describe distribution plan].

COMMENT: Provisions must be added to state the recipient of trust assets upon the death of the beneficiary. The second sentence in the paragraph is not essential, but in most situations it is desirable. As can be seen, this sentence requires the trust to terminate and be distributed in the event a court or government agency treats the trust as a resource for the beneficiary. Obviously, the recipient of the trust assets must be someone the grantor believes will maintain the trust assets for the benefit of the beneficiary even though those assets will then be owned by that person.

5. <u>Protection from Creditors.</u> The trust beneficiary shall not have the right to sell, transfer, assign, alienate, pledge, or in any way encumber trust assets, including income and principal, nor shall trust assets be subject to execution, levy, sale, garnishment, attachment, bankruptcy, or other legal proceedings. Any such actions by the trust beneficiary or a third party seeking to enforce a claim against the trust assets shall not be recognized under any circumstances by the trustee. These provisions do not prevent the trustee from making distributions for the benefit of the trust beneficiary in such amounts and at such times as the trustee determines necessary for the trust beneficiary's maintenance, support, health and education.

COMMENT: This is a standard paragraph that precludes the trust assets from being attached by claims of creditors, including government agencies seeking reimbursement for payments made by them under a Medicaid or other government program.

6. <u>Trustee Powers.</u> In the administration of the trusts, the trustee shall have the following powers and rights and all others granted by law:

a. To sell publicly or privately any trust property, for cash or on time, without an order of court and upon such terms and conditions as my trustee deems proper; and no person dealing with my trustee shall have any obligation to look to the application of the purchase money.

b. To invest and reinvest all or any part of the principal of the trust in any stocks, bonds, mortgages, shares or interests in common trust funds, mutual funds, or other securities or property, real, personal, or mixed, and of any kind or nature whatsoever, as the trustee deems proper, and without diversification if the trustee deems it advisable, irrespective of whether or not such securities or property are eligible for trust investment under state or any other law, and may change any investment received or made by the trustee, and may hold cash if the trustee deems it advisable.

c. To exercise broad discretion as to diversification of trust property, and shall not be required to reduce any concentrated holdings merely because of such concentration, and shall have full discretion as to the percentage to be invested in fixed income securities, and is specifically relieved from any requirements, legal or otherwise, as to the percentage of the trust assets to be invested in fixed income securities, and may invest or retain invested any trust estates wholly in common stocks.

d. To sell, convey, lease or mortgage, repair and improve, and take any and all other steps with regard to any real estate that may at any time be a part of the principal of the trust; and any lease of such real property or contract with regard thereto made by the trustee shall be binding for the full period of the lease or contract, even though the period shall extend beyond the termination of the trust.

e. To vote shares of stock held in the trust at stockholders' meetings in person or by special, limited, or general proxy, with or without power of substitution, as seems best to the trustee.

f. To participate in the liquidation, reorganization, consolidation, incorporation and reincorporation, or any other financial readjustment of any corporation, limited liability company or business in which the trust is, or shall be financially interested.

g. To borrow money from any source for any purpose connected with the protection, preservation, improvement or development of the trust hereunder, whenever in the trustee's judgment the trustee deems it advisable, and as security to mortgage or pledge any real estate or personal property forming a part of the trust upon such terms and conditions as the trustee may deem advisable.

h. To hold any and all securities in bearer form, in the trustee's own name, or the name of some other person, partnership, or corporation, or in the name of a duly appointed nominee, with or without disclosing the fiduciary ownership.

i. To divide the principal of the trust property into parts or shares and to distribute or allot same, and to make such division in cash or in kind or both. For the purpose of such division or allotment, the judgment of the trustee concerning the propriety thereof and relative value of property so distributed or allotted shall be binding and conclusive with respect to all interested persons.

j. To merge and consolidate the trust property of any separate trust held hereunder with other trusts and then to administer such trust property as a single trust provided the separate trust is for the benefit of the same persons with substantially the same terms, conditions and federal tax consequences.

k. To pay such income and principal during the minority or incapacity of any beneficiary for whose benefit income and principal may be expended, in any one or more of the following ways: (1) directly to the beneficiary; (2) to the legal guardian or committee of the beneficiary; (3) to a relative of the beneficiary to be expended by the relative for the maintenance, health, and education of the beneficiary; or (4) by expending the same directly for the maintenance, health, and education of the beneficiary. The trustee shall not be obliged to see to the application of the funds so expended, but the receipt of such person shall be full acquittance to the trustee.

l. To continue and operate any business owned by me at my death and to do any and all things deemed appropriate by the trustee, including the power to form a limited liability company or incorporate the business and to put additional capital into the business, for such time as the trustee deems advisable, without liability for loss resulting from the continuance or operation of the business except for the trustee's own negligence; and to close out, liquidate, or sell the business at such time and upon such terms as the trustee deems proper, and in this connection a sale may be made (pursuant to an agreement entered into by me during my lifetime, or otherwise) to a partner, officer, member, employee or beneficiary under this trust. I am aware of the fact that certain risks are inherent in the operation of any business and, therefore, my trustee shall not be liable for any loss resulting from the retention and operation of any business unless such loss results directly from my trustee's gross negligence or willful misconduct.

m. To have the same powers, authorities, and discretions in the management of the trust as I would have in the management and control of my own personal assets. The trustee may continue to exercise any powers and discretions granted in this instrument for a reasonable period after the termination of any trust under this instrument.

COMMENT: The above powers are a set of standard powers that appear throughout this book. The powers should be reviewed to be certain that you the lawyer understand each power, the client is in agreement with each of the powers granted and that the powers granted are needed. Because this is a generic and broad statement of powers, some of these powers may not be necessary. For example, powers to sell or lease real estate are not needed if the grantor knows the trust will consist only of cash and other intangible investments.

7. <u>Limitation on Powers of Individual Trustee.</u> Notwithstanding any other powers granted to my trustee in this instrument, an individual trustee (a) shall have no power to make payments or distributions that would discharge the trustee's legal obligation to support the trust beneficiary, (b) shall not exercise any power or discretion in any manner that would be deemed to be a general power of appointment under Internal Revenue Code Section 2041, (c) shall be limited by the ascertainable standard of "maintenance, support, health and education" when making payments or distributions to the trustee personally or to anyone for whom the trustee has a beneficial interest, and (d) shall possess no incidence of ownership or powers with respect to life insurance in which the trustee is the insured and has fiduciary power over such life insurance.

COMMENT: There are some situations in which an individual trustee may have adverse estate or income tax consequences when given broad powers as trustee. If a corporate trustee is used, then this paragraph is not needed. But an individual trustee must be certain that acting as trustee does not result in any adverse estate or income tax consequences. This paragraph is intended to ensure that adverse tax consequences are avoided if overly broad powers are granted in the trust instrument. The lawyer is urged to exercise caution when using individual trustees coupled with broad discretionary powers of income and principal distribution to a trust beneficiary because of possible adverse tax consequences. An ABA resource to acquaint oneself with these issues is L. Rush Hunt and Lara Rae Hunt, *A Lawyer's Guide to Estate Planning*, American Bar Association (Chicago: 2004) §14.4.

8. <u>Trustee Resignation.</u> My trustee may resign at any time by giving written notice to my successor trustee named below, if any, and if none, then written notice shall be given to each current adult income beneficiary who is then living.

COMMENT: If a trustee resigns, there must be some method of notice and appointment of a successor trustee. This paragraph provides a method of notification. It is not an essential trust provision, but is a helpful one.

9. <u>Trustee Succession and Appointment.</u> The initial trustee shall be [name of trustee]. If my initial trustee ceases to act as trustee due to death, incompetency, resignation or any other reason, then [name of successor trustee] shall be successor trustee. My successor trustee may name [his or her] own successor trustee by a written instrument delivered to the successor trustee, or by will. The successor trustee shall be an individual or a financial institution possessing trust powers under state or federal law. Any further vacancy in the office of trustee shall be filled by decision of the probate court where I resided at the time of my death. No trustee or successor trustee shall be required to post a surety bond for serving as trustee or successor trustee.

COMMENT: A decision must be made as to succession of trustees and the method of appointing a successor trustee if all of those named successor trustees are unable to serve. It is also essential to clarify whether successor trustees must only be financial institutions or if individuals may also be considered. Once a decision is made as to the succession of trustees, then the last three sentences should be reviewed to be certain to what extent each of those are needed.

10. <u>Powers of Successor Trustee.</u> Each successor trustee shall have the same rights, titles, powers, duties, discretions, and immunities and otherwise be in the same position as if originally named trustee. No successor trustee shall be personally liable for any act or failure to act of a predecessor trustee. Further, a successor trustee may accept the account furnished and the property delivered by or for a predecessor trustee without liability for so doing, and such acceptance shall be a full and complete discharge to the predecessor trustee.

COMMENT: This paragraph clarifies that a successor trustee has the same powers as the initial trustee. Further, the paragraph relieves the successor trustee from liability for the prior acts of the resigning trustee and waives any requirements of audit or inquiry into the activities of the prior trustee. This is essential for any successor trustee.

11. <u>Compensation of Trustee.</u> **OPTION 1: Corporate trustee compensation** A corporate trustee shall receive compensation in accordance with its regular schedule of fees in effect at the time such services are rendered.

OPTION 2: Individual does not receive compensation An individual trustee shall not be paid any compensation, but shall be reimbursed for out-of-pocket expenses.

OPTION 3: Individual does receive compensation An individual trustee shall be paid [insert amount of compensation] as compensation for such services and shall be reimbursed for out-of-pocket expenses.

COMMENT: Three options are provided, but the actual drafting of this paragraph may be different than each of these options. If the only trustee to be used is a corporate trustee, then Option 1 is a standard trust provision. If there is a possibility of individual trustees, then care should be given to the method for setting this fee. If no fee is to be paid because the trustee is a close family member, then it is suggested that Option 2 be used. If the grantor expects a fee to be charged, then an amount or a formula, such as a percentage of income or principal, must be set. It is unwise to simply provide for compensation to be a reasonable fee, as that leaves an individual trustee with great uncertainty as to the fee to be charged. Without the grantor clarifying compensation, the trustee could find him or herself in litigation with the beneficiary or the beneficiary's guardian.

12. <u>Appointment of Personal Representative.</u> My [husband or wife], shall be the personal representative of my estate. If my [husband or wife] fails to qualify as personal representative, or having qualified, dies, becomes incompetent, resigns, or declines to continue to serve, then my [relationship of successor PR] [name of successor PR] shall serve as my successor personal representative. Neither my [husband or wife] nor my successor personal representative shall be required to furnish any surety bond for serving as my personal representative.

COMMENT: The full names of the personal representative and successor personal representative are required as is a decision concerning the waiver of a surety bond. The form, as drafted, assumes the intent to waive such bond.

13. <u>Powers of Personal Representative.</u> I hereby grant to my personal representative (including my successor personal representative) the absolute power to deal with any property, real or personal, held in my estate, as freely as I might in the handling of my own affairs. This power may be exercised independently and without the approval of any court, and no person dealing with my personal representative shall be required to inquire into the propriety of the actions of my personal representative. Without in any way limiting the generality of the foregoing provisions, I grant to my personal representative in addition to those powers specified under state law the following powers:

a. To sell, exchange, assign, transfer and convey any security or property, real or personal, held in my estate at public or private sale, at such time and at such reasonable price and upon such reasonable terms and conditions (including credit) as my personal representative may determine; and without regard to whether or not such sale is necessary in order to settle my estate.

b. To lease any real estate for such term, or terms, and upon such reasonable conditions and rentals and in such manner as my personal representative deems proper, and any lease so made shall be valid and binding for its full term even though such lease term extends beyond the duration of the administration of my estate; to make repairs, replacements and improvements, structural or otherwise, to any such real estate; to subdivide real estate, dedicate real estate to public use and grant easements as my personal representative deems proper.

c. To employ accountants, attorneys and such other agents as my personal representative deems necessary; to pay reasonable compensation for such services and to charge same to (or apportion same between) income and principal as my personal representative deems proper.

d. To join with my [husband or wife] on my behalf in filing income tax returns, or to consent for gift tax purposes to having gifts made by either of us during my life considered as made one-half by each of us, and any resulting tax liability shall be paid by my estate, except such portion as my personal representative and my [husband or wife] agree should be paid by my [husband or wife].

COMMENT: A statement of the powers of the personal representative is not essential, as those powers are specified by state law; however, those state laws may not be sufficiently broad. Often state laws do not include power over real estate. Paragraph 13.c may not be essential, but this writer prefers to clarify that the personal representative may hire at the expense of the estate professionals to assist in estate settlement. Paragraph 13.d deals with the signing of tax returns and, while not essential, still is appropriate in most situations.

14. Certification of Incompetency. **OPTION 1: Decided by treating physician** Any person acting or named to act in a fiduciary capacity in this will is considered to be unable to serve or to continue serving when a physician whom such person has consulted within the prior three years has certified as to such consultation and the certification states that the person is incapable of managing the affairs of my estate or any trust I have established, regardless of cause and regardless of whether there is an adjudication of incompetency. No person is liable to anyone for actions taken in reliance on the physician's certification or for dealing with a personal representative or trustee other than the one removed for incompetency based on these certifications.

OPTION 2: Decided by two physicians Any person acting or named to act in a fiduciary capacity in this will is considered to be unable to serve or to continue serving when a written certification is received from two (2) physicians, both of whom have personally examined the person and at least one (1) of whom is board-certified in the specialty most closely associated with the health condition alleged to cause such incompetency. The certification must state that the person is incapable of managing his or her own finances, regardless of cause and regardless of whether there is an adjudication of incompetence, or need for a conservator, guardian, or other personal representative. No person is liable to anyone for actions taken in reliance on these certifications, or for dealing with a personal representative or trustee other than the one removed for incompetency based on these certifications.

COMMENT: This provision relates both to paragraph 9 concerning the succession of trustees, paragraph 12 regarding the successor personal representative, and paragraph 15 concerning the appointment of an alternate guardian. It defines incompetency, which is one of those events requiring a successor trustee, personal representative or an alternate guardian. The first option involves consultation with the person's personal physician, whereas Option 2 involves a panel of two physicians, one of whom is board certified in the speciality most closely associated with the health condition of the person acting in a fiduciary capacity. Clients differ as to which provision they prefer. Absent a strong preference by the testator, Option 1 is the provision most frequently used.

15. Appointment of Guardian. If my [husband or wife] does not survive me, my [relationship to guardian], [name of guardian], shall be guardian of each child for whom it is necessary to appoint a guardian. If [name of guardian] does not act as guardian, or having qualified dies, becomes incompetent, resigns, or declines to continue to serve, then my [relationship to alternate guardian], [name of alternate guardian] shall be guardian of each child for whom it is necessary to appoint a guardian. No surety bond shall be required of my guardians.

COMMENT: This is a standard paragraph naming a guardian for any children for whom a guardian is necessary, which includes the handicapped child in this drafting situation and may include other children. Some drafting changes may be needed due to state law requirements if the handicapped child is an adult child for whom the testator is the court-appointed guardian. If there is only one possible guardian and no alternate guardian, then the second sentence can be omitted. This paragraph omits the requirement of a surety bond.

16. <u>Employment of Attorney.</u> I request but do not require that my personal representative employ the law firm of [insert name of law firm], [city], [state] to be my estate's attorney as the attorneys in that law firm are the most familiar with my intentions expressed in this will.

COMMENT: This paragraph may be appropriate when the client is expecting the lawyer who drafted the will to be available to settle the estate. Often the children do not know the parent's preference for a lawyer, thus the provision is inserted. The employment of the testator's lawyer is made permissive to avoid any appearance of self-dealing by the lawyer preparing the will. There will be situations in which the client insists the wording be made mandatory. If so, the lawyer may wish to document this fact by memo to the file, signed by the client.

IN TESTIMONY WHEREOF, I, [full name of client], sign my name to this instrument this _____ day of _____, [current year], and being first duly sworn, do hereby declare to the undersigned authority that I sign and execute this instrument as my last will and that I sign it willingly, that I execute it as my free and voluntary act for the purposes therein expressed, and that I am 18 years of age or older, of sound mind, and under no constraint or undue influence.

_____

[full name of client]

We _____ and _____, the witnesses, sign our names to this instrument, being first duly sworn, and do hereby declare to the undersigned authority that [full name of client] signs and executes this instrument as [his or her Last Will and Testament dated _____, [current year], and that [he or she] signs it willingly and that each of us, in the presence and hearing of [full name of client] and in the presence of the other subscribing witness, hereby signs this Last Will and Testament as witness to [full name of client]'s signing, and that to the best of their knowledge, [full name of client] is eighteen (18) years of age or older, of sound mind and under no constraint or undue influence, all on this _____ day of _____, [current year].

_____

Witness

_____

Witness

_____

Address

_____

Address

STATE OF [State of Notary]   )

)SCT.

COUNTY OF [County of Notary])

Subscribed, sworn to, and acknowledged before me by [full name of client], and subscribed and sworn to before me by _____ and _____, witnesses, this the _____ day of _____, [current year].

_____

Notary Public, State at Large

My Commission Expires:_____

COMMENT: The above provisions are in compliance with the writer's own state law to avoid the necessity of locating witnesses to the will at a later date. This provision should be modified to meet the requirement of the lawyer's own state law.

PREPARED BY:

_____

[Name of Attorney]
[Name of Law Firm]
Attorneys at Law
[Street Address]
[City], [State] [Zip Code]
[Telephone Number]

INTER VIVOS TRUST FOR HANDICAPPED CHILD OR PERSON/ SPECIAL NEEDS TRUST/SUPPLEMENTAL CARE TRUST WORKSHEET

1. **Grantor and Trustee Information**

   Grantor Acting as Trustee? <u>Yes / No</u>

   If yes, Grantor Name _____

   Grantor City and State _____

   If no, Separate Trustee Name _____

   Trustee City and State _____

2. **Name of Trust**

   " _____ Trust"

3. **Name of Beneficiary**

   _____

4. **Distribution, upon the Death of the Handicapped Child or Person:**

   _____

   _____

   _____

5. **Powers**

   Environmental Powers? <u>Yes / No</u> (See Single Trust Paragraph 11 at page 73)

   Farm Powers? <u>Yes / No</u> (See Single Trust Paragraph 12 at page 73)

   Limitation on Trustee Powers? <u>Yes / No</u>

6. **Trustees**

   Name of first successor trustee: _____

   Name of second successor trustee: _____

   Corporate trustee compensation? (Option 1) <u>Yes / No</u>

   Individual reimbursed for expenses but no compensation? (Option 2) <u>Yes / No</u>

   Individual receives compensation? (Option 3) <u>Yes / No</u>

   Amount of compensation: $_____

7. **Incompetency**

   One physician decides? (Option 1) <u>Yes / No</u>

   Two physicians decide and one board certified? (Option 2) <u>Yes / No</u>

8. **Power to Amend**

   Irrevocable? <u>Yes / No</u>

   Revocable, becoming irrevocable upon death of grantor? <u>Yes / No</u>

INTER VIVOS TRUST FOR HANDICAPPED CHILD OR PERSON/
SPECIAL NEEDS TRUST/SUPPLEMENTAL CARE TRUST

This trust is one that may be used when provisions need to be made for a child or other person who has a disability that is severe enough for the person to qualify for Medicaid and SSI benefits. These types of trusts have several different common names, but the essence of the trust is that its benefits are paid only after state Medicaid and any other state or federal benefits. Thus, the trust operates as a supplement to those governmental benefits. An excellent ABA resource is Clifton B. Kruse, Jr., *Third Party and Self-Created Trusts*, 3rd edition, American Bar Association (Chicago, 2002).

I, [grantor's name], currently of [grantor's city], [grantor's state], as grantor and [trustee's name], currently of [trustee's city], [trustee's state], as trustee hereby enter into this trust agreement, and I transfer to my trustee the property described in Schedule A. This property and all investments, reinvestments and additions which may sometimes be referred to in this instrument as the "trust property" or "trust assets" are to be held subject to the following provisions:

COMMENT: This trust provides for a separate trustee from the grantor. If the grantor and trustee are to be the same person, then in lieu of this paragraph, the first paragraph on the Single Person Inter Vivos Trust at page 58 can be used.

1. Name of Trust. This instrument and the initial trust hereby established may be named the "[full name of handicapped child] Trust."

COMMENT: It is not essential that a trust have a name, but it has become common practice in recent years. Thus, the beneficiary's name or some abbreviation of it may be used. If the lawyer prefers, some other name may be used.

2. Beneficiary Information. My child, [full name of handicapped child] whose date of birth is [insert date of birth], is the beneficiary of this trust and references to "my child" or "the beneficiary" are only to [him or her].

COMMENT: This paragraph is drafted for a handicapped beneficiary who is the child of the grantor. If the beneficiary is not a child, then the relationship should be inserted in lieu of the word "child" followed by the full name of the person who is the beneficiary. If the beneficiary is someone other than a child, then appropriate changes should be made to change the reference to "my child" to the appropriate relationship or to delete the phrase entirely. It is not essential to include the beneficiary's date of birth. This can be retained or deleted as deemed appropriate.

3. Trust Provisions for Beneficiary. The trustee shall hold and administer the trust property, including property which the trustee receives under my will or from any other source as follows:

a. Throughout the lifetime of the beneficiary, unless this trust is sooner terminated, the trustee shall pay or use all, part, or none of the income and principal of the trust to or for the benefit of the beneficiary, to provide for [his or her] extra and supplemental care, maintenance, support and education, in addition to the benefits my child otherwise receives as a result of [his or her] handicap or disability from any local, state or federal government, or from any public or private agencies, any of which provide services or benefits to persons who are handicapped.

COMMENT: This is a typical wording for a special needs trust. The intent is to give the trustee sole discretion in making distributions and to clarify that all distributions are supplemental to other benefits the beneficiary receives.

---

    b. It is the express purpose of this trust to supplement other benefits which the beneficiary is entitled to receive. This trust is not intended to provide basic support, but rather is to be a discretionary trust to provide for supplemental needs of the beneficiary which are not otherwise provided for by various public and private assistance. To this end, the trustee may provide benefits for the beneficiary which the trustee considers necessary for [his or her] care, maintenance, support and education that cannot, in the trustee's opinion, be provided by the aforementioned public and private assistance programs. This includes but is not limited to such items as vacation, entertainment and recreational trips and the expenses of a traveling companion to accompany the beneficiary on such trips; personal items such as radios, televisions and other electronic entertainment devices; healthcare services, supplies, and special equipment; training programs; and rehabilitation supplemental to those the beneficiary is entitled to receive under any public or private assistance program. The trustee's obligation to make such payments is entirely discretionary; provided, however, the trustee may not exercise any discretion in making distributions from this trust that would make the beneficiary ineligible for any public or private benefits otherwise available to the beneficiary from any agency, private or public, including state or federal social service agencies.

COMMENT: This paragraph continues to clarify that the trust is supplemental to basic needs that are provided by state or federal programs, such as SSI or Medicaid. The third and fourth sentences are not essential and may be omitted. The final sentence in the paragraph makes it clear that the trustee is not permitted to make any distributions that would cause ineligibility for assistance benefits, such as SSI and Medicaid.

---

    c. Any payments from this trust shall be paid directly to the person or business which supplies such services or benefits.

COMMENT: This paragraph may not be essential in some states. It is inserted to avoid the result of a distribution being treated as a resource for the beneficiary if it is paid to an account such as a guardianship account held for the benefit of the beneficiary, from which payments are made for services or benefits received by the beneficiary. Some states take the position that such a distribution is a resource, which will then create partial or total ineligibility for government benefits. Making direct distributions to the provider of the services or benefits should avoid this unintended result.

---

    d. This trust shall terminate upon the death of the beneficiary and shall be distributed to [describe distribution plan]. In the event of a determination by any agency or court of competent jurisdiction that the income or principal of this trust is liable for the basic maintenance, support and medical care of the beneficiary which would otherwise be provided for the beneficiary by local, state, or federal government agencies or programs, or from any public or private agencies, then and in such event this trust shall terminate and the then remaining trust assets shall be distributed to [describe distribution plan].

COMMENT: Provisions must be added to state the recipient of trust assets upon the death of the beneficiary. The second sentence in the paragraph is not essential, but in most situations it is desirable. As can be seen, this sentence requires the trust to terminate and be distributed in the event a court or government agency treats the trust as a resource for the beneficiary. Obviously, the recipient of the trust assets must be someone the grantor believes will maintain the trust assets for the benefit of the beneficiary even though those assets will then be owned by that person.

4. Protection from Creditors. The trust beneficiary shall not have the right to sell, transfer, assign, alienate, pledge, or in any way encumber trust assets, including income and principal, nor shall trust assets be subject to execution, levy, sale, garnishment, attachment, bankruptcy, or other legal proceedings. Any such actions by the trust beneficiary or a third party seeking to enforce a claim against the trust assets shall not be recognized under any circumstances by the trustee. These provisions do not prevent the trustee from making distributions for the benefit of the trust beneficiary in such amounts and at such times as the trustee determines necessary for the trust beneficiary's maintenance, support, health and education.

COMMENT: This is a standard paragraph that precludes the trust assets from being attached by claims of creditors, including government agencies seeking reimbursement for payments made by them under a Medicaid or other government program.

5. Trustee Powers. In the administration of the trusts, the trustee shall have the following powers and rights and all others granted by law:

a. To sell publicly or privately any trust property, for cash or on time, without an order of court, upon such terms and conditions as shall seem best to the trustee; and no person dealing with the trustee shall have any obligation to look to the application of the purchase money therefor.

b. To invest and reinvest all or any part of the principal of the trust assets in any stocks, bonds, mortgages, shares, or interests in common trust funds, mutual funds, or other securities or property, real, personal, or mixed, and of any kind or nature whatsoever, as the trustee deems advisable, and without diversification if the trustee deems it advisable, irrespective of whether or not such securities or property are eligible for trust investment under state or any other law, and may change any investment received or made by the trustee, and may hold cash if the trustee deems it advisable.

c. To exercise broad discretion as to diversification of trust property, and shall not be required to reduce any concentrated holdings merely because of such concentration, and shall have full discretion as to the percentage to be invested in fixed income securities, and is specifically relieved from any requirements, legal or otherwise, as to the percentage of the trust assets to be invested in fixed income securities, and may invest and retain invested any trust estate wholly in common stocks.

d. To sell, convey, lease or mortgage, repair and improve, and take any and all other steps with regard to any real estate that may at any time be a part of the principal of the trust; and any lease of such real property or contract with regard thereto made by the trustee shall be binding for the full period of the lease or contract, though said period shall extend beyond the termination of the trust.

e. To vote shares of stock held in the trust at stockholders' meetings in person or by special, limited, or general proxy, with or without power of substitution, as to the trustee seems best.

f. To participate in the liquidation, reorganization, consolidation, incorporation and reincorporation, or any other financial readjustment of any limited liability company, corporation or business in which the trust is or shall be financially interested.

g. To borrow money from any source for any purpose connected with the protection, preservation, improvement or development of the trust hereunder, whenever in the trustee's judgment the trustee deems it advisable, and as security to mortgage or pledge any real estate or personal property forming a part of the trust upon such terms and conditions as the trustee may deem advisable.

h. To hold any and all securities in bearer form, in the trustee's own name, or the name of some other person, partnership, or corporation, or in the name of a duly appointed nominee, with or without disclosing the fiduciary ownership thereof.

i. To divide the principal of the trust property into parts or shares and to distribute or allot same, the trustee is authorized to make such division in cash or in kind or both; and for the purpose of such division or allotment, the judgment of the trustee concerning the propriety thereof and relative value of property so distributed or allotted shall be binding and conclusive with respect to all persons interested herein.

j. To merge and consolidate the trust property of any separate trust held hereunder with other trusts and then to administer such trust property as a single trust provided the separate trust is for the benefit of the same persons with substantially the same terms, conditions and federal tax consequences.

k. To pay such income and principal during the minority or incapacity of any beneficiary to whom income is herein directed to be paid, or for whose benefit income and principal may be expended, in any one or more of the following ways: (1) directly to said beneficiary; (2) to the legal guardian or committee of said beneficiary; (3) to a relative of said beneficiary to be expended by such relative for the maintenance, health, and education of said beneficiary; or (4) by expending the same directly for the maintenance, health, and education of said beneficiary. The trustee shall not be obliged to see to the application of the funds so paid, but the receipt of such person shall be full acquittance to the trustee.

l. To continue and operate any business owned by me at my death and to do any and all things deemed appropriate by the trustee, including the power to form a limited liability company or incorporate the business and to put additional capital into the business, for such time as the trustee deems advisable, without liability for loss resulting from the continuance or operation of the business except for the trustee's own negligence; and to close out, liquidate, or sell the business at such time and upon such terms as the trustee deems proper, and in this connection a sale may be made (pursuant to an agreement entered into by me during my lifetime, or otherwise) to a partner, officer, member, employee or beneficiary under this trust. I am aware of the fact that certain risks are inherent in the operation of any business and, therefore, my trustee shall not be liable for any loss resulting from the retention and operation of any business unless such loss results directly from my trustee's gross negligence or willful misconduct.

m. To have the same powers, authorities, and discretions in the management of the trust as I would have in the management and control of my own personal assets. The trustee may continue to exercise any powers and discretions hereunder for a reasonable period after the termination of any trust under this instrument.

COMMENT: The above powers are a set of standard powers that appear throughout this book. The powers should be reviewed to be certain that you the lawyer understand each power, the client is in agreement with each of the powers granted and that the powers granted are needed.

Because this is a generic and broad statement of powers, some of these powers may not be necessary. For example, powers to sell or lease real estate are not needed if the grantor knows the trust will consist only of cash and other intangible investments.

6. <u>Limitation on Powers of Individual Trustee.</u> Notwithstanding any other powers granted to my trustee in this instrument, an individual trustee (a) shall have no power to make payments or distributions that would discharge the trustee's legal obligation to support the trust beneficiary, (b) shall not exercise any power or discretion in any manner that would be deemed to be a general power of appointment under Internal Revenue Code Section 2041, (c) shall be limited by the ascertainable standard of "maintenance, support, health and education" when making payments or distributions to the trustee personally or to anyone for whom the trustee has a beneficial interest, and (d) shall possess no incidence of ownership or powers with respect to life insurance in which the trustee is the insured and has fiduciary power over such life insurance.

COMMENT: There are some situations in which an individual trustee may have adverse estate or income tax consequences when given broad powers as trustee. If a corporate trustee is used, then this paragraph is not needed. But an individual trustee must be certain that acting as trustee does not result in any adverse estate or income tax consequences. This paragraph is intended to ensure that adverse tax consequences are avoided if overly broad powers are granted in the trust instrument. The lawyer is urged to exercise caution when using individual trustees coupled with broad discretionary powers of income and principal distribution to a trust beneficiary because of possible adverse tax consequences. An ABA resource to acquaint oneself with these issues is L. Rush Hunt and Lara Rae Hunt, *A Lawyer's Guide to Estate Planning*, American Bar Association (Chicago: 2004) §14.4.

7. <u>Trustee Resignation.</u> My trustee may resign at any time by giving written notice to my successor trustee named below, if any, and if none, then written notice shall be given to each current adult income beneficiary who is then living.

COMMENT: If a trustee resigns, there must be some method of notice and appointment of a successor trustee. This paragraph provides a method of notification. It is not an essential trust provision, but is a helpful one.

8. <u>Trustee Succession and Appointment.</u> If [trustee's name] dies, becomes incompetent, resigns or ceases to serve for any reason, then [insert name of first successor trustee] shall serve as successor trustee. If [insert name of first successor trustee] dies, becomes incompetent, resigns or ceases to serve for any reason, then [insert name of second successor trustee] shall serve as successor trustee. The last serving successor trustee may name [his or her] own successor trustee by a written instrument delivered to the successor trustee or by will. The successor trustee may be an individual or a financial institution possessing trust powers under state or federal law. Any further vacancy in the office of trustee shall be filled by decision of the probate court where I resided at the time of my death.

COMMENT: A decision must be made as to succession of trustees and the method of appointing a successor trustee if all of those named successor trustees are unable to serve. It is also essential to clarify whether successor trustees must only be financial institutions or if individuals may also be considered. Once a decision is made as to the succession of trustees, then the last three sentences should be reviewed to be certain to what extent each of those are needed.

9. <u>Powers of Successor Trustee.</u> Each successor trustee shall have the same rights, titles, powers, duties, discretions, and immunities and otherwise be in the same position as if originally named trustee. No successor trustee shall be personally liable for any act or failure to act of a predecessor trustee. Further, a successor trustee may accept the account furnished and the property delivered by or for a predecessor trustee without liability for so doing, and such acceptance shall be a full and complete discharge to the predecessor trustee.

COMMENT: This paragraph clarifies that a successor trustee has the same powers as the initial trustee. Further, the paragraph relieves the successor trustee from liability for the prior acts of the resigning trustee and waives any requirements of audit or inquiry into the activities of the prior trustee. This is essential for any successor trustee.

10. <u>Compensation of Trustee.</u> **OPTION 1: Corporate trustee compensation** A corporate trustee shall receive compensation in accordance with its regular schedule of fees in effect at the time such services are rendered.

OPTION 2: Individual does not receive compensation An individual trustee shall not be paid any compensation, but shall be reimbursed for out-of-pocket expenses.

OPTION 3: Individual does receive compensation An individual trustee shall be paid [insert amount of compensation] as compensation for such services and shall be reimbursed for out-of-pocket expenses.

COMMENT: Three options are provided, but the actual drafting of this paragraph may be different than each of these options. If the only trustee to be used is a corporate trustee, then Option 1 is a standard trust provision. If there is a possibility of individual trustees, then care should be given to the method for setting this fee. If no fee is to be paid because it is a close family member, then it is suggested that Option 2 be used. If the grantor expects a fee to be charged, then an amount or a formula, such as a percentage of income or principal, must be set. It is unwise to simply provide for compensation to be a reasonable fee, as that leaves an individual trustee with great uncertainty as to the fee to be charged. Without the grantor clarifying compensation, the trustee could find him or herself in litigation with the beneficiary or the beneficiary's guardian.

11. <u>Court Accountings.</u> To the extent such requirements can be waived, the trustee shall not be required (a) to file any inventory of trust property or accounts or reports of the administration of the trusts, or to register the trusts, in any court, (b) to furnish any bond or other security for the proper performance of the trustee's duties or (c) to obtain authority from a court for the exercise of any power conferred on the trustee by this instrument. This waiver does not preclude the trustee from registering any trust created in this instrument and petitioning a court having jurisdiction over registered trusts for a judicial ruling on any matter relating to administration of any trust created by this instrument.

COMMENT: The first sentence is to clarify the normal situation that an inter vivos trust is not subject to judicial oversight. The second sentence may be omitted, but is suggested as a potential benefit in some states. In a state in which a trust can be registered, it may be possible to have minor trust matters resolved by the court in which the trust is registered. This creates a simplified process for dealing with minor administrative matters. Without this provision, a court might be reluctant to decide matters for a trust which is not required to be registered under state law.

12. <u>Severability.</u> If any provisions of this trust shall be unenforceable, the remaining provisions shall nevertheless be carried into effect.

COMMENT: This is the same type of standard provision often seen in contracts that is intended to save the document if a particular provision is found to be invalid or void. It is doubtful this provision will have any practical effect in most trust situations, but it is a "boilerplate" provision that is frequently found in trust instruments and for which there is no disadvantage.

---

13. <u>Certification of Incompetency.</u> **OPTION 1: Decided by treating physician** Any person acting or named to act as a trustee in this instrument is considered to be unable to serve or to continue serving when a physician whom such person has consulted within the prior three years has certified as to such consultation and the certification states that the person is incapable of managing the affairs of the trusts I have established in this instrument, regardless of cause and regardless of whether there is an adjudication of incompetency. No person shall be liable to anyone for actions taken in reliance on the physician's certification, or for dealing with a trustee other than the one removed for incompetency based on such certification.

OPTION 2: Decided by two physicians Any person acting or named to act as a trustee in this instrument is considered to be unable to serve or to continue serving when a written certification is received from two (2) physicians, both of whom have personally examined the person and at least one (1) of whom is board-certified in the specialty most closely associated with the health condition alleged to cause such incompetency. The certification must state that the person is incapable of managing the affairs of this trust, regardless of cause and regardless of whether there is an adjudication of incompetence. No person is liable to anyone for actions taken in reliance on these physician's certifications, or for dealing with a trustee other than the one removed for incompetency based on these certifications.

COMMENT: This provision relates back to paragraph 8 concerning the succession of trustees. It defines incompetency, which is one of those events requiring a successor trustee. The first option involves consultation with the trustee's personal physician, whereas Option 2 involves a panel of two physicians, one of whom is board certified in the speciality most closely associated with the health condition of the trustee. Clients differ as to which provision they prefer and are more concerned about the provision when the grantor is also the initial trustee. Absent a strong preference by the grantor, Option 1 is the provision most frequently used.

---

14. <u>Titles and References.</u> The underscored titles of paragraphs in this instrument are for information purposes only and shall be given no legal effect.

COMMENT: This is another common "boilerplate" provision that is perhaps not essential, but for which there is no disadvantage.

---

15. <u>Choice and Effect of Law.</u> This trust agreement is entered into and executed in the [State or Commonwealth] of [name of state]. It shall be administered in accordance with the laws of that state.

COMMENT: It is a standard provision in both trust instruments and in contracts to specify the state law that applies in interpretation of the instrument. This will usually be the grantor's state of residency, but also should be the state in which the lawyer is licensed to practice.

16. <u>Power to Amend or Revoke.</u> I reserve the right from time to time by written instrument delivered to the trustee to amend or revoke this instrument and the trusts hereby evidenced, in whole or in part.

COMMENT: The trust instrument should specify whether it is revocable or irrevocable. This particular trust is a revocable trust that becomes irrevocable upon the death of the grantor. This is because the trust will be an unfunded trust and will only receive assets after the grantor's death. In some situations, the lawyer or client will want the trust to be irrevocable, such as, situations in which the grantor will currently transfer assets to the trust. This is not as easy as it seems. Such a transfer will raise gift tax considerations that must be addressed before making the trust irrevocable and transferring assets to the trust. The general recommendation is that the trust remain revocable.

The undersigned have signed this instrument and have established the foregoing trust on this the _____ day of _____, [Current Year]._____

GRANTOR:

_____
[grantor's name]

TRUSTEE:

_____
[trustee's name]

STATE OF [State of Notary]   )

) SCT.

COUNTY OF [County of Notary])

The undersigned, a Notary Public within and for the state and county aforesaid, does hereby certify that the foregoing trust agreement executed by [grantor's name], as grantor, was on this day produced to me in my county by [grantor's name], who executed, acknowledged and swore the same before me to be [his or her] act and deed in due form of law.

Given under my hand and notarial seal on this the ___ day of _____, [Current Year].

_____

Notary Public, State at Large

My commission expires:_____

STATE OF [State of Notary]   )

) SCT.

COUNTY OF [County of Notary])

The undersigned, a Notary Public within and for the state and county aforesaid, does hereby certify that the foregoing trust agreement executed by [trustee's name], as trustee, was on this day produced to me in my county by [trustee's name], who executed, acknowledged and swore the same before me to be [his or her] act and deed in due form of law.

Given under my hand and notarial seal on this the ___ day of _____, [Current Year].

_____

Notary Public, State at Large

My commission expires:_____

PREPARED BY:

_____

[Name of Attorney]
[Name of Law Firm]
Attorneys at Law
[Street Address]
[City], [State] [Zip Code]
[Telephone Number]

SCHEDULE A

[NAME OF TRUST] TRUST

Cash. . . . . $ 10.00

The lawyer will note on schedule A, a deposit of $10 in the trust. State law will determine the necessity of an initial deposit. An unfunded trust that contains no principal may be deemed a "dry" trust under state law, meaning that it is not a valid document. Some lawyers go to the added step of affixing a $10 bill to schedule A, while others are satisfied with a cash deposit which does have the disadvantage of not being traceable. If there is the possibility of a contest of the trust, the cautious practice is to affix a $10 bill to schedule A.

QUALIFYING INCOME TRUST WORKSHEET

1. **Grantor Information**

   1.1 Grantor Name_____

   1.2 Grantor City and State _____

   1.3 Acting through Attorney-in-Fact? <u>Yes / No</u>

       If Yes, Name of Attorney-in-Fact _____

2. **Trustee Information**

   2.1 Trustee Name _____

   2.2 Trustee City and State _____

3. **Name of Trust**

   "_____ Qualifying Income Trust"

4. **Name of Beneficiary**

   _____

5. **Name of Successor Trustee**

   _____

   If no successor named, name of court that shall name successor:

   _____

6. **State Law**

   _____

QUALIFYING INCOME TRUST

On occasion, a qualifying income trust is needed for a person in nursing home care who seeks to be Medicaid eligible but whose income is greater than the income cap under that particular state's Medicaid laws. The person otherwise qualifies for Medicaid, as they do not have sufficient resources to be disqualified, but under Medicaid law, the person is still deemed ineligible due to the amount of their income, such as social security and other pension income. To become Medicaid eligible, a qualifying income trust (QIT) or Miller trust (as it is sometimes termed) is required. The basics of the trust are that the income above the cap is distributed to the QIT. Then the person's remaining income is within the amount of the income cap and by a legal fiction, the excess income held in the QIT is not considered income in excess of the cap. This typically results in two checking accounts from which distribution is made to the nursing home. For those who have interest in understanding these trusts more fully, see Clifton B. Kruse, Jr., *Third Party and Self-Created Trusts*, 3rd edition, American Bar Association (Chicago, 2002). Also, the reader is cautioned that state law should be considered. The trust provided may need to be modified to meet the requirements of the lawyer's own state Medicaid office.

I, [grantor's name], by and through my attorney-in-fact, [attorney-in-fact's name], currently of [grantor's city], [grantor's state], acting as grantor and [trustee's name], currently of [trustee's city], [trustee's state], as trustee hereby enter into this trust agreement, which shall be held subject to the following provisions:

COMMENT: If the nursing home patient is mentally competent, he or she can act as the grantor of the trust. Otherwise, the person acting as the grantor's power of attorney may sign. Some states do not allow a third party to act as grantor, creating the oddity of an incompetent person signing a trust document if they do not have a person acting as their power of attorney. Hopefully, the lawyer drafting one of these trusts lives in a state whose Medicaid office is more reasonable than the one in the writer's own state.

---

1. <u>Name of Trust.</u> This instrument and the initial trust hereby established may be named the "[name of beneficiary] Qualifying Income Trust."

COMMENT: The trust is typically named after the beneficiary followed by the phrase "Qualifying Income Trust."

---

2. <u>Beneficiary Information.</u> The beneficiary of this trust is [name of beneficiary] and any references to "the beneficiary" are only to [him or her].

COMMENT: The beneficiary's name is inserted in this paragraph.

---

3. <u>Trust Purpose.</u> The grantor establishes this trust for the benefit of [name of beneficiary] in strict accordance with the limitations imposed by this instrument.

a. This trust is created pursuant to § 1917(d)(4)(B) of the Social Security Act [42USC 1396p] and [insert applicable state statute or regulation]; and is created in order to enable the beneficiary to qualify for Medicaid benefits and to provide for the administration and disposition of the trust estate during and after the lifetime of the beneficiary, in accordance with the terms and conditions of this trust.

b. No distributions of income or principal may be made by the trustee to the beneficiary except in accordance with the terms set out in this agreement.

c. All interpretations and actions taken by the trustee pursuant to this trust shall be done for and with the purpose of creating, establishing, and maintaining the beneficiary's eligibility for Medicaid benefits. Any provisions of this trust which are deemed to be inconsistent or contrary to such purpose shall be deemed to be void and of no force or effect.

COMMENT: The essence of this trust is that distributions can only be made as permitted by state and federal Medicaid laws. The applicable state statute or regulation should be inserted in 3.a and any modifications required by the lawyer's own state should be made.

---

4. <u>Trust Assets.</u> The trust assets held in this trust shall be subject to the following restrictions.

a. The grantor shall transfer to the trustee by deposit to the bank account which has been established solely for receiving funds under this trust, the monthly income the beneficiary receives from pensions, social security, and other income permitted an individual under Section 1917(d)(4)(B) of the Social Security Act.

b. All such assets when transferred to the trust shall be registered or titled in the name of the trustee.

c. The trustee shall hold, invest, administer, and distribute the trust assets in accordance with the terms of this agreement and as required to maintain Medicaid eligibility for the beneficiary.

d. No assets may be transferred to the trust other than the beneficiary's income as defined above.

COMMENT: These are requirements from the writer's own state imposed by state regulation. The lawyer should consult his/her own state Medicaid regulations to be certain of any provisions that need to be added or any modifications that need to be made to these provisions.

---

5. <u>Distribution of Income and Principal.</u> The trustee shall make distributions of income and principal from the trust as follows:

a. During the lifetime of the beneficiary, the trustee shall distribute to the beneficiary or for the beneficiary's benefit all income, no less often than monthly as permitted by the [name of state agency handling Medicaid services], or other appropriate state or federal agency.

b. Currently it is anticipated that permissible trustee distributions include the beneficiary's personal needs allowance, a monthly maintenance needs allowance for the beneficiary's spouse and any dependent family members, the beneficiary's health insurance premiums, the amount the beneficiary is required to pay for nursing home or community-based health care, and such other expenses that may be determined by the [name of state agency handling Medicaid services] to be permissible.

c. The trustee shall have no discretion concerning distributions to the beneficiary or for the beneficiary's benefit. No payments from the trust may be made to any other person during the beneficiary's lifetime.

COMMENT: The Medicaid regulations are very specific regarding distributions from the trust. Those regulations require compliance. While these provisions are generally standard, there may be some variation from state to state; therefore some modifications may be necessary. Paragraph 5.b should be modified if the grantor is not married.

6. <u>Termination of Trust.</u> At the death of the beneficiary, the trust shall terminate and the remaining trust assets shall be distributed in an amount sufficient to pay the [State or Commonwealth] of [name of state] the amount of medical assistance paid by it on behalf of the beneficiary under the Medicaid program. The balance of the trust assets, if any, shall be distributed to the beneficiary's estate.

COMMENT: Any amounts held in the trust will be paid to the state Medicaid office after the death of the beneficiary to offset payments made by the Medicaid program for that person. Any excess funds can be distributed to that person's estate, but as a practical matter, there will be none.

7. <u>Non-assignability of Interest.</u> This is a spendthrift trust. None of the principal or income of the trust estate or any interest in the trust shall be anticipated, assigned, encumbered, or be subject to any creditors' claims or to any legal process.

COMMENT: This is a standard provision required by the writer's state Medicaid office.

8. <u>Trustee Succession.</u> In the event the initial trustee ceases to act due to death, incompetency, resignation or otherwise ceases to serve for any reason, then [name of successor trustee] shall serve as successor trustee. The last serving successor trustee may name his or her own successor trustee by a written instrument delivered to the successor trustee or by will. The successor trustee may be an individual or a financial institution possessing trust powers under state or federal law. If no successor trustee is named, then a successor trustee shall be named by the [name of court]. No trustee shall be required to post surety or personal bond while serving as trustee.

COMMENT: The method of trustee succession should be determined as in any trust.

9. <u>Trustee Powers.</u> In the administration of this trust, the trustee shall have all powers granted to trustees under state law, except as limited by the terms of this trust and as specifically limited by the following provisions.

a. If any trust funds remain after the required monthly distributions provided for hereinabove, such funds shall remain in the trust and cannot be sold or reserved.

b. No powers may be exercised that are inconsistent with regulations of the [name of state agency handling Medicaid services].

c. The trustee shall have the power to open bank accounts, to issue checks on, and make withdrawals from such account. Any and all bank accounts, including checking, certificates of deposit, and savings accounts, established in the name of the trust by the trustee shall be subject to withdrawal, and all checks, drafts and other obligations of the trust shall be honored by said depositories upon the signature of the trustee.

d. The trustee shall report to the [name of state agency handling Medicaid services] and any court of competent jurisdiction as required by regulation or court order.

e. The trustee may invest in non-income producing property.

f. The trustee shall take whatever legal steps may be necessary to initiate or continue any public assistance program for which the beneficiary is or may become eligible.

COMMENT: A broad statement of powers may result in the trust failing to meet Medicaid eligibility standards. Therefore, the powers contained in this trust are limited to those approved by the writer's own state Medicaid office.

---

10. <u>Grantor Trust.</u> This trust is a grantor trust; and pursuant to IRC Section 672(e) the trust income is taxed to the beneficiary.

COMMENT: This provision is inserted to clarify that the income is still taxed to the Medicaid eligible beneficiary.

---

11. <u>Irrevocability.</u> This trust is irrevocable and the grantor has no right to alter, amend, or revoke any provision of this agreement; however, the trustee is granted the limited right to amend this trust in order to comply with any provisions now or in the future required of the [name of state agency handling Medicaid services] in order for this trust to be treated as a qualifying income trust.

COMMENT: This trust must be irrevocable to meet Medicaid requirements.

---

12. <u>Choice and Effect of Law.</u> This trust agreement is entered into and executed in the [State or Commonwealth] of [name of state]. It shall be administered in accordance with the laws of that state.

COMMENT: It is a standard provision in both trust instruments and in contracts to specify the state law that applies in interpretation of the instrument. This will be the grantor's home state.

The undersigned have signed this instrument and have established the foregoing trust on this the _____ day of _____, [Current Year].

GRANTOR:

_____

[grantor's name]

TRUSTEE:

_____

[trustee's name]

STATE OF [State of Notary]   )

) SCT.

COUNTY OF [County of Notary])

The undersigned, a Notary Public within and for the state and county aforesaid, does hereby certify that the foregoing trust agreement executed by [attorney in fact's name], on behalf of the grantor and in [his or her] capacity as trustee, was on this day produced to me in my county by [attorney in fact's name], who executed, acknowledged and swore the same before me to be [his or her] act and deed in due form of law.

Given under my hand and notarial seal on this the ___ day of _____, [Current Year].

                                                    _____

                                                    Notary Public, State at Large

                                                    My commission expires:_____

PREPARED BY:

_____
[Name of Attorney]
[Name of Law Firm]
Attorneys at Law
[Street Address]
[City], [State] [Zip Code]
[Telephone Number]

SCHEDULE A

[NAME OF BENEFICIARY] TRUST

Cash. . . . . $ 10.00

The lawyer will note on schedule A, a deposit of $10 in the trust. State law will determine the necessity of an initial deposit. An unfunded trust that contains no principal may be deemed a "dry" trust under state law, meaning that it is not a valid document. Some lawyers go to the added step of affixing a $10 bill to schedule A, while others are satisfied with a cash deposit which does have the disadvantage of not being traceable. If there is the possibility of a contest of the trust, the cautious practice is to affix a $10 bill to schedule A.

SPENDTHRIFT TRUST WORKSHEET

1. **Grantor and Trustee Information**

   Grantor Acting as Trustee? Yes / No

   If yes, Grantor Name _____

   Grantor City and State _____

   If no, Separate Trustee Name _____

   Trustee City and State _____

2. **Name of Trust**

   " _____ Trust"

3. **Beneficiary Information**

   Name of Beneficiary: _____

   Relationship to Grantor (child, etc.)_____

4. **Distribution, upon the Death of the Beneficiary**:

   A. Power of appointment: (See Single Person Inter Vivos Trust Paragraph 5.f at page 62)

       Limited to descendants/charities? (Option 1) Yes / No

       Broad? (Option 2) Yes / No

       Limited and age restricted? (Option 3) Yes / No

       Broad and age restricted? (Option 4) Yes / No

   If power of appointment not exercised and a child is deceased (Can be modified if no power of appointment is granted):

   Deceased child's share distributed
   to such child's estate? (Option 1) Yes / No

   or Deceased child's share per stirpes
   to lineal descendants? (Option 2) Yes / No

   B. Provision for educational incentive? Yes / No
       (See Single Person Inter Vivos Trust Paragraph 5.c at page 61)

   C. Provision for trustee authority to withhold? Yes / No
       (See Single Person Inter Vivos Trust Paragraph 5.e at page 61)

   Other provisions/instructions _____

   _____

   _____

5.   **Powers**

Environmental Powers? <u>Yes</u> / <u>No</u> (See Single Person Inter Vivos Trust Paragraph 11 at page 73)

Farm Powers? <u>Yes</u> / <u>No</u> (See Single Person Inter Vivos Trust Paragraph 12 at page 73)

Limitation on Trustee Powers? <u>Yes / No</u>

6.   **Trustees**

Name of first successor trustee: _____

Name of second successor trustee: _____

Corporate trustee compensation? (Option 1) <u>Yes / No</u>

Individual reimbursed for expenses but no compensation? (Option 2) <u>Yes / No</u>

Individual receives compensation? (Option 3) <u>Yes / No</u>

Amount of compensation: $_____

7.   **Incompetency**

One physician decides? (Option 1) <u>Yes / No</u>

Two physicians decide and one board certified? (Option 2) <u>Yes / No</u>

8.   **Power to Amend**

Irrevocable? <u>Yes / No</u>

Revocable, becoming irrevocable upon death of grantor? <u>Yes / No</u>

9.   **No Contest**

Is No Contest provision needed? <u>Yes / No</u>

SPENDTHRIFT TRUST

This trust is designed to protect a beneficiary from creditor claims. As drafted, it has a child as the beneficiary. Obviously, the form can be changed to provide for any individual. The trust is broad in scope and will require editing to streamline it for the particular situation presented.

I, [Grantor's name], currently of [Grantor's city], [Grantor's state], acting as grantor and trustee hereby transfer to myself, as trustee, the property described in Schedule A. This property and all investments, reinvestments and additions which may sometimes be referred to in this instrument as the "trust property" or "trust assets" are to be held subject to the following provisions:

COMMENT: This trust provides for the grantor acting as trustee. In some situations it will be more appropriate for a third party to be the trustee. If a third party trustee is needed, the Inter Vivos Trust for a Handicapped Person beginning at page 222 contains an introductory paragraph with a separate initial trustee and a signature page for the grantor and trustee and separate notarizations. Also, Paragraph 10 must be modified.

1. <u>Name of Trust.</u> This instrument and the initial trust hereby established may be named the "[Name of trust] Trust."

COMMENT: The trust may have any name, but it is commonly named after the beneficiary.

2. <u>Beneficiary Information.</u> My child [name of child] is the beneficiary of this trust and references to "my child" or "the beneficiary" are only to [him or her].

COMMENT: This trust is drafted for the grantor's child being the beneficiary, in which case the child's name is inserted. If another person is named the beneficiary, then the term "child" must be changed to the correct relationship. Also, changes will be necessary in paragraph 3 as it uses the term "child."

3. <u>Trust Provisions for Child.</u> The trustee shall hold and administer the trust property, including property which the trustee receives under my will or from any other source as follows:

a. The trustee may pay to or use all, part or none, of the income and principal of my child's trust as the trustee believes appropriate for the reasonable maintenance, support, health and education (including college or graduate, professional or vocational school education) of my child, considering my child's income or assets and all other circumstances and factors the trustee believes pertinent. It is my desire that distributions of income and principal not impair my child's motivation to be productive and self-supporting, thus my trustee shall not make distributions of income and principal from my child's trust if my child is not productive, mature, and responsible. If any net income remains undistributed at the end of each calendar year (excluding income distributed during the sixty-five [65] day period under Internal Revenue Code Section 663), the trustee shall add it to the principal of my child's trust.

COMMENT: The first sentence provides broad discretion to the trustee in making distributions for the child. The second sentence establishes a broad restriction on distributions. Greater restrictions follow in paragraph 3.b. The third sentence may be eliminated, but is provided for situations in which income is not distributed before year end; and to set the time at which accumulated income is added to trust principal.

b. In addition to the restrictions provided in the above paragraph and as a condition precedent to distributions under that paragraph, my trustee shall withhold or postpone any or all distributions of income or principal from my child's trust if my trustee believes a distribution to my child could result in the loss of some part or all of the distribution due to any possible civil or criminal legal action involving my child or my child's spouse, or due to my child or my child's spouse being addicted to alcohol or any legal or illegal controlled substance. The decision of my trustee shall be final and binding and shall not be subject to question by any person or in any court.

COMMENT: If the client is faced with a child who has a substance abuse or other serious problem which makes distributions from the trust unwise, then this paragraph or a variation should be considered. This provision is designed to give the trustee full authority to withhold all distributions of income and principal when a child is facing substance abuse or other significant personal problems.

c. Upon the death of my child, the trustee shall distribute the trust assets (specify distribution plan).

COMMENT: The distribution of the trust assets after the child's death must be determined. This paragraph provides for the grantor to make that decision. Paragraph 5.f and 5.g (page 62) of the Single Person Inter Vivos Trust provide multiple drafting options for the lawyer to consider.

4. <u>Default Provisions.</u> Any trust property not disposed of by any of the above provisions shall be distributed on the date of such failure of disposition to [default provisions].

COMMENT: If there are a limited number of beneficiaries, then it may be wise to insert a default provision providing for the ultimate recipient should all the beneficiaries named in paragraph 3 be deceased.

5. <u>Protection from Creditors.</u> The trust beneficiary shall not have the right to sell, transfer, assign, alienate, pledge, or in any way encumber trust assets, including income and principal, nor shall trust assets be subject to execution, levy, sale, garnishment, attachment, bankruptcy, or other legal proceedings. Any such actions by the trust beneficiary or by a third party seeking to enforce a claim against the trust assets shall not be recognized under any circumstances by the trustee. These provisions do not prevent the trustee from making distributions for the benefit of a trust beneficiary in such amounts and at such times as the trustee determines necessary for the trust beneficiary's maintenance, support, health and education, provided such distributions are otherwise permitted in this trust.

COMMENT: This is a standard paragraph that precludes the trust assets from being attached by claims of creditors. The lawyer should check state law before advising a client of the effect of this provision.

6. <u>Definitions.</u> For all purposes of this instrument, the following shall apply:

a. The words "child," "children," "descendant" or "descendants" shall exclude adopted persons unless they are adopted prior to [insert age] years; and shall include only persons legitimately born unless a decree of adoption terminates the parental rights of the natural mother during her lifetime, or the natural father signs a written notarized instrument during his lifetime in which he irrevocably states that the child is to be considered legitimately born for purposes of inheriting under this will.

COMMENT: Some clients will want to restrict distribution for an adopted descendant to preclude a child adopted as an adult. Thus, many clients will use the age 18 or perhaps a slightly older age such as 20 or 21. Other clients may wish to restrict the age to a younger adopted child, such as one under the age of 10. The issue of illegitimate descendants should also be considered. In many situations, a child or more remote descendant should be treated the same as any other child, in which case the portion of this paragraph that deals with illegitimate children can be deleted. In other situations there may be a limited or no relationship with the child, in which event no distribution should be made to that child. This form gives the father of the child the right to allow the child to inherit if the father signs a written document allowing the inheritance.

b. Whenever assets are to be divided and allocated per stirpes, the assets to be divided or allocated shall be divided into as many equal shares as are necessary to divide or allocate one share to each then living child of such person and to provide one share collectively for the then living descendants of each child of such person who then is deceased leaving one or more descendants then living. Any collective share shall be divided and allocated per stirpes among the descendants of such deceased person in accordance with the preceding sentence.

COMMENT: Since the term per stirpes is used often in this document, a definition is provided of that term. The lawyer should modify this definition to conform with his or her own state law should it differ any from this definition. Of course, a definition is not essential, since the term will be defined under state law. But since it is a term that clients are not familiar with, it is often helpful to define it for them in the document. An excellent ABA resource that explains the term per stirpes and its variations is Jeffrey N. Penell and Alan Newman, *Estate and Trust Planning*, American Bar Association (Chicago, 2005) pp. 19–26.

7. <u>Trustee Powers.</u> In the administration of the trusts, the trustee shall have the following powers and rights and all others granted by law:

a. To sell publicly or privately any trust property, for cash or on time, without an order of court and upon such terms and conditions as my trustee deems proper; and no person dealing with my trustee shall have any obligation to look to the application of the purchase money.

b. To invest and reinvest all or any part of the principal of the trust in any stocks, bonds, mortgages, shares or interests in common trust funds, mutual funds, or other securities or property, real, personal, or mixed, and of any kind or nature whatsoever, as the trustee deems proper, and without diversification if the trustee deems it advisable, irrespective of whether or not such securities or property are eligible for trust investment under state or any other law, and may change any investment received or made by the trustee, and may hold cash if the trustee deems it advisable.

c. To exercise broad discretion as to diversification of trust property, and shall not be required to reduce any concentrated holdings merely because of such concentration, and shall have full discretion as to the percentage to be invested in fixed income securities, and is specifically relieved from any requirements, legal or otherwise, as to the percentage of the trust assets to be invested in fixed income securities, and may invest or retain invested any trust estates wholly in common stocks.

d. To sell, convey, lease or mortgage, repair and improve, and take any and all other steps with regard to any real estate that may at any time be a part of the principal of the trust; and any lease of such real property or contract with regard thereto made by the trustee shall be binding for the full period of the lease or contract, even though the period shall extend beyond the termination of the trust.

e. To vote shares of stock held in the trust at stockholders' meetings in person or by special, limited, or general proxy, with or without power of substitution, as seems best to the trustee.

f. To participate in the liquidation, reorganization, consolidation, incorporation and reincorporation, or any other financial readjustment of any corporation, limited liability company or business in which the trust is, or shall be financially interested.

g. To borrow money from any source for any purpose connected with the protection, preservation, improvement or development of the trust hereunder, whenever in the trustee's judgment the trustee deems it advisable, and as security to mortgage or pledge any real estate or personal property forming a part of the trust upon such terms and conditions as the trustee may deem advisable.

h. To hold any and all securities in bearer form, in the trustee's own name, or the name of some other person, partnership, or corporation, or in the name of a duly appointed nominee, with or without disclosing the fiduciary ownership.

i. To divide the principal of the trust property into parts or shares and to distribute or allot same, and to make such division in cash or in kind or both. For the purpose of such division or allotment, the judgment of the trustee concerning the propriety thereof and relative value of property so distributed or allotted shall be binding and conclusive with respect to all interested persons.

j. To merge and consolidate the trust property of any separate trust held hereunder with other trusts and then to administer such trust property as a single trust provided the separate trust is for the benefit of the same persons with substantially the same terms, conditions and federal tax consequences.

k. To pay such income and principal during the minority or incapacity of any beneficiary for whose benefit income and principal may be expended, in any one or more of the following ways: (1) directly to the beneficiary; (2) to the legal guardian or committee of the beneficiary; (3) to a relative of the beneficiary to be expended by the relative for the maintenance, health, and education of the beneficiary; or (4) by expending the same directly for the maintenance, health, and education of the beneficiary. The trustee shall not be obliged to see to the application of the funds so expended, but the receipt of such person shall be full acquittance to the trustee.

l. To continue and operate any business owned by me at my death and to do any and all things deemed appropriate by the trustee, including the power to form a limited liability company or incorporate the business and to put additional capital into the business, for such time as the trustee deems advisable, without liability for loss resulting from the continuance or operation of the business except for the trustee's own negligence; and to close out, liquidate, or sell the business at such time and upon such terms as the trustee deems proper; and in this connection a sale may be made (pursuant to an agreement entered into by me during my lifetime, or otherwise) to a partner, officer, member, employee or beneficiary under this trust. I am aware of the fact that certain risks are inherent in the operation of any business and, therefore, my trustee shall not be liable for any loss resulting from the retention and operation of any business unless such loss results directly from my trustee's gross negligence or willful misconduct.

m. To have the same powers, authorities, and discretions in the management of the trust as I would have in the management and control of my own personal assets. The trustee may continue to exercise any powers and discretions granted in this instrument for a reasonable period after the termination of any trust under this instrument.

COMMENT: The above powers are a set of standard powers that appear throughout this book. The powers should be reviewed to be certain that you the lawyer understand each power, the client is in agreement with each of the powers granted and that the powers granted are needed. Because this is a generic and broad statement of powers, some of these powers may not be necessary. For example, powers to sell or lease real estate are not needed if the grantor knows the trust will consist only of cash and other intangible investments.

---

8. <u>Limitation of Trustee Powers.</u> Notwithstanding any other powers granted to my trustee in this instrument, an individual trustee (a) shall have no power to make payments or distributions that would discharge the trustee's legal obligation to support the trust beneficiary, (b) shall not exercise any power or discretion in any manner that would be deemed to be a general power of appointment under Internal Revenue Code Section 2041, (c) shall be limited by the ascertainable standard of "maintenance, support, health and education" when making payments or distributions to the trustee personally or to anyone for whom the trustee has a beneficial interest, and (d) shall possess no incidence of ownership or powers with respect to life insurance in which the trustee is the insured and has fiduciary power over such life insurance.

COMMENT: There are some situations in which an individual trustee may have adverse estate or income tax consequences when given broad powers as trustee. If a corporate trustee is used, then this paragraph is not needed. But an individual trustee must be certain that acting as trustee does not result in any adverse estate or income tax consequences. This paragraph is intended to ensure that adverse tax consequences are avoided if overly broad powers are granted in the trust instrument. The lawyer is urged to exercise caution when using individual trustees coupled with broad discretionary powers of income and principal distribution to a trust beneficiary because of possible adverse tax consequences. An ABA resource to acquaint oneself with these issues is L. Rush Hunt and Lara Rae Hunt, *A Lawyer's Guide to Estate Planning*, American Bar Association (Chicago: 2004) §14.4.

---

9. <u>Trustee Resignation.</u> My trustee may resign at any time by giving written notice to my successor trustee named below, if any, and if none, then written notice shall be given to each current adult income beneficiary who is then living.

COMMENT: If a trustee resigns, there must be some method of notice and appointment of a successor trustee. This paragraph provides a method of notification. It is not an essential trust provision, but is a helpful one.

---

10. <u>Trustee Succession and Appointment.</u> If I cease to act as trustee due to death, incompetency, resignation or cease to serve for any reason, then [Name of successor trustee] shall serve as successor trustee. If [Name of successor trustee] dies, becomes incompetent, resigns or ceases to serve for any reason, then [Name of second successor trustee] shall serve as successor trustee. The last serving successor trustee may name [his or her] own successor trustee by a written instrument delivered to the successor trustee or by will. The successor trustee may be an individual or a financial institution possessing trust powers under state or federal law. Any further vacancy in the office of trustee shall be filled by decision of the probate court where I resided at the time of my death.

COMMENT: A decision must be made as to succession of trustees and the method of appointing a successor trustee if those named successor trustees are unable to serve. It is also essential to clarify whether successor trustees must only be financial institutions or if individuals may also be considered. Once a decision is made as to the succession of trustees, then the last three sentences should be reviewed to be certain to what extent each of those are needed.

11. <u>Powers of Successor Trustee.</u> Each successor trustee shall have the same rights, titles, powers, duties, discretions, and immunities and otherwise be in the same position as if originally named trustee. No successor trustee shall be personally liable for any act or failure to act of a predecessor trustee. Further, a successor trustee may accept the account furnished and the property delivered by or for a predecessor trustee without liability for so doing, and such acceptance shall be a full and complete discharge to the predecessor trustee.

COMMENT: This paragraph clarifies that a successor trustee has the same powers as the initial trustee. Further, the paragraph relieves the successor trustee from liability for the prior acts of the resigning trustee and waives any requirements of audit or inquiry into the activities of the prior trustee. This is essential for any successor trustee.

12. <u>Compensation of Trustee.</u> **OPTION 1: Corporate trustee compensation** A corporate trustee shall receive compensation in accordance with its regular schedule of fees in effect at the time such services are rendered.

OPTION 2: Individual does not receive compensation An individual trustee shall not be paid any compensation, but shall be reimbursed for out-of-pocket expenses.

OPTION 3: Individual does receive compensation An individual trustee shall be paid <insert amount of compensation> as compensation for such services and shall be reimbursed for out-of-pocket expenses.

COMMENT: Three options are provided, but the actual drafting of this paragraph may be different than each of these options. If the only trustee to be used is a corporate trustee, then Option 1 is a standard trust provision. If there is a possibility of individual trustees, then care should be given to the method for setting this fee. If no fee is to be paid because the trustee is a close family member, then it is suggested that Option 2 be used. If the grantor expects a fee to be charged, then an amount or a formula, such as a percentage of income or principal, must be set. It is unwise to simply provide for compensation to be a reasonable fee, as that leaves an individual trustee with great uncertainty as to the fee to be charged. Without the grantor clarifying compensation, the trustee could find him or herself in litigation with the beneficiary.

13. <u>Court Accountings.</u> To the extent such requirements can be waived, the trustee shall not be required (a) to file any inventory of trust property or accounts or reports of the administration of the trusts, or to register the trusts, in any court, (b) to furnish any bond or other security for the proper performance of the trustee's duties or (c) to obtain authority from a court for the exercise of any power conferred on the trustee by this instrument. This waiver does not preclude the trustee from registering any trust created in this instrument and petitioning a court having jurisdiction over registered trusts for a judicial ruling on any matter relating to administration of any trust created in this instrument.

COMMENT: The first sentence is to clarify the normal situation that an inter vivos trust is not subject to judicial oversight. The second sentence may be omitted, but is suggested as a potential benefit in some states. In a state in which a trust may be registered, it may be possible to have minor trust matters resolved by the court in which the trust is registered. This creates a simplified process for dealing with minor administrative matters. Without this provision, a court might be reluctant to decide matters for a trust which is not required to be registered under state law.

14. <u>Severability.</u> If any provisions of this trust shall be unenforceable, the remaining provisions shall nevertheless be carried into effect.

COMMENT: This is the same type of standard provision often seen in contracts that is intended to save the document if a particular provision is found to be invalid or void. It is doubtful this provision will have any practical effect in most trust situations, but it is a "boilerplate" provision that is frequently found in trust instruments and for which there is no disadvantage.

15. <u>Certification of Incompetency.</u> **OPTION 1: Decided by treating physician** Any person acting or named to act as a trustee in this instrument is considered to be unable to serve or to continue serving when a physician whom such person has consulted within the prior three years has certified as to such consultation and the certification states that the person is incapable of managing the affairs of the trusts I have established in this instrument, regardless of cause and regardless of whether there is an adjudication of incompetency. No person shall be liable to anyone for actions taken in reliance on the physician's certification or for dealing with a trustee other than the one removed for incompetency based on such certification.

OPTION 2: Decided by two physicians Any person acting or named to act as a trustee in this instrument is considered to be unable to serve or to continue serving when a written certification is received from two (2) physicians, both of whom have personally examined the person and at least one (1) of whom is board-certified in the specialty most closely associated with the health condition alleged to cause such incompetency. The certification must state that the person is incapable of managing the affairs of this trust, regardless of cause and regardless of whether there is an adjudication of incompetence. No person is liable to anyone for actions taken in reliance on these certifications, or for dealing with a trustee other than the one removed for incompetency based on these certifications.

COMMENT: This provision relates back to paragraph 10 concerning the succession of trustees. It defines incompetency, which is one of those events requiring a successor trustee. The first option involves consultation with the trustee's personal physician, whereas Option 2 involves a panel of two physicians, one of whom is board certified in the speciality most closely associated with the health condition of the trustee. Clients differ as to which provision they prefer and are more concerned about the provision when the grantor is also the initial trustee. Absent a strong preference by the grantor, Option 1 is the provision most frequently used.

16. <u>Titles and References.</u> The underscored titles of paragraphs in this instrument are for information purposes only and shall be given no legal effect.

COMMENT: This is another common "boilerplate" provision that is perhaps not essential, but for which there is no disadvantage.

17. <u>Governing Law.</u> The laws of the State of [insert state] shall govern the interpretation and validity of the provisions of this instrument and all questions relating to the management, administration, investment, and distribution of the trusts hereby created; provided, however, my trustee shall have the power, exercisable in the trustee's sole discretion, to declare, by written instrument that this trust shall be governed and interpreted by the law of some other state which shall then be the forum for the administration of this trust. In selecting a new state as the forum for this trust my trustee shall give consideration to selecting a state whose laws will carry out my desire that the trust property be preserved for my beneficiary.

COMMENT: It is a standard provision in both trust instruments and in contracts generally to specify the state law that applies in interpretation of the instrument. Here, the trustee is granted the power to remove the trust to another state so that it is administered and interpreted according to the laws of another state whose laws are more favorable for asset protection.

18. <u>No-Contest.</u> If any beneficiary of this trust, or the guardian or legal representative of such beneficiary, contests the validity of this trust or of any of its provisions or shall institute or join in (except as a party defendant) any proceeding to contest the validity of this trust or to prevent any provision of it from being carried out in accordance with its terms (regardless of whether or not such proceedings are instituted in good faith and with probable cause), then all benefits provided for such beneficiary hereunder are revoked and such benefits shall pass as if such beneficiary and such beneficiary's descendants all had predeceased me.

COMMENT: This provision or some variation of it should be considered if there is any concern that a beneficiary or heir-at-law may challenge the trust. The lawyer may need to modify this provision to meet any requirements of state law.

19. **OPTION 1** <u>Power To Amend or Revoke.</u> I reserve the right from time to time by written instrument delivered to the trustee to amend or revoke this instrument and the trust hereby evidenced, in whole or in part.

OPTION 2 <u>Irrevocability.</u> This trust agreement shall be absolutely irrevocable, and I have no right whatsoever to withdraw any property from the trust, to modify the trust in any manner, or to exercise any control over the trust property.

COMMENT: If the grantor is only funding this trust with a nominal amount, then the grantor may prefer the trust to be revocable so that future changes can be made in the document. On the other hand, if the trust is going to be currently funded, then the trust will usually be irrevocable.

The trust as drafted contemplates it being a revocable trust with only a nominal $10 transfer to the trust. Then the grantor by his or her last will and testament will transfer assets into the trust. When used in this manner, a pour over will transfers the grantor's assets into this trust.

The undersigned has signed this instrument and has established the foregoing trust on this the _____ day of _____, [Current year].

GRANTOR AND TRUSTEE:

_____
[Grantor's name]

STATE OF [State of Notary]   )

) SCT.

COUNTY OF [County of Notary])

The undersigned, a Notary Public within and for the state and county aforesaid, does hereby certify that the foregoing trust agreement executed by [Grantor's name], as grantor and trustee, was on this day produced to me in my county by [Grantor's name], who executed, acknowledged and swore the same before me to be [his or her] act and deed in due form of law.

Given under my hand and notarial seal on this the _____ day of _____, [Current year].

_____
Notary Public, State at Large
My commission expires:_____

PREPARED BY:

_____
[Name of Attorney]
[Name of Law Firm]
Attorneys at Law
[Street Address]
[City], [State] [Zip Code]
[Telephone Number]

SCHEDULE A

[NAME OF TRUST] TRUST

Cash. . . . . $ 10.00

The lawyer will note a deposit of $10 in the trust. State law will determine the necessity of an initial deposit. An unfunded trust that contains no principal may be deemed a "dry" trust under state law, meaning that it is not a valid document. Some lawyers go to the added step of affixing a $10 bill to schedule A, while others are satisfied with a cash deposit which does have the disadvantage of not being traceable. If there is the possibility of a contest of the trust, the cautious practice would be to affix a $10 bill to schedule A.

PART V—ESTATE TAX SAVINGS TRUSTS

Irrevocable Life Insurance Trust

Marital and Credit Shelter Trust

5

IRREVOCABLE LIFE INSURANCE TRUST WORKSHEET

1. **Grantor Information**

   1.1 Grantor Name_____

   1.2 Grantor City and State _____

2. **Trustee Information**

   2.1 Trustee Name _____

   2.2 Trustee City and State _____

3. **Name of Trust**

   "_____ Life Insurance Trust"

4. **Family Information**

   4.1 Name of Spouse _____

   4.2 Names of Children _____

   _____

   _____

   4.3 Are any of the above-named children step-children? <u>Yes / No</u>

   4.4 Are provisions needed for after-born children? <u>Yes / No</u>

   4.5 Are provisions needed for adopted and/or illegitimately born children? <u>Yes / No</u>
   (See Paragraph 11)

5. **Withdrawal Rights for Children**

   Greater of $5,000 or 5% of principal value? (Option 1) <u>Yes / No</u>

   Amount of annual federal gift tax exclusion? (Option 2) <u>Yes / No</u>

6. **Trust upon Grantor's Death** (Separate Trust for Each Child)

   A. Provision for educational incentive? <u>Yes / No</u>
   (See Paragraph 8.b)

   B. Provision for distribution to beneficiary's descendants? <u>Yes / No</u>
   (See Paragraph 8.c)

C. Provision for trustee authority to withhold? Yes / No
   (See Paragraph 8.d)

D. If a child is deceased:

Deceased child's share distributed
to such child's estate? (Option 1) Yes / No
(See Paragraph 8.f)

or Deceased child's share per stirpes
to lineal descendants? (Option 2) Yes / No
(See Paragraph 8.f)

7.   **Default Provisions (if needed) if All Named Beneficiaries Deceased:**

_____

_____

_____

8.   **Definition of "Child" and "Descendant"**

Include adopted prior to age _____ (18, 21, etc.)

Include provision for illegitimate children (treated same, etc.)? Yes / No

9.   **Powers**

Environmental Powers? Yes / No (See Master Will Paragraph 15)

Farm Powers? Yes / No (See Master Will Paragraph 16)

Limitation on Trustee Powers? Yes / No

10.   **Trustees**

Name of initial trustee: _____

Name of first successor trustee: _____

Name of second successor trustee: _____

Corporate trustee compensation? (Option 1) Yes / No

Individual reimbursed for expenses but no compensation? (Option 2) Yes / No

Individual receives compensation? (Option 3) Yes / No

        Amount of compensation: $_____

11.   **Incompetency**

One physician decides? (Option 1) Yes / No

Two physicians decide and one board certified? (Option 2) Yes / No

12.   **No-Contest**

Is No-Contest provision needed? Yes / No

IRREVOCABLE LIFE INSURANCE TRUST

This type of trust is used when a grantor is purchasing life insurance that the grantor does not want to be subject to federal estate tax. Thus, this trust is only needed in larger sized estates in which there are federal estate tax concerns. There are a number of intricacies and details with this type of trust. A helpful ABA resource is Louis A. Mezzullo, *An Estate Planner's Guide to Life Insurance*, American Bar Association (Chicago: 2000).

I, [grantor's name], currently of [grantor's city], [grantor's state], as grantor and [trustee's name], currently of [trustee's city], [trustee's state], as trustee hereby enter into this trust agreement, and I transfer to my trustee the property described in Schedule A. This property and all investments, reinvestments and additions which may sometimes be referred to in this instrument as the "trust property" or "trust assets" are to be held subject to the following provisions:

***

COMMENT: The grantor cannot be the trustee of this trust. A financial institution or other independent individual trustee is required. In some situations it is possible for the spouse to be the trustee, but this writer suggests reading the above-cited ABA publication or another resource before naming a spouse as the trustee.

***

1. <u>Name of Trust.</u> This instrument and the initial trust hereby established may be named the "[Name of trust] Trust."

***

COMMENT: Any named can be used for this trust, but commonly the grantor's name followed by the words "life insurance trust" is used.

***

2. <u>Family Information.</u> My [husband or wife]'s name is [husband or wife's name], and all references in this will to "my [husband or wife]" are only to [him or her].

OPTION 1: Naming of all children My [child is or children are], [names of children], and all references in this will to "my [child is or children are]" only to [him her or them].

OPTION 2: Inclusion of step-children Even though some of the above-named children are step-children it is my intent that each of the above-named children be treated for purposes of this instrument as if they and their lineal descendants are my natural born children and descendants.

OPTION 3: After-born children If subsequent to the execution of this instrument there shall be an additional child or children born to me, then such child or children shall share in the benefits of the trusts established in this instrument to the same extent as my above-named children and their descendants; and the provisions of this instrument shall be deemed modified to the extent necessary to carry out this intent.

***

COMMENT: The full name of the other spouse and children should be inserted. If step-children are involved, Option 2 should be considered. Also, Option 3 may be appropriate if there is the possibility of additional children. The lawyer's state law may provide for this contingency, but it may still be appropriate to add this provision to the trust. Paragraph 11 in this trust considers adopted and illegitimate children and descendants.

***

3. <u>Rights in Policies of Life Insurance.</u> My trustee is hereby vested with all right, title, and interest in and to any policy or policies of life insurance transferred to my trustee, and is authorized to exercise, for the purposes of the trust herein created, and as absolute owner of such

policy or policies of life insurance, all the options, benefits, rights and privileges under such policy or policies, including the right to borrow upon such policy or policies and to pledge such policy or policies for a loan or loans. I hereby relinquish all rights and powers in such policy or policies of life insurance and will, at the request of the trustee, execute instruments reasonably required to carry out this intent.

COMMENT: This paragraph is intended to clarify that the grantor has no ownership rights in the life insurance. It is essential that the grantor have no such rights, and while this paragraph is not dispositive of the issue of whether or not the grantor retained ownership rights, it is still important as it evidences the intent to relinquish all rights in life insurance on the grantor's life.

---

4. <u>Rights and Duties Relating to Life Insurance Policies.</u> After the death of the insured when the life insurance policies shall become payable, my trustee shall promptly furnish proof of loss to the life insurance companies, and shall collect and receive the proceeds of the policies. My trustee shall have power to execute and deliver receipts and other instruments and to take such action as is appropriate for this collection. If my trustee deems it necessary to institute legal action for the collection of any policies, [he, she or it] shall be indemnified for all costs, including attorney's fees.

No life insurance company under any policy of insurance deposited with my trustee shall be responsible for the application or disposition of the proceeds of such policy by my trustee. Payment to my trustee of such life insurance proceeds shall be a full discharge of the liability of such life insurance company under such policy.

My trustee, in [his, her or its] sole discretion, may accept any of the optional modes of payment provided in any of such policies where such modes of payment are permitted to the trustee by the life insurance company.

COMMENT: The above three paragraphs simply establish that the trustee has full authority to make demand for the life insurance death proceeds and that the life insurance company has no liability to the trustee or trust beneficiary once the life insurance death proceeds have been paid to the trustee.

My trustee shall not be liable for any investment in life insurance policies, or the retention of any life insurance policies in this trust. Nor shall my trustee have any liability over the selection of life insurance products or the continued ownership of any life insurance products in this trust. My trustee is relieved of all fiduciary responsibilities and liability as to any life insurance policy or policies held in this trust until following receipt of life insurance proceeds following the death of the insured and upon such proceeds being payable to this trust.

COMMENT: It is important to absolve the trustee of any personal liability for the life insurance owned in the trust. A trustee has fiduciary liability for improper trust investments. A trustee will always be concerned that, in the event a life insurance company becomes insolvent, that the trust beneficiary will bring suit against the trustee claiming a breach of fiduciary duties for failing to monitor trust investments. Thus, this paragraph is essential.

---

5. <u>Withdrawal Rights for Children.</u> Following any addition to the trust, my children shall have the unrestricted right to withdraw an amount equal to such child's proportionate share of any such addition. A child's proportionate share shall be the amount of such addition divided by the

number of my children living at the time of the addition. Each child's right of withdrawal shall not exceed in any one calendar year **OPTION 1:** the greater of five thousand dollars ($5,000) or five percent (5%) of the value of the principal of the trust. **OPTION 2:** the amount of the annual per-donee federal gift tax exclusion, including the amount of the gift tax exclusion if gift-splitting is elected by the donor of the gift. This right of withdrawal is non-cumulative and shall lapse thirty (30) calendar days following the date of the addition, but in no event later than December 31 in the year of the addition. In the event a child of mine is under the age of eighteen (18) years or under any legal disability, this right of withdrawal may be exercised by such child's legal guardian, if any, and if none, the trustee shall designate an appropriate adult individual (other than myself) who may make the demand on behalf of such child. My trustee shall provide written notice to my children, or to my children's guardian or the adult designated by my trustee, as soon as it is reasonably possible to do so after the trustee receives the addition to the trust.

COMMENT: There is a gift tax problem associated with a gift to a person who does not exercise the withdrawal right in paragraph 5 below. The problem exists due to the annual gift tax exclusion ($13,000 per donee, or $26,000 with gift-splitting) exceeding the $5,000 or 5% of the value of the trust assets requirement under the power of appointment rules in IRC Section 2514(e). The problem arises because the demand power is a general power of appointment, and to the extent it exceeds the greater of $5,000 or 5% of the trust assets, the failure to exercise the power (which should not be exercised) by the beneficiary results in a taxable gift to the contingent remainder beneficiaries. Option 1 in the withdrawal power in paragraph 5 limits the withdrawal to the "5 and 5" requirement which eliminates the gift tax problem. Until the trust principal exceeds $100,000, this solution limits the annual gift to $5,000. If this option is selected, paragraph 8.e can be modified as desired as the requirement of a general appointment is not needed. If Option 2 in paragraph 5 is used in order to increase the annual gift to the trust to the $13,000 annual gift to the trust or $26,000 with gift-splitting, then paragraph 8.e should be used. An excellent ABA resource that provides a further discussion of this tax problem and its various other solutions is Louis A. Mezzullo, *An Estate Planner's Guide to Life Insurance*, American Bar Association (Chicago, 2000).

COMMENT: To ensure that the child has the opportunity to exercise the right of withdrawal, the trustee must send a letter to the child, the child's guardian, or the person designated by the trustee to receive notice and make demand on behalf of the child of the gift to the trust. This should be a letter from the trustee to that person stating the amount of the gift, the date of the gift, and the period of time during which the person may exercise this right. This requirement must be adhered to and no effort should be made to have the right waived. A letter must be given each time a gift is made to the trust. Wise practice is for the trustee to retain copies of all letters.

6. <u>Withdrawal Rights for [Husband or Wife].</u> In the event any of the life insurance proceeds payable to my trustee upon my death shall be includable in my gross estate due to the three-year rule under Internal Revenue Code 2035, or otherwise, my [husband or wife] shall have the power to demand distribution of any and all amounts of income and principal as [he or she] may desire.

COMMENT: If the grantor transfers life insurance owned by the grantor into the trust, there is a three year rule under which the life insurance death benefits are includable in the gross estate of the grantor. Since the beneficiary of the trust is not the spouse, those death benefits would then be subject to federal estate tax. This could result in a disastrous result. Therefore, any existing life insurance must be subject to this trust provision until the three-year time limit expires. If death occurs within three years, then the surviving spouse will make demand for those benefits. In this event, those benefits will qualify for the marital deduction, eliminating any federal estate tax.

7. <u>Trust During Grantor's Life.</u> During my life, my trustee shall hold and administer all trust property remaining after the exercise or lapse of the withdrawal powers created above as follows:

a. <u>Payment of Premiums.</u> My trustee may apply for and purchase life insurance policies on my life and my trustee shall pay the premiums on such policies first from trust income, if any, and if none, then from trust principal. If the trust assets are insufficient to pay such premiums, my trustee shall be under no obligation to pay any premiums which may be due and may allow such policies to lapse. Further, my trustee shall have no obligation to notify any person of a non-payment of premiums or seek to have any other person pay such premiums.

b. <u>Other Distributions.</u> After making the payments required above, my trustee shall distribute to or for the benefit for my children as much of the trust's net income and principal as the trustee deems appropriate for the reasonable maintenance, support and education of my children. Whether or not distributions are made to my children shall be determined in the sole discretion of my trustee, and in the event any distributions are made to my children, such distributions need not be made in equal shares among my children.

COMMENT: Both of these paragraphs define how distributions will be made from the trust during the lifetime of the grantor. Typically there will be no assets in the trust other than the life insurance policies and a cash contribution from the grantor to the trust in an amount sufficient to pay the life insurance premiums. The amount transferred from the grantor to the trust will be used under paragraph 7.a to pay life insurance premiums and there will be no balance for distribution during the lifetime of the grantor.

8. <u>Trust upon Grantor's Death.</u> Upon my death, the trustee shall divide and allocate the trust property, including any funds received on account of my death, among my children in equal shares. If a child is deceased, my deceased child's share shall be distributed to the child's then living lineal descendants per stirpes, if any, otherwise such share shall be distributed to my then-living lineal descendants per stirpes, and property so allocated shall be retained in trust as a separate trust which shall be named for that person subject to the following provisions:

COMMENT: If the client wants the surviving spouse to have benefits from the trust following the grantor's death, then provisions for the spouse will need to be added to paragraph 8.

a. The trustee may pay to or use all, part or none, of the income and principal of such person's trust as the trustee believes appropriate for the reasonable maintenance, support, health, and education (including college or graduate, professional or vocational school education) of such person, considering such person's income or assets and all other circumstances and factors the trustee believes pertinent. It is my desire that distributions of income and principal not impair such person's motivation to be productive and self-supporting, thus my trustee shall not make distributions of income and principal from such person's trust if such person is not productive, mature, and responsible. If any net income remains undistributed at the end of each calendar year (excluding income distributed during the sixty-five (65) day period under Internal Revenue Code Section 663), the trustee shall add it to the principal of the trust.

COMMENT: The first sentence provides broad discretion to the trustee in making distributions for the child, but is limited to avoid adverse tax consequences that may befall an individual trustee. The second sentence is not essential, but is provided to illustrate a possible restriction that the grantor may desire. The third sentence can be eliminated, but is provided for situations in which income is not distributed before year end; and to set the time at which accumulated income is added to trust principal.

b. Notwithstanding the above paragraphs, following high school graduation, if a person for whom a trust is held hereunder fails to pursue post-secondary education leading to a bachelor's degree from an accredited college or university, all trust distributions, except for health care needs, shall cease until such person reaches the age of twenty-three (23) years. A person pursuing post-secondary education must annually maintain a 2.50 GPA based on a 4.0 grading scale in order to receive trust distributions, except for health care needs, prior to the age of twenty-three (23) years. If a person for whom a trust is named earns a bachelor's degree from an accredited college or university before such person reaches the age of twenty-three (23) years, the trustee shall within ninety (90) days of such person's graduation distribute [enter number] percent ([enter number]%) of the trust assets to such person free of trust.

COMMENT: This provision is intended to provide a model for the lawyer to consider in addressing an incentive for a child or more remote descendant to pursue post-secondary education and to maintain an adequate grade point average. This paragraph may need to be moved to become part of paragraph a or as a separate paragraph b. In this form, the decision was made to place it in this location as it and the following paragraphs are offered as supplemental provisions that some clients will want and others will not. Be certain to modify the reference in the first sentence to the phrase "nothwithstanding . . . paragraphs" if it is moved elsewhere in the document.

c. In addition, the trustee may pay to or use for the benefit of any one or more of the descendants of a person for whom a trust is held hereunder such part or all of the principal of such person's trust at such time or times and in such equal or unequal proportions among them as the trustee believes appropriate for the reasonable maintenance, support, health and education (including college or graduate, professional or vocational school education) of such descendants as a group, considering their respective incomes or assets and all other circumstances and factors the trustee believes pertinent.

COMMENT: In some situations, the grantor may desire for the trust beneficiary's own descendants to receive distributions from the trust. This provision permits such distributions, but such distributions are limited to trust principal only and not to income or principal. If that flexibility is desired, then a minor modification may be made to this paragraph.

d. In addition to the restrictions provided in the above paragraphs and as a condition precedent to distributions under those paragraphs, my trustee shall withhold or postpone any or all distributions of income or principal from a person's trust if my trustee believes a distribution to such person could result in the loss of some part or all of the distribution due to any possible civil or criminal legal action involving such person or such person's spouse, or due to such person or such person's spouse being addicted to alcohol or any legal or illegal controlled substance. The decision of my trustee shall be final and binding and shall not be subject to question by any person or in any court.

COMMENT: If the client is faced with a child or more remote descendant who has substance abuse or other serious problems making distributions from the trust unwise, or if the client is concerned about such possibility, then paragraph e or a variation of it may be helpful. It is designed to give the trustee full authority to withhold all distributions of income and principal when a child or more remote descendant is facing substance abuse or other significant personal problems.

e. Upon the death of a person for whom a trust held under this paragraph is named, any part or all of the principal of such person's trust and any accrued or undistributed income thereof shall be distributed to or for the benefit of one or more persons or entities as such person may appoint by specific reference to the power of appointment in such person's last will and testament, including the power of such person to appoint the trust property or any part of it to such person's own estate, such person's creditors or the creditors of such person's estate. If such person fails to exercise this power of appointment, then the trust principal and undistributed income of such person's trust shall be divided and allocated per stirpes among the then living lineal descendants of such person, if any, otherwise such person's trust shall be divided and allocated per stirpes among the then living lineal descendants of the nearest lineal ancestor of such person who also was a descendant of mine and of whom one or more descendants then are living, or, if none, such person's trust shall be divided and allocated per stirpes among my then living lineal descendants.

COMMENT: This form provides that the trust continues until the beneficiary's death. If the trust is to terminate earlier, a modification should be made. If the trust is to avoid estate tax in the beneficiary's own estate, then a limited power of appointment can be used. For further discussion, refer to Louis A. Mezzullo, *An Estate Planner's Guide to Life Insurance*, American Bar Association (Chicago: 2000). An additional resource concerning a per stirpes distribution is Jeffrey N. Ponnell and Alan Newman, *Estate and Trust Planning*, American Bar Association (Chicago: 2005) pp 19–26.

f. If the power of appointment under paragraph 8.e is not exercised, then distribution shall be made outright to such descendant or descendants unless: (i) distribution is to be made to a descendant for whom a trust then held under this trust instrument is named in which event such distribution shall be added to that trust, or (ii) distribution is to be made to a descendant who has not reached the age of [Age of remote descendants] years in which event, the trustee shall retain any property otherwise distributable to such descendant as a separate trust named for such descendant to be distributed to such descendant when he or she reaches the age of [Age for remote descendants] years. If such descendant is already [Age for remote descendants] years of age, then such descendant shall receive his or her share outright. Until such descendant reaches [Age for remote descendants] years of age, the trustee shall distribute the income and principal of a trust so retained in such amounts, if any, and at such times as the trustee believes appropriate for the reasonable maintenance, support, health and education (including college or graduate, professional or vocational school education) of the descendant for whom the trust is named, considering such descendant's income or assets and all other circumstances and factors the trustee believes pertinent. It is my desire that distributions of income and principal not impair a descendant's motivation to be productive and self-supporting, thus my trustee shall not make distributions of income and principal from a descendant's trust if my descendant is not productive, mature, and responsible. If any net income remains undistributed at the end of each calendar year (excluding income distributed during the sixty-five (65) day period under Internal Revenue Code Section 663), the trustee shall add it to the principal of the trust.

OPTION 1: If a descendant for whom a trust held under this paragraph is named dies prior to termination of such descendant's trust, then such descendant's trust shall terminate and shall be distributed to such descendant's own estate.

OPTION 2: On the death of a descendant for whom a trust held under this paragraph is named, any principal and undistributed income of such descendant's trust shall be divided and allocated per stirpes among the then living lineal descendants of such descendant, if any, otherwise such person's trust shall be divided and allocated per stirpes among my then living lineal descendants.

COMMENT: The above provisions permit a distribution to a more remote descendant to be distributed to that person's own trust if he or she is a recipient of a trust under this instrument, or if not and the remote descendant is under a specified minimum age, then the trustee may hold that person's share in trust until that person reaches the minimum age with the trust property to be used for that person until distribution. If this option is used, then Option 1 or 2 above should be selected to determine to whom the trust property is distributed should that remote descendant die before termination of the trust. Care must be taken to be certain that the per stirpes distribution provided in this form is adequate. This provision should not be used routinely without an analysis of its effect under the facts of the particular estate plan. An additional resource concerning a per stirpes distribution is Jeffrey N. Ponnell and Alan Newman, *Estate and Trust Planning*, American Bar Association (Chicago: 2005) pp 19–26.

---

9. <u>Default Provisions.</u> Any trust property not disposed of by any of the above provisions shall be distributed on the date of such failure of disposition to [insert default provisions].

COMMENT: If there are a limited number of beneficiaries, then it may be wise to insert a default provision providing for the ultimate recipient should all the beneficiaries in paragraph 8 and their descendants be deceased. If this is too remote of a possibility, some clients may direct that this paragraph be deleted.

---

10. <u>Protection from Creditors.</u> No trust beneficiary shall have the right to sell, transfer, assign, alienate, pledge, or in any way encumber trust assets, including income and principal, nor shall trust assets be subject to execution, levy, sale, garnishment, attachment, bankruptcy, or other legal proceedings. Any such actions by a trust beneficiary or a third party seeking to enforce a claim against the trust assets shall not be recognized under any circumstances by the trustee. These provisions do not prevent the trustee from making distributions for the benefit of a trust beneficiary in such amounts and at such times as the trustee determines necessary for the trust beneficiary's maintenance, support, health and education.

COMMENT: This is a standard paragraph that precludes the trust assets from being attached by claims of creditors.

---

11. <u>Definitions.</u> For all purposes of this instrument, the following shall apply:

a. The words "child," "children," "descendant" or "descendants" shall exclude adopted persons unless they are adopted prior to [insert age] years; and shall include only persons legitimately born unless a decree of adoption terminates the parental rights of the natural mother during her lifetime, or the natural father signs a written notarized instrument during his lifetime in which he irrevocably states that the child is to be considered legitimately born for purposes of inheriting under this will.

COMMENT: Some clients will want to restrict distribution for an adopted child to preclude a child adopted as an adult. Thus, many will use the age 18 or perhaps a slightly older age such as 20 or 21. Other clients may wish to restrict the age to a younger adopted child, such as under the age of 10. The issue of illegitimate children should also be addressed. In many situations, a child or more remote descendant should be treated the same as any other child, in which case the portion of this paragraph that deals with illegitimate children can be deleted. In other situations there may be a limited or no relationship with the child, in which event no distribution should be made to that child. This form gives the father of the child the right to allow the child to inherit by the father signing a written document allowing inheritance.

b. Whenever assets are to be divided and allocated per stirpes, the assets to be divided or allocated shall be divided into as many equal shares as are necessary to divide or allocate one share to each then living child of such person and to provide one share collectively for the then living descendants of each child of such person who then is deceased leaving one or more descendants then living. Any collective share shall be divided and allocated per stirpes among the descendants of such deceased person in accordance with the preceding sentence.

COMMENT: Since the term per stirpes is used often in this document, a definition is provided of that term. The lawyer should modify this definition to conform with his or her own state law should it differ any from this definition. Of course, a definition is not essential, since the term will be defined under state law. But since it is a term that clients are not familiar with, it is often helpful to define it for them in the document. An excellent ABA resource that discusses this issue in detail is Jeffrey N. Penell and Alan Newman, *Estate and Trust Planning*, American Bar Association (Chicago, 2005) pp. 19–26.

12. <u>Trustee Powers.</u> In the administration of the trusts, the trustee shall have the following powers and rights and all others granted by law:

a. To purchase from the my estate any stock, bond, security or other property, real or personal, offered for sale by my personal representative (even though such personal representative may also be trustee herein) irrespective of whether or not such security or property is eligible for investment by fiduciaries under any statute or law; and the trustee shall incur no responsibility or liability for any loss resulting to the trust estate from any such purchase or from retention of any asset so acquired.

b. To invest and reinvest all or any part of the principal of the trust in any stocks, bonds, mortgages, shares or interests in common trust funds, mutual funds, or other securities or property, real, personal, or mixed, and of any kind or nature whatsoever, as the trustee deems proper, and without diversification if the trustee deems it advisable, irrespective of whether or not such securities or property are eligible for trust investment under state or any other law, and may change any investment received or made by the trustee, and may hold cash if the trustee deems it advisable.

c. To exercise broad discretion as to diversification of trust property, and shall not be required to reduce any concentrated holdings merely because of such concentration, and shall have full discretion as to the percentage to be invested in fixed income securities, and is specifically relieved from any requirements, legal or otherwise, as to the percentage of the trust assets to be invested in fixed income securities, and may invest or retain invested any trust estates wholly in common stocks.

d. To sell, convey, lease or mortgage, repair and improve, and take any and all other steps with regard to any real estate that may at any time be a part of the principal of the trust; and any lease of such real property or contract with regard thereto made by the trustee shall be binding for the full period of the lease or contract, even though the period shall extend beyond the termination of the trust.

e. To vote shares of stock held in the trust at stockholders' meetings in person or by special, limited, or general proxy, with or without power of substitution, as seems best to the trustee.

f. To participate in the liquidation, reorganization, consolidation, incorporation and reincorporation, or any other financial readjustment of any corporation, limited liability company or business in which the trust is, or shall be financially interested.

g. To borrow money from any source for any purpose connected with the protection, preservation, improvement or development of the trust hereunder, whenever in the trustee's judgment the trustee deems it advisable, and as security to mortgage or pledge any real estate or personal property forming a part of the trust upon such terms and conditions as the trustee may deem advisable.

h. To hold any and all securities in bearer form, in the trustee's own name, or the name of some other person, partnership, or corporation, or in the name of a duly appointed nominee, with or without disclosing the fiduciary ownership.

i. To divide the principal of the trust property into parts or shares and to distribute or allot same, and to make such division in cash or in kind or both. For the purpose of such division or allotment, the judgment of the trustee concerning the propriety thereof and relative value of property so distributed or allotted shall be binding and conclusive with respect to all interested persons.

j. To merge and consolidate the trust property of any separate trust held hereunder with other trusts and then to administer such trust property as a single trust provided the separate trust is for the benefit of the same persons with substantially the same terms, conditions and federal tax consequences.

k. To pay such income and principal during the minority or incapacity of any beneficiary for whose benefit income and principal may be expended, in any one or more of the following ways: (1) directly to the beneficiary; (2) to the legal guardian or committee of the beneficiary; (3) to a relative of the beneficiary to be expended by the relative for the maintenance, health, and education of the beneficiary; or (4) by expending the same directly for the maintenance, health, and education of the beneficiary. The trustee shall not be obliged to see to the application of the funds so expended, but the receipt of such person shall be full acquittance to the trustee.

l. To continue and operate any business owned by me at my death and to do any and all things deemed appropriate by the trustee, including the power to form a limited liability company or incorporate the business and to put additional capital into the business, for such time as the trustee deems advisable, without liability for loss resulting from the continuance or operation of the business except for the trustee's own negligence; and to close out, liquidate, or sell the business at such time and upon such terms as the trustee deems proper, and in this connection a sale may be made (pursuant to an agreement entered into by me during my lifetime, or otherwise) to a partner, officer, member, employee or beneficiary under this trust. I am aware of the fact that certain risks are inherent in the operation of any business and, therefore, my trustee shall not be liable for any loss resulting from the retention and operation of any business unless such loss results directly from my trustee's gross negligence or willful misconduct.

m. To have the same powers, authorities, and discretions in the management of the trust as I would have in the management and control of my own personal assets. The trustee may continue to exercise any powers and discretions granted in this instrument for a reasonable period after the termination of any trust under this instrument.

COMMENT: The above powers are a set of standard powers that appear throughout this book. The powers should be reviewed to be certain that you the lawyer understand each power, the client is in agreement with each of the powers granted and that the powers granted are needed. Because this is a generic and broad statement of powers, some of these powers may not be necessary. For example, powers to sell or lease real estate are not needed if the grantor knows the trust will consist only of cash and other intangible investments.

13. <u>Limitation on Powers of Individual Trustee.</u> Notwithstanding any other powers granted to my trustee in this instrument, an individual trustee (a) shall have no power to make payments or distributions that would discharge the trustee's legal obligation to support the trust beneficiary, (b) shall not exercise any power or discretion in any manner that would be deemed to be a general power of appointment under Internal Revenue Code Section 2041, (c) shall be limited by the ascertainable standard of "maintenance, support, health and education" when making payments or distributions to the trustee personally or to anyone for whom the trustee has a beneficial interest, and (d) shall possess no incidence of ownership or powers with respect to life insurance in which the trustee is the insured and has fiduciary power over such life insurance.

COMMENT: There are some situations in which an individual trustee may have adverse estate or income tax consequences when given broad powers as trustee. If a corporate trustee is used, then this paragraph is not needed. But an individual trustee must be certain that acting as trustee does not result in any adverse estate or income tax consequences. This paragraph is intended to ensure that adverse tax consequences are avoided if overly broad powers are granted in the trust instrument. The lawyer is urged to exercise caution when using individual trustees coupled with broad discretionary powers of income and principal distribution to a trust beneficiary because of possible adverse tax consequences. An ABA resource to acquaint oneself with these issues is L. Rush Hunt and Lara Rae Hunt, *A Lawyer's Guide to Estate Planning*, American Bar Association (Chicago: 2004) §14.4.

14. <u>Trustee Resignation.</u> My trustee may resign at any time by giving written notice to my successor trustee named below, if any, and if none, then written notice shall be given to each current adult income beneficiary who is then living.

COMMENT: If a trustee resigns, there must be some method of notice and appointment of a successor trustee. This paragraph provides a method of notification. It is not an essential trust provision, but is a helpful one.

15. <u>Trustee Succession and Appointment.</u> If [trustee's name] dies, becomes incompetent, resigns or ceases to serve for any reason, then [insert name of first successor trustee] shall serve as successor trustee. If [insert name of first successor trustee] dies, becomes incompetent, resigns or ceases to serve for any reason, then [insert name of second successor trustee] shall serve as successor trustee. The last serving successor trustee may name [his or her] own successor trustee by a written instrument delivered to the successor trustee or by will. The successor trustee may be an individual or a financial institution possessing trust powers under state or federal law. Any further vacancy in the office of trustee shall be filled by decision of the probate court where I resided at the time of my death.

COMMENT: A decision must be made as to succession of trustees and the method of appointing a successor trustee if all of those named successor trustees are unable to serve. It is also essential to clarify whether successor trustees must only be financial institutions or if individuals may also be considered. Once a decision is made as to the succession of trustees, then the last three sentences should be reviewed to be certain to what extent each of those are needed.

16. <u>Powers of Successor Trustee.</u> Each successor trustee shall have the same rights, titles, powers, duties, discretions, and immunities and otherwise be in the same position as if originally named trustee. No successor trustee shall be personally liable for any act or failure to act of a predecessor trustee. Further, a successor trustee may accept the account furnished and the property delivered by or for a predecessor trustee without liability for so doing, and such acceptance shall be a full and complete discharge to the predecessor trustee.

COMMENT: This paragraph clarifies that a successor trustee has the same powers as the initial trustee. Further, the paragraph relieves the successor trustee from liability for the prior acts of the resigning trustee and waives any requirements of audit or inquiry into the activities of the prior trustee. This is essential for any successor trustee.

17. <u>Compensation of Trustee.</u> **OPTION 1: Corporate trustee compensation** A corporate trustee shall receive compensation in accordance with its regular schedule of fees in effect at the time such services are rendered.

OPTION 2: Individual does not receive compensation An individual trustee shall not be paid any compensation, but shall be reimbursed for out-of-pocket expenses.

OPTION 3: Individual does receive compensation An individual trustee shall be paid [insert amount of compensation] as compensation for such services and shall be reimbursed for out-of-pocket expenses.

COMMENT: Three options are provided, but the actual drafting of this paragraph may be different than each of these options. If the only trustee to be used is a corporate trustee, then Option 1 is a standard trust provision. If there is a possibility of individual trustees, then care should be given to the method for setting this fee. If no fee is to be paid because the trustee is a close family member, then it is suggested that Option 2 be used. If the grantor expects a fee to be charged, then an amount or a formula, such as a percentage of income or principal, must be set. It is unwise to simply provide for compensation to be a reasonable fee, as that leaves an individual trustee with great uncertainty as to the fee to be charged. Without the grantor clarifying compensation, the trustee could find him or herself in litigation with the beneficiary.

18. <u>Court Accountings.</u> To the extent such requirements can be waived, the trustee shall not be required (a) to file any inventory of trust property or accounts or reports of the administration of the trusts, or to register the trusts, in any court, (b) to furnish any bond or other security for the proper performance of the trustee's duties or (c) to obtain authority from a court for the exercise of any power conferred on the trustee by this instrument. This waiver does not preclude the trustee from registering any trust created in this instrument and petitioning a court having jurisdiction over registered trusts for a judicial ruling on any matter relating to administration of any trust created by this instrument.

COMMENT: The first sentence is to clarify the normal situation that an inter vivos trust is not subject to judicial oversight. The second sentence may be omitted, but is suggested as a potential benefit in some states. In a state in which a trust can be registered, it may be possible to have minor trust matters resolved by the court in which the trust is registered. This creates a simplified process for dealing with minor administrative matters. Without this provision, a court might be reluctant to decide matters for a trust which is not required to be registered under state law.

19. <u>Severability.</u> If any provisions of this trust shall be unenforceable, the remaining provisions shall nevertheless be carried into effect.

COMMENT: This is the same type of standard provision often seen in contracts that is intended to save the document if a particular provision is found to be invalid or void. It is doubtful this provision will have any practical effect in most trust situations, but it is a "boilerplate" provision that is frequently found in trust instruments and for which there is no disadvantage.

20. <u>Certification of Incompetency.</u> **OPTION 1: Decided by treating physician** Any person acting or named to act as a trustee in this instrument is considered to be unable to serve or to continue serving when a physician whom such person has consulted within the prior three years has certified as to such consultation and the certification states that the person is incapable of managing the affairs of the trusts I have established in this instrument, regardless of cause and regardless of whether there is an adjudication of incompetency. No person shall be liable to anyone for actions taken in reliance on the physician's certification, or for dealing with a trustee other than the one removed for incompetency based on such certification.

OPTION 2: Decided by two physicians Any person acting or named to act as a trustee in this instrument is considered to be unable to serve or to continue serving when a written certification is received from two (2) physicians, both of whom have personally examined the person and at least one (1) of whom is board-certified in the specialty most closely associated with the health condition alleged to cause such incompetency. The certification must state that the person is incapable of managing the affairs of this trust, regardless of cause and regardless of whether there is an adjudication of incompetence. No person is liable to anyone for actions taken in reliance on these physicians' certifications, or for dealing with a trustee other than the one removed for incompetency based on these certifications.

COMMENT: This provision relates back to paragraph 15 concerning the succession of trustees. It defines incompetency, which is one of those events requiring a successor trustee. The first option involves consultation with the trustee's personal physician, whereas Option 2 involves a panel of two physicians, one of whom is board certified in the speciality most closely associated with the health condition of the trustee. Clients differ as to which provision they prefer and are more concerned about the provision when the grantor is also the initial trustee. Absent a strong preference by the grantor, Option 1 is the provision most frequently used.

21. <u>Titles and References.</u> The underscored titles of paragraphs in this instrument are for information purposes only and shall be given no legal effect.

COMMENT: This is another common "boilerplate" provision that is perhaps not essential, but for which there is no disadvantage.

22. <u>Governing Law.</u> The laws of the State of [insert state] shall govern the interpretation and validity of the provisions of this instrument and all questions relating to the management, administration, investment, and distribution of the trusts hereby created.

COMMENT: It is a standard provision in both trust instruments and in contracts to specify the state law that applies in interpretation of the instrument. This will usually be the grantor's state of residency but also the state in which the lawyer is licensed to practice.

---

23. <u>No-Contest.</u> If any beneficiary of this trust, or the guardian or legal representative of such beneficiary, contests the validity of this trust or of any of its provisions or shall institute or join in (except as a party defendant) any proceeding to contest the validity of this trust or to prevent any provision of it from being carried out in accordance with its terms (regardless of whether or not such proceedings are instituted in good faith and with probable cause), then all benefits provided for such beneficiary hereunder are revoked and such benefits shall pass as if such beneficiary and such beneficiary's descendants all had predeceased me.

COMMENT: This provision or some variation of it should be considered if there is any concern that a beneficiary or heir-at-law may challenge the trust. The lawyer may need to modify this provision to meet any requirements of state law.

---

24. <u>Irrevocability.</u> This trust agreement shall be absolutely irrevocable, and I have no right whatsoever to withdraw any property from the trust, to modify the trust in any manner, or to exercise any control over the trust property.

COMMENT: This type of trust must be irrevocable. Otherwise the life insurance death benefits will be a taxable asset of the grantor's estate.

The undersigned have signed this instrument and have established the foregoing trusts on this the _____ day of _____, [Current Year].

GRANTOR:

_____

[grantor's name]

TRUSTEE:

_____

[trustee's name]

STATE OF [State of Notary]   )

) SCT.

COUNTY OF [County of Notary])

The undersigned, a Notary Public within and for the state and county aforesaid, does hereby certify that the foregoing trust agreement executed by [grantor's name], as grantor, was on this day produced to me in my county by [grantor's name], who executed, acknowledged and swore the same before me to be [his or her] act and deed in due form of law.

Given under my hand and notarial seal on this the ___ day of _____, [Current Year].

_____
Notary Public, State at Large

My commission expires:_____

STATE OF [State of Notary]   )

) SCT.

COUNTY OF [County of Notary])

The undersigned, a Notary Public within and for the state and county aforesaid, does hereby certify that the foregoing trust agreement executed by [trustee's name], as trustee, was on this day produced to me in my county by [trustee's name], who executed, acknowledged and swore the same before me to be [his or her] act and deed in due form of law.

Given under my hand and notarial seal on this the ___ day of _____, [Current Year].

_____
Notary Public, State at Large

My commission expires:_____

PREPARED BY:

_____
[Name of Attorney]
[Name of Law Firm]
Attorneys at Law
[Street Address]
[City], [State] [Zip Code]
[Telephone Number]

SCHEDULE A

[NAME OF TRUST] TRUST

Cash. . . . . $ 10.00

The lawyer will note on schedule A, a deposit of $10 in the trust. State law will determine the necessity of an initial deposit. An unfunded trust that contains no principal may be deemed a "dry" trust under state law, meaning that it is not a valid document. Some lawyers go to the added step of affixing a $10 bill to schedule A, while others are satisfied with a cash deposit which does have the disadvantage of not being traceable. If there is the possibility of a contest of the trust, the cautious practice is to affix a $10 bill to schedule A.

MARITAL AND CREDIT SHELTER TRUST WORKSHEET

1. **Grantor and Trustee Information**

   Name _____

   City and State _____

2. **Name of Trust**

   "_____ Trust"

3. **Children**

   3.1 Names of Children _____

   _____

   _____

   3.2 Are any of the above-named children step-children? <u>Yes / No</u>

   3.3 Are provisions needed for after-born children? <u>Yes / No</u>

4. **Payment of Death Taxes (if provision needed)**

   4.1 Are taxes on probate and nonprobate assets, including apportionment property, to be paid from the trust principal? (Option 1)

   | Yes / No |

   4.2 Are taxes to be paid by beneficiary and taxes collected on apportionment property? (Option 2)

   | Yes / No |

   4.3 Are taxes on probate and nonprobate assets to be paid from trust principal, but taxes on apportionment property to be collected? (Option 3)

   | Yes / No |

   4.4 Other tax provisions _____

   _____

5. **Qualifying for Marital Deduction**

   5.1 Marital Trust coupled with general power of appointment? <u>Yes / No</u>
   (Then use 5.d option 1 and 5.e)

   If yes, limit surviving spouse's rights to
   principal? (5.b) <u>Yes / No</u>

   If no, Marital Trust qualifies for
   Q-TIP election? <u>Yes / No</u>
   Omit 5.b? <u>Yes / No</u>
   Omit 5.d option 1 and 5.e; use 5.d option 2
   And reletter Paragraph 5 if 5.b omitted

5.2 Exempt Trust

    A. Exempt Trust net income paid only to surviving spouse? <u>Yes / No</u>

        If no, net income to surviving spouse and other beneficiaries? <u>Yes / No</u>

        If no, net income paid only to other beneficiaries? <u>Yes / No</u>

        If yes, describe _____

    B. Exempt Trust upon death of surviving spouse

        Exempt Trust to continue upon death
of surviving spouse plus added provisions? (Option 1) <u>Yes / No</u>

        Exempt Trust to terminate and be distributed
to beneficiaries? (Option 2) <u>Yes / No</u>

        Exempt Trust distributed as directed by
will of surviving spouse? (Option 3) <u>Yes / No</u>

6.   **Special Provisions**:

    Residential Real Estate? <u>Yes / No</u>

    Rule against Perpetuities? <u>Yes / No</u>

    Subchapter S Stock? <u>Yes / No</u>

    Reliance on Will? <u>Yes / No</u>

    Method of Payment? <u>Yes / No</u>

    Accrued Income and Termination:

        Distributed to such interested person's estate? (Option 1) <u>Yes / No</u>

        Remain an asset of the trust (not distributed)? (Option 2) <u>Yes / No</u>

    Life Insurance Policies? <u>Yes / No</u>

7.   **Default Provisions (if needed), if All Named Beneficiaries are Deceased**:

_____

_____

_____

8.   **Definition of "Child" and "Descendant"**

Include children adopted prior to age _____ (18, 21, etc.).

Include provision for illegitimate children (treated same, etc.)? <u>Yes / No</u>

9.   **Powers**

    Environmental Powers? <u>Yes / No</u>

    Farm Powers? <u>Yes / No</u>

    Limitation on Trustee Powers? <u>Yes / No</u>

10. **Trustees**

Name of first successor trustee: _____

Name of second successor trustee: _____

Corporate trustee compensation? (Option 1) <u>Yes / No</u>

Individual reimbursed for expenses but no compensation? (Option 2) <u>Yes / No</u>

Individual receives compensation? (Option 3) <u>Yes / No</u>

   Amount of compensation: $_____

Provision needed for children to act as trustee of own trust? <u>Yes / No</u>

11. **Incompetency**

One physician decides? (Option 1) <u>Yes / No</u>

Two physicians decide and one board certified? (Option 2) <u>Yes / No</u>

12. **No-Contest**

Is No-Contest provision needed? <u>Yes / No</u>

MARITAL AND CREDIT SHELTER TRUST

In those situations in which the client's estate is large enough to require tax planning due to federal estate taxes being owed, then marital deduction planning coupled with a credit shelter trust is the common solution. This is a complicated area of estate planning and thus not one to be undertaken lightly. The form that follows provides only one of a number of alternative ways of trust drafting when dealing with these tax issues. An ABA resource that provides an initial overview of this area of law is L. Rush Hunt and Lara Rae Hunt, *A Lawyer's Guide to Estate Planning*, American Bar Association (Chicago: 2004); and Thomas M. Featherston, Jr. et al., *Drafting for Tax and Administrative Issues*, American Bar Association (Chicago: 2000).

I, [Grantor's name], currently of [Grantor's city], [Grantor's state], acting as grantor and trustee hereby transfer to myself, as trustee, the property described in Schedule A. This property and all investments, reinvestments and additions which may sometimes be referred to in this instrument as the "trust property" or "trust assets" are to be held subject to the following provisions:

COMMENT: In this trust the grantor will also act as trustee during his or her lifetime. The trust may be funded at the time it is created or the grantor may choose to fund the trust at a later date. Thus, this trust has the benefit of being a so-called living trust, which is intended to simplify estate settlement, as well as, providing for the benefit of the grantor, his or her spouse and the children or other estate beneficiaries.

1. <u>Name of Trust.</u> This instrument and the initial trust hereby established may be named the "[Name of trust] Trust."

COMMENT: The trust may have any name the grantor desires. Often times, the grantor will simply name the trust after him or herself.

2. <u>Family Information.</u> My [husband or wife]'s name is [husband or wife's name], and all references in this will to "my [husband or wife]" are only to [him or her].

OPTION 1: Naming of all children My [child is or children are], [names of children], and all references in this will to "[my child is or children are]" only to [him her or them].

OPTION 2: Inclusion of step-children Even though some of the above named children are step-children it is my intent that each of the above-named children be treated for purposes of this instrument as if they and their lineal descendants are my natural born children.

OPTION 3: After-born children If subsequent to the execution of this instrument there shall be an additional child or children born to me, then such child or children shall share in the benefits of the trusts established in this instrument to the same extent as my above named children and their descendants; and the provisions of this instrument shall be deemed modified to the extent necessary to carry out this intent.

COMMENT: The full name of the spouse should be inserted, as well as the names of the children. If step-children are involved, Option 2 should be considered. Also, Option 3 may be appropriate if there is the possibility of additional children. The lawyer's state law should provide for this contingency, but it still may be appropriate to add this provision to the will. Concerns about adopted or illegitimate children inheriting and the extent to that inheritance are considered in paragraph 11.a.

---

3. <u>Provisions During My Lifetime.</u> During my lifetime, I shall be paid the net trust income and the principal of the trust property as I direct. If my successor trustee determines that I am unable to manage my financial affairs based on the criteria in paragraph 22 below, the trustee shall pay to or use all, part or none, of the income and principal of the trust property as the trustee believes appropriate for my reasonable maintenance, support, and health. If any net income remains undistributed at the end of each calendar year (excluding income distributed during the sixty-five (65) day period under Internal Revenue Code Section 663), the trustee shall add it to the principal of the trust.

COMMENT: These are basic provisions to provide that, during the lifetime of the grantor, all income and principal is for the sole benefit of the grantor. In order to maintain privacy, the grantor may elect to transfer brokerage accounts and other assets to the trust. In this way, those assets need not be reported to the probate court in settlement of the grantor's estate. Throughout the grantor's lifetime, he or she acts as trustee in making distributions to him or herself with a successor trustee making distributions in the event of disability. Please note that this form cross-references paragraph 22 which defines incompetency. Care must be taken to insert the correct paragraph number, as if any of the ensuing paragraphs are deleted, this will change the paragraph numbers.

---

4. **OPTION 1: Death taxes paid from trust** <u>Payment of Debts, Death Taxes and Funeral Expenses.</u> On my death the trustee shall pay all of my just debts, my funeral expenses, costs of estate administration, and death taxes, if any, from trust principal and the trustee shall not seek contribution toward or recovery of any such payments; provided, however, such obligations and death taxes shall be paid by the trustee only to the extent the personal representative of my probate estate certifies in writing to the trustee that the residue of my probate estate is insufficient to pay such obligations and death taxes. Death taxes means any estate or inheritance taxes, but not generation-skipping transfer taxes, imposed under the laws of any jurisdiction due to my death on any property passing by reason of my death. Any generation-skipping transfer taxes shall be paid from the property that incurred such tax.

OPTION 2: Death taxes paid by beneficiary and collecting taxes on apportionment property <u>Payment of Debts, Death Taxes and Funeral Expenses.</u> On my death the trustee shall pay all of my just debts, my funeral expenses and costs of estate administration from trust principal as soon as possible after my death. Any death taxes owed shall be charged against the trust share passing to the person whose share generated such tax. Death taxes means any estate or inheritance taxes, but not generation-skipping transfer taxes, imposed under the laws of any jurisdiction due to my death on any property passing by reason of my death. With regard to apportionment property, my trustee shall take such actions as are necessary to obtain reimbursement with respect to apportionment property, including withholding distribution. Apportionment property means (a) any property with respect to which my trustee may be entitled to recover federal estate tax under Internal Revenue Code Section 2207, 2207A, or 2207B and (b) any policies of insurance, or the proceeds of policies of insurance, on my life which are not owned by me at my death. Any generation-skipping transfer taxes shall be paid from the property that incurred such tax.

OPTION 3: Death taxes paid from residue but collecting taxes on apportionment property <u>Payment of Debts, Death Taxes and Funeral Expenses.</u> On my death the trustee shall pay all of my just debts, my funeral expenses and costs of estate administration from trust principal as soon as possible after my death. I further direct that my death taxes, if any, be paid out of trust principal, other than apportionment property, without proration and my trustee shall not seek contribution toward or recovery of any such payments. Death taxes means any estate or inheritance taxes, but not generation-skipping transfer taxes, imposed under the laws of any jurisdiction due to my death on any property passing by reason of my death whether or not such property passes under this will. With regard to apportionment property, my trustee shall take such actions as are necessary to obtain reimbursement with respect to apportionment property, including withholding distribution. Apportionment property means (a) any property with respect to which my trustee may be entitled to recover federal estate tax under Internal Revenue Code Section 2207, 2207A, or 2207B and (b) any policies of insurance, or the proceeds of policies of insurance, on my life which are not owned by me at my death. Any generation-skipping transfer taxes shall be paid from the property that incurred such tax.

COMMENT: If the grantor owns sufficient assets in his or her individual name, rather than all assets being titled in the trust, then this provision is not needed to pay final expenses. The concern giving rise to this provision is that all assets will be owned in the trust and there will not be sufficient estate assets with which to pay final expenses. The more difficult question becomes the payment of death taxes. In many situations, there will be no death taxes anticipated, thus in some situations, these provisions can be deleted. Otherwise, a decision must be made as to who bears the burden of paying these taxes. An excellent ABA resource discussing tax payment clauses, apportionment property and the GST tax is Thomas M. Featherston, Jr. et al., *Drafting for Tax and Administrative Issues*, American Bar Association (Chicago: 2000).

---

5. <u>Establishing Trust Funds.</u> After my death, the trustee shall hold and administer the trust property, including property which the trustee receives under my will or from any other sources, as follows:

COMMENT: There are several different approaches to drafting the Marital and Exempt (credit shelter) Trusts, as well as some technical tax law considerations. This form only provides one approach. Excellent ABA resources are Thomas M. Featherston, Jr. et al., *Drafting for Tax and Administrative Issues*, American Bar Association (Chicago: 2000); and L. Rush Hunt and Lara Rae Hunt, *A Lawyer's Guide to Estate Planning*, American Bar Association (Chicago: 2004).

---

a. If my [husband or wife] survives me, the trustee shall divide the trust property into two (2) parts: one part shall be known as the Marital Trust and the other part shall be known as the Exempt Trust.

The trustee shall allocate to the Marital Trust (undiminished by any estate or inheritance taxes) an amount, if any, which is equal to the maximum marital deduction allowable to my estate for federal estate tax purposes, less (i) the value of all other property interests included in my gross estate for federal estate tax purposes which pass or have passed to or for the benefit of my [husband or wife] under my last will and testament or otherwise in such manner as to qualify for the marital deduction, and (ii) an amount, if any, needed to increase my taxable estate to the largest amount that will result in the smallest, if any, federal estate tax being imposed on my estate after allowing for the applicable credit amount against the federal estate tax. The remaining trust property, or all of the trust property if my [husband or wife] either does not survive me, or if my estate is not large enough to require the filing of a federal estate tax return, shall constitute the Exempt Trust.

COMMENT: This is a pecuniary share formula clause that provides the Exempt Trust receives an amount, including cash and specific property, equal to the amount needed to result in the smallest or no federal estate tax. This will be an increasing amount depending on the year of death ($3,500,000 in 2009; and thereafter it is expected there will be future changes in the law).

    b. The words "gross estate," "taxable estate," "marital deduction," "pass," and "applicable credit amount," shall have the same meaning as these words have in the Internal Revenue Code of 1986, as amended.

COMMENT: This clarifies the meaning of various technical terms of the federal estate tax law and includes the meanings of these terms as they may be modified by future legislative changes.

    c. In making the computations to determine the amount of property to be set aside as the Marital Trust, the final determinations for federal estate tax purposes shall control, and only property which qualifies for the marital deduction shall be allocated to the Marital Trust.

COMMENT: Setting values based on final estate tax values is needed for administrative convenience in making allocation between the two trusts. Also, this sentence is designed to avoid the tainted asset rule in I.R.C. Section 2056(b)(2). Also, see Treas. Reg. Section 20.2056(b)-2.

    d. The trustee may allocate to the Marital Trust money or property in kind, or partly in money and partly in kind; provided, however, that any property transferred in kind shall be valued at its fair market value determined as of the date or dates it is allocated to the Marital Trust. Allocations of property may be made to the Marital Trust and the Exempt Trust without regard to the income tax basis of the property so transferred, irrespective of the fact that my trustee's decision may affect a beneficiary's interest in the trust estate.

COMMENT: This clause is required to satisfy Revenue Procedure 64-19, which applies to pecuniary bequests. Without this clause, Rev. Proc. 64-19 may disallow the marital deduction. This clause will cause any appreciation after the date of death (or alternate valuation date) to be a taxable income gain to the estate at the time of distribution. The final sentence affords the trustee some liability protection when allocating assets between the two trust funds.

    e. My trustee may estimate the amount of property to be allocated to the Marital Trust and the Exempt Trust, and may make a tentative allocation in satisfaction thereof; making any final adjustments as may be necessary to preserve the deductibility of the Marital Trust as the marital deduction trust in determining my taxable estate. The Marital Trust and the Exempt Trust shall carry with them (as income and not as principal) their proportionate part of the income received by my trustee until such trusts are fully funded.

COMMENT: This clause is administrative and permits an early funding of the two trusts pending final adjustment on settlement of the estate and the estate tax audit.

f. It is my express intent that the Marital Trust be available for the federal estate tax marital deduction and all questions applicable to the creation and funding of the Marital Trust shall be resolved so as to achieve such deduction for my estate. Any provision of this instrument which cannot be so interpreted or limited, or which is inconsistent with such intent shall be void. The powers, duties, and discretions given to my trustee with respect to the Marital Trust and with respect to its administration shall not be exercised or exercisable except in a manner to preserve the deductibility of the Marital Trust as the marital deduction.

COMMENT: A savings clause is commonly used in an effort to save the marital deduction if some power or act of the trustee could jeopardize the entitlement to the marital deduction.

g. Any property transferred to my trustee under the terms of my last will and testament or my [husband's or wife's] last will and testament shall be added to the Marital Trust and the Exempt Trust as provided by my or my [husband's or wife's] last will and testament. Further, the trustee may accept the property delivered to [him, her or it] by my or my [husband's or wife's] personal representative as all the property it is entitled to receive without having to examine the records and accounts of the Personal Representatives.

COMMENT: This paragraph is largely administrative. If the trustee and personal representative are the same, the second sentence can be deleted.

6. <u>Marital Trust.</u> The trustee shall hold and dispose of the trust property held in this trust as follows:

a. The net income of the Marital Trust shall be paid to my [husband or wife] in quarterly or more frequent installments, or used for [his or her] benefit if [he or she] is disabled. Any income accrued and undistributed at the death of my [husband or wife] shall be paid to [his or her] personal representative.

COMMENT: There are two approaches to qualifying the Marital Trust for the marital deduction. One approach is the Marital Trust coupled with a general power of appointment for the surviving spouse. The other approach is the Marital Trust being a terminable interest but still qualifying for the marital deduction by the personal representative making a Q-TIP election. The option of an outright bequest of the Marital Trust to the surviving spouse is not considered in these forms, but it can be accomplished very easily by naming the Marital Trust a Marital Share and then specifying that it is distributed outright to the grantor's spouse.

b. My trustee is authorized at any time and from time to time to distribute to my [husband or wife] or apply to [his or her] benefit from the principal of the Marital Trust (even to the point of completely exhausting the same) such amounts as the trustee deems necessary to provide for [his or her] reasonable health, maintenance, and support. In determining the amounts of principal to be so disbursed, the trustee may take into consideration any other income which my [husband or wife] may have from any other source, and also [his or her] capital resources other than household goods, residence, and personal effects.

COMMENT: If the invasion of principal for the surviving spouse needs to be limited, this paragraph can be used with paragraphs d and e below, which is a general power of appointment. If paragraphs d and e are not appropriate, they may be deleted and the marital deduction can still be obtained by the personal representative making a Q-TIP election. If appropriate for the client's needs, this paragraph permitting an invasion of principal can be omitted.

c. My [husband or wife] may at any time by written notice, require the trustee to make any nonproductive property of the Marital Trust productive or to convert such nonproductive property to productive property within a reasonable time.

OPTION 1 d. At the time of [his or her] death, my [husband or wife] may appoint, by specifically referring to this power in [his or her] last will and testament, part or all of the principal of the Marital Trust, in such amounts and in trust or outright, to [his or her] estate, or to any person, or any corporation. To the extent this power is not effectively exercised, the principal of the Marital Trust shall be added to the principal of the Exempt Trust and shall be administered and distributed in accordance with paragraph 7 et seq.

COMMENT: See comment following 6.b.

e. The trustee may consider any writing probated in a proper court as the last will and testament of my [husband or wife] and shall not be liable for [his, her or its] actions in reliance thereon. Likewise, if no writing purporting to be [his or her] last will and testament is duly offered for probate within three months of [his or her] death, my trustee may conclusively presume that [he or she] left no last will and testament and shall not be liable for [his, her or its] actions in reliance thereon. However, this provision shall not limit or qualify a donee of the power of appointment conferred upon my [husband or wife] to pursue any funds affected by the exercise of it, irrespective of the place of probate or time of discovery of [his or her] last will and testament.

COMMENT: This paragraph is for administrative clarity and is used with the general power-of-appointment approach only when Option 1 above is used.

OPTION 2 d. Following the death of my [husband or wife], the Marital Trust shall be added to the principal of the Exempt Trust and shall be administered and distributed in accordance with paragraph 7 et seq.

COMMENT: This paragraph will be used with the Q-TIP approach, but is not needed with the general-power-of-appointment approach if Option 1 is used.

7. <u>Exempt Trust.</u> After my death, my trustee shall hold and dispose of the trust property held in this trust as follows:

a. The net income of the Exempt Trust shall be paid to my [husband or wife] in quarterly or more frequent installments, or used for [his or her] benefit if [he or she] is disabled.

COMMENT: If desired, all of the income can be paid to the surviving spouse, or it can be paid to multiple beneficiaries or even accumulated.

b. My trustee is authorized at any time and from time to time to distribute to my [husband or wife] or apply to [his or her] benefit from the principal of the Exempt Trust (even to the point of completely exhausting the same) such amounts as the trustee deems necessary to provide for [his or her] reasonable health, maintenance, and support. In determining the amounts of principal to be so disbursed, the trustee may take into consideration any other income which my [husband or wife] may have from any other source, and also [his or her] capital resources other than household goods, residence, and personal effects.

COMMENT: This paragraph permits the principal to be expended for the surviving spouse, if needed. Other beneficiaries may also receive distributions of trust principal. Although not required, this flexibility is normally desired.

---

c. **OPTION 1** Upon the death of my [husband or wife] after my death or upon my death if my [husband or wife] does not survive me, the remaining trust fund and any property transferred to the trustee under the last will and testament of my [husband or wife] shall be held, administered, and distributed by the trustee in accordance with the terms and conditions hereinafter set out.

COMMENT: This paragraph will be used if the grantor desires for the trust to continue for some period of time for the benefit of other beneficiaries following the death of the surviving spouse. See the Single Person Inter Vivos Trust beginning at page 60 for sample dispositive provisions.

---

c. **OPTION 2** Upon the death of my [husband or wife] after my death or upon my death if my [husband or wife] does not survive me, the remaining trust fund and any property transferred to the trustee under the last will and testament of my [husband or wife] shall be distributed by the trustee to my then living lineal descendants, per stirpes.

COMMENT: If the children are of sufficient maturity, the trust can terminate at the surviving spouse's death and be distributed outright to the ultimate trust beneficiaries.

---

c. **OPTION 3** Upon the death of my [husband or wife] after my death, the remaining trust fund shall be distributed, in trust or otherwise, among my children, my remote descendants and public charities in such proportions as my [husband or wife] may direct by specific reference to this power in [his or her] last will and testament. The trustee may rely upon an instrument admitted to probate in any jurisdiction as the last will and testament of my [husband or wife] and if no such instrument is offered for probate within three months after [his or her] death, the trustee may presume [he or she] died intestate. In default of the exercise of this limited power of appointment the trust estate shall be distributed to my descendants, per stirpes.

COMMENT: The surviving spouse may be given a limited power of appointment without the Exempt Trust being taxed in his or her estate. This adds greater flexibility, which may be, but is not always, needed. A limited power of appointment is one that cannot be exercised in favor of the donee, his or her estate, and the creditors of either. This power is more limited than this requirement, but is used because it includes the distributees most clients will want to see inherit the trust property.

---

8. <u>Special Provisions.</u> In addition to the other provisions of this trust agreement:

COMMENT: The following are various provisions that may be needed in a given situation, but rarely will all of these paragraphs be needed.

a. <u>Residential Real Estate.</u> In the event any residential real estate is included among the trust assets and my [husband or wife] is then living, [he or she] may occupy such residence rent-free during [his or her] lifetime. My [husband or wife] shall pay all property taxes, insurance premiums, and the expenses of ordinary maintenance and repair. Further, my [husband or wife] may purchase any such residential real estate at its then appraised value as determined by a professional real estate appraiser.

COMMENT: In the event the grantor desires for his or her personal residence to be available for the surviving spouse or another trust beneficiary, then this paragraph, or a modification of it, may be appropriate.

b. <u>Rule Against Perpetuities</u>. If not sooner terminated, twenty-one years after the death of the last to die of my [husband or wife], myself, and my descendants who are living at the time of the death of the first to die of my [husband or wife] or me, my trustee shall distribute the trust property to each person for whom a trust is held under this trust agreement.

COMMENT: The lawyer will need to determine if there is any concern over the rule against perpetuities, and if so, the above provision, or a modification of it, will be necessary. In most drafting situations, there will not be the possibility of violating this rule, thus the lawyer may want to omit this paragraph.

c. <u>Subchapter S Stock.</u> In the event a trust under this agreement holds Subchapter S stock, then the terms of this trust are hereby modified so that this trust qualifies as a Qualified Subchapter S Trust ("QSST") under section 1361(d) of the Internal Revenue Code. Therefore, any trust that has more than one permissible beneficiary shall be divided on a prorata basis into separate trusts for those beneficiaries, resulting in each trust having only one beneficiary who shall be the only recipient of trust income and principal until the earlier of the beneficiary's death or the termination of the trust.

COMMENT: One of the general tax law requirements for a corporation being taxed as a Subchapter S corporation, which allows the corporate income to flow to the owners and be taxed to them rather than facing the possible double-taxation of the traditional corporate tax law, is that a trust cannot be an owner. Of course, with the tax law there are always exceptions. There are several situations in which a trust can be a stockholder of a Subchapter S corporation. This paragraph is intended to ensure that the corporation will maintain its status as a Subchapter S corporation, even though some of its stock is held in trust. This is a technical and somewhat tricky tax trap. An excellent ABA resource addressing this issue is Thomas M. Featherston, Jr. et al., *Drafting for Tax and Administrative Issues*, American Bar Association (Chicago: 2000).

d. <u>Reliance on Will.</u> The trustee may rely on a will admitted to probate in any jurisdiction as the last will and testament of such person, or may assume (absent actual knowledge to the contrary) the person had no will if a will has not been admitted to probate within three months after such person's death.

COMMENT: This is a "boilerplate" provision that is helpful, but this provision must be reviewed to be certain that it is needed, and to make any modifications that are required.

---

e. <u>Method of Payment.</u> If a person entitled to receive income or principal distributions is unable to manage his or her financial affairs due to any type of mental or physical incapacity, then distributions may be made to or for such person's benefit, including making distributions to such person's guardian, conservator, committee, or a custodian under a Uniform Gift or Transfer to Minors Act.

COMMENT: This is a "boilerplate" provision that is usually inserted in a trust instrument.

---

f. <u>Accrued Income and Termination.</u> Income accrued and undistributed at the termination of a person's interest in trust property **OPTION 1** shall be distributed to such person's estate. **OPTION 2** shall remain an asset of the trust and shall not be distributed to such person's estate.

COMMENT: This is a helpful provision for administrative reasons to clarify for the trustee whether accumulated but undistributed income should remain in the trust after the beneficiary's death or if it should be distributed to that beneficiary's estate. One of the two options should be selected. Note this paragraph must be consistent with paragraph 6.a.

---

g. <u>Rights and Duties Relating to Life Insurance Policies.</u> After my death when life insurance policies become payable to the trust, my trustee shall promptly furnish proof of loss to the life insurance companies, and shall collect and receive the proceeds of the policies. My trustee shall have power to execute and deliver receipts and other instruments and to take such action as is appropriate for this collection. If my trustee deems it necessary to institute legal action for the collection of any policies, [he, she or it] shall be indemnified for all costs, including attorney's fees.

My trustee, in [his, her or its] sole discretion, may accept any of the optional modes of payment provided in any of such policies where such modes of payment are permitted to the trustee by the life insurance company. No life insurance company under any policy of insurance deposited with my trustee shall be responsible for the application or disposition of the proceeds of such policy by my trustee. Payment to my trustee of such life insurance proceeds shall be a full discharge of the liability of the life insurance company under such policy.

COMMENT: This paragraph is needed only if life insurance is made payable to the trust. The provisions are customary and are intended to avoid liability for the life insurance company and the trustee over receipt of life insurance death proceeds and the selection of the mode of payment. While these are routine provisions, the lawyer should review them to be certain that they are appropriate.

---

9. <u>Default Provisions.</u> Any trust property not disposed of by any of the above provisions shall be distributed on the date of such failure of disposition to [default provisions].

COMMENT: If there are a limited number of beneficiaries, then it may be wise to insert a default provision providing for the ultimate recipient should all the beneficiaries who could receive under paragraphs 5-7 and their descendants be deceased. If this is too remote of a possibility, some clients may direct that this paragraph be deleted.

---

10. <u>Protection from Creditors.</u> No trust beneficiary shall have the right to sell, transfer, assign, alienate, pledge, or in any way encumber trust assets, including income and principal, nor shall trust assets be subject to execution, levy, sale, garnishment, attachment, bankruptcy, or other legal proceedings. Any such actions by a trust beneficiary or a third party seeking to enforce a claim against the trust assets shall not be recognized under any circumstances by the trustee. These provisions do not prevent the trustee from making distributions for the benefit of a trust beneficiary in such amounts and at such times as the trustee determines necessary for the trust beneficiary's maintenance, support, health and education.

COMMENT: This is a standard paragraph that precludes the trust assets from being attached by claims of creditors.

---

11. <u>Definitions.</u> For all purposes of this instrument, the following shall apply:

a. The words "child," "children," "descendant" or "descendants" shall exclude adopted persons unless they are adopted prior to [insert age] years; and shall include only persons legitimately born unless a decree of adoption terminates the parental rights of the natural mother during her lifetime, or the natural father signs a written notarized instrument during his lifetime in which he irrevocably states that the child is to be considered legitimately born for purposes of inheriting under this will.

COMMENT: Some clients will want to restrict distribution for an adopted child to preclude a child adopted as an adult. Thus, many will use the age 18 or perhaps a slightly older age such as 20 or 21. Other clients may wish to restrict the age to a younger adopted child, such as under the age of 10. The issue of illegitimate children should also be addressed. In many situations, a child or more remote descendant should be treated the same as any other child, in which case the portion of this paragraph that deals with illegitimate children can be deleted. In other situations there may be a limited or no relationship with the child, in which event no distribution should be made to that child. This form gives the father of the child the right to allow the child to inherit by the father signing a written document allowing inheritance.

---

b. Whenever assets are to be divided and allocated per stirpes, the assets to be divided or allocated shall be divided into as many equal shares as are necessary to divide or allocate one share to each then living child of such person and to provide one share collectively for the then living descendants of each child of such person who then is deceased leaving one or more descendants then living. Any collective share shall be divided and allocated per stirpes among the descendants of such deceased person in accordance with the preceding sentence.

COMMENT: Since the term per stirpes is used often in this document, a definition is provided of that term. The lawyer should modify this definition to conform with his or her own state law should it differ any from this definition. Of course, a definition is not essential, since the term will be defined under state law. But since it is a term that clients are not familiar with, it is often helpful to define it for them in the document. An excellent ABA resource that discusses this issue in detail is Jeffrey N. Penell and Alan Newman, *Estate and Trust Planning*, American Bar Association (Chicago, 2005) pp. 19–26.

12. <u>Trustee Powers.</u> In the administration of the trusts, the trustee shall have the following powers and rights and all others granted by law:

a. To sell publicly or privately any trust property, for cash or on time, without an order of court and upon such terms and conditions as my trustee deems proper; and no person dealing with my trustee shall have any obligation to look to the application of the purchase money.

b. To invest and reinvest all or any part of the principal of the trust in any stocks, bonds, mortgages, shares or interests in common trust funds, mutual funds, or other securities or property, real, personal, or mixed, and of any kind or nature whatsoever, as the trustee deems proper, and without diversification if the trustee deems it advisable, irrespective of whether or not such securities or property are eligible for trust investment under state or any other law, and may change any investment received or made by the trustee, and may hold cash if the trustee deems it advisable.

c. To exercise broad discretion as to diversification of trust property, and shall not be required to reduce any concentrated holdings merely because of such concentration, and shall have full discretion as to the percentage to be invested in fixed income securities, and is specifically relieved from any requirements, legal or otherwise, as to the percentage of the trust assets to be invested in fixed income securities, and may invest or retain invested any trust estates wholly in common stocks.

d. To sell, convey, lease or mortgage, repair and improve, and take any and all other steps with regard to any real estate that may at any time be a part of the principal of the trust; and any lease of such real property or contract with regard thereto made by the trustee shall be binding for the full period of the lease or contract, even though the period shall extend beyond the termination of the trust.

e. To vote shares of stock held in the trust at stockholders' meetings in person or by special, limited, or general proxy, with or without power of substitution, as seems best to the trustee.

f. To participate in the liquidation, reorganization, consolidation, incorporation and reincorporation, or any other financial readjustment of any corporation, limited liability company or business in which the trust is, or shall be financially interested.

g. To borrow money from any source for any purpose connected with the protection, preservation, improvement or development of the trust hereunder, whenever in the trustee's judgment the trustee deems it advisable, and as security to mortgage or pledge any real estate or personal property forming a part of the trust upon such terms and conditions as the trustee may deem advisable.

h. To hold any and all securities in bearer form, in the trustee's own name, or the name of some other person, partnership, or corporation, or in the name of a duly appointed nominee, with or without disclosing the fiduciary ownership.

i. To divide the principal of the trust property into parts or shares and to distribute or allot same, and to make such division in cash or in kind or both. For the purpose of such division or allotment, the judgment of the trustee concerning the propriety thereof and relative value of property so distributed or allotted shall be binding and conclusive with respect to all interested persons.

j. To merge and consolidate the trust property of any separate trust held hereunder with other trusts and then to administer such trust property as a single trust provided the separate trust is for the benefit of the same persons with substantially the same terms, conditions and federal tax consequences.

k. To pay such income and principal during the minority or incapacity of any beneficiary for whose benefit income and principal may be expended, in any one or more of the following ways: (1) directly to the beneficiary; (2) to the legal guardian or committee of the beneficiary; (3) to a relative of the beneficiary to be expended by the relative for the maintenance, health, and education of the beneficiary; or (4) by expending the same directly for the maintenance, health, and education of the beneficiary. The trustee shall not be obliged to see to the application of the funds so expended, but the receipt of such person shall be full acquittance to the trustee.

l. To continue and operate any business owned by me at my death and to do any and all things deemed appropriate by the trustee, including the power to form a limited liability company or incorporate the business and to put additional capital into the business, for such time as the trustee deems advisable, without liability for loss resulting from the continuance or operation of the business except for the trustee's own negligence; and to close out, liquidate, or sell the business at such time and upon such terms as the trustee deems proper; and in this connection a sale may be made (pursuant to an agreement entered into by me during my lifetime, or otherwise) to a partner, officer, member, employee or beneficiary under this trust. I am aware of the fact that certain risks are inherent in the operation of any business and, therefore, my trustee shall not be liable for any loss resulting from the retention and operation of any business unless such loss results directly from my trustee's gross negligence or willful misconduct.

m. To have the same powers, authorities, and discretions in the management of the trust as I would have in the management and control of my own personal assets. The trustee may continue to exercise any powers and discretions granted in this instrument for a reasonable period after the termination of any trust under this instrument.

COMMENT: The above powers are a set of standard powers that appear throughout this book. The powers should be reviewed to be certain that you the lawyer understand each power, the client is in agreement with each of the powers granted and that the powers granted are needed. Because this is a generic and broad statement of powers, some of these powers may not be necessary. For example, powers to sell or lease real estate are not needed if the grantor knows the trust will consist only of cash and other intangible investments.

---

13. Environmental Concerns. In the administration of this trust, my trustee shall have the power and authority to inspect, assess and evaluate any assets held in this trust, or proposed to be added to this trust, to determine if any environmental concerns exist with such asset or assets, and if so, my trustee may take any remedial action my trustee believes necessary to prevent, abate or remedy any environmental concerns whether or not my trustee is required to do so by any governmental agency. Further, my trustee may refuse to accept or may disclaim any asset or assets proposed to be added to the trust if my trustee believes there are possible environmental concerns that could result in liability to the trust or the trustee. Also, my trustee may settle or compromise any claims or lawsuits alleging environmental concerns which have been asserted

by a private party or governmental agency. The decisions of my trustee regarding environmental concerns shall be final and binding on all parties and shall not be subject to question by anyone or in any court.

COMMENT: In many situations, it will be appropriate to address concerns of the trustee if the trust holds, or is expected to receive by will or other transfer, an asset that may have environmental concerns. This paragraph, or a variation of it, is helpful to the trustee in addressing this oftentimes difficult fiduciary problem. If there is any possibility the trust may hold assets that have environmental concerns, then the lawyer should address those issues fully with the client and with the trustee, including successor trustees, to avoid the situation in which a named trustee refuses to serve due to concerns over personal liability of the fiduciary for environmental cleanup costs.

---

14. <u>Trustee Powers as to Farms and Farm Real Estate.</u> In the administration of any farms and farmland held in this trust, the trustee shall have the following powers and rights:

a. To formulate and carry out a general farm plan of operation.

b. To make leases and enter into contracts with tenants, either on shares or for stated compensation, or to employ and pay such labor as might be employed.

c. To buy, breed, raise, and sell all kinds of livestock, either on shares with a tenant or solely on behalf of the trust estate.

d. To plant, cultivate, fertilize, produce, and market all crops raised on the farm, and to collect, receive and receipt for all shares, rent, and other income from the farm.

e. To ditch and drain so much of the land as might be considered desirable, and to make such repairs and improvements to building, land, and other items of property as may be consistent with good farm management.

f. To enter into contracts with the United States Department of Agriculture, or other Federal or State governmental agencies, for crop reductions or soil conservation practices.

g. To pay all taxes and assessments against the farm property and insure the improvements against loss by fire, windstorm, and other casualties.

h. To credit receipts and charge expenditures to and against the income account or the principal account as may be appropriate under applicable rules of trust accounting. In this regard, it is especially provided that any capital improvements made by the trustee in the exercise of prudent trust management shall be allocated between the income account and the principal account on the basis of the ratio of the life expectancy of the income beneficiary at that time to the normally expected useful life of the capital improvement.

i. To employ farm management services to the extent that this may be considered desirable for the proper formulation of farming plans and the active management of farm properties under the supervision and responsibility of the trustee.

j. To borrow monies which may be required from time to time to finance the farm operations, and to encumber trust assets to secure such loans.

k. To do any and all other things consistent with the provisions of this trust to facilitate an orderly distribution of our assets calculated to accomplish the purposes herein set out in an economically feasible manner.

COMMENT: In the event the trust will include a farm that will continue to be owned in trust, then these additional trust provisions should be considered. The general trustee powers should be sufficient, but when drafting for a farming client these more specific trustee powers are usually helpful.

15. <u>Limitation of Trustee Powers.</u> Notwithstanding any other powers granted to my trustee in this instrument, an individual trustee (a) shall have no power to make payments or distributions that would discharge the trustee's legal obligation to support the trust beneficiary, (b) shall not exercise any power or discretion in any manner that would be deemed to be a general power of appointment under Internal Revenue Code Section 2041, (c) shall be limited by the ascertainable standard of "maintenance, support, health and education" when making payments or distributions to the trustee personally or to anyone for whom the trustee has a beneficial interest, and (d) shall possess no incidence of ownership or powers with respect to life insurance in which the trustee is the insured and has fiduciary power over such life insurance.

COMMENT: There are some situations in which an individual trustee may have adverse estate or income tax consequences when given broad powers as trustee. If a corporate trustee is used, then this paragraph is not needed. But an individual trustee must be certain that acting as trustee does not result in any adverse estate or income tax consequences. This paragraph is intended to ensure that adverse tax consequences are avoided if overly broad powers are granted in the trust instrument. The lawyer is urged to exercise caution when using individual trustees coupled with broad discretionary powers of income and principal distribution to a trust beneficiary because of possible adverse tax consequences. An ABA resource to acquaint oneself with these issues is L. Rush Hunt and Lara Rae Hunt, *A Lawyer's Guide to Estate Planning*, American Bar Association (Chicago: 2004) §14.4.

16. <u>Trustee Resignation.</u> My trustee may resign at any time by giving written notice to my successor trustee named below, if any, and if none, then written notice shall be given to each current adult income beneficiary who is then living.

COMMENT: If a trustee resigns, there must be some method of notice and appointment of a successor trustee. This paragraph provides a method of notification. It is not an essential trust provision, but is a helpful one.

17. <u>Trustee Succession and Appointment.</u> If I cease to act as trustee due to death, incompetency, resignation or cease to serve for any reason, then [Name of successor trustee] shall serve as successor trustee. If [Name of successor trustee] dies, becomes incompetent, resigns or ceases to serve for any reason, then [Name of second successor trustee] shall serve as successor trustee. The last serving successor trustee may name his or her own successor trustee by a written instrument delivered to the successor trustee or by will. The successor trustee may be an individual or a financial institution possessing trust powers under state or federal law. Any further vacancy in the office of trustee shall be filled by decision of the probate court where I resided at the time of my death.

COMMENT: A decision must be made as to succession of trustees and the method of appointing a successor trustee if all of those named successor trustees are unable to serve. It is also essential to clarify whether successor trustees must only be financial institutions or if individuals may also be considered. Once a decision is made as to the succession of trustees, then the last three sentences should be reviewed to be certain to what extent each of those are needed.

18. <u>Powers of Successor Trustee.</u> Each successor trustee shall have the same rights, titles, powers, duties, discretions, and immunities and otherwise be in the same position as if originally named trustee. No successor trustee shall be personally liable for any act or failure to act of a predecessor trustee. Further, a successor trustee may accept the account furnished and the property delivered by or for a predecessor trustee without liability for so doing, and such acceptance shall be a full and complete discharge to the predecessor trustee.

COMMENT: This paragraph clarifies that a successor trustee has the same powers as the initial trustee. Further, the paragraph relieves the successor trustee from liability for the prior acts of the resigning trustee and waives any requirements of audit or inquiry into the activities of the prior trustee. This is essential for any successor trustee.

19. <u>Compensation of Trustee.</u> **OPTION 1: Corporate trustee compensation** A corporate trustee shall receive compensation in accordance with its regular schedule of fees in effect at the time such services are rendered.

OPTION 2: Individual does not receive compensation An individual trustee shall not be paid any compensation, but shall be reimbursed for out-of-pocket expenses.

OPTION 3: Individual does receive compensation An individual trustee shall be paid [insert amount of compensation] as compensation for such services and shall be reimbursed for out-of-pocket expenses.

COMMENT: Three options are provided, but the actual drafting of this paragraph may be different than each of these options. If the only trustee to be used is a corporate trustee, then Option 1 is a standard trust provision. If there is a possibility of individual trustees, then care should be given to the method for setting this fee. If no fee is to be paid because the trustee is a close family member, then it is suggested that Option 2 be used. If the grantor expects a fee to be charged, then an amount or a formula, such as a percentage of income or principal, must be set. It is unwise to simply provide for compensation to be a reasonable fee, as that leaves an individual trustee with great uncertainty as to the fee to be charged. Without the grantor clarifying compensation, the trustee could find him or herself in litigation with the beneficiary.

20. <u>Court Accountings.</u> To the extent such requirements can be waived, the trustee shall not be required (a) to file any inventory of trust property or accounts or reports of the administration of the trusts, or to register the trusts, in any court, (b) to furnish any bond or other security for the proper performance of the trustee's duties or (c) to obtain authority from a court for the exercise of any power conferred on the trustee by this instrument. This waiver does not preclude the trustee from registering any trust created in this instrument and petitioning a court having jurisdiction over registered trusts for a judicial ruling on any matter relating to administration of any trust created in this instrument.

COMMENT: The first sentence is to clarify the normal situation that an inter vivos trust is not subject to judicial oversight. The second sentence may be omitted, but is suggested as a potential benefit in some states. In a state in which a trust can be registered, it may be possible to have minor trust matters resolved by the court in which the trust is registered. This creates a simplified process for dealing with minor administrative matters. Without this provision, a court might be reluctant to decide matters for a trust which is not required to be registered under state law.

21. <u>Severability.</u> If any provisions of this trust shall be unenforceable, the remaining provisions shall nevertheless be carried into effect.

COMMENT: This is the same type of standard provision often seen in contracts that is intended to save the document if a particular provision is found to be invalid or void. It is doubtful this provision will have any practical effect in most trust situations, but it is a "boilerplate" provision that is frequently found in trust instruments and for which there is no disadvantage.

22. <u>Certification of Incompetency.</u> **OPTION 1: Decided by treating physician** Any person acting or named to act as a trustee in this instrument is considered to be unable to serve or to continue serving when a physician whom such person has consulted within the prior three years has certified as to such consultation and the certification states that the person is incapable of managing the affairs of the trusts I have established in this instrument, regardless of cause and regardless of whether there is an adjudication of incompetency. No person shall be liable to anyone for actions taken in reliance on the physician's certification or for dealing with a trustee other than the one removed for incompetency based on such certification.

OPTION 2: Decided by two physicians Any person acting or named to act as a trustee in this instrument is considered to be unable to serve or to continue serving when a written certification is received from two (2) physicians, both of whom have personally examined the person and at least one (1) of whom is board-certified in the specialty most closely associated with the health condition alleged to cause such incompetency. The certification must state that the person is incapable of managing the affairs of this trust, regardless of cause and regardless of whether there is an adjudication of incompetence. No person is liable to anyone for actions taken in reliance on these certifications, or for dealing with a trustee other than the one removed for incompetency based on these certifications.

COMMENT: This provision relates back to paragraph 17 concerning the succession of trustees. It defines incompetency, which is one of those events requiring a successor trustee. The first option involves consultation with the trustee's personal physician, whereas Option 2 involves a panel of two physicians, one of whom is board certified in the speciality most closely associated with the health condition of the trustee. Clients differ as to which provision they prefer and are more concerned about the provision when the grantor is also the initial trustee. Absent a strong preference by the grantor, Option 1 is the provision most frequently used.

23. <u>Titles and References.</u> The underscored titles of paragraphs in this instrument are for information purposes only and shall be given no legal effect.

COMMENT: This is another common "boilerplate" provision that is perhaps not essential, but for which there is no disadvantage.

24. <u>Governing Law.</u> The laws of the State of [insert state] shall govern the interpretation and validity of the provisions of this instrument and all questions relating to the management, administration, investment, and distribution of the trusts hereby created.

COMMENT: It is a standard provision in both trust instruments and in contracts to specify the state law that applies in interpretation of the instrument. This will usually be the grantor's state of residency but also the state in which the lawyer is licensed to practice.

Notwithstanding the foregoing, my trustee shall have the power, exercisable in the trustee's sole and absolute discretion, to declare, by written instrument that the forum for this trust and all trusts established herein shall be another state in which event the laws of that state shall govern the interpretation and validity of the provisions of this instrument and all questions relating to the management, administration, investment, and distribution of the trusts hereby created.

COMMENT: In those situations in which the trust is drafted to provide asset protection for trust beneficiaries other than the grantor, it may be wise to include the power for the trustee to change the situs of the trust to another state whose laws are more favorable to the protection of the trust assets should the trustee find that the laws of the home state are less favorable to asset protection.

25. <u>No-Contest.</u> If any beneficiary of this trust, or the guardian or legal representative of such beneficiary, contests the validity of this trust or of any of its provisions or shall institute or join in (except as a party defendant) any proceeding to contest the validity of this trust or to prevent any provision of it from being carried out in accordance with its terms (regardless of whether or not such proceedings are instituted in good faith and with probable cause), then all benefits provided for such beneficiary hereunder are revoked and such benefits shall pass as if such beneficiary and such beneficiary's descendants all had predeceased me.

COMMENT: This provision or some variation of it should be considered if there is any concern that a beneficiary or heir-at-law may challenge the trust. The lawyer may need to modify this provision to meet any requirements of state law.

26. <u>Power To Amend or Revoke.</u> I reserve the right from time to time by written instrument delivered to the trustee to amend or revoke this instrument and the trusts hereby evidenced, in whole or in part.

COMMENT: This instrument is revocable thus permitting the grantor to make any amendments he or she chooses or to revoke the trust in its entirety.

The undersigned has signed this instrument and has established the foregoing trusts on this the _____ day of _____, [Current year].

GRANTOR AND TRUSTEE:

_____
[Grantor's name]

STATE OF [State of Notary]   )

) SCT.

COUNTY OF [County of Notary])

The undersigned, a Notary Public within and for the state and county aforesaid, does hereby certify that the foregoing trust agreement executed by [Grantor's name], as grantor and trustee, was on this day produced to me in my county by [Grantor's name], who executed, acknowledged and swore the same before me to be [his or her] act and deed in due form of law.

Given under my hand and notarial seal on this the _____ day of _____, [Current year].

_____
Notary Public, State at Large

My commission expires:_____

PREPARED BY:

_____
[Name of Attorney]
[Name of Law Firm]
Attorneys at Law
[Street Address]
[City], [State] [Zip Code]
[Telephone Number]

SCHEDULE A

[NAME OF TRUST] TRUST

Cash. . . . . $ 10.00

The lawyer will note a deposit of $10 in the trust. State law will determine the necessity of an initial deposit. An unfunded trust that contains no principal may be deemed a "dry" trust under state law, meaning that it is not a valid document. Some lawyers go to the added step of affixing a $10 bill to schedule A, while others are satisfied with a cash deposit which does have the disadvantage of not being traceable. If there is the possibility of a contest of the trust, the cautious practice would be to affix a $10 bill to schedule A.

Index